With the purchase of a new book

You Can Access the Real Financial Data that the Experts Use!

*If you purchased a used book, see other side for access information

This card entitles the purchaser of a new textbook to a semester of access to the Educational Version of Standard & Poor's Market Insight®, a rich online resource featuring hundreds of the most-often researched companies in the Market Insight database.

For over 1000 Canadian, U.S., and international companies, this Web site provides you:

- Access to six years' worth of fundamental financial data from the renowned Standard & Poor's COMPUSTAT® database

- 12 Excel Analytics Reports, including annual and quarterly balance sheets, income statements, ratio reports, and cash flow statements; daily, weekly, and monthly adjusted price reports, and profitability; forecasted values and monthly valuation data reports

- Access to Financial Highlights Reports including key ratios

- S&P Stock Reports offering fundamental, quantitative, and technical analysis

- Industry Surveys, written by S & P's Equity analysts

- Charting, providing powerful, interactive JavaCharts with price and volume data, incorporating over 100 different technical studies, user-specific watch lists, easy-to-customize parameters and drawing tools. Delayed real-time pricing available.

- News feeds (updated hourly) for companies and industries

STANDARD
&POOR'S

Mc Graw Hill **McGraw-Hill Ryerson**

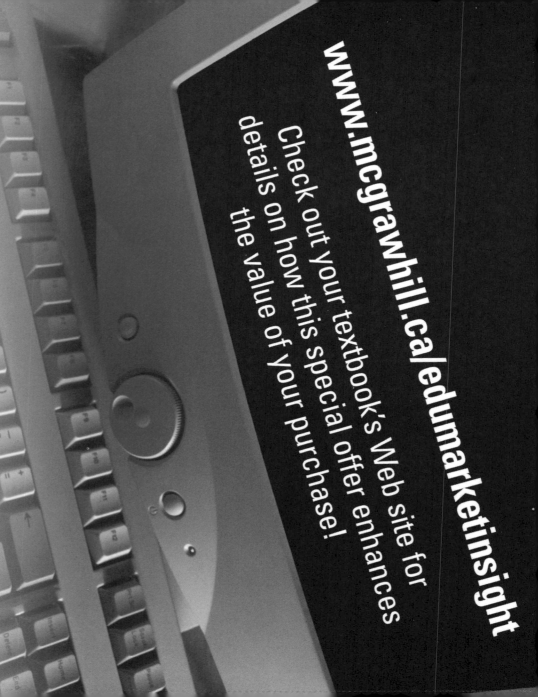

www.mcgrawhill.ca/edumarketinsight

Check out your textbook's Web site for details on how this special offer enhances the value of your purchase!

Welcome to the Educational Version of Market Insight!

1. To get started, use your web browser to go to **www.mcgrawhill.ca/edumarketinsight**

2. Enter your site ID exactly as it appears below.

3. You may be prompted to enter the site ID for future use—please keep this card

Your site ID is:

ta165845

If you purchased a used book, this site ID may have expired. For new password purchase, please go to **www.mcgrawhill.ca/edumarketinsight**. Password activation is good for a six month duration.

Corporate Finance

FOURTH CANADIAN EDITION

Stephen A. Ross
Sloan School of Management
Massachusetts Institute of Technology

Randolph W. Westerfield
Marshall School of Business
University of Southern California

Jeffrey F. Jaffe
Wharton School of Business
University of Pennsylvania

Gordon S. Roberts
Schulich School of Business
York University

McGraw-Hill Ryerson

Toronto Montréal Boston Burr Ridge, IL Dubuque, IA Madison, WI New York
San Francisco St. Louis Bangkok Bogotá Caracas Kuala Lumpur Lisbon London
Madrid Mexico City Milan New Delhi Santiago Seoul Singapore Sydney Taipei

The McGraw-Hill Companies

Mc Graw Hill

McGraw-Hill Ryerson

Corporate Finance
Fourth Canadian Edition

Copyright © 2005, 2003, 1999, 1995 by McGraw-Hill Ryerson Limited, a Subsidiary of The McGraw-Hill Companies. All rights reserved. No part of this publication may be reproduced or transmitted in any form or by any means, or stored in a data base or retrieval system, without the prior written permission of McGraw-Hill Ryerson Limited, or in the case of photocopying or other reprographic copying, a license from The Canadian Copyright Licensing Agency (Access Copyright). For an Access Copyright licence, visit www.accesscopyright.ca or call toll free to 1-800-893-5777.

ISBN: 0-07-09653-X

3 4 5 6 7 8 9 10   TCP   09876

Printed and bound in Canada.

Care has been taken to trace ownership of copyright material contained in this text; however, the publisher will welcome any information that enables them to rectify any reference or credit for subsequent editions.

Executive Sponsoring Editor: Lynn Fisher
Developmental Editor: Maria Chu
Senior Marketing Manager: Kelly Smyth
Supervising Editor: Jaime Smith
Editorial Associate: Stephanie Hess
Copy Editor: Laurel Sparrow
Senior Production Coordinator: Madeleine Harrington
Page Layout: Bookman Typesetting Co. Inc.
Cover Design: Dianna Little
Cover Image: © Eduardo Garcia/Gettyimages
Printer: Transcontinental Printing Group

Library and Archives Canada Cataloguing in Publication

Corporate finance / Stephen A. Ross ... [et al.]. — 4th Canadian ed.

Includes index.
ISBN 0-07-090653-X

1. Corporations—Finance.   2. Corporations—Canada—Finance.
I. Ross, Stephen A.

HG4026.C64 2005   658.15   C2004-907350-8

About the Authors

STEPHEN A. ROSS *Sloan School of Management, Massachusetts Institute of Technology* Stephen Ross is presently the Franco Modigliani Professor of Financial Economics at the Sloan School of Management, Massachusetts Institute of Technology. One of the most widely published authors in finance and economics, Professor Ross is recognized for his work in developing the Arbitrage Pricing Theory, as well as for having made substantial contributions to the discipline through his research in signalling, agency theory, option pricing, and the theory of the term structure of interest rates, among other topics. A past president of the American Finance Association, he currently serves as an associate editor of several academic and practitioner journals. He is a trustee of CalTech, and a director of the College Retirement Equity Fund (CREF), Freddie Mac, and Algorithmics, Inc. He is also the co-chairman of Roll and Ross Asset Management Corporation.

RANDOLPH W. WESTERFIELD *Marshall School of Business, University of Southern California* Randolph W. Westerfield is Dean of the University of Southern California's Marshall School of Business and holder of the Robert R. Dockson Dean's Chair of Business Administration.

He came to USC from the Wharton School, University of Pennsylvania, where he was the chairman of the finance department and a member of the finance faculty for 20 years. He is a member of several public company boards of directors including Health Management Associates, Inc., William Lyon Homes, and the Nicholas Applegate growth fund. His areas of expertise include corporate financial policy, investment management, and stock market price behaviour.

JEFFREY F. JAFFE *Wharton School of Business, University of Pennsylvania* Jeffrey F. Jaffe has been a frequent contributor to finance and economic literature in such journals as the *Quarterly Economic Journal, The Journal of Finance, The Journal of Financial and Quantitative Analysis, The Journal of Financial Economics,* and *The Financial Analysts Journal.* His best known work concerns insider trading, where he showed both that corporate insiders earn abnormal profits from their trades and that regulation has little effect on these profits. He has also made contributions concerning initial public offerings, regulation of utilities, the behaviour of marketmakers, the fluctuation of gold prices, the theoretical effect of inflation on the interest rate, the empirical effect of inflation on capital asset prices, the relationship between small capitalization stocks and the January effect, and the capital structure decision.

GORDON S. ROBERTS *Schulich School of Business, York University* Gordon Roberts is Canadian Imperial Bank of Commerce Professor of Financial Services at the Schulich School of Business, York University. His extensive teaching experience includes finance classes for undergraduate and MBA students, managers, and bankers. Professor Roberts conducts research on duration models for bond portfolio management, corporate finance, and banking. He serves on the editorial boards of several Canadian and international academic journals. Professor Roberts has been a consultant to a number of organizations, including the Office of the Superintendent of Financial Institutions, the Canada Deposit Insurance Corporation, and Canada Investment and Savings, as well as the Debt Management Office of New Zealand. He has appeared as an expert witness on utility rates of return and capital structures in regulatory hearings in Nova Scotia, Quebec, Ontario, and Alberta.

Brief Contents

Contents

C h a p t e r 1 3
Risk, Return, and Capital Budgeting   353

Executive Summary   353

Preface

The teaching and practice of corporate finance in Canada is more challenging and exciting than ever before. The last decade has seen fundamental changes in financial markets and financial instruments. In the early years of the 21st century, we still see announcements in the financial press about such matters as takeovers, junk bonds, financial restructuring, initial public offerings, bankruptcy, and derivatives. In addition, there is the new recognition of "real" options (Chapters 21 and 22), private equity and venture capital (Chapter 19), and the disappearing dividend (Chapter 18). The world's financial markets are more integrated than ever before. Both the theory and practice of corporate finance have been moving ahead with uncommon speed, and our teaching must keep pace.

These developments place new burdens on the teaching of corporate finance. On one hand, the changing world of finance makes it more difficult to keep materials up to date. On the other hand, the teacher must distinguish the permanent from the temporary and avoid the temptation to follow fads. Our solution to this problem is to emphasize the modern fundamentals of the theory of finance and make the theory come to life with contemporary examples. All too often, the beginning student views corporate finance as a collection of unrelated topics that are unified largely because they are bound together between the covers of one book. As in the previous editions, our aim is to present corporate finance as the working of a small number of integrated and powerful institutions.

The Intended Audience of This Book

This book has been written for the introductory courses in corporate finance at the MBA level, and for the intermediate courses in many undergraduate programs. Some instructors will find our text appropriate for the introductory course at the undergraduate level as well.

We assume that most students either will have taken, or will be concurrently enrolled in, courses in accounting, statistics, and economics. This exposure will help students understand some of the more difficult material. However, the book is self-contained, and a prior knowledge of these areas is not essential. The only mathematics prerequisite is basic algebra.

New to the Fourth Canadian Edition

Following are key revisions and updates to this edition:

- Significant reorganization of material on **financial accounting, cash flows, and growth.** Corporate financial models and long-term planning are now included with the early chapters (Chapter 3) to provide earlier, expanded coverage of **cash flow** (Chapter 2) and **sustainable growth** (Chapter 3) to bridge accounting and valuation concepts.
- New material on **alternatives to NPV** such as modified Internal Rate of Return (IRR) and better treatment of the profitability index is presented in Chapter 7. There is also new

Learning Solutions

material on **capital budgeting "best practices,"** where the authors relate what companies actually do to theoretical models, showcasing the latest research and scholarship.

- **New material on risk analysis and real options** (Chapter 9) is reflected in the new chapter title, Risk Analysis, Real Options, and Capital Budgeting. This reinforces the capital budgeting material from the previous chapter. New coverage of real options is now earlier in the book, as is coverage of Monte Carlo simulation techniques.
- Chapter 14 includes new material on **efficient markets behavioural finance.** This content covers a new way of thinking about financial markets and behavioural users versus efficient markets theory.
- Incorporates the latest theoretical developments in **capital budgeting, capital structure, and dividends** throughout Chapters 8, 16, 17, and 19.
- **New problems** added in most chapters.

Below are the new and updated fourth edition features.

Executive Summary

Keeping the theory and concepts current and up-to-date is only one phase of developing a corporate finance text. To be an effective teaching tool, the text must present the theory and concepts in a coherent way that can be easily learned. With this in mind, we have included several study features:

EXECUTIVE SUMMARY

Air Canada has long been the nation's largest airline. As a result of numerous setbacks in the travel industry, the company entered bankruptcy protection in 2003, with cash flows falling significantly short of $12 billion, owing to creditors. As of April 2004, the company had $900 million in available cash, despite suffering a loss of $1.9 billion in the previous year.[1] In the face of insolvency, Air Canada's unions agreed to take $850 million in job and pay cuts in an attempt to alleviate cash flow pressures on the company in 2004. At the time of writing, Air Canada is negotiating with investors in order to secure operations for the future. Air Canada's experience illustrates the basic concepts of corporate finance (discussed in Section 1.1):

Executive Summary

Each chapter begins with a "roadmap" that describes the objectives of the chapter and how it connects with concepts already learned in previous chapters. Real company examples that will be discussed are highlighted in this section.

In Their Own Words Boxes

Located throughout the chapters, this unique series consists of articles written by distinguished scholars or practitioners on key topics in the text.

In Their Own Words

Bombardier Didn't Heed Teachers on Share Structure

As one of Canada's first families of business now knows, the country's biggest money managers are starting to play hardball on corporate governance.

Bombardier Inc. executives made the rounds at the big pension funds this winter, as newly named CEO Paul Tellier explored the idea of selling stock to rebuild a debt-heavy balance sheet. The **Ontario Teachers Pension Plan Board** was among the first stops.

Brian Gibson, senior vice-president of the $68-billion fund, revealed this week at the Association of Investment...

...success, Bombardier opted for family interests over the best equity deal.

As a result of the stock sale, existing shareholders suffered massive dilution. But with the dual share structure, members of a Bombardier clan who were at the controls when the company went off the rails were able to maintain the status quo on ownership.

While he's a bit frustrated with shortsighted shareholders who don't make full use of their clout, content instead to remain second-class owners, Mr. Gibson is...

Concept Questions

Included after each major section in a chapter, Concept Questions point to essential material and allow students to test their recall and comprehension before moving forward.

Figures and Tables

This text makes extensive use of real data and presents them in various figures and tables. Explanations in the narrative, examples, and end-of-chapter problems will refer to many of these exhibits.

Examples

Separate called-out examples are integrated throughout the chapters. Each example illustrates an intuitive or mathematical application in a step-by-step format. There is enough detail in the explanations that the student doesn't have to look elsewhere for additional information.

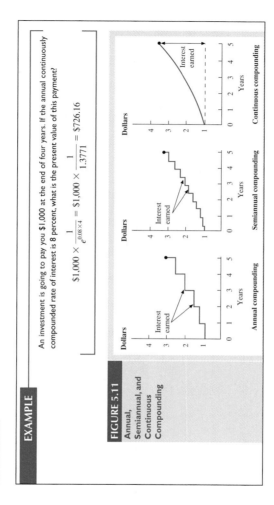

EXAMPLE

An investment is going to pay you $1,000 at the end of four years. If the annual continuously compounded rate of interest is 8 percent, what is the present value of this payment?

$$\$1,000 \times \frac{1}{e^{0.08 \times 4}} = \$1,000 \times \frac{1}{1.3771} = \$726.16$$

FIGURE 5.11

Annual, Semiannual, and Continuous Compounding

Equations

Key equations are numbered and highlighted for easy reference.

Highlighted Concepts

Throughout the text, important ideas are pulled out and presented in a box—signalling to students that this material is particularly relevant and critical to their understanding.

Relevant Data from Example of Supertech and Slowpoke

Item	Symbol	Value
Expected return on Supertech	$\bar{R}_{Super}$	0.175 = 17.5%
Expected return on Slowpoke	$\bar{R}_{Slow}$	0.055 = 5.5%
Variance of Supertech	σ^2_{Super}	0.066875
Variance of Slowpoke	σ^2_{Slow}	0.013225
Standard deviation of Supertech	σ_{Super}	0.2586 = 25.86%
Standard deviation of Slowpoke	σ_{Slow}	0.1150 = 11.50%
Covariance between Supertech and Slowpoke	$\sigma_{Super, Slow}$	−0.004875
Correlation between Supertech and Slowpoke	$\rho_{Super, Slow}$	−0.1639

Case Study

Four case studies are highlighted in the Fourth Canadian Edition that present situations with real companies and how they rationalized the decisions they made to solve various problems. They provide extended examples of the material covered in the chapter. The cases are highlighted in the detailed Table of Contents.

IPOs in Practice: The Case of Air Canada

In October 1988, the Government of Canada sold 30.8 million shares of Air Canada stock in a successful partial privatization.[22] The IPO was priced at $8 per share and generated $234 million after flotation costs. The airline (government-owned since its inception as Trans-Canada Air Lines in 1937) was to remain under government majority ownership, but the government promised to refrain from taking an active role in management. At the time, the airline industry was enjoying strong growth in revenue passenger miles domestically and more moderate growth in international markets. Deregulation improved flexibility and was expected to benefit Air Canada. Net income was volatile due to fluctuating fuel prices, but had hit a high of $46 million in 1987.

The shares issued were voting shares, but non-Canadian shareholders were restricted from voting more than 25 percent of the shares. Proceeds of the issue were roughly split between retir-

End-of-Chapter Material

The end-of-chapter material reflects and builds upon the concepts learned from the chapter and study features.

Summary and Conclusions

The numbered summary provides a quick review of key concepts in the chapter.

10.6 SUMMARY AND CONCLUSIONS

1. This chapter explores capital market history. Such history is useful because it tells us what to expect in the way of returns from risky assets. We summed up our study of market history with two key lessons:

   a. Risky assets, on average, earn a risk premium. There is a reward for bearing risk.

   b. The greater the risk from a risky investment, the greater is the required reward.

   These lessons' implications for the financial manager are discussed in the chapters ahead.

2. The statistical measures in this chapter are necessary building blocks for the next three chapters. Standard deviation and variance measure the variability of the return on an individual security.

List of Key Terms

A list of the boldfaced key terms in the text with page numbers is included for easy reference.

Suggested Readings

Each chapter is followed by a short, annotated list of books, articles, and websites to which interested students can refer for additional information on key topics.

Questions and Problems

Because solving problems is so critical to a student's learning, new questions and problems have been added, and existing questions and problems have been revised. All problems have also been thoroughly reviewed and accuracy-checked.

Problems have been grouped according to the concepts they test on, with the concept headings listed at the beginning of each group.

Additionally, we have tried to make the problems in the critical "concept" chapters, such as those on value, risk, and capital structure, especially challenging and interesting.

We provide answers to selected problems in Appendix B located on the OLC at www.mcgrawhill.ca/college/ross.

S&P Problems

New! Now included in the end-of-chapter material are problems directly incorporating the Educational Version of Market Insight, a service based on Standard & Poor's renowned Compustat database. These problems provide you with an easy method of including current real-world data into the finance course. This web-based resource is available with each new copy of the text.

S & P
PROBLEM

STANDARD
&POOR'S

5.56 Under the "Excel Analytics" link find the "Mthly. Adj. Price" for BCE stock. What was your annual return over the last four years assuming you purchased the stock at the close price four years ago? (Assume no dividends were paid.) Using this same return, what price will BCE stock sell for five years from now? ten years from now? What if the stock prices increases at 11 percent per year?

Excel Problems

EXCEL

Indicated by the Excel icon in the margin, these problems can be found at the end of almost all chapters. Located on the book's website (see Technology Solutions), Excel templates have been created for each of these problems, where students can use the data in the problem to work out the solution using Excel skills.

Minicase

This end-of-chapter feature, located in Chapters 13 and 30, parallels the Case Study feature found in various chapters. These Minicases apply what is learned in a number of chapters to a real-world type of scenario. After presenting the facts, the student is given guidance in rationalizing a sound business decision.

MINICASE: AlliedProducts

AlliedProducts, Inc., has recently won approval from Transport Canada for its Enhanced Ground Proximity Warning System (GPWS). This system is designed to give airplane pilots additional warning of approaching ground danger and, thus, help prevent crashes. AlliedProducts has spent $10 million in research and development over the past four years developing GPWS. The GPWS will be put on the market beginning this year and AlliedProducts expects it to stay on the market for five years.

As a financial analyst specializing in the aerospace industry for United Pension & Investment, Inc., you are asked by your managing partner, Adam Smith, to evaluate the potential of this new GPWS project.

Initially, AlliedProducts will need to acquire $42 million in production equipment to make the GPWS. The equipment is expected to have a seven-year useful life. This equipment can be sold for $12 million at the end of five years. AlliedProducts intends to sell two different versions of the GPWS:

airplane manufacturing industry. Airline industry analysts have the following production expectations, depending on the annual state of the economy for the next five years:

State of economy	Probability of State	New Aircraft (year 1)	Annual Growth
Strong growth	0.15	350	0.15
Moderate growth	0.45	250	0.10
Mild recession	0.30	150	0.06
Severe recession	0.10	50	0.03

While probabilities of each state of the economy do not change during the next five years, airplane production for each state will increase, as shown in the table, each year after year 1. Transport Canada requires that each of these planes have a new ground proximity warning system, of which there are a number of manufacturers besides AlliedProducts.

Technology Solutions

Online Learning Centre

More and more students are studying online. That is why we offer an Online Learning Centre (OLC) that follows *Corporate Finance* chapter by chapter. You don't have to build or maintain anything and it's ready to go the moment you and your students type in the URL:

www.mcgrawhill.ca/college/ross

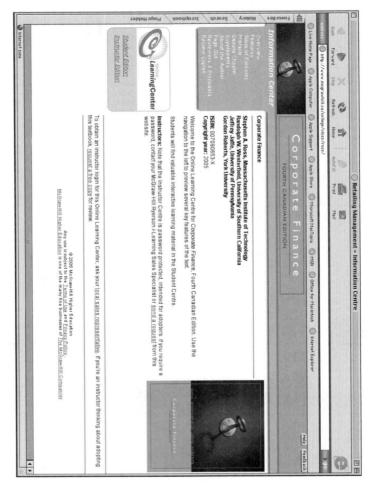

As your students study, they can refer to the OLC website for such benefits as:

- Online Quizzes
- Access to the Educational Version of Standard & Poor's Market Insight
- S&P Problems
- Essay Questions
- Problems
- Annotated Web Links
- *Globe and Mail* Headline Links
- Appendix B (Answers to selected End-of-Chapter Problems)

- Finance Around the World
- Study to Go
- Excel templates tied to end-of-chapter text material
- Glossary and Key Terms
- Summary and Conclusions
- Additional Material
- Videos

Remember, the *Corporate Finance* OLC content is flexible enough to use with any course management platform currently available. If your department or school is already using a platform, we can help. For information on our course management services, contact your iLearning Sales Specialist or see "Superior Service" on page xxii.

Classroom Performance System (CPS)

Bring interactivity into the classroom or lecture hall.

CPS, by eInstruction, is a student response system using wireless connectivity. It gives instructors and students immediate feedback from the entire class. The response pads are remotes that are easy to use and engage students.

- CPS helps you to increase student preparation, interactivity, and active learning so you can receive immediate feedback and know what students understand.
- CPS allows you to administer quizzes and tests, and provide immediate grading.
- With CPS you can create lecture questions that can be multiple-choice, true/false, and subjective. You can even create questions on-the-fly as well as conduct group activities.
- CPS not only allows you to evaluate classroom attendance, activity, and grading for your course as a whole, but CPS Online allows you to provide students with an immediate study guide. All results and scores can easily be imported into Excel and can be used with various classroom management systems.

CPS-ready content is available for use with Ross, *Corporate Finance*. Please contact your *i*Learning Sales Specialist for more information on how you can integrate CPS into your corporate finance classroom.

Mobile Learning

STUDY TO GO The businesses and companies of today want their new employees to be adept in all aspects of the changing business environment. They are quick to tell us they want graduates with the skills of tomorrow . . . today. From laptops to cell phones to PDAs, the new medium is mobility.

As a leader in technology and innovation, McGraw-Hill Ryerson has developed material providing students with optimum flexibility for use anytime, anywhere they need to study—whether with a laptop, PDA, or tablet. These innovations provide instructors with a number of exciting ways to integrate technology into the learning process.

With **Study To Go** we have introduced wireless activities as a part of our Online Learning Centre. Now, whether you are waiting in line, riding on transit, or just filling some spare time, homework and practice are just a click away.

POWERWEB AND POWERWEB TO GO Keeping your course current can be a job in itself, and now McGraw-Hill Ryerson can do it for you. **PowerWeb** extends the learning experience beyond the core textbook by offering all the latest news and developments pertinent to your course via the Internet, without all the clutter and dead links of a typical online search.

PowerWeb offers current articles related to corporate finance, weekly updates with assessment tools, informative and timely world news culled by a finance expert, refereed web links, and more. In addition, PowerWeb provides an array of helpful learning aids, including self-grading quizzes and interactive glossaries and exercises. Students may also access study tips, conduct online research, and learn about different career paths. Visit the PowerWeb site at *http://www.dushkin.com/powerweb* and see firsthand what PowerWeb can mean to your course.

PowerWeb To Go is a new McGraw-Hill content offering designed specifically for use on handheld devices. PowerWeb To Go content consists of current news stories, weekly updates, and magazine articles developed specifically for corporate finance. It is revised daily, giving you the most up-to-date, course-specific information available and is easily loaded onto your Pocket PC or Palm OS handheld device. Visit the PowerWeb To Go site at *www.powerwebtogo.com* for information on how you can sign up today.

Superior Service

Course Management

PAGEOUT McGraw-Hill Ryerson's course management system, PageOut, is the easiest way to create a website for your corporate finance course. There is no need for HTML coding, graphic design, or a thick how-to book. Just fill in a series of boxes in plain English and click on one of our professional designs. In no time, your course is online!

For the integrated instructor, we offer *Corporate Finance* content for complete online courses. Whatever your needs, you can customize the *Corporate Finance* Online Learning Centre content and author your own online course materials. It is entirely up to you. You can offer online discussion and message boards that will complement your office hours, and reduce the lines outside your door. Content cartridges are also available for course management systems, such as **WebCT** and **Blackboard**. Ask your *i*Learning Sales Specialist for details.

Superior Service

SUPERIOR SERVICE Service takes on a whole new meaning with McGraw-Hill Ryerson and *Corporate Finance*. More than just bringing you the textbook, we have consistently raised the bar in terms of innovation and educational research—both in finance and in education in general. These investments in learning and the education community have helped us to understand the needs of students and educators across the country, and allowed us to foster the growth of truly innovative, integrated learning.

INTEGRATED LEARNING Your Integrated Learning Sales Specialist is a McGraw-Hill Ryerson representative who has the experience, product knowledge, training, and support to help you assess and integrate any of our products, technology, and services into your course for optimum teaching and learning performance. Whether it's helping your students improve their grades, or putting your entire course online, your *i*Learning Sales Specialist is there to help you do it. Contact your *i*Learning Sales Specialist today to learn how to maximize all of McGraw-Hill Ryerson's resources!

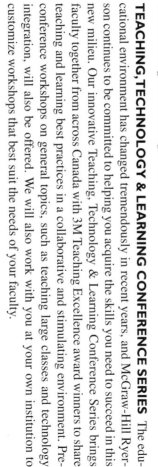

iLEARNING SERVICES McGraw-Hill Ryerson offers a unique *i*Service package designed for Canadian faculty. Our mission is to equip providers of higher education with superior tools and resources required for excellence in teaching. For additional information, visit *www.mcgrawhill.ca/highereducation/iservices*.

TEACHING, TECHNOLOGY & LEARNING CONFERENCE SERIES The educational environment has changed tremendously in recent years, and McGraw-Hill Ryerson continues to be committed to helping you acquire the skills you need to succeed in this new milieu. Our innovative Teaching, Technology & Learning Conference Series brings faculty together from across Canada with 3M Teaching Excellence award winners to share teaching and learning best practices in a collaborative and stimulating environment. Preconference workshops on general topics, such as teaching large classes and technology integration, will also be offered. We will also work with you at your own institution to customize workshops that best suit the needs of your faculty.

RESEARCH REPORTS INTO MOBILE LEARNING AND STUDENT SUCCESS These landmark reports, undertaken in conjunction with academic and private sector advisory boards, are the result of research studies into the challenges professors face in helping students succeed and the opportunities that new technology presents to impact teaching and learning.

Comprehensive Teaching and Learning Package

For the Instructor

As with the text, extraordinary quality and utility was the primary objective in developing supplements. Each component in the supplements package underwent extensive review and revision.

Instructor's Online Learning Centre (www.mcgrawhill.ca/college/ross)

The Online Learning Centre includes a password-protected website for instructors. The site offers downloadable supplements, solutions to the Excel spreadsheets found on the student site, and PageOut, the McGraw-Hill Ryerson course website and development centre.

Instructor's CD-ROM

This CD-ROM includes the following Instructors Supplements:

Instructor's Manual
Prepared by Ingrid McLeod-Dick, Schulich School of Business, York University. Part I of the Instructor's Manual contains, by chapter, a brief chapter outline, an introduction, and an annotated outline. This outline provides additional explanations, examples and teaching tips. Part II consists of answers to all Concept Check questions. Part III of the Instructor's Manual consists of solutions for all end-of-chapter problems and has been thoroughly reviewed for accuracy.

PowerPoint Presentation System
Prepared by Gady Jacoby, University of Manitoba, these slides contain useful outlines, summaries, and exhibits from the text.

Test Bank
Prepared by Sanjay Banerji, McGill University, the test bank provides a variety of question formats, multiple-choice questions, problems, and essay questions and levels of difficulty to meet any instructor's testing needs.

For the Students

Student Online Learning Centre (www.mcgrawhill.ca/college/ross)

The Online Learning Centre prepared by Ian Rakita, Concordia University, includes online study material including quizzes, essay questions, problems, annotated web links, Mobile Resources, Excel templates tied to end-of-chapter test material, video clips, S&P Problems, Appendix B (Answers to selected End-of-Chapter Problem) and a link to the S&P site. There is also a link to *Finance Around the World*, a tremendous resource that takes students to important and popular finance websites throughout the world.

Standard & Poor's Educational Version of Market Insight

McGraw-Hill Ryerson and the Institutional Market Services division of Standard & Poor's is pleased to announce an exclusive partnership that offers instructors and students FREE access to the educational version of Standard & Poor's Market Insight with each new textbook. The Educational Version of Market Insight is a rich online resource that provides six years of fundamental financial data for over 1000 companies in the database. S&P-specific problems can be found at the end of almost all chapters in this text. For more details, please see the bound-in card inside the front cover of this text, or visit www.mcgrawhill.ca/edumarketinsight.

Acknowledgments

Many people have contributed their time and expertise to the development and writing of this text. We extend our thanks once again for their assistance and countless insights. For the Fourth Canadian Edition, we thank the following reviewers:

Syed W. Ahmed, *University of Toronto*
Harjeet S. Bhabra, *Concordia University*
Susan Christoffersen, *McGill University*
François Derrien, *University of Toronto*
Wajeeh Elali, *McGill University*
Richard Hudson, *Mount Allison University*
Teresa Longobardi, *University of Manitoba*
Wendy Rotenberg, *University of Toronto*
Jacques Schnabel, *Wilfrid Laurier University*
David A. Stangeland, *University of Manitoba*
Ken Vetzal, *University of Waterloo*

A special thank-you must be given to Jacques Schnabel, Wilfrid Laurier University, for his vigilant efforts as the technical reviewer for the text. His keen eye and attention to detail have contributed greatly to the quality of the final product.

In addition, thanks must be extended to Alex Faseruk, Memorial University for his contributions to the text and to Chantal Allard, Queen's University for providing technical reviews of the solutions and answers.

Much credit must go to a first-class group of people at McGraw-Hill Ryerson who worked on the Fourth Canadian Edition and the support package. Especially important were Lynn Fisher, Executive Sponsoring Editor, and Maria Chu, Developmental Editor. Lynn Fisher championed the project, ensuring that it was well launched. Maria Chu had hands-on responsibility for the revision, fielding queries and juggling deadlines with aplomb. Copy editing of the manuscript was handled ably by Laurel Sparrow with the in-house supervision of Jaime Smith.

Jashar Grewal, Li Hao, and Priya Malik were the research assistants for this project.

Through the development of this edition, we have taken great care to discover and eliminate errors. Our goal is to provide the best Canadian textbook available on this subject. Please write and tell us how to make this a better text. Forward your comments to:

Professor Gordon S. Roberts
Schulich School of Business
4700 Keele Street
York University
North York, Ontario
M3J 1P3

Or, e-mail your comments to *groberts@schulich.yorku.ca*

Stephen A. Ross   **Jeffrey F. Jaffe**
Randolph W. Westerfield   **Gordon S. Roberts**

Part I

Overview

To engage in business, the financial managers of a corporation must find answers to three kinds of important questions. First, what long-term investments should the firm take on? This is the capital budgeting decision. Second, how can cash be raised for the required investments? We call this the financing decision. Third, what short-term investments should the firm take on and how should they be financed? These decisions involve short-term finance.

In Chapter 1 we discuss these important questions, briefly introducing the basic ideas of this book and describing the nature of the modern corporation and why it has emerged as the leading form of the business firm. Using a perspective that views the firm as a set of contracts, the chapter discusses the goals of the modern corporation. Though the goals of shareholders and managers may not always be the same, conflicts usually will be resolved in favour of the shareholders. Finally, the chapter reviews some salient features of modern financial markets. This preliminary material will be familiar to students who have some background in accounting, finance, and economics.

Chapter 2 examines the basic accounting statements. It is review material for students with an accounting background. We describe the balance sheet and the income statement. The point of the chapter is to show the ways of converting data from accounting statements into cash flow. Understanding how to identify cash flow from accounting statements is especially important for later chapters on capital budgeting.

Chapter 3 presents corporate financial planning models. These models play an important role in integrating corporate financial decisions into a feasible plan. The chapter also introduces the concept of sustainable growth and shows how a firm's growth rate depends on its spending characteristics (profit margin and asset turnover) and financial policies (dividend policy and capital structure).

 1

Introduction to Corporate Finance

 2

Accounting Statements and Cash Flow

3

Financial Planning and Growth

Chapter 1

Introduction to Corporate Finance

EXECUTIVE SUMMARY

Air Canada has long been the nation's largest airline. As a result of numerous setbacks in the travel industry, the company entered bankruptcy protection in 2003, with cash flows falling significantly short of $12 billion, owing to creditors. As of April 2004, the company had $900 million in available cash, despite suffering a loss of $1.9 billion in the previous year.[1] In the face of insolvency, Air Canada's unions agreed to take $850 million in job and pay cuts in an attempt to alleviate cash flow pressures on the company in 2004. At the time of writing, Air Canada is negotiating with investors in order to secure operations for the future. Air Canada's experience illustrates the basic concerns of corporate finance (discussed in Section 1.1):

1. What long-term investment strategy should a company take on?
2. How can cash be raised?
3. How much short-term cash flow does a company need to pay its bills?

These are not the only questions of corporate finance. For example, another important question covered in this text is, how should a company divide earnings between payouts to shareholders (dividends) and reinvestment? The three on our list are, however, among the most important questions and, taken in order, they provide a rough outline of our book.

One way that companies raise cash to finance their investment activities is by selling or "issuing" securities. The securities, sometimes called *financial instruments* or *claims*, may be roughly classified as equity or debt, loosely called stocks or bonds. The difference between equity and debt is a basic distinction in the modern theory of finance. All securities of a firm are claims that depend on or are contingent on the value of the firm.[2] In Section 1.2 we show how debt and equity securities depend on the firm's value, and we describe them as different contingent claims.

In Section 1.3 we discuss different organizational forms and the pros and cons of the decision to become a corporation.

In Section 1.4 we take a close look at the goals of the corporation and discuss why maximizing shareholder wealth is likely to be its primary goal. Throughout the rest of the book, we assume that the firm's performance depends on the value of their shares is increased by the firm's decisions.

A company raises cash by issuing securities in the financial markets. In Section 1.5 we describe some of the basic features of the financial markets. Roughly speaking, there are two types of financial markets: money markets and capital markets.

Section 1.6 covers trends in financial markets and management, and the last section of this chapter (1.7) outlines the rest of the book.

[1] "Air Canada Unions Dig In As Rescue Falters," *Airwise News*, April 19, 2004.

[2] We tend to use the words *firm, company,* and *business* interchangeably. However, there is a difference between these and a corporation. We discuss this difference in Section 1.3.

1.1 What Is Corporate Finance?

Suppose you decide to start a firm to make tennis balls. To do this, you hire managers to buy raw materials, and you assemble a workforce that will produce and sell finished tennis balls. In the language of finance, you make an investment in assets such as inventory, machinery, land, and labour. The amount of cash you invest in assets must be matched by an equal amount of cash raised by financing. When you begin to sell tennis balls, your firm will generate cash. This is the basis of value creation. The purpose of the firm is to create value for you, the owner (shareholder). In other words, the goal of the firm and its managers should be to maximize the value of the shareholders' wealth. The value is reflected in the framework of the simple balance-sheet model of the firm.

The Balance-Sheet Model of the Firm

Suppose we take a financial snapshot of the firm and its activities at a single point in time. Figure 1.1, a graphic conceptualization of the balance sheet, will help introduce you to corporate finance.

The assets of the firm are on the left side of the balance sheet. These assets can be thought of as current and fixed. *Fixed assets* are those that will last a long time, such as a building. Some fixed assets are tangible, such as machinery and equipment. Other fixed assets are intangible, such as patents, trademarks, and the quality of management. The other category of assets, *current assets*, comprises those that have short lives, such as inventory. The tennis balls that your firm has made but has not yet sold are part of its inventory. Unless you have overproduced, they will leave the firm shortly.

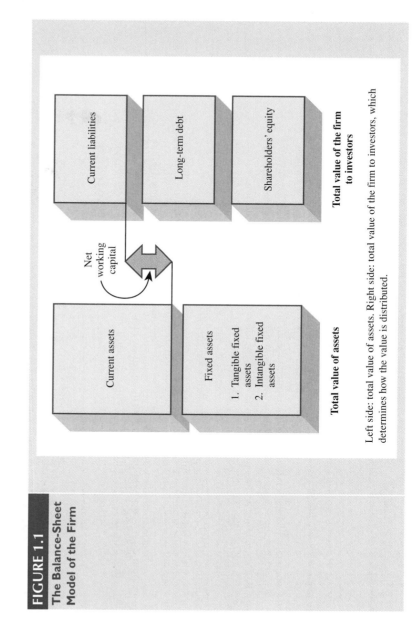

FIGURE 1.1

The Balance-Sheet Model of the Firm

Net working capital

Current assets

Fixed assets

1. Tangible fixed assets
2. Intangible fixed assets

Total value of assets

Current liabilities

Long-term debt

Shareholders' equity

Total value of the firm to investors

Left side: total value of assets. Right side: total value of the firm to investors, which determines how the value is distributed.

Before a company can invest in an asset, it must obtain financing, which means that it must raise the money to pay for the investment. The forms of financing are represented on the right side of the balance sheet. A firm will issue (sell) pieces of paper called *debt* (loan agreements) or *equity shares* (share certificates). Just as assets are classified as long-lived or short-lived, so too are liabilities. A short-term debt is called a *current liability*. Short-term debt represents loans and other obligations that must be repaid within one year. Long-term debt is debt that does not have to be repaid within one year. Shareholders' equity represents the difference between the value of the assets and the debt of the firm. In this sense it is a residual claim on the firm's assets.

From the balance-sheet model of the firm it is easy to see why finance can be thought of as the study of the following three questions:

1. In what long-lived assets should the firm invest? This question concerns the left side of the balance sheet. Of course, the type and proportions of assets the firm needs tend to be set by the nature of the business. We use the terms **capital budgeting** and *capital expenditure* to describe the process of making and managing expenditures on long-lived assets.

2. How can the firm raise cash for required capital expenditures? This question concerns the right side of the balance sheet. The answer involves the firm's **capital structure,** which represents the proportions of the firm's financing from current and long-term debt and equity.

3. How should short-term operating cash flows be managed? This question concerns the upper portion of the balance sheet. There is a mismatch between the timing of cash inflows and cash outflows during operating activities. Furthermore, the amount and timing of operating cash flows are not known with certainty. The financial managers must attempt to manage the gaps in cash flow. From an accounting perspective, short-term management of cash flow is associated with a firm's **net working capital.** Net working capital is defined as current assets minus current liabilities. From a financial perspective, the short-term cash flow problem comes from the mismatching of cash inflows and outflows. It is the subject of short-term finance.

Capital Structure

Financing arrangements determine how the value of the firm is sliced up like a pie. The persons or institutions that buy debt from the firm are called *creditors*.[3] The holders of equity shares are called *shareholders*.

Sometimes it is useful to think of the firm as a pie. Initially, the size of the pie will depend on how well the firm has made its investment decisions. After a firm has made its investment decisions, financial markets determine the value of its assets (e.g., its buildings, land, and inventories).

The firm can then determine its capital structure. It might initially have raised the cash to invest in its assets by issuing more debt than equity; now it can consider changing that mix by issuing more equity and using the proceeds to buy back some of its debt. Financing decisions like this can be made independently of the original investment decisions. The decisions to issue debt and equity affect how the pie is sliced.

The pie we are thinking of is depicted in Figure 1.2. The size of the pie is the value of the firm in the financial markets. We can write the value of the firm, V, as

$$V = B + S$$

where B is the value of the debt (bonds) and S is the value of the equity (shares).

---

[3] We tend to use the words *creditors*, *debtholders*, and *bondholders* interchangeably. In later chapters we examine the differences among the kinds of creditors.

FIGURE 1.2

Two Pie Models of the Firm

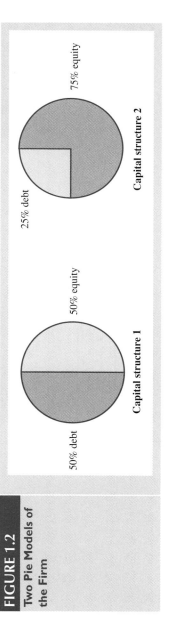

50% debt

50% equity

Capital structure 1

25% debt

75% equity

Capital structure 2

The pie diagram considers two ways of slicing the pie: 50 percent debt and 50 percent equity, and 25 percent debt and 75 percent equity. The way the pie is sliced could affect its value. If so, the goal of the financial manager will be to choose the ratio of debt to equity that makes the value of the pie—that is, the value of the firm, V—as large as it can be.

The Financial Manager

In large firms the finance activity is usually associated with a senior officer of the firm (such as a vice-president of finance) and some lesser officers. Figure 1.3 depicts one example of a general organizational structure emphasizing the finance activity within the firm. Reporting to the vice-president of finance are the treasurer and controller. The treasurer is responsible for handling cash flows, analyzing capital expenditures, and making financing plans. The controller handles the accounting function, which includes taxes, cost and financial accounting, and information systems. Our discussion of corporate finance is much more relevant to the treasurer's function.

We think that a financial manager's most important job is to create value from the firm's capital budgeting, financing, and liquidity activities. How do financial managers create value?

1. The firm should try to buy assets that generate more cash than they cost.
2. The firm should sell bonds, shares, and other financial instruments that raise more cash than they cost.

Thus, the firm must create more cash flow than it uses. The cash flow paid to bondholders and shareholders of the firm should be higher than the cash flows put into the firm by the bondholders and shareholders. To see how this is done, we can trace the cash flows from the firm to the financial markets and back again.

The interplay of the firm's finance with the financial markets is illustrated in Figure 1.4. To finance its planned investment the firm sells debt and equity shares to participants in the financial markets. The resulting cash flows from the financial markets to the firm (A). This cash is invested in the investment activities of the firm (B) by the firm's management. The cash generated by the firm (C) is paid to shareholders and bondholders (F). Shareholders receive cash from the firm in the form of dividends or as share repurchases; bondholders who lent funds to the firm receive interest and, when the initial loan is repaid, principal. Not all of the firm's cash is paid out to shareholders and bondholders. Some is retained (D), and some is paid to governments as taxes (E).

Over time, if the cash paid to shareholders and bondholders (F) is greater than the cash raised in the financial markets (A), value will be created.

FIGURE 1.3
Hypothetical
Organization Chart

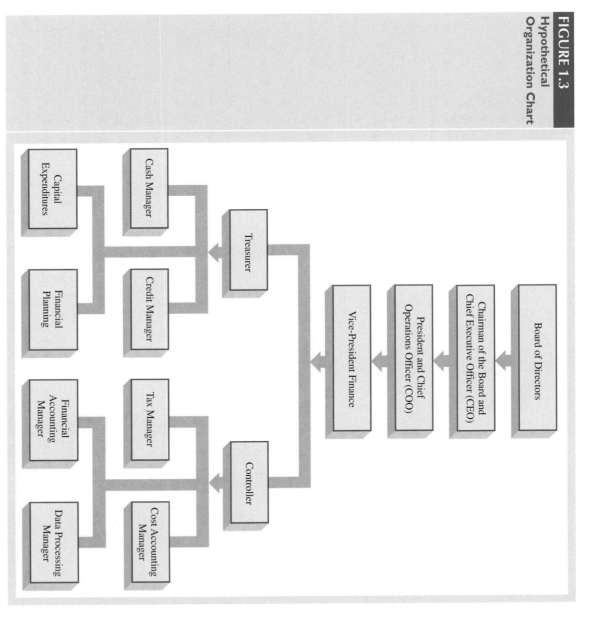

Identification of Cash Flows

Unfortunately, it is not all that easy to observe cash flows directly. Much of the information we obtain is in the form of accounting statements, and much of the work of financial analysis is to extract cash flow information from accounting statements. The following example illustrates how this is done.

The Midland Company refines and trades gold. At the end of the year it sold some gold for $1 million. The company had acquired the gold for $900,000 at the beginning of the year. The company paid cash for the gold when it was purchased. Unfortunately, it has yet to collect from the customer to whom the gold was sold.

The following is a standard accounting of Midland's financial circumstances at year-end:

THE MIDLAND COMPANY
Accounting View
Income Statement
Year Ended December 31

Sales	$1,000,000
Costs	− 900,000
Profit	$ 100,000

By generally accepted accounting principles (GAAP), the sale is recorded even though the customer has yet to pay. It is assumed that the customer will pay soon. From the accounting perspective, Midland seems to be profitable. The perspective of corporate finance is different. It focuses on cash flows:

THE MIDLAND COMPANY
Corporate Finance View
Income Statement
Year Ended December 31

Cash inflow	0
Cash outflow	−$900,000
	−$900,000

The perspective of corporate finance examines whether cash flows are being created by the gold trading operations of Midland. Value creation depends on cash flows. For Midland, value creation depends on whether and when it actually receives $1 million.

FIGURE 1.4

Cash Flows Between the Firm and the Financial Markets

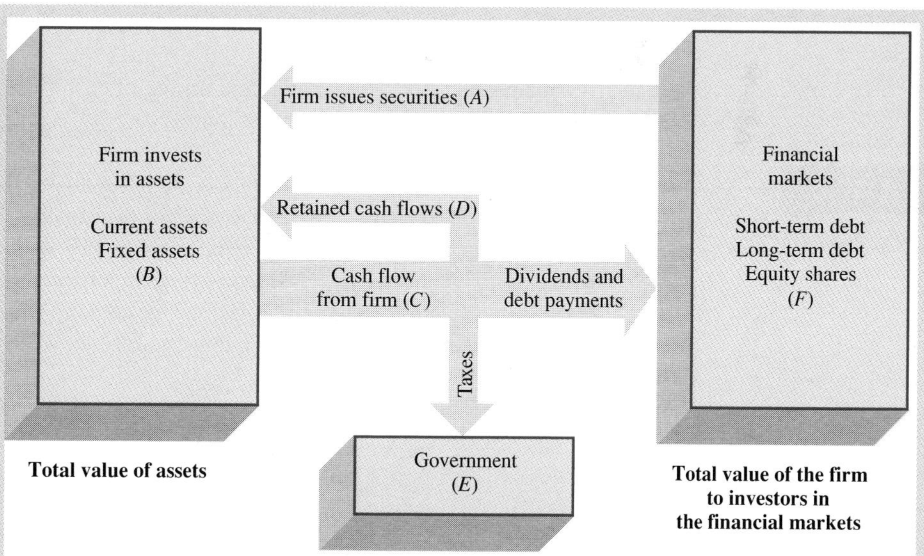

(A) Firm issues securities to raise cash (the financing decision).
(B) Firm invests in assets (capital budgeting).
(C) Firm's operations generate cash flow.
(D) Retained cash flows are reinvested in firm.
(E) Cash is paid to government as taxes.
(F) Cash is paid out to investors in the form of interest and dividends.

Timing of Cash Flows

The value of an investment made by the firm depends on the timing of cash flows. One of the most important principles of finance is that individuals prefer to receive cash flows earlier rather than later. One dollar received today is worth more than one dollar received next year because today's dollar can be invested today to earn interest. This time preference plays a role in stock and bond prices.

The Midland Company is attempting to choose between two proposals for new products. Both proposals will provide cash flows over a four-year period and will initially cost $10,000. The cash flows from the proposals are as follows:

Year	New Product A	New Product B
1	0	$ 4,000
2	0	4,000
3	0	4,000
4	$20,000	4,000
Total	$20,000	$16,000

At first it appears that new product A would be better. However, the cash flows from proposal B come earlier than those of A. Without more information we cannot decide which set of cash flows would create greater value. It depends on whether the value of getting cash from B up front outweighs the extra total cash from A. Bond and stock prices reflect this preference for earlier cash, and we will see how to use them to decide between A and B.

Risk of Cash Flows

The firm must consider risk. The amount and timing of cash flows are not usually known with certainty. Most investors have an aversion to risk.

The Midland Company is considering expanding operations overseas. It is evaluating Europe and Japan as possible sites. Europe is considered to be relatively safe, whereas Japan is seen as very risky. In both cases the company would close down operations after one year.

After doing a complete financial analysis, Midland has come up with the following cash flows of the alternative plans for expansion under three equally likely scenarios: pessimistic, most likely, and optimistic:

	Pessimistic	Most Likely	Optimistic
Europe	$75,000	$100,000	$125,000
Japan	0	150,000	200,000

If we ignore the pessimistic scenario, perhaps Japan is the better alternative. When we take the pessimistic scenario into account, the choice is unclear. Japan appears to be riskier, but it may also offer a higher expected level of cash flow. What is risk and how can it be defined? We must try to answer this important question. Corporate finance cannot avoid coping with risky alternatives, and much of our book is devoted to developing methods for evaluating risky opportunities.

Concept
Questions

- What are three basic questions of corporate finance?
- Describe capital structure.
- List three reasons why value creation is difficult.

1.2 Corporate Securities as Contingent Claims on Total Firm Value

What is the essential difference between debt and equity? The answer can be found by thinking about what happens to the payoffs to debt and equity when the value of the firm changes.

The basic feature of debt is that it is a promise by the borrowing firm to repay a fixed dollar amount by a certain date.

EXAMPLE

The Canadian Corporation promises to pay $100 to the True North Insurance Company at the end of one year. This is a debt of the Canadian Corporation. Holders of the Canadian Corporation's debt will receive $100 if the value of the Canadian Corporation's assets equals $100 or more at the end of the year.

Formally, the debtholders have been promised an amount F at the end of the year. If the value of the firm, X, is equal to or greater than F at year-end, debtholders will get F. Of course, if the firm does not have enough to pay off the promised amount, the firm will be "broke." It may be forced to liquidate its assets for whatever they are worth, and bondholders will receive X. Mathematically this means that the debtholders have a claim to X or F, whichever is smaller. Figure 1.5 illustrates the general nature of the payoff structure to debtholders.

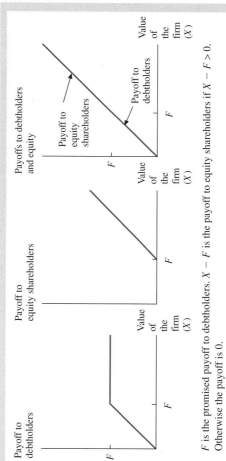

F is the promised payoff to debtholders. $X - F$ is the payoff to equity shareholders if $X - F > 0$. Otherwise the payoff is 0.

FIGURE 1.5
Debt and Equity as Contingent Claims

Suppose at year-end the Canadian Corporation's value is $100. The firm has promised to pay the True North Insurance Company $100, so the debtholders will get $100.

Now suppose the Canadian Corporation's value is $200 at year-end and the debtholders are promised $100. How much will the debtholders receive? It should be clear that they will receive the same amount as when the Canadian Corporation was worth $100.

Suppose the firm's value is $75 at year-end and debtholders are promised $100. How much will the debtholders receive? In this case the debtholders will get $75.

The shareholders' claim on firm value at the end of the period is the amount that remains after the debtholders are paid. Of course, shareholders get nothing if the firm's value is equal to or less than the amount promised to the debtholders.

EXAMPLE

The Canadian Corporation will sell its assets for $200 at year-end. The firm has promised to pay the insurance company $100 at that time. The shareholders will get the residual value of $100.

Algebraically, the shareholders' claim is $X - F$ if $X > F$ and zero if $X \leq F$. This is depicted in Figure 1.5. The sum of the debtholders' claim and the shareholders' claim is always the value of the firm at the end of the period.

The debt and equity securities issued by a firm derive their value from the total value of the firm. In the words of finance theory, debt and equity securities are **contingent claims** on the total firm value.

When the value of the firm exceeds the amount promised to debtholders, the shareholders obtain the residual of the firm's value over the amount promised the debtholders, and the debtholders obtain the amount promised. When the value of the firm is less than the amount promised to the bondholders, the shareholders receive nothing and the debtholders get the value of the firm.

Concept Questions

- **What is a contingent claim?**
- **Describe equity and debt as contingent claims.**

1.3 The Corporate Firm

The firm is a way of organizing the economic activity of many individuals. There are many reasons why so much economic activity is carried out by firms and not by individuals. The theory of firms, however, does not tell us much about why most large firms are corporations rather than any of the other legal forms that firms can assume.

A basic problem of the firm is how to raise cash. The corporate form of business (that is, organizing the firm as a corporation) is the standard method for solving problems encountered in raising large amounts of cash. However, business can take other forms. In this section we consider the three basic legal forms of organizing firms (sole proprietorship, partnership, and corporation) and we see how firms go about the task of raising large amounts of money under each form. We also introduce the income trust, a new non-corporate form of business organization.

The Sole Proprietorship

A **sole proprietorship** is a business owned by one person. Suppose you decide to start a business to produce mousetraps. Going into business is simple: You announce to all who will listen, "Today I am going to build a better mousetrap."

Most large cities require that you obtain a business licence. Afterward, you can try to hire as many people as you need and borrow whatever money you need. At year-end all the profits and the losses will be yours.

Here are some important factors in considering a sole proprietorship:

1. The sole proprietorship is the cheapest type of business to form. No formal charter is required, and few government regulations must be satisfied.

2. A sole proprietorship pays no corporate income taxes. All profits of the business are taxed as individual income.

3. The sole proprietorship has unlimited liability for business debts and obligations. No distinction is made between personal and business assets.

4. The life of the sole proprietorship is limited by the life of the sole proprietor.

5. Because the only money invested in the firm is the proprietor's, the equity money that can be raised by the sole proprietor is limited to the proprietor's personal wealth.

The Partnership

Any two or more persons can get together and form a **partnership.** Partnerships fall into two categories: general partnerships and limited partnerships.

In a *general partnership* all partners agree to provide some fraction of the work and cash and to share the profits and losses. Each partner is liable for the debts of the partnership. A partnership agreement specifies the nature of the arrangement. The partnership agreement may be an oral agreement or a formal document setting forth the understanding.

Limited partnerships permit the liability of some of the partners to be limited to the amount of cash each has contributed to the partnership. Limited partnerships usually require that (1) at least one partner be a general partner and (2) the limited partners do not participate in managing the business.

Here are some points that are important when considering a partnership:

1. Partnerships are usually inexpensive and easy to form. In complicated arrangements, including general and limited partnerships, written documents are required. Business licences and filing fees may be necessary.

2. General partners have unlimited liability for all debts. The liability of limited partners is usually limited to the contribution each has made to the partnership. If one general partner is unable to meet his or her commitment, the shortfall must be made up by the other general partners.

3. The general partnership is terminated when a general partner dies or withdraws (but this is not so for a limited partner). It is difficult for a partnership to transfer ownership without dissolving. Usually, all general partners must agree. However, limited partners may sell their interest in a business.

4. It is difficult for a partnership to raise large amounts of cash. Equity contributions are limited to a partner's ability and desire to contribute to the partnership. Sometimes the partners have no choice about contributing. For example, in 2001, a major global management consulting firm, McKinsey & Company, called on its partners to contribute up to $300,000 each to finance growing accounts receivable. Many companies, such as Apple Computer, start life as a proprietorship or partnership, but at some point they need to convert to corporate form.

5. Income from a partnership is taxed as personal income to the partners.

6. Management control resides with the general partners. Usually a majority vote is required on important matters, such as the amount of profit to be retained in the business.

It is very difficult for large business organizations to exist as sole proprietorships or partnerships. The main advantage is the cost of getting started. Afterward, the disadvantages, which may become severe, are (1) unlimited liability, (2) limited life of the enterprise, and (3) difficulty of transferring ownership. These three disadvantages lead to (4) the difficulty of raising cash.

The Corporation

Of the many forms of business enterprise, the **corporation** is by far the most important. Most large Canadian firms, such as Bank of Montreal and Bombardier, are organized as corporations. As a distinct legal entity, a corporation can have a name and enjoy many of the legal powers of natural persons. For example, corporations can acquire and exchange property. Corporations may enter into contracts and may sue and be sued. For jurisdictional purposes, the corporation is a citizen of its province of incorporation. (It cannot vote, however.)

Starting a corporation is more complicated than starting a proprietorship or partnership. The incorporators must prepare articles of incorporation and a set of bylaws. The articles of incorporation must include:

1. Name of the corporation
2. Business purpose
3. Number of shares that the corporation is authorized to issue, with a statement of limitations and rights of different classes of shares
4. Nature of the rights granted to shareholders
5. Number of members of the initial board of directors.

A Comparison of Partnerships and Corporations

	Corporation	Partnership
Liquidity and marketability	Common stock can be listed on stock exchange.	Units are subject to substantial restrictions on transferability. There is no established trading market for partnership units.
Voting rights	Usually each share of common stock entitles each holder to one vote per share on matters requiring a vote and on the election of the directors. Directors determine top management.	Some voting rights by limited partners. However, general partner has exclusive control and management of operations.
Taxation	Corporate income is taxable. Dividends to shareholders are also taxable with partial integration through use of the dividend tax credit.	Partnership income is taxable.
Reinvestment and dividend payout	Corporations have broad latitude on dividend payout decisions.	Partnerships are generally prohibited from reinvesting partnership cash flow. All net cash flow is distributed to partners.
Liability	Shareholders are not personally liable for obligations of the corporation.	Limited partners are not liable for obligations of partnerships. General partners may have unlimited liability.
Continuity of existence	Corporations have perpetual life.	Partnerships have a limited life.

The bylaws (the rules to be used by the corporation to regulate its own existence) concern its shareholders, directors, and officers. Bylaws range from the briefest possible statement of rules for the corporation's management to hundreds of pages of text.

In its simplest form, the corporation comprises three sets of distinct interests: the shareholders (the owners), the directors, and the corporation officers (the top management). Traditionally, the shareholders control the corporation's direction, policies, and activities. The shareholders elect a board of directors, who in turn select top management who serve as corporate officers.

The separation of ownership from management gives the corporation several advantages over proprietorships and partnerships:

1. Because ownership in a corporation is represented by shares, ownership can be readily transferred to new owners. Because the corporation exists independently of those who own its shares, there is no limit to the transferability of shares as there is in partnerships.

2. The corporation has unlimited life. Because the corporation is separate from its owners, the death or withdrawal of an owner does not affect its existence. The corporation can continue on after the original owners have withdrawn.

3. The shareholders' liability is limited to the amount invested in the ownership shares. For example, if a shareholder purchased $1,000 in shares of a corporation, the potential loss would be $1,000. In a partnership, a general partner with a $1,000 contribution could lose the $1,000 plus any other indebtedness of the partnership.

Limited liability, ease of ownership transfer, and perpetual succession are the major advantages of the corporate form of business organization. These give the corporation an enhanced ability to raise cash.

There is, however, one great disadvantage to incorporation. Federal and provincial governments tax corporate income. Corporate dividends received by shareholders are also taxable. The dividend tax credit for individual shareholders and a corporate dividend exclusion provide a degree of tax integration for Canadian corporations. These tax provisions are discussed in Appendix 1A.

The Income Trust

Starting in 2001, the income trust, a non-corporate form of business organization, has been growing in importance in Canada. As of December 2003, there were over 200 income trusts listed on the Toronto Stock Exchange with a sector market capitalization of $60 billion.[4] These trusts (also called income funds) hold the debt and equity of an underlying business and distribute the income generated to unitholders. Because income trusts are not corporations, unitholders do not enjoy the protection of limited liability. Further, income trusts are not subject to corporate income tax and their income is typically taxed only in the hands of unitholders. As a result, investors see trusts as tax-efficient and the federal government has recently moved to curb their attractiveness due to concerns about lost taxes.

? Concept
Questions

- **Define a proprietorship, a partnership, a corporation, and an income trust.**
- **What are the advantages of the corporate form of business organization?**

---

[4]For a discussion of income trusts, see R. Carrick, "Weekly Insight: Is the Party Over for Income Trusts?" Globefund.com, December 23, 2003, and M. R. King, "Income Trusts: A Growing Asset Class," *Canadian Investment Review* 17 (Spring 2004).

1.4 Goals of the Corporate Firm

What is the primary goal of the corporation? The traditional answer is that managers in a corporation make decisions for the shareholders because the shareholders own and control the corporation. If so, the goal of the corporation is to add value for the shareholders. This goal is a little vague and so we will try to come up with a precise formulation. It is also impossible to give a definitive answer to this important question because the corporation is an artificial being, not a natural person. It exists in the "contemplation of the law."[5]

It is necessary to precisely identify who controls the corporation. We shall consider the **set-of-contracts viewpoint**. This viewpoint suggests the corporate firm will attempt to maximize the shareholders' wealth by taking actions that increase the current value per share of existing stock of the firm.

Agency Costs and the Set-of-Contracts Perspective

The set-of-contracts theory of the firm states that the firm can be viewed as nothing more than a set of contracts.[6] One of the contract claims is a residual claim (equity) on the firm's assets and cash flows. The equity contract can be defined as a principal–agent relationship. The members of the management team are the agents hired to act on behalf of the equity investors (shareholders), who are the principals. This discussion focuses on conflict between shareholders and managers. It is assumed that each of the two groups, left alone, will attempt to act in its own self-interest. We also assume that shareholders are unanimous in defining their self-interest; we explain how perfect markets make this happen in Chapter 3.

The shareholders, however, can discourage the managers from diverging from the shareholders' interests by devising appropriate incentives for managers and then monitoring their behaviour. Doing so, unfortunately, is complicated and costly. The costs of resolving the conflicts of interest between managers and shareholders are special types of costs called **agency costs**. These costs include the monitoring costs of the shareholders and the incentive fee paid to the managers. It can be expected that contracts will be devised that will provide the managers with appropriate incentives to maximize the shareholders' wealth. Thus, agency problems do not mean that the corporate firm will not act in the best interests of shareholders, only that it is costly to make it do so. However, agency problems can never be perfectly solved, and managers may not always act in the best interests of shareholders. *Residual losses* are the lost wealth of the shareholders due to divergent behaviour of the managers.

Managerial Goals

Managerial goals are different from those of shareholders. What will managers maximize if they are left to pursue their own goals rather than shareholders' goals?

Williamson proposes the notion of *expense preference*.[7] He argues that managers obtain value from certain kinds of expenses. In particular, company cars, office furniture, office location, and funds for discretionary investment have value to managers beyond that which comes from their productivity.

---

[5] These are the words of U.S. Chief Justice John Marshall from *The Trustees of Dartmouth College v. Woodward*, 4, Wheaton 636 (1819).

[6] M. C. Jensen and W. Meckling, "Theory of the Firm: Managerial Behavior, Agency Costs and Ownership Structure," *Journal of Financial Economics* 3 (1976).

[7] O. Williamson, "Managerial Discretion and Business Behavior," *American Economic Review* 53 (1963).

Donaldson conducted a series of interviews with chief executives of several large companies.[8] He concluded that managers are influenced by three underlying motivations in defining the corporate mission:

1. *Survival.* Organizational survival means that management must always command sufficient resources to support the firm's activities.

2. *Independence.* This is the freedom to make decisions and take action without encountering external parties or depending on outside financial markets.

3. *Self-sufficiency.* Managers do not want to depend on external parties.

These motivations lead to what Donaldson concludes is the basic financial objective of managers: the maximization of corporate wealth. Corporate wealth is that wealth over which management has effective control; it is closely associated with corporate growth and corporate size. Corporate wealth is not necessarily shareholder wealth. Corporate wealth tends to lead to increased growth by providing funds for growth and limiting the extent to which equity is raised. Increased growth and size are not necessarily the same thing as increased shareholder wealth.

Separation of Ownership and Control

Some people argue that shareholders do not control the corporation. They argue that shareholder ownership is too diffuse and fragmented for effective control of management. A striking feature of the modern large corporation is the diffusion of ownership among thousands of investors. For example, Table 1.1 shows that the largest corporations in Canada are widely held with no shareholder owning 10 percent or more of the shares. While this argument is certainly worth considering, it is less true in Canada than in the United States. Over 70 percent of U.S. corporations were widely held compared to only 15 percent in Canada. Many domestically owned Canadian corporations have controlling shareholders.[9] Still, controlling agency costs through re-examining the rules of corporate governance is of considerable interest in corporate Canada.

As we discussed earlier, one of the most important advantages of the corporate form of business organization is that it allows ownership of shares to be transferred. The resulting diffuse ownership, however, brings with it the separation of ownership and control of

TABLE 1.1	The Largest Canadian Corporations, 2003		
	Number of Shares Outstanding	Market Value (in $ millions)	Ownership
Nortel Networks Corp.	3,838,000,000	45,252.9	Widely held
Royal Bank of Canada	656,021,000	41,631.1	Widely held
The Bank of Nova Scotia	505,353,000	34,707.7	Widely held
The Toronto-Dominion Bank	649,800,000	29,659.7	Widely held
The Thomson Corp.	651,150,484	27,931.6	Widely held

Source: *National Post BUSINESS*, 2004 edition and individual annual reports.

[8]G. Donaldson, *Managing Corporate Wealth: The Operations of a Comprehensive Financial Goals System* (New York: Praeger, 1984).

[9]Important exceptions are chartered banks. The *Bank Act* prohibits any one interest from owning more than 20 percent of the shares.

the large corporation. The possible separation of ownership and control raises an important question: Who controls the firm?

Do Shareholders Control Managerial Behaviour?   The claim that managers can ignore the interests of shareholders is deduced from the fact that ownership in large corporations is widely dispersed. As a consequence, it is often claimed that individual shareholders cannot control management. There is some merit in this argument, but it is too simplistic.

The extent to which shareholders can control managers depends on (1) the costs of monitoring management, (2) the costs of implementing the control devices, and (3) the benefits of control.

When a conflict of interest exists between management and shareholders, who wins? Do managers or shareholders control the firm? Ownership in large corporations is diffuse compared to the closely held corporation. However, shareholders have several control devices (some more effective than others) to bond management to the self-interest of shareholders.

1. Shareholders determine the membership of the board of directors by voting. Thus, shareholders control the directors, who in turn select the management team.

2. Contracts with management and arrangements for compensation, such as stock option plans, can be made so that management has an incentive to pursue shareholders' goals. Similarly, management may be given loans to buy the firm's shares.

3. If the price of a firm's stock drops too low because of poor management, the firm may be acquired by a group of shareholders, by another firm, or by an individual. This is called a takeover. In a takeover, top management of the acquired firm may find itself out of a job. For example, the CEO of Chapters Inc. lost his job when the bookseller was taken over by Indigo in 2001. This pressures management to make decisions in the shareholders' interests. Fear of a takeover gives managers an incentive to take actions that will maximize stock prices.

4. Competition in the managerial labour market may force managers to perform in the best interest of shareholders. Otherwise they will be replaced. Firms willing to pay the most will lure good managers. These are likely to be firms that compensate managers based on the value they create. Compensation design is far from perfect, however, and many firms have come under intense criticism for having high rates of executive compensation amid corporate governance scandals. One example that sparked controversy in 2002 was the case of Eleanor Clitheroe, the former CEO of Hydro One, who earned over $2.2 million in salaries and perks for her work on behalf of the publicly owned corporation.

The available evidence and theory are consistent with the idea of shareholder control. However, there can be no doubt that, at times, corporations pursue managerial goals at the expense of shareholders. In addition to the issue of excessive executive compensation already discussed, management may change the firm's corporate governance rules by removing independent directors who might challenge management. Major pension funds such as the Alberta Teachers' Retirement Fund Board and the Ontario Teachers' Pension Plan Board have joined with professional money managers to form the Canadian Coalition for Good Governance. The Coalition has set up detailed governance guidelines backed by action in voting its shares at annual meetings.[10]

[10] www.ccgg.ca.

Stakeholders   In addition to shareholders and management, employees, customers, suppliers, and the public all have a financial interest in the firm and its decisions. This enlarged stakeholder group may introduce alternative goals such as preserving the environment or avoiding alcohol, tobacco, gambling, nuclear power, and military weapons. Stakeholder concerns are attaining additional clout through the growth of interest in ethical or **socially responsible investing.** Such funds screen and select securities based on social or environmental criteria. For example, ethical investors like Canadian Hydro, a small electric utility in Alberta, B.C., and Ontario, is noted for its green power projects with renewable energy sources and low emissions.[11] Critics argue that socially responsible investing will lower returns and increase risk by excluding profitable investments that do not meet the screening criteria. While some studies find that socially responsible investment practices do not impact portfolio returns and risk consistently, the most recent study supports the critics.[12]

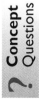

Concept Questions

· **What are two types of agency costs?**
· **How are managers bonded to shareholders?**
· **Can you recall some managerial goals?**
· **What is the set-of-contracts perspective?**
· **What is socially responsible investing?**

1.5 Financial Institutions, Financial Markets, and the Corporation

We have seen that the primary advantages of the corporate form of organization are that (1) ownership can be transferred more quickly and easily than with other forms and (2) money can be raised more readily. Both advantages are significantly enhanced by the existence of financial institutions and markets. Financial markets play an extremely important role in corporate finance.

Financial Institutions

Financial institutions act as intermediaries between investors (funds suppliers) and firms raising funds. (Federal and provincial governments and individuals also raise funds in financial markets but our examples will focus on firms.) Financial institutions justify their existence by providing a variety of services that promote efficient allocation of funds. Canadian financial institutions include chartered banks and other depository institutions (trust companies and credit unions) as well as nondepository institutions (investment dealers, insurance companies, pension funds, and mutual funds).[13]

Table 1.2 ranks Canada's top 10 financial institutions by total assets. They include the "Big Six" domestically owned chartered banks, one credit union (Caisses Desjardins), a

[11] J. Schreiner, "Ethics team applauds Canadian Hydro," *National Post* (February 2, 2001), D3.

[12] A Canadian study supporting the view that socially responsible investing does not harm returns is P. Amundson and S. R. Foerster, "Socially Responsible Investing: Better for Your Soul or Your Bottom Line?" *Canadian Investment Review,* Winter 2001, pp. 26–34. A contrary U.S. study is C. Geczy, R. F. Stambaugh, and D. Levin, "Investing in Socially Responsible Mutual Funds," Wharton School Working Paper, May 2003.

[13] Our discussion of Canadian financial institutions draws on L. Kryzanowski and G. S. Roberts, "Bank Structure in Canada," in *Banking Structure in Major Countries,* ed. G. G. Kaufman (Boston: Kluwer, 1992).

pension fund (Caisse de dépôt), and two financial holding companies (Power Financial and Fairfax Financial).

Because they are allowed to diversify by operating in all provinces, Canada's chartered banks are good-sized on an international scale. Table 1.2 shows that the chartered banks also held the top slots domestically in 2003. Over time, pension funds and financial holding companies offering one-stop financial shopping are gaining on the banks.

Chartered banks operate under federal regulation, accepting deposits from suppliers of funds and making commercial loans to mid-sized businesses, corporate loans to large companies, and personal loans and mortgages to individuals. Banks make the majority of their income from the spread between the interest paid on deposits and the higher rate earned on loans. This process is called indirect finance because banks receive funds in the form of deposits and engage in a separate lending contract with funds demanders. Figure 1.6's top panel illustrates indirect finance.

Chartered banks also provide other services that generate fees instead of spreading income. For example, a large corporate customer seeking short-term debt funding can borrow directly from another large corporation with funds to supply through a banker's acceptance. This is an interest-bearing IOU that is stamped by a bank guaranteeing the borrower's credit. Instead of spread income, the bank receives a stamping fee. Banker's acceptances are an example of direct finance as illustrated in Figure 1.6's lower panel. Notice that in this case, funds do not pass through the bank's balance sheet in the form of a deposit and loan. This is often called securitization because a security (the banker's acceptance) is created.

Trust companies also accept deposits and make loans. In addition, trust companies engage in fiduciary activities—managing assets for estates, registered retirement savings plans, and so on. Banks own all the major trust companies. Like trust companies, credit unions also accept deposits and make loans.

Investment dealers are nondepository institutions that assist firms in issuing new securities in exchange for fee income. Investment dealers also aid investors in buying and selling securities. Chartered banks own majority stakes in Canada's top investment dealers.

Insurance companies include property and casualty insurance and health and life insurance companies. Life insurance companies accept funds in a form similar to deposits and make loans.

TABLE 1.2   The Largest Financial Institutions in Canada, 2003

	Rank by Total Assets	Assets (in $ millions)
Royal Bank of Canada	1	403,033
The Bank of Nova Scotia	2	285,892
Canadian Imperial Bank of Commerce	3	277,147
The Toronto-Dominion Bank	4	273,532
Bank of Montreal	5	256,494
Caisse de dépôt et placement du Québec	6	118,838
Power Financial Corp.	7	105,960
Le mouvement des caisses Desjardins	8	94,652
National Bank of Canada	9	82,423
Fairfax Financial Holdings Ltd.	10	32,436

Source: National Post BUSINESS, 2004 edition.

FIGURE 1.6

**Two Types of
Finance**

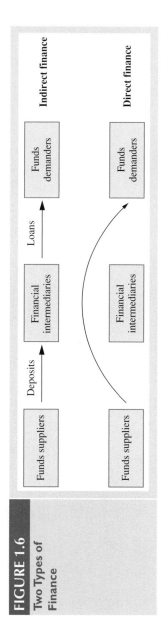

Pension funds invest contributions from employers and employees in securities offered by financial markets. Mutual funds pool individual investments to purchase a diversified portfolio of securities.

We base this survey of the principal activities of financial institutions on their main activities today. Recent deregulation now allows chartered banks, insurance companies, and investment dealers to engage in most activities of the others with one exception: Chartered banks are not allowed to sell life insurance through their branch networks. Although not every institution plans to become a one-stop financial supermarket, the different types of institutions will likely continue to become more alike.

Like financial institutions, financial markets differ. Principal differences concern the types of securities that are traded, how trading is conducted, and who the buyers and sellers are. Some of these differences are discussed next.

Money Versus Capital Markets

Financial markets can be classified as either money markets or capital markets. Short-term debt securities of many varieties are bought and sold in **money markets.** These short-term debt securities are often called money-market instruments and are essentially IOUs. For example, a banker's acceptance represents short-term borrowing by large corporations and is a money-market instrument. Treasury bills are an IOU of the Government of Canada. **Capital markets** are the markets for long-term debt and shares of stock, so the Toronto Stock Exchange, for example, is a capital market.

The money market is a dealer market. Generally speaking, dealers buy and sell something for themselves at their own risk. A car dealer, for example, buys and sells automobiles. In contrast, brokers and agents match buyers and sellers, but they do not actually own the commodity. A real estate agent or broker, for example, does not normally buy and sell houses.

The largest money-market dealers are chartered banks and investment dealers. Their trading facilities, along with other market participants, are connected electronically via telephone and computer so the money market has no actual physical location.

Primary Versus Secondary Markets

Financial markets function as both primary and secondary markets for debt and equity securities. The term *primary market* refers to the original sale of securities by governments and corporations. The secondary markets are where these securities are bought and sold after the original sale. Equities are, of course, issued solely by corporations. Debt securities are issued by both governments and corporations. The following discussion focuses on corporate securities only.

Primary Markets   In a primary market transaction, the corporation is the seller and raises money through the transaction. For example, in 1999 and early 2000, many untested dot-com companies issued public shares for the first time in initial public offerings (IPOs). Corporations engage in two types of primary market transactions: public offerings and private placements. A public offering, as the name suggests, involves selling securities to the general public, while a private placement is a negotiated sale involving a specific buyer. These topics are detailed in Chapters 20 and 21 so we only introduce the bare essentials here.

Most publicly offered debt and equity securities are underwritten. In Canada, underwriting is conducted by investment dealers specializing in marketing securities. Three of Canada's largest underwriters are RBC Dominion, Merrill Lynch, and CIBC World Markets.

When a public offering is underwritten, an investment dealer or a group of investment dealers (called a *syndicate*) typically purchases the securities from the firm and markets them to the public. The underwriters hope to profit by reselling the securities to investors at a higher price than they paid the firm for them.

By law, public offerings of debt and equity must be registered with provincial authorities, the most important being the Ontario Securities Commission (OSC). Registration requires the firm to disclose a great deal of information before selling any securities. The accounting, legal, and underwriting costs of public offerings can be considerable.

Partly to avoid the various regulatory requirements and the expense of public offerings, debt and equity are often sold privately to large financial institutions such as life insurance companies or pension funds. Such private placements do not have to be registered with the OSC and do not require the involvement of underwriters.

Secondary Markets   A secondary market transaction involves one owner or creditor selling to another. It is therefore the secondary markets that provide the means for transferring ownership of corporate securities. There are two kinds of secondary markets: auction markets and dealer markets.

Dealer markets in stocks and long-term debt are called over-the-counter (OTC) markets. Today, like the money market, a significant fraction of the market for stocks and all of the market for long-term debt has no central location; the many dealers are connected electronically. Nasdaq in the U.S. is a well-known over-the-counter market. As Table 1.3 shows, it is the third-largest stock market in the world. The name comes from the National Association of Securities Dealers (NASD), which sets up the automated quotation (AQ) system. Many smaller technology stocks are listed on Nasdaq, and the Nasdaq 100 index reflects the rise and fall of tech stocks.

The equity shares of most large firms in Canada trade in organized auction and dealer markets. The largest stock market in Canada is the Toronto Stock Exchange (TSX). Table 1.3 shows the top 10 stock exchanges in the world in 2002. The TSX ranked seventh. Smaller exchanges in Canada include the Montreal Exchange and the CDNX, which consists primarily of smaller oil and gas, mining, IT, and biotechnology companies.

Auction markets differ from dealer markets in two ways. First, an auction market or exchange, unlike a dealer market, has a physical location (like Bay Street or Wall Street). Second, in a dealer market, most buying and selling is done by the dealer. The primary purpose of an auction market, on the other hand, is to match those who wish to sell with those who wish to buy. Dealers play a limited role. For example, the TSX has computerized its floor trading, replacing the trading floor with a wide-area computer network. This technological shift makes the TSX a hybrid of auction and dealer markets.

TABLE 1.3	The Largest Stock Markets in the World by Market Capitalization in 2002	
	Market Value (in U.S. $ billions)	Rank in 2002
New York	9,015.3	1
Tokyo	2,069.3	2
Nasdaq	1,994.5	3
London	1,800.7	4
Euronext	1,538.7	5
Deutsche Borse	686.0	6
Toronto	570.2	7
Switzerland	547.0	8
Italy	477.1	9
Hong Kong	463.1	10

Source: World Federation of Exchanges at www.world-exchanges.org.

Listing

Stocks that trade on an organized exchange are said to be *listed* on that exchange. Companies seek exchange listing in order to enhance the liquidity of their shares, making them more attractive to investors by facilitating raising equity.[14] To be listed, firms must meet certain minimum criteria concerning, for example, the number of shares and shareholders and the market value. These criteria differ for different exchanges. To be listed on the TSX, a company must have at least one million shares trading, at least 300 public shareholders, and a market value of $4 million. There are additional requirements for earnings and assets that depend on the industry and whether the company is established and profitable or a junior firm. For example, profitable industrial firms must have earnings before tax of at least $200,000 in the year before listing and net tangible assets of $2 million. In contrast, technology firms with no earnings are allowed to list provided they have $10 million in the treasury and a market value of at least $50 million.

Foreign Exchange Market

The **foreign exchange market** is undoubtedly the world's largest financial market. It is the market where one country's currency is traded for another's. Most of the trading takes place in a few currencies: the U.S. dollar ($), the euro (€), British pound sterling (£), Japanese yen (¥), and Swiss franc (SF).

The foreign exchange market is an over-the-counter market. There is no single location where traders get together. Instead, traders are located in the major commercial and investment banks around the world. They communicate using computer terminals, telephones, and other telecommunication devices. One element in the communications network for foreign transactions is the *Society for Worldwide Interbank Financial Telecommunications* (SWIFT). It is a Belgian not-for-profit cooperative. A bank in Toronto can send messages to a bank in London via SWIFT's regional processing centres. The connections are through data-transmission lines.

[14]Two relevant studies of Canadian companies listing in the U.S. are S. R. Foerster and G. A. Karolyi, "The Effects of Market Segmentation and Investor Recognition on Asset Prices: Evidence from Foreign Listings in the U.S.," *Journal of Finance* 54 (June 1999), pp. 981–1013 and U. R. Mittoo, "The Winners and Losers of Listings in the U.S.", *Canadian Investment Review* (Fall 1998), pp. 13–17.

The many different types of participants in the foreign exchange market include the following:

1. Importers who convert their domestic currency to foreign currency to pay for goods from foreign countries
2. Exporters who receive foreign currency and may want to convert to the domestic currency
3. Portfolio managers who buy and sell foreign stocks and bonds
4. Foreign exchange brokers who match buy and sell orders
5. Traders who make the market in foreign exchange.

? Concept
Questions

- **Distinguish between money markets and capital markets.**
- **What is listing?**
- **What is the difference between a primary market and a secondary market?**
- **What are the principal financial institutions in Canada? What is the principal role of each?**
- **What are direct and indirect finance? How do they differ?**
- **What is a dealer market? How do dealer and auction markets differ?**
- **What is the largest auction market in Canada?**

1.6 Trends in Financial Markets and Management

Like all markets, financial markets are experiencing rapid globalization. At the same time, interest rates, foreign exchange rates, and other macroeconomic variables have become more volatile. The toolkit of available financial management techniques has expanded rapidly in response to a need to control increased risk from volatility and to track complexities arising from dealings in many countries. Improved computer technology makes new financial engineering applications practical.

When financial managers or investment dealers design new securities or financial processes, their efforts are referred to as financial engineering. Successful financial engineering reduces and controls risk and minimizes taxes. Financial engineering creates a variety of debt securities and reinforces the trend toward securitization of credit introduced earlier. In addition, options and optionlike securities are becoming important in risk management.

Financial engineering also seeks to reduce financing costs of issuing securities as well as the costs of complying with rules laid down by regulatory authorities. An example is the Prompt Offering Prospectus (POP), which allows firms that frequently issue new equity to bypass repetitive OSC registration requirements.

In addition to financial engineering, advances in computer technology also create opportunities to combine different types of financial institutions to take advantage of economies of scale and scope. Large institutions operate in all provinces and internationally, enjoying more lax regulations in some jurisdictions than in others. Financial institutions pressure authorities to deregulate in a push–pull process called the regulatory dialectic.

Deregulation is opening the possibility for further changes. For example, in 2001, financial services legislation reopened discussion on bank mergers. Two pairs of banks had been unsuccessful in their plans to merge several years earlier, and the industry revived this issue to pressure for government approval for future mergers. Starting in January 2002, life insurance company mergers were allowed. This means that large Canadian life insurers such as Manulife can acquire smaller companies, leading to industry consolidation.

These trends have made financial management a much more complex and technical activity. For this reason, many business students find introductory finance one of their most challenging subjects. The trends we reviewed have also increased the stakes. In the face of increased competition globally, the payoff for good financial management is great. The finance function is also becoming important in corporate strategic planning. The good news is that career opportunities (and compensation) in financial positions are highly competitive.

Concept Question

- **How do key trends in financial markets affect Canadian financial institutions?**

1.7 Outline of the Text

Now that we have taken the quick tour through all of corporate finance, we can take a closer look at this book. The book is divided into seven parts. The long-term investment decision is covered first. Financing decisions and working capital are covered next. Finally, a series of special topics is covered. Here are the seven parts:

Part I:	Overview
Part II:	Value and Capital Budgeting
Part III:	Risk
Part IV:	Capital Structure and Dividend Policy
Part V:	Long-Term Financing
Part VI:	Options, Futures, and Corporate Finance
Part VII:	Short-Term Finance
Part VIII:	Special Topics

Part II describes how investment opportunities are valued in financial markets. This part contains the basic theory. Because finance is a subject that builds understanding from the ground up, the material is very important. The most important concept in Part II is net present value. We develop the net present value rule into a tool for valuing investment alternatives. We discuss general formulas and apply them to a variety of different financial instruments.

Part III introduces basic measures of risk. The capital asset pricing model (CAPM) and the arbitrage pricing theory (APT) are used to devise methods for incorporating risk in valuation. As part of this discussion, we describe the famous beta coefficient. Finally, we use the preceding pricing models to handle capital budgeting under risk.

Part IV examines two interrelated topics: capital structure and dividend policy. Capital structure is the extent to which the firm relies on debt. It cannot be separated from the amount of cash dividends the firm decides to pay out to its equity shareholders.

Part V concerns long-term financing. We describe the securities that corporations issue to raise cash as well as the mechanics of offering securities for public sale. Here we discuss call provisions and leasing.

Part VI covers options and futures and their use in risk management. We introduce these derivatives and show how understanding the underlying concepts opens up new insights into corporate finance. Next we focus on warrants and convertibles—two important kinds of corporate securities with options embedded in them. In the final chapter in this section, we introduce the important topic of risk management.

Part I   Overview

Part VII is devoted to short-term finance. We focus on managing the firm's current assets and current liabilities. We describe aspects of the firm's short-term financial management. Separate chapters on cash management and credit management are included.

Part VIII covers two important special topics: mergers and international corporate finance.

KEY TERMS

Agency costs 14	Foreign exchange market 21
Capital budgeting 4	Money markets 19
Capital gains 26	Net working capital 4
Capital markets 19	Partnership 11
Capital structure 4	Set-of-contracts viewpoint 14
Contingent claims 10	Socially responsible investing 17
Corporation 12	Sole proprietorship 10

SUGGESTED READING

A survey of trends affecting chartered banks and other Canadian financial institutions is found in:

A. Saunders and H. Thomas, *Financial Institutions Management*, 2nd Canadian ed., Toronto: McGraw-Hill Ryerson, 2001.

Do managers pay too little attention to shareholders? This is the question posed in:

M. Miller, "Is American Corporate Governance Fatally Flawed?" *Journal of Applied Corporate Finance* (Winter 1994).

Evidence is provided on the tax factor in choosing to incorporate in:

J. K. Mackie-Mason and R. H. Gordon, "How Much Do Taxes Discourage Incorporation?" *Journal of Finance* (June 1997).

What are the patterns of corporate ownership around the world? This is the question posed by:

R. La Porta, F. Lopez-De-Silanes, and A. Shleifer, "Corporate Ownership Around the World," *Journal of Finance* 54 (1999).

A recent survey of international corporate governance can be found in:

D. K. Denis and J. S. McConnell, "International Corporate Governance," *Journal of Financial and Quantitative Analysis* 38 (March 2003).

F. Barca and M. Becht, *The Corporate Control of Europe*, Oxford University Press, 2002.

QUESTIONS & PROBLEMS

1.1   Suppose you were the financial manager of an incorporated business. What kinds of goals do you think would be appropriate? Suppose that you changed jobs to become financial manager of a not-for-profit organization. How would this change your answer?

1.2   Can our goal of maximizing the value of the shareholders' wealth conflict with other goals such as avoiding unethical or illegal behaviour? In particular, do you think that topics such as customer and employee safety, the environment, and the general good of society fit into this framework? Think of some specific scenarios to illustrate your answer.

1.3   Who owns a corporation? Describe the process whereby the owners control the firm's management. What is the main reason that an agency relationship exists in the corporate form of organization? In this context, what kinds of problems can arise?

1.4   Corporate ownership varies around the world. Historically, individuals have owned the majority of shares in public corporations in the United States. In Canada this is also the case, but ownership is more often concentrated in the hands of a majority shareholder. In Germany and Japan, banks, other financial institutions, and large companies own most of the shares in public corporations. How do you think these ownership differences affect the severity of agency costs in different countries?

1.5   What are the major types of financial institutions and financial markets in Canada?

1.6   What are some major trends in Canadian financial markets? Explain how these trends affect the practice of financial management in Canada.

1.7   On the Market Insight Home Page, follow the "industry" link. From the pull-down menu, you can select various industries. Answer the following questions for these industries: Aerospace & Defense, Application Software, Diversified Capital Markets, Homebuilding, Personal Products, Restaurants, and Precious Metals & Minerals.

    a. How many companies are in each industry?

    b. What are the total sales of each industry?

    c. Does the industry with the largest total sales have the largest number of competitors? What does this tell you about the competition in each industry?

Appendix 1A	# Taxes

Taxes are very important since cash flows are measured after taxes. In this section, we examine corporate and personal tax rates and how taxes are calculated. We apply this knowledge to see how different types of income are taxed in the hands of individuals and corporations.

The size of the tax bill is determined through tax laws and regulations in the annual budgets of the federal government (administered by the Canada Revenue Agency) and provincial governments. If the various rules of taxation seem a little bizarre or convoluted to you, keep in mind that tax law is the result of political forces as well as economic forces. The tax law is continually evolving, so our discussion cannot make you a tax expert. Rather, it will give you an understanding of the tax principles important for financial management along with the ability to ask the right questions when consulting a tax expert.

Individual Tax Rates

Individual tax rates in effect for federal and selected provincial taxes for 2004 are shown in Table 1A.1. These rates apply to income from employment (wages and salary) and from unincorporated businesses. Investment income is also taxable. Interest income is taxed at the same rates as employment income, but special provisions reduce the taxes payable on dividends and capital gains. We discuss these in detail later in the appendix.

In making financial decisions it is frequently important to distinguish between average and marginal tax rates. The percentage rates shown in Table 1A.1 are all marginal rates. To illustrate, suppose you live in Ontario and have a taxable income of $120,000. Your tax on the next dollar is:[15]

$$40.16\% = \text{Federal tax rate} + \text{Provincial tax rate} = 29\% + 11.16\%$$

Tax rates vary somewhat across provinces. For example, in Quebec the same taxable income faces tax on the next dollar at 53 percent.

With the exception of Quebec residents, taxpayers file one tax return. In computing your tax, you first find the federal tax and then calculate the provincial tax as a percentage of the federal tax.

Taxes on Investment Income

A dividend tax credit provides a degree of integration between corporate and individual taxation. This credit applies only to dividends paid by Canadian corporations. The result is to

---

[15] Actual rates for 2004 are somewhat higher as we ignore surtaxes that apply in higher brackets.

TABLE 1A.1   Individual Income Tax Rates, 2004

	Taxable Income	Tax Rate
Federal Taxes	$0–35,000	16.00%
	$35,001–70,000	22.00
	$70,001–113,804	26.00
	$113,805 and over	29.00
British Columbia	$0–32,476	6.05%
	$32,477–64,954	9.15
	$64,955–74,575	11.70
	$74,576–90,555	13.70
	$90,556 and over	14.70
Alberta	All income	10.00%
Ontario	$0–33,375	6.05%
	$33,376–66,752	9.15
	$66,753 and over	11.16
Quebec	$0–27,635	16.0%
	$27,636–55,280	20.0
	$55,281 and over	24.00
Nova Scotia	$0–29,590	8.79%
	$29,591–59,180	13.58
	$59,181 and over	15.17

Reproduced with permission from *Canadian Income Tax Act with Regulations, 77th Edition, 2004,* published by and copyright CCH Canadian Limited, Toronto, Canada.

encourage Canadian investors to invest in Canadian companies as opposed to foreign ones.[16]

To see how dividends are taxed we start with common shares held by individual investors. Table 1A.2 shows how the dividend tax credit reduces the effective tax rate on dividends for investors in the top federal tax bracket. The steps follow the instructions on federal tax returns. Actual dividends are grossed up by 25 percent and federal tax is calculated on the grossed-up figure. A dividend tax credit of 16⅔ percent of the actual dividend is subtracted from the federal tax to get the federal tax payable. The provincial tax (for Ontario in this example) is calculated and added. Note that each province has its own dividend tax credit.

Individual Canadian investors also benefit from a tax reduction for **capital gains.** Capital gains arise when an investment increases in value above its purchase price. Only half of capital gains are taxable.

Additionally, capital gains are lightly taxed since individuals only pay taxes on realized capital gains when shares are sold. Since many individuals hold shares for a long time (have unrealized capital gains), the time value of money dramatically reduces the effective tax rate on capital gains.

Corporate Taxes

Canadian corporations, like individuals, are subject to corporate taxes levied by the federal and provincial governments. Table 1A.3 shows corporate tax rates using Ontario as an

[16]Evidence that the dividend tax credit causes investors to favour Canadian stocks is provided in L. Booth, "The Dividend Tax Credit and Canadian Ownership Objectives," *Canadian Journal of Economics* 20 (May 1987).

TABLE 1A.2   Investment Income Tax Treatment for Ontario Residents in Top Bracket (over $113,805) for 2004

Interest Tax Treatment

Interest	$1,000.00
Federal tax at 29%	290.00
Provincial tax at 11.16%	111.60
Total tax	$ 401.60

Capital Gains Tax Treatment

Capital gains	$1,000.00
Taxable capital gains (50% × $1,000)	500.00
Federal tax at 29%	145.00
Provincial tax at 11.16%	55.80
Total tax	$ 200.80

Dividend Tax Treatment

Dividends	$1,000.00
Gross up at 25%	250.00
Grossed up dividend	1,250.00
Federal tax at 29%	362.50
Less dividend tax credit (13.33% × $1,250)	(166.70)
Federal tax payable	195.80
Provincial tax at 11.16%	139.50
Less dividend tax credit (5.13% × $1,250)	(64.13)
Provincial tax payable	75.37
Total tax	$ 271.17

Source: Adapted from KPMG, *www.kpmg.ca/english/services/docs/tax/rates/kpmg2004ptr.pdf.*

example. You can see from the table that small corporations (income under $250,000) and, to a lesser degree, manufacturing and processing companies, pay tax at lower rates.

Comparing the rates in Table 1A.3 with the personal tax rates in Table 1A.1 appears to reveal a tax advantage for small businesses and professionals in forming a corporation. The tax rate on corporate income of, say, $150,000 is less than the personal tax rate assessed on income of unincorporated businesses. But this is oversimplified because dividends paid to the owners are also taxed, as we saw earlier.

Taxable Income

Interest and dividends are treated differently in calculating corporate tax. Interest paid is deducted from EBIT (earnings before interest and taxes) in calculating taxable income, but

TABLE 1A.3   Corporate Tax Rates in Percentages in 2004

	Federal	Ontario	Combined
Basic corporations	22.1%	14.0%	36.1%
Manufacturing and processing	22.1%	12.0%	34.1%
All small corporations with a taxable income less than $250,000	13.1%	5.5%	18.6%

dividends paid are not. Because interest is a tax-deductible expense, debt financing has a tax advantage over financing with common stock.

The tables are turned when we contrast interest and dividends earned by the firm. Interest earned is fully taxable just like any other form of ordinary income. Dividends on common and preferred shares received from other Canadian corporations qualify for a 100 percent exemption and are received tax-free.[17]

Capital Gains, Carryforward, and Carryback

If a firm disposes of an asset for more than it paid originally, the difference is a capital gain. As with individuals, firms' capital gains are taxed at 50 percent of the tax rate.

When calculating capital gains for tax purposes, a firm nets out all capital losses in the same year. If capital losses exceed capital gains, the net capital loss may be carried back to reduce taxable income in the three prior years. Any capital losses remaining may be carried forward indefinitely. Under the carryback feature, a firm files a revised tax return and receives a refund of prior years' taxes.

A similar carryback and carryforward provision applies to operating losses. In this case, the carryback period is three years and carryforward is allowed for up to seven years.

Investment Tax Credits

An investment tax credit applies in certain regions of the country—presently Atlantic Canada but applied more broadly in past years. An investment tax credit allows a qualified firm to subtract a set percentage of an investment directly from taxes payable.

Appendix Questions and Problems

1.A1 Distinguish between an average tax rate and a marginal tax rate.

1.A2 How does tax treatment of investment income differ among interest, dividends, and capital gains?

1.A3 Explain how carryback/carryforward provisions and investment tax credits reduce corporate taxes.

Marginal Versus Average Tax Rates

1.A4 (Refer to Table 1A.3.) Corporation X has $100,000 in taxable income, and Corporation Y, a manufacturer, has $1 million in taxable income.

   a. What is the tax bill for each firm in Ontario?

   b. Suppose both firms have identified a new project that will increase taxable income by $10,000. How much in additional taxes will each firm pay? Why aren't these amounts the same?

Taxes on Investment Income

1.A5 Mary Song, a Toronto investor, receives $10,000 in dividends from B.C. Forest Products shares, $10,000 in interest from a deposit in a chartered bank, and a $10,000 capital gain from selling Central B.C. Mines shares. Use the information in Table 1A.2 to calculate the after-tax cash flow from each investment. Ms. Song's federal tax rate is 16 percent.

---

[17] We ignore refundable taxes on dividends here and discuss them in Chapter 14.

Chapter 2

Accounting Statements and Cash Flow

EXECUTIVE SUMMARY

Chapter 2 describes the basic accounting statements used for reporting corporate activity. It focuses on practical details of cash flow. It will become obvious in the next several chapters that knowing how to determine cash flow helps the financial manager make better decisions. The increasing number of corporate accounting scandals with companies such as Enron, WorldCom, and Nortel has highlighted the importance of accurate financial reporting. Students who have had accounting courses will not find the material new and can think of it as a review with an emphasis on finance. We discuss cash flow further in later chapters.

2.1 The Balance Sheet

The **balance sheet** is an accountant's snapshot of the firm's accounting value on a particular date, as though the firm momentarily stood still. The balance sheet has two sides: On the left are the *assets* and on the right the *liabilities* and *shareholders' equity*. The balance sheet states what the firm owns and how it is financed. The accounting definition that underlies the balance sheet and describes the balance is:

$$\text{Assets} \equiv \text{Liabilities} + \text{Shareholders' equity}$$

We have put a three-line equality in the balance sheet equation to indicate that it must always hold, by definition. In fact, the shareholders' equity is defined to be the difference between the assets and the liabilities of the firm. In principle, equity is what the shareholders would have remaining after the firm discharged its obligations.

Table 2.1 gives the 20X5 and 20X4 balance sheet for the fictitious Canadian Composite Corporation. The assets in the balance sheet are listed in order by the length of time it normally takes a going concern to convert them to cash. The asset side depends on the nature of the business and how management chooses to conduct it. Management must make decisions about cash versus marketable securities, credit versus cash sales, whether to make or buy commodities, whether to lease or purchase items, the types of business in which to engage, and so on. The liabilities and the shareholders' equity are listed in the order in which they must be paid.

The liabilities and shareholders' equity side reflects the types and proportions of financing, which depend on management's choice of capital structure, as between debt and equity and between current debt and long-term debt.

When analyzing a balance sheet, the financial manager should be aware of at least three concerns: accounting measures of liquidity, debt versus equity, and value versus cost.

TABLE 2.1   Balance Sheet of the Canadian Composite Corporation

CANADIAN COMPOSITE CORPORATION
Balance Sheet
20X5 and 20X4
(in $ millions)

Assets	20X5	20X4	Liabilities (debt) and Shareholders' Equity	20X5	20X4
Current assets:			Current liabilities:		
Cash and equivalents	$ 140	$ 107	Accounts payable	$ 213	$ 197
Accounts receivable	294	270	Notes payable	50	53
Inventories	269	280	Accrued expenses	223	205
Other	58	50	Total current liabilities	486	455
Total current assets	761	707			
Long-term assets:			Long-term liabilities:		
Property, plant, and equipment	1,423	1,274	Deferred taxes	117	104
Less accumulated depreciation	(550)	(460)	Long-term debt	471	458
Net property, plant, and equipment	873	814	Total long-term liabilities	588	562
Intangible assets and others	245	221	Shareholders' equity:		
			Preferred shares	39	39
			Common shares	376	339
Total long-term assets	1,118	1,035	Accumulated retained earnings	390	347
			Total equity	805	725
Total assets	$1,879	$1,742	Total liabilities and shareholders' equity	$1,879	$1,742

Liquidity

Liquidity refers to the ease and speed with which assets can be converted to cash. Current assets are the most liquid and include cash and those assets that can reasonably be expected to be turned into cash within a year from the date of the balance sheet. Accounts receivable are the amount not yet collected from customers for goods or services sold to them (after adjustment for potential bad debts). Inventory is composed of raw materials to be used in production, work in process, and finished goods. Fixed assets are the least liquid kind of asset. Tangible fixed assets include property, plant, and equipment. These assets do not convert to cash from normal business activity, and they are not usually used to pay expenses, such as payroll.

Some fixed assets are not tangible. Intangible assets have no physical existence but can be very valuable. Examples of intangible assets are the value of a trademark, the value of a patent, and the value of customer recognition. The more liquid a firm's assets, the less likely the firm is to experience problems meeting short-term obligations. Thus, the probability that a firm will avoid financial distress can be linked to its liquidity. Unfortunately, liquid assets frequently have lower rates of return than fixed assets; for example, cash generates no investment income. To the extent a firm invests in liquid assets, it sacrifices an opportunity to invest in more profitable investment vehicles.

Debt Versus Equity

Liabilities are obligations of the firm that require a payout of cash within a stipulated time period. Many liabilities involve contractual obligations to repay a stated amount with interest over a period. Thus, liabilities are debts and are frequently associated with nominally fixed cash burdens, called *debt service*, that put the firm in default of a contract if they are not paid. *Shareholders' equity* is a claim against the firm's assets that is residual and not fixed. In general terms, when the firm borrows, it gives the bondholders first claim on the firm's cash flow.[1] Bondholders can sue if the firm defaults on its bond contracts. This may lead the firm to declare itself bankrupt. Shareholders' equity is the residual difference between assets and liabilities:

$$\text{Assets} - \text{Liabilities} \equiv \text{Shareholders' equity}$$

This is the shareholders' share in the firm stated in accounting terms. The accounting value of shareholders' equity increases when retained earnings are added. This occurs when the firm retains part of its earnings instead of paying them out as dividends.

Value Versus Cost

The accounting value of a firm's assets is frequently referred to as the *carrying value* or the *book value* of the assets.[2] Under **generally accepted accounting principles (GAAP)**, audited financial statements of firms in Canada carry the assets at historical cost adjusted for depreciation. Thus the terms *carrying value* and *book value* are unfortunate. They specifically say "value," when in fact the accounting numbers are based on cost. This misleads many readers of financial statements into thinking that the firm's assets are recorded at true market values. *Market value* is the price at which willing buyers and sellers trade the assets. It would be only a coincidence if accounting value and market value were the same. In fact, management's job is to create a value for the firm that is higher than its cost. When market values are considerably below book values, it is customary accounting practice to write down assets. For example, in March 2003, the Ontario Municipal Employees' Retirement System (OMERS), a large pension fund, announced $600 million in write-downs as a result of changes in the value of real estate holdings, private equity, and infrastructure projects.[3] Sometimes, huge write-offs are also indicative of overstated profits in previous years, as assets were not expensed properly.

There are many users of a firm's balance sheet and each may seek different information from it. A banker may look at a balance sheet for evidence of liquidity and working capital. A supplier may also note the size of accounts payable, which reflects the general promptness of payments. Many users of financial statements, including managers and investors, want to know the value of the firm, not its cost. This is not found on the balance sheet. In fact, many of a firm's true resources (good management, proprietary assets, and so on) do not appear on the balance sheet.

Concept Questions

- What is the balance sheet equation?
- What three things should be kept in mind when looking at a balance sheet?

---

[1] Bondholders are investors in the firm's debt. They are creditors of the firm. In this discussion, the term *bondholder* means the same thing as *creditor*.

[2] Confusion often arises because many financial accounting terms have the same meaning. This presents a problem with jargon for the reader of financial statements. For example, the following terms usually refer to the same thing: *assets minus liabilities, net worth, shareholders' equity, owner's equity,* and *equity capitalization.*

[3] E. Church, "OMERS Taking Huge Writedown," globeinvestor.com, March 31, 2004. This process does not work the other way—accounting principles are conservative and carry assets at adjusted cost when market values are higher.

2.2 The Income Statement

The **income statement** measures performance over a specific period of time (say, a year). The accounting definition of income is:

$$\text{Revenue} - \text{Expenses} \equiv \text{Income}$$

If the balance sheet is like a snapshot, the income statement is like a video recording of what happened between two snapshots. Table 2.2 gives the income statement for the Canadian Composite Corporation for 20X5.

The income statement usually includes several sections. The operations section reports the firm's revenues and expenses from principal operations. Among other things, the non-operating section of the income statement includes all financing costs, such as interest expense. Usually a second section reports as a separate item the amount of taxes levied on income. The last item on the income statement is the bottom line, or net income. Net income is frequently expressed per share of common stock, that is, earnings per share.

When analyzing an income statement, the financial manager should keep in mind GAAP, noncash items, time, and costs.

Generally Accepted Accounting Principles (GAAP)

As pointed out earlier, the focus in financial decisions is on market value, which depends on cash flow. However, like the balance sheet, the income statement has many different users and the accounting profession has developed GAAP to provide information for a broad audience not necessarily concerned with cash flow. For this reason, it is necessary to make adjustments to information on income statements to obtain cash flow.

For example, revenue is recognized on an income statement when the earnings process is virtually completed and an exchange of goods or services has occurred. Therefore, the

TABLE 2.2	Income Statement of the Canadian Composite Corporation

CANADIAN COMPOSITE CORPORATION
Income Statement
20X5
(in $ millions)

Total operating revenues	$ 2,262
Cost of goods sold	(1,655)
Selling, general, and administrative expenses	(327)
Depreciation	(90)
Operating income	190
Other income	29
Earnings before interest and taxes	219
Interest expense	(49)
Pretax income	170
Taxes	(84)
Current: $71	
Deferred: $13	
Net income	$ 86
Retained earnings: $43	
Dividends: $43	

unrealized appreciation in owning property will not be recognized as income. This provides a device for smoothing income by selling appreciated property at convenient times. For example, if the firm owns a tree farm that has doubled in value, then in a year when its earnings from other businesses are down, it can raise overall earnings by selling some trees. The matching principle of GAAP dictates that revenues be matched with expenses. Thus, income is reported when it is earned or accrued, even though no cash flow has necessarily occurred. (For example, when goods are sold for credit, sales and profits are reported.)

Noncash Items

The economic value of assets is intimately connected to their future incremental cash flows. However, cash flow does not appear on an income statement. There are several **noncash items** that are expenses against revenues, but do not affect cash flow directly.[4] The most important of these is *depreciation*. Depreciation reflects the accountant's estimate of the cost of equipment used up in the production process.[5] For example, suppose an asset with a five-year life and no resale value is purchased for $1,000. According to accountants, the $1,000 cost must be expensed over the useful life of the asset. If straight-line depreciation is used, there will be five equal installments and $200 of depreciation expense will be incurred each year. From a finance perspective, the cost of the asset is the actual negative cash flow incurred when the asset is acquired (that is, $1,000, not the accountant's smoothed $200-per-year depreciation expense).

Another noncash expense is *deferred taxes*. Deferred taxes result from differences between accounting income and true taxable income.[6] Notice that the accounting tax shown on the income statement for the Canadian Composite Corporation is $84 million. It can be broken down as current taxes and deferred taxes. The current tax portion is actually sent to the tax authorities (for example, Canada Revenue Agency). The deferred tax portion is not. However, the theory is that if taxable income is less than accounting income in the current year, it will be more than accounting income later. Consequently, taxes that are not paid today will have to be paid in the future, and they represent a liability of the firm. It shows up on the balance sheet as deferred tax liability. From the cash flow perspective, though, deferred tax is not a cash outflow.

Time and Costs

It is often useful to think of the future as having two distinct parts: the *short run* and the *long run*. The short run is that period in which certain equipment, resources, and commitments of the firm are fixed; but it is long enough for the firm to vary its output by using more labour and raw materials. The short run is not a precise period of time that will be the same for all industries. However, all firms making decisions in the short run have some fixed costs, that is, costs that will not change because of the fixed commitments. In real business activity, examples of fixed costs are bond interest, overhead, and property taxes. Costs that are not fixed are variable. Variable costs change as the output of the firm

---

[4] Although it is a noncash expense, depreciation has tax implications (discussed later) that affect cash flow.

[5] Depreciation is the form of amortization that applies to capital assets.

[6] One situation in which taxable income may be lower than accounting income is when the firm uses capital cost allowance (CCA) depreciation expense procedures for calculating taxes but uses straight-line procedures allowed by GAAP for reporting purposes. We discuss CCA in Chapter 7. Accountants refer to deferred taxes as a future income tax liability.

changes; some examples are raw materials and wages for production line workers. In the long run, all costs are variable.[7]

Financial accountants do not distinguish between variable costs and fixed costs. Instead, accounting costs usually fit into a classification that distinguishes product costs from period costs. Product costs are the total production costs (raw materials, direct labour, and manufacturing overhead) incurred during a period and are reported on the income statement as the cost of goods sold. Both variable and fixed costs are included in product costs. Period costs are costs that are allocated to a time period; they are called *selling, general,* and *administrative expenses*. One period cost would be the company president's salary.

Concept
Questions

- **What is the income statement equation?**
- **What are three things to keep in mind when looking at an income statement?**
- **What are noncash expenses?**

2.3   Net Working Capital

Net working capital is current assets minus current liabilities. Net working capital is positive when current assets are greater than current liabilities. This means the cash that will become available over the next 12 months is greater than the cash that must be paid out. The net working capital of the Canadian Composite Corporation is $275 million in 20X5 and $252 million in 20X4:

Current assets ($ millions)	−	Current liabilities ($ millions)	=	Net working capital ($ millions)
20X5	$761	−	$486	=	$275
20X4	$707	−	$455	=	$252

In addition to investing in fixed assets (capital spending), a firm can invest in net working capital—called the *change in net working capital*. The **change in net working capital** in 20X5 is the difference between the net working capital in 20X5 and 20X4; that is, $275 million − $252 million = $23 million. The change in net working capital is usually positive in a growing firm because higher levels of net working capital are necessary for increased sales.

Concept
Questions

- **What is net working capital?**
- **What is the change in net working capital?**

2.4   Financial Cash Flow

Perhaps the most important item that can be extracted from financial statements is the actual **cash flow**. There is an accounting statement called the *statement of changes in financial position*. This statement helps to explain the change in accounting cash and equivalents, which for Canadian Composite is $33 million in 20X5. (See Appendix 2B.) Notice in Table 2.1 that cash and equivalents increases from $107 million in 20X4 to

[7] When one famous economist was asked about the difference between the long run and the short run, he said, "In the long run we are all dead."

$140 million in 20X5. However, we will look at cash flow from a different perspective, the perspective of finance. In finance, the value of the firm is its ability to generate financial cash flow. (We will talk more about financial cash flow in Chapter 7.)

The first point we should mention is that cash flow is not the same as net working capital. For example, increasing inventory requires using cash. Because both inventories and cash are current assets, this does not affect net working capital. In this case, an increase in a particular net working capital account, such as inventory, is associated with decreasing cash flow.

Just as we established that the value of a firm's assets is always equal to the value of the liabilities plus the value of the equity, the cash flows from the firm's assets generated by its operating activities, CF(*A*), must equal the cash flows to the firm's creditors, CF(*B*), and equity investors, CF(*S*):

$$CF(A) = CF(B) + CF(S)$$

The first step in determining a firm's cash flows is to figure out the *cash flow from operations*. Table 2.3 shows that operating cash flow is the cash flow generated by business activities, including sales of goods and services. Operating cash flow reflects tax payments, but not financing, capital spending, or changes in net working capital.

	(in $ millions)
Earnings before interest and taxes	$219
Depreciation	90
Current taxes	(71)
Operating cash flow	$238

Another important component of cash flow involves *changes in long-term assets*. For example, when Canadian Composite sold its power systems subsidiary in 20X5 it generated $25 in cash flow. The net change in long-term assets equals sales of long-term assets

TABLE 2.3	Financial Cash Flow of the Canadian Composite Corporation

CANADIAN COMPOSITE CORPORATION
Financial Cash Flow 20X5
(in $ millions)

Cash Flow of the Firm	
Operating cash flow	$ 238
(Earnings before interest and taxes plus depreciation minus taxes)	
Capital spending	(173)
(Acquisitions of long-term assets minus sales of long-term assets)	
Additions to net working capital	(23)
Total	$ 42

Cash Flow to Investors in the Firm	
Debt	$ 36
(Interest plus retirement of debt minus long-term debt financing)	
Equity	6
(Dividends plus repurchase of equity minus new equity financing)	
Total	$ 42

minus the acquisition of long-term assets. The result is the cash flow used for capital spending:

Acquisition of long-term assets	$198
Sales of fixed assets	(25)
Capital spending	$173

We can arrive at the same number by adding the increase in property, plant, and equipment ($149) to the increase in intangible assets ($24). Cash flows are also used for making investments in net working capital ($24) to the increase in net working capital. In the Canadian Composite Corporation in 20X5, *additions to net working capital are*

Additions to net working capital	$23

Total cash flows generated by the firm's assets are the sum of

Operating cash flow	$ 238
Capital spending	(173)
Additions to net working capital	(23)
Total cash flow of the firm	$ 42

The total outgoing cash flow of the firm can be separated into cash flows paid to creditors and cash flows paid to shareholders. The cash flow paid to creditors represents a regrouping of the data in Table 2.3 and an explicit recording of interest expense from Table 2.2. An important source of cash flow comes from selling new debt. Thus, an increase in long-term debt is the net effect of new borrowing and repayment of maturing obligations plus interest expense.

Cash Flow Paid to Creditors
($ millions)

Interest	$ 49
Net proceeds from long-term debt sales	(13)
Total	$ 36

Cash flow of the firm also is paid to the shareholders. It is the sum of dividends plus net new equity from repurchasing outstanding shares of stock and issuing new shares of stock.

Cash Flow to Shareholders
($ millions)

Dividends	$ 43
Net new equity	(37)
Total	$ 6

Some important observations can be drawn from our discussion of cash flow:

1. Several types of cash flow are relevant to understanding the financial situation of the firm. **Cash flow from operations,** defined as earnings before interest and depreciation minus taxes, measures the cash generated from operations not counting capital spending or working capital requirements. It should usually be positive; a firm is in trouble if operating cash flow is negative for a long time because the firm is not generating enough cash to pay operating costs.

Total cash flow of the firm includes adjustments for capital spending and additions to net working capital. It will frequently be negative. When a firm is growing at a rapid rate, spending on inventory and fixed assets can be higher than cash flow from sales. On the other hand, positive total cash flow is not always a sign of financial health. An unprofitable firm with negative cash flow from operations could show positive total cash flow temporarily by selling assets. This was a common occurrence in the airline industry in the early 1990s.

2. Net income is not cash flow. The net income of the Canadian Composite Corporation in 20X5 was $86 million, whereas cash flow was $42 million. The two numbers are not usually the same. In determining the economic and financial condition of a firm, cash flow is more revealing.

3. Cash flow from assets sometimes goes by a different name, **free cash flow**. The term refers to cash that the firm is free to distribute to creditors and shareholders because it is not needed for working capital or fixed asset investment. (We return to free cash flow in Chapter 29.)

Concept
Questions

- **How is cash flow different from changes in net working capital?**
- **What is the difference between operating cash flow and total cash flow of the firm?**
- **What is free cash flow?**

2.5 SUMMARY AND CONCLUSIONS

Besides introducing you to corporate accounting, the purpose of this chapter has been to teach you how to determine cash flow from the accounting statements of a typical company.

1. Cash flow is generated by the firm and paid to creditors and shareholders. It can be classified as
   a. Cash flow from operations.
   b. Cash flow from changes in fixed assets.
   c. Cash flow from changes in working capital.

2. There is a cash flow identity that says that cash flow from assets equals cash flow to bondholders and shareholders.

3. Calculations of cash flow are not difficult, but they require care and particular attention to detail in properly accounting for noncash expenses such as depreciation and deferred taxes. It is especially important that you do not confuse cash flow with changes in net working capital and net income.

KEY TERMS

Balance sheet 29
Cash flow 34
Cash flow from operations 36
Change in net working capital 34
Free cash flow 37

Generally accepted accounting principles
   (GAAP) 31
Income statement 32
Noncash items 33
Total cash flow of the firm 36

SUGGESTED READING

There are many excellent textbooks on accounting. One that we have found helpful is:
R. H. Garrison, G. R. Chesley, and R. F. Carroll. *Managerial Accounting Concepts for Planning, Control, Decision Making,* 6th Canadian ed. Homewood III: Richard D. Irwin, 2004.

QUESTIONS & PROBLEMS

The Balance Sheet

2.1   Prepare a December 31 balance sheet using the following data. Given that the residual amount for the figures listed below is common stock, first calculate the amount of common equity and then prepare a balance sheets at December 31.

Cash	$ 4,000
Patents	82,000
Accounts payable	6,000
Accounts receivable	8,000
Taxes payable	2,000
Machinery	34,000
Bonds payable	7,000
Accumulated retained earnings	6,000
Preferred stock	19,000

2.2   The following table presents the long-term liabilities and shareholders' equity of Information Control Corp. of one year ago.

Long-term debt	$ 50,000,000
Preferred shares	30,000,000
Common shares	100,000,000
Retained earnings	20,000,000

During the past year, Information Control issued $10 million of new common shares. The firm generated $5 million of net income and paid $3 million of dividends. Construct today's balance sheet reflecting the changes that occurred at Information Control Corp. during the year.

The Income Statement

2.3   Prepare an income statement using the following data.

Sales	$500,000
Cost of goods sold	200,000
Administrative expenses	100,000
Interest expense	50,000

The firm's tax rate is 40 percent.

2.4   The Flying Lion Corporation reported the following data on the income statement of one of its divisions. Flying Lion Corporation has other profitable divisions.

	2004	2005
Net sales	$800,000	$500,000
Cost of goods sold	560,000	320,000
Operating expenses	75,000	56,000
Depreciation	300,000	200,000
Tax rate (%)	40	40

a. Prepare an income statement for each year.
b. Determine the operating cash flow during each year.

Financial Cash Flow

2.5   What are the differences between accounting profit and cash flow?

2.6   During 2005, the Senbet Discount Tire Company had gross sales of $1 million. The firm's cost of goods sold and selling expenses were $300,000 and $200,000, respectively. These figures do not include depreciation. Senbet also had notes payable of $1 million. These notes carried an interest rate of 10 percent. Depreciation was $100,000. Senbet's tax rate in 2004 was 40 percent.

a. What was Senbet's net operating income?

b. What were the firm's earnings before taxes?

c. What was Senbet's net income?

d. What was Senbet's operating cash flow?

2.7 The Stancil Corporation provided the following current information:

Proceeds from short-term borrowing	$ 6,000
Proceeds from long-term borrowing	20,000
Proceeds from the sale of common shares	1,000
Purchases of fixed assets	1,000
Purchases of inventories	4,000
Payment of dividends	22,000

Determine the cash flow of the Stancil Corporation.

2.8 Ritter Corporation's accountants prepared the following financial statements for year-end 2005.

RITTER CORPORATION
Income Statement
2005

Revenue	$400
Expenses	250
Depreciation	50
Net income	$100
Dividends	$ 50

RITTER CORPORATION
Balance Sheets
December 31

	2004	2005
Assets		
Cash	$ 25	$ 5
Other current assets	125	95
Net fixed assets	200	100
Total assets	$350	$200
Liabilities and Equity		
Current liabilities	$ 75	$ 50
Long-term debt	75	0
Shareholders' equity	200	150
Total liabilities and equity	$350	$200

a. Explain the change in cash during the year 2005.

b. Determine the change in net working capital in 2005.

c. Determine the cash flow of the firm during the year 2005.

Appendix 2A

Financial Statement Analysis

This appendix shows how to rearrange data from financial statements into financial ratios that provide information about five areas of financial performance:

1. *Short-term solvency*—the firm's ability to meet its short-run obligations.
2. *Activity*—the firm's ability to control its investment in assets.
3. *Financial leverage*—the extent to which a firm relies on debt financing.
4. *Profitability*—the extent to which a firm is profitable.
5. *Value*—the value of the firm.

This appendix also discusses the interpretation, uses, and shortcomings of financial ratios.

Our discussion covers a representative sampling of ratios chosen to be consistent with the practice of experienced financial analysis and the output of commercially available financial analysis software.

For each of the ratios discussed, several questions are important:

1. How is the ratio calculated?
2. What is it intended to measure, and why might we be interested?
3. What might a high or low value be telling us? How might such values be misleading?
4. How could this measure be improved?

We consider each question in turn. The Canadian Composite Corporation financial statements in Tables 2.1, 2.2, and 2.3 provide inputs for the examples that follow. (Monetary values are given in millions of dollars.)

Short-Term Solvency

Ratios of short-term solvency measure the firm's ability to meet recurring financial obligations (that is, to pay its bills). To the extent that a firm has sufficient cash flow, it can avoid defaulting on its financial obligations and thus avoid financial distress. Liquidity measures short-term solvency and is often associated with net working capital, the difference between current assets and current liabilities. Recall that current liabilities are debts due within one year from the date of the balance sheet. One source from which to pay these debts is current assets.

The most widely used measures of liquidity are the current ratio and the quick ratio.

Current Ratio   To find the current ratio, divide current assets by current liabilities. For the Canadian Composite Corporation, the figure for 20X5 is

$$\text{Current ratio} = \frac{\text{Total current assets}}{\text{Total current liabilities}} = \frac{761}{486} = 1.57$$

If a firm is having financial difficulty, it may not be able to pay its bills (accounts payable) on time or it may need to extend its bank credit (notes payable). As a consequence, current liabilities may rise faster than current assets and the current ratio may fall. This could be the first sign of financial trouble. Of course, a firm's current ratio should be calculated over several years for historical perspective, and it should be compared to the current ratios of other firms with similar operating activities.

While a higher current ratio generally indicates greater liquidity, it is possible for the current ratio to be too high. A current ratio far above the industry average could indicate excessive inventory or difficulty in collecting accounts receivable.

Quick Ratio   The quick ratio is computed by subtracting inventories from current assets and dividing the difference (called *quick assets*) by current liabilities:

$$\text{Quick ratio} = \frac{\text{Quick assets}}{\text{Total current liabilities}} = \frac{492}{486} = 1.01$$

Quick assets are those current assets that are quickly convertible into cash. Inventories are the least liquid current assets. Many financial analysts believe it is important to determine a firm's ability to pay off current liabilities without relying on the sale of inventories. Comparing the quick ratio to the industry average may help to detect cases in which a high current ratio reflects excessive inventory.

Activity

Activity ratios are constructed to measure how effectively the firm's assets are being managed. The level of a firm's investment in assets depends on many factors. For example, The Bay might have a large stock of toys at the peak of the Christmas season; yet that same inventory in January would be undesirable. How can the appropriate level of investment in assets be measured? One logical starting point is to compare assets with sales for the year to arrive at turnover. The idea is to find out how quickly assets are used to generate sales and we come back to these ideas in Chapter 27.

Total Asset Turnover   The total asset turnover ratio is determined by dividing total operating revenues for the accounting period by the average of total assets. The total asset turnover ratio for the Canadian Composite Corporation for 20X5 is:

$$\text{Total asset turnover} = \frac{\text{Total operating revenues}}{\text{Average total assets}} = \frac{2,262}{1,810.5} = 1.25$$

$$\text{Average total assets} = \frac{1,879 + 1,742}{2} = 1,810.5$$

This ratio is intended to indicate how effectively a firm is using its assets. If the asset turnover ratio is high, the firm is presumably using its assets effectively in generating sales. If the ratio is low, the firm is not using its assets up to their capacity and must either increase sales or dispose of some of the assets. Total asset turnover differs across industries. Firms with relatively small investments in fixed assets, such as retail and wholesale trade firms, tend to have high ratios of total asset turnover when compared with firms that require a large investment in fixed assets, such as manufacturing firms. One problem in interpreting this ratio is that it is maximized by using older assets because their accounting value is lower than newer assets.

Receivables Turnover   The receivables turnover ratio is calculated by dividing sales by average receivables during the accounting period. If the number of days in the year (365) is divided by the receivables turnover ratio, the average collection period can be determined. Net receivables are used for these calculations.[8] The average receivables,

---

[8] Net receivables are determined after an allowance for potential bad debts.

receivables turnover ratio, and average collection period for the Canadian Composite Corporation are:

$$\text{Average receivables} = \frac{294 + 270}{2} = 282$$

$$\text{Receivables turnover} = \frac{\text{Total operating revenues}}{\text{Average receivables}} = \frac{2,262}{282} = 8.02$$

$$\text{Average collection period} = \frac{\text{Days in period}}{\text{Receivables turnover}} = \frac{365}{8.02} = 45.5 \text{ days}$$

The receivables turnover ratio and the average collection period provide some information on the success of the firm in managing its investment in accounts receivable. The actual value of these ratios reflects the firm's credit policy. If a firm has a liberal credit policy, the amount of its receivables will be higher than under a restrictive credit policy. One common rule of thumb that financial analysts use is that the average collection period of a firm should not exceed the time allowed for payment in the credit terms by more than 10 days.

Inventory Turnover   The ratio of inventory turnover is calculated by dividing the cost of goods sold by average inventory. Because inventory is always stated in terms of historical cost, it must be divided by cost of goods sold instead of sales. (Sales include a margin for profit and are not commensurate with inventory.) The number of days in the year divided by the inventory turnover ratio yields the *days in inventory ratio* (the number of days it takes to get goods produced and sold). It is called *shelf life* for retail and wholesale trade firms. The inventory ratios for the Canadian Composite Corporation are

$$\text{Average inventory} = \frac{269 + 280}{2} = 274.5$$

$$\text{Inventory turnover} = \frac{\text{Cost of goods sold}}{\text{Average inventory}} = \frac{1,655}{274.5} = 6.03$$

$$\text{Days in inventory} = \frac{\text{Days in period}}{\text{Inventory turnover}} = \frac{365}{6.03} = 60.5 \text{ days}$$

The inventory ratios measure how quickly inventory is produced and sold. They are significantly affected by the production technology of goods being manufactured. It takes longer to produce a gas turbine engine than a loaf of bread. The ratios are also affected by the perishability of the finished goods. A large increase in the ratio of days in inventory could suggest either an ominously high inventory of unsold finished goods or a change in the firm's product mix to goods with longer production periods.

The method of inventory valuation can materially affect the computed inventory ratios. Thus, financial analysts should be aware of the different inventory valuation methods and how they might affect the ratios.

Financial Leverage

Financial leverage measures the extent to which a firm relies on debt financing rather than equity. Measures of financial leverage are tools in determining the probability that the firm will default on its debt contracts. The more debt a firm has, the more likely it is that the firm will become unable to fulfill its contractual obligations. In other words, too much debt can lead to a higher probability of insolvency and financial distress.

On the positive side, debt is an important form of financing, and provides a significant tax advantage because interest payments are tax deductible. If a firm uses debt, creditors and equity investors may have conflicts of interest. Creditors may want the firm to invest in less risky ventures than those the equity investors prefer.

We discuss the advantages and disadvantages of debt in depth in Chapters 16 and 17.

Debt Ratio   The debt ratio is calculated by dividing total debt by total assets. We can also use several other ways to express the extent to which a firm uses debt, such as the debt–equity ratio and the equity multiplier (that is, total assets divided by equity). The debt ratios for the Canadian Composite Corporation for 20X5 are:

$$\text{Debt ratio} = \frac{\text{Total debt}}{\text{Total assets}} = \frac{1,074}{1,879} = 0.57$$

$$\text{Debt--equity ratio} = \frac{\text{Total debt}}{\text{Total equity}} = \frac{1,074}{805} = 1.33$$

$$\text{Equity multiplier} = \frac{\text{Total assets}}{\text{Total equity}} = \frac{1,879}{805} = 2.33$$

Debt ratios provide information about protection of creditors from insolvency and the ability of firms to obtain additional financing for potentially attractive investment opportunities. However, debt is carried on the balance sheet simply as the unpaid balance. Consequently, no adjustment is made for the current level of interest rates (which may be higher or lower than when the debt was originally issued) or risk. Thus, the accounting value of debt may differ substantially from its market value. Some forms of debt, such as pension liabilities or lease obligations, may not appear on the balance sheet at all.

Interest Coverage   The interest coverage ratio is calculated by dividing earnings (before interest and taxes) by interest. This ratio emphasizes the ability of the firm to generate enough income to cover interest expense. For the Canadian Composite Corporation, this ratio is

$$\text{Interest coverage} = \frac{\text{Earnings before interest and taxes}}{\text{Interest expense}} = \frac{219}{49} = 4.5$$

Interest expense is an obstacle that a firm must surmount if it is to avoid default. The interest coverage ratio is directly connected to the firm's ability to pay interest. However, since interest is paid in cash, it would probably make sense to add back depreciation (a noncash expense) to income in computing this ratio and to include other financing expenses paid in cash, such as payments of principal and lease payments.

A large debt burden is a problem only if the firm's cash flow is insufficient to make the required debt service payments. This is related to the uncertainty of future cash flows. Firms with predictable cash flows are frequently said to have more *debt capacity* than firms with highly uncertain cash flows. Therefore, it makes sense to compute the variability of the firm's cash flows. One possible way to do this is to calculate the standard deviation of cash flows relative to the average cash flow.

Profitability

One of the most difficult attributes of a firm to conceptualize and to measure is profitability. In a general sense, accounting profits are the difference between revenues and costs. Unfortunately, there is no completely unambiguous way to know when a firm is profitable. At best, a financial analyst can measure current or past accounting profitability. Many business opportunities, however, involve sacrificing current profits for future profits. For example, all new products require large start-up costs and, as a consequence, produce low initial profits. Thus, current profits can be a poor reflection of true future profitability.

Different industries employ different amounts of capital and differ in risk. For this reason, benchmark measures of profitability differ among industries.

Profit Margin   Profit margins are computed by dividing profits by total operating revenue. Thus, they express profits as a percentage of total operating revenue. The most important margin is the net profit margin. The net profit margin for the Canadian Composite Corporation is

$$\text{Net profit margin} = \frac{\text{Net income}}{\text{Total operating revenue}} = \frac{86}{2,262} = 0.038 \ (3.8\%)$$

In general, profit margins reflect the firm's ability to produce a product or service at a low cost or to sell it at a high price. Profit margins are not direct measures of profitability because they are based on total operating revenue, not on the investment made in assets by the firm or the equity investors. Trade firms tend to have low margins and service firms tend to have high margins.

Return on Assets   One common measure of managerial performance is the ratio of income to average total assets, both before tax and after tax. These ratios for the Canadian Composite Corporation for 20X5 are:

$$\text{Net return on assets} = \frac{\text{Net income}}{\text{Average total assets}} = \frac{86}{1,810.5} = 0.0475 \ (4.75\%)$$

$$\text{Gross return on assets} = \frac{\text{Earnings before interest and taxes}}{\text{Average total assets}} = \frac{219}{1,810.5} = 0.121 \ (12.1\%)$$

One of the most interesting aspects of return on assets (ROA) is how some financial ratios can be linked together to compute ROA in the *DuPont system of financial control*. This system expresses ROA in terms of the profit margin and asset turnover. The basic components of the system are as follows:

$$\text{ROA} = \text{Profit margin} \times \text{Asset turnover}$$

$$\text{ROA (net)} = \frac{\text{Net income}}{\text{Total operating revenue}} \times \frac{\text{Total operating revenue}}{\text{Average total assets}}$$

$$0.0475 = 0.038 \times 1.25$$

$$\text{ROA (gross)} = \frac{\text{Earnings before interest and taxes}}{\text{Total operating revenue}} \times \frac{\text{Total operating revenue}}{\text{Average total assets}}$$

$$0.121 = 0.097 \times 1.25$$

Firms can increase ROA by increasing profit margins or asset turnover. Of course, competition limits their ability to do so simultaneously. Thus, firms tend to face a trade-off between turnover and margin. In retail trade, for example, mail-order companies have low margins and high turnover whereas high-quality jewellery stores have high margins and low turnover.

It is often useful to describe financial strategies in terms of margins and turnover. Suppose a firm selling pneumatic equipment is thinking about providing customers with more liberal credit terms. This will probably decrease asset turnover (because receivables would increase more than sales). Thus, the margins will have to go up to keep ROA from falling.

Return on Equity   This ratio (ROE) is defined as net income after interest and taxes divided by average common shareholders' equity, which for the Canadian Composite Corporation is

$$\text{ROE} = \frac{\text{Net income}}{\text{Average shareholders' equity}} = \frac{86}{765} = 0.112 \ (11.2\%)$$

$$\text{Average shareholders' equity} = \frac{805 + 725}{2} = 765$$

The difference between ROA and ROE is due to financial leverage. To see this, consider the following breakdown of ROE expanding the DuPont equation:

$$\text{ROE} = \text{Profit margin} \times \text{Asset turnover} \times \text{Equity multiplier}$$

$$= \frac{\text{Net income}}{\text{Total operating revenue}} \times \frac{\text{Total operating revenue}}{\text{Average total assets}} \times \frac{\text{Average total assets}}{\text{Average shareholders' equity}}$$

$$0.112 = 0.038 \times 1.25 \times 2.36$$

From the preceding numbers, it would appear that financial leverage always magnifies ROE. Actually, this occurs only when ROA (gross) is greater than the interest rate on debt.

Payout Ratio   The *payout ratio* is the proportion of net income paid out in cash dividends. For the Canadian Composite Corporation:

$$\text{Payout ratio} = \frac{\text{Cash dividends}}{\text{Net income}} = \frac{43}{86} = 0.5$$

The *retention ratio* is the proportion of net income added to annual retained earnings. For the Canadian Composite Corporation this ratio is:

$$\text{Retention ratio} = \frac{\text{Annual retained earnings}}{\text{Net income}} = \frac{43}{86} = 0.5$$

$$\text{Retained earnings} = \text{Net income} - \text{Dividends}$$

The Sustainable Growth Rate

One ratio that is very helpful in financial analysis is called the sustainable growth rate. It is the maximum rate of growth a firm can sustain by self-generated financing. The precise value of sustainable growth can be calculated as

$$\text{Sustainable growth rate} = \text{ROE} \times \text{Retention ratio}$$

For the Canadian Composite Corporation, ROE is 11.2 percent. The retention ratio is 1/2, so we can calculate the sustainable growth rate as

$$\text{Sustainable growth rate} = 11.2 \times (1/2) = 5.6\%$$

The Canadian Composite Corporation can expand at a maximum rate of 5.6 percent per year with no external equity financing or without increasing financial leverage. (We discuss sustainable growth in Chapters 3 and 6.)

Part 1 Overview

Market Value Ratios

We can learn many things from a close examination of balance sheets and income statements. However, one very important characteristic of a firm that cannot be found on an accounting statement is its market value.

Market Price   The market price of a share of common stock is the price that buyers and sellers establish when they trade the stock. The market value of the common equity of a firm is the market price of a share of common stock multiplied by the number of shares outstanding.

Sometimes the words *fair market value* are used to describe market prices. Fair market value is the price at which common stock would change hands between a willing buyer and a willing seller, both having knowledge of the relevant facts. Thus, market prices give guesses about the true worth of the assets of a firm. In an efficient stock market, market prices reflect all relevant facts about firms, and thus reveal the true value of the firm's underlying assets.

The market value of Imperial Oil is many times greater than that of Rio Alta. This may suggest nothing more than the fact that Imperial Oil is a bigger firm than Rio Alta (hardly a surprising revelation). Financial analysts construct ratios to extract information that is independent of a firm's size.

Price–Earnings (P/E) Ratio   The price–earnings (P/E) ratio is the ratio of market price for a stock to its current annual earnings per share. The following table shows average P/Es for three selected companies on the TSX on April 26, 2004.

	P/E	Div. Yield
Research in Motion (RIM-T)	167.70	0.00
Royal Bank of Canada (RY-T)	14.00	3.34
Alcan (AL-T)	49.10	1.36

The P/E ratio shows how much investors are willing to pay for $1 of earnings per share. For the average TSX stock this was around $18.00 on April 26, 2004. Looking at our example, Research in Motion and Alcan were far above average and financial services somewhat below.

The price–earnings ratio reflects investors' views of the growth potential of different sectors. The reason an investor would pay $167.70 for a dollar of earnings in a tech stock like RIM is that the investor expects large earnings growth. If this expectation is realized, high P/E stocks will have high returns. If earnings do not grow to meet expectations, these stocks will be very risky. We return to P/E ratios in Chapter 6.

Dividend Yield   The dividend yield is calculated by annualizing the last observed dividend payment of a firm and dividing by the current market price:

$$\text{Dividend yield} = \frac{\text{Dividend per share}}{\text{Market price per share}}$$

The table above shows dividend yields for selected indexes. Like P/E ratios, dividend yields are related to the market's perception of future growth prospects for firms. Firms with high growth prospects will generally have lower dividend yields.

Market-to-Book (M/B) Value and the Q Ratio   The market-to-book value ratio is calculated by dividing the market price per share by the book value per share. Since book value per share is an accounting number, it reflects historical costs. In a loose sense, the market-to-book ratio therefore compares the market value of the firm's assets to their cost. A value less than 1 could mean that the firm has not been successful overall in creating value for its shareholders.

There is another ratio, called Tobin's Q, that is very much like the M/B ratio. Tobin's Q ratio divides the market value of all of the firm's debt plus equity by the replacement value of the firm's assets. The Q ratios for several firms in the past were:[9]

High Qs	
Coca-Cola	4.20
IBM	4.20
Low Qs	
National Steel	0.53
U.S. Steel	0.61

The Q ratio differs from the M/B ratio in that the Q ratio uses market value of the debt plus equity. It also uses the replacement value of all assets and not the historical cost value.

If a firm has a Q ratio above 1 it provides an incentive to invest that is probably greater than for a firm with a Q ratio below 1. Firms with high Q ratios tend to be those firms with attractive investment opportunities or a significant competitive advantage.

Using Financial Ratios

Financial ratios have a variety of uses within a firm. Among the most important is performance evaluation. For example, managers are frequently evaluated and compensated on the basis of accounting measures of performance such as profit margin and return on equity. Also, firms with multiple divisions frequently compare their performance using financial statement information. Another important internal use is planning for the future. Historical financial statement information is very useful for generating projections about the future and for checking the realism of assumptions made in those projections.

Financial statements are useful to parties outside the firm, including short-term and long-term creditors and potential investors. For example, such information is quite useful in deciding whether or not to grant credit to a new customer.[10] When firms borrow from chartered banks, loan agreements almost always require that financial statements be submitted periodically. Most bankers use computer software to prepare common-size statements expressing income statement items as percentages of sales and balance sheet items as percentages of total assets. They also calculate ratios for their accounts. More advanced software uses expert system technology to generate a preliminary diagnosis of the borrower by comparing the company's ratios against benchmark parameters selected by the banker.

Table 2A.1 shows such a table prepared for the financial statement ratios for our example, the Canadian Composite Corporation.

Choosing a Benchmark

The firm's historical ratios are standard benchmarks for financial ratio analysis. Historical benchmarks are used to establish a trend. Another means of establishing a benchmark is to identify firms that are similar in the sense that they compete in the same markets, have

[9] E. B. Lindberg and S. Ross, "Tobin's Q and Industrial Organization," *Journal of Business* 54 (January 1981).

[10] Chapter 29 shows how statistical models based on ratios are used to predict insolvency.

Part 1   Overview

TABLE 2A.1   Selected Ratios for Canadian Composite Corporation

	2005	Industry	Rating
Short-Term Solvency			
Current ratio	1.57	1.52	OK
Quick ratio	1.01	1.10	OK
Activity			
Total asset turnover	1.25	1.31	OK
Receivables turnover	8.02	7.80	OK
Average collection period (days)	45.5	46.79	OK
Inventory turnover	6.03	7.12	−
Days in inventory	60.5	51.26	−
Financial Leverage			
Debt ratio	0.57	0.60	OK
Debt–equity ratio	1.33	1.33	OK
Equity multiplier	2.33	2.33	OK
Interest coverage	4.5	4.0	OK
Profitability			
Profit margin	3.8%	2.3%	+
Net return on assets	4.8%	3.0%	+
Return on equity	11.2%	7.0%	+
Payout ratio	0.5	0.3	OK
Retention ratio	0.5	0.7	OK
Sustainable growth rate	5.6%	4.9%	+

similar assets, and operate in similar ways. In practice, establishing such a peer group involves judgment on the part of the analyst since no two companies are identical.

Various benchmarks are available.[11] Statistics Canada publications include typical balance sheets, income statements, and selected ratios for firms in around 180 industries. Dun & Bradstreet Canada provides key business ratios for Canadian corporations. Other sources of benchmarks for Canadian companies include financial databases available from *The Financial Post* and *InfoGlobe*.[12] Several financial institutions gather their own financial ratio databases by compiling information on their loan customers. In this way, they seek to obtain more current, industry-specific information than is available from services like Statistics Canada and Dun & Bradstreet.

Obtaining current information is not the only challenge facing the financial analyst. Most large Canadian corporations do business in several industries, so the analyst often compares the company against several industry averages. Further, it is necessary to recognize that the industry average is not necessarily optimal. For example, agricultural analysts know that farmers are suffering with painfully low average profitability coupled with excessive debt. Despite these shortcomings, the industry average is a useful benchmark for ratio analysis.

[11] This discussion draws on L. Kryzanowski, M. To, and R. Seguin, *Business Solvency Risk Analysis* (Institute of Canadian Bankers, 1990), Chapter 3.
[12] Analysts examining U.S. companies will find comparable information available from Robert Morris Associates.

Potential Pitfalls of Financial Ratio Analysis

Financial ratio analysis is not based on any underlying theory to help identify which quantities to examine and to guide in establishing benchmarks. For this reason, individual judgment guided by experience plays an important role. Recognizing this, chartered banks are investing in expert system technology to pool the experience of many individual lenders and to standardize judgment.

Several other general problems frequently crop up. Different firms end their fiscal years at different times. For firms in seasonal businesses (such as a retailer with a large Christmas season), this can lead to difficulties in comparing balance sheets because of fluctuations in accounts during the year. For any particular firm, unusual or transient events, such as a one-time profit from an asset sale, may affect financial performance. In comparing firms, such events can give misleading signals.

SUMMARY AND CONCLUSIONS

Much research indicates that accounting statements provide important information about the value of the firm. Financial analysts and managers learn how to rearrange financial statements to squeeze out the maximum amount of information. In particular, analysts and managers use financial ratios to summarize the firm's liquidity, activity, financial leverage, and profitability. When possible, they also use market values. This appendix describes the most popular financial ratios. The following points should be kept in mind when trying to interpret financial statements:

1. Measures of profitability such as return on equity suffer from several potential deficiencies as indicators of performance. They do not take into account the risk or timing of cash flows.

2. Financial ratios are linked to one another. For example, return on equity is determined from the profit margins, the asset turnover ratio, and the financial leverage.

3. Financial ratio analysis seldom looks at ratios in isolation. As we have illustrated, financial analysts compare a firm's present ratios against historical ratios and industry averages.

4. Because ratio analysis is based on experience rather than on theory, special care must be taken to achieve consistent interpretations. Since financial ratios are based on accounting numbers, ratios may be misleading if management engages in accounting window dressing to improve reported performance. The hardest performance measures for management to manipulate are those based on market values because the market can usually see through attempts to manipulate accounting numbers.

Appendix 2B

Statement of Cash Flows

There is an official accounting statement called the statement of cash flows. This statement helps explain the change in accounting cash, which for Canadian Composite is $33 million in 20X5. It is very useful in understanding financial cash flow. Notice in Table 2.1 that cash increases from $107 million in 20X4 to $140 million in 20X5.

The first step in determining the change in cash is to figure out cash flow from operating activities. This is the cash flow that results from the firm's normal activities producing and selling goods and services. The second step is to make an adjustment for cash flow from investing activities. The final step is to make an adjustment for cash flow from financing activities. Financing activities are the net payments to creditors and owners (excluding interest expense) made during the year.

The three components of the statement of cash flows are determined below.

Cash Flow from Operating Activities

To calculate cash flow from operating activities we start with net income. Net income can be found on the income statement and is equal to $86. We now need to add back noncash expenses and adjust for changes in current assets and liabilities (other than cash). The result is cash flow from operating activities.

CANADIAN COMPOSITE CORPORATION
Cash Flow from Operating Activities
20X5
(in $ millions)

Net income	$ 86
Depreciation	90
Deferred taxes	13
Change in assets and liabilities	
Accounts receivable	(24)
Inventories	11
Accounts payable	16
Accrued expense	18
Notes payable	(3)
Other	(8)
Cash flow from operating activities	**$199**

Cash Flow from Investing Activities

Cash flow from investing activities involves changes in capital assets: acquisition of fixed assets and sales of fixed assets (i.e., net capital expenditures). The result for Canadian Composite follows.

CANADIAN COMPOSITE CORPORATION
Cash Flow from Investing Activities
20X5
(in $ millions)

Acquisition of fixed assets	$(198)
Sales of fixed assets	25
Cash flow from investing activities	**$(173)**

Cash Flow from Financing Activities

Cash flows to and from creditors and owners include changes in equity and debt.

CANADIAN COMPOSITE CORPORATION
Cash Flow from Financing Activities
20X5
(in $ millions)

Retirement of debt (includes notes)	$(73)
Proceeds from long-term debt sales	86
Dividends	(43)
Repurchase of stock	(6)
Proceeds from new stock issue	43
Cash flow from financing activities	**$ 7**

The statement of cash flows is the addition of cash flows from operations, cash flows from investing activities, and cash flows from financing activities, and is produced in Table 2B.1.

TABLE 2B.1   Statement of Consolidated Cash Flows of the Canadian Composite Corporation

CANADIAN COMPOSITE CORPORATION
Statement of Cash Flows
20X5
(in $ millions)

Operations	
Net income	$ 86
Depreciation	90
Deferred taxes	13
Changes in assets and liabilities	
Accounts receivable	(24)
Inventories	11
Accounts payable	16
Accrued expenses	18
Notes payable	(3)
Other	(8)
Total cash flow from operations	**$ 199**
Investing activities	
Acquisition of fixed assets	$(198)
Sales of fixed assets	25
Total cash flow from investing activities	**$(173)**
Financing activities	
Retirement of debt (including notes)	$ (73)
Proceeds of long-term debt	86
Dividends	(43)
Repurchase of stock	(6)
Proceeds from new stock issues	43
Total cash flow from financing activities	**$ 7**
Change in cash (on the balance sheet)	**$ 33**

Appendix Questions and Problems

2.A1 What effect would the following actions have on a firm's current ratio? Assume that net working capital is positive.

a. Inventory is purchased for cash.

b. A supplier is paid.

c. A bank loan is repaid.

d. A long-term debt matures and is paid.

e. A customer pays off an account.

f. Inventory is sold.

2.A2 If a company reports a 6 percent profit margin, a total asset turnover of 1.5, and a total debt ratio of 0.60, what are its ROA and ROE?

2.A3 Consider the following information for the PVI Corporation:

Credit sales	$17,655
Cost of goods sold	12,063
Accounts receivable	2,640
Accounts payable	1,926

How long does it take PVI to collect on its sales? How long does PVI take to pay its suppliers?

Use the following financial statement information for Stowe Enterprises to work Problems 2.A4 through 2.A8.

STOWE ENTERPRISES
2005 Income Statement

Sales	$6,300.00
Cost of goods sold	3,150.00
Depreciation	900.00
Earnings before interest and taxes	$2,250.00
Interest paid	675.00
Taxable income	$1,575.00
Taxes	535.50
Net income	$1,039.50
Addition to retained earnings	$ 279.00
Dividends	$ 760.50

STOWE ENTERPRISES
Abbreviated Balance Sheet, 2004–2005

Assets	2004	2005	Liabilities and Owners' Equity	2004	2005
Current assets			Current liabilities		
Cash	$ 900.00	$ 2,542.50	Accounts payable	$ 2,250.00	$ 2,385.00
Accounts receivable	2,925.00	3,096.00	Notes payable	2,443.50	2,070.00
Inventory	4,702.50	3,150.00	Other	963.00	823.50
Fixed assets			Long-term debt	4,936.50	5,328.00
Net plant and equipment	6,705.00	7,600.50	Owners' equity		
			Common stock	2,655.00	3,519.00
			Accumulated retained earnings	1,984.50	2,263.50
Total assets	$15,232.50	$16,389.00	Total liabilities and owners' equity	$15,232.50	$16,389.00

Chapter 2   Accounting Statements and Cash Flow

2.A4 Compute the following ratios for Stowe Enterprises for 2004 and 2005:

Short-Term Solvency Ratios	Asset Management Ratios	Long-Term Solvency Ratios	Profitability Ratios
Current ratio	Total asset turnover	Debt ratio	Profit margin
Quick ratio	Inventory turnover	Debt–equity ratio	Return on assets
Cash ratio	Receivables turnover	Equity multiplier	Return on equity
		Times interest earned	
		Cash coverage ratio	

2.A5 Construct the DuPont identity for Stowe Enterprises for 2005.

2.A6 Prepare a statement of cash flows for Stowe.

2.A7 For how many days in 2005 could Stowe continue to operate if its production were suspended?

2.A8 Stowe has 80 shares outstanding in 2005. The price per share is $40. What are the P/E ratio and market-to-book ratio?

2.A9 Select an industry featured in recent financial news. Then obtain annual reports on two companies in that industry and conduct a ratio analysis for the most recent two years. Make the relevant comparisons between the companies and against industry norms. Based on your ratio analysis, how do the two companies differ? Compare your comments against recent newspaper articles on the industry. (Note: This question is much easier to answer using ratio analysis software.)

2.A10 Enter the ticker symbol "IPS" for IPSCO Inc. and follow the "Excel Analytics" link. You will find the annual balance sheets for IPS for each of the past five years. Calculate the change in the net working capital for each year. How has net working capital changed over this entire period?

2.A11 Under the "Excel Analytics" link for Alcan, download the annual income statements and balance sheets for Alcan Inc. (AL). Calculate the operating cash flow, cash flow to creditors, and cash flow to shareholders for the most recent year. After you have completed your calculations, download the annual cash flow report and compare the given numbers to your calculations.

Chapter 3

Financial Planning and Growth

EXECUTIVE SUMMARY

Corporate financial planning establishes guidelines for change in the firm. These guidelines should include (1) an identification of the firm's financial goals, (2) an analysis of the differences between these goals and the current financial status of the firm, and (3) a statement of the actions needed for the firm to achieve its financial goals. In other words, as one member of GM's board was heard to say, "Planning is a process that at best helps the firm avoid stumbling into the future backwards."

The basic elements of financial planning comprise (1) the investment opportunities the firm elects to take advantage of, (2) the amount of debt the firm chooses to employ, and (3) the amount of cash the firm thinks is necessary and appropriate to pay shareholders. These are the financial policies that the firm must decide upon for its growth and profitability.

Almost all firms identify a companywide growth rate as a major component of their financial planning.[1] In one famous case, International Business Machines' stated growth goal was simple but typical: to match the growth of the computer industry, which was projected to be 15 percent per year through the end of the 1990s. Though we may have had some doubts about IBM's ability to sustain a 15 percent growth rate, we are certain there are important financial implications of the strategies that IBM will adopt to achieve that rate. There are direct connections between the growth that a company can achieve and its financial policy. One purpose of this chapter is to look at the financial aspects of how fast a firm can grow.

The chapter first describes what is usually meant by financial planning. This enables us to make an important point: Investment and financing decisions frequently interact. The different interactions of investment and financing decisions can be analyzed in the financial statements. We show how financial statements can be used to better understand how growth is achieved.

3.1 What Is Financial Planning?

Financial planning formulates the method by which financial goals are to be achieved. It has two dimensions: a time frame and a level of aggregation.

A financial plan is a statement of what is to be done in a future time. The GM board member was right on target when he explained the virtues of financial planning. Most decisions have long lead times, which means they take a long time to implement. In an uncertain world, this requires that decisions be made far in advance of their implementation. If a firm wants to build a factory in 2008, it may need to line up contractors in 2006. It is sometimes useful to think of the future as having a short run and a long run. The short run,

---

[1] We think that a firm's growth should be a consequence of its trying to achieve maximum shareholder value.

in practice, is usually the coming 12 months. We focus our attention on financial planning over the long run, which is usually taken to be a two-year to five-year period of time.

Financial plans are compiled from the capital-budgeting analyses of each of a firm's projects. In effect, the smaller investment proposals of each operational unit are added up and treated as a big project. This process is called **aggregation.**

Financial plans always entail alternative sets of assumptions. For example, suppose a company has two separate divisions: one for consumer products and one for gas turbine engines. The financial planning process might require each division to prepare three alternative business plans for the next three years.

1. *A Worst Case.* This plan would require making the worst possible assumptions about the company's products and the state of the economy. It could mean divestiture and liquidation.

2. *A Normal Case.* This plan would require making the most likely assumptions about the company and the economy.

3. *A Best Case.* Each division would be required to work out a case based on the most optimistic assumptions. It could involve new products and expansion.

Because the company is likely to spend a lot of time preparing proposals on different scenarios that will become the basis for the company's financial plan, it seems reasonable to ask what the planning process will accomplish.

1. *Interactions.* The financial plan must make the linkages between investment proposals for the different operating activities of the firm and the financing choices available to the firm explicit. IBM's 15 percent growth target goes hand in hand with its financing program.

2. *Options.* The financial plan provides the opportunity for the firm to work through various investment and financing options. The firm addresses questions of what financing arrangements are optimal and evaluates options of closing plants or marketing new products.

3. *Feasibility.* The different plans must fit into the overall corporate objective of maximizing shareholder wealth.

4. *Avoiding Surprises.* Financial planning should identify what may happen in the future if certain events take place. Thus, one of the purposes of financial planning is to avoid surprises.

Concept Questions

- What are the two dimensions of the financial planning process?
- Why should firms draw up financial plans?

3.2 A Financial Planning Model: The Ingredients

Just as companies differ in size and products, financial plans are not the same for all companies. However, there are some common elements:

1. **Sales forecast.** All financial plans require a sales forecast. Perfectly accurate sales forecasts are not possible, because sales depend on the uncertain future state of the economy. Firms can get help from businesses specializing in macroeconomic and industry projections. A good sales forecast should be the consequence of having identified all valuable investment opportunities.

EXAMPLE

2. **Pro forma statements.** The financial plan will have a forecast balance sheet, an income statement, and a sources-and-uses statement. These are called *pro forma statements*, or *pro formas*.

3. **Asset requirements.** The plan will describe projected capital spending. In addition, it will discuss the proposed uses of net working capital.

4. **Financial requirements.** The plan will include a section on financing arrangements. This part of the plan should discuss dividend policy and debt policy. Sometimes firms will expect to raise equity by selling new shares of stock. In this case the plan must consider what kinds of securities must be sold and what methods of issuance are most appropriate.

5. **Plug.** Suppose a financial planner assumes that sales, costs, and net income will rise at a particular rate, g_1. Further suppose that the planner wants assets and liabilities to grow at a different rate, g_2. These two different growth rates may be incompatible unless a third variable is also adjusted. For example, compatibility may only be reached if outstanding stock grows at a different rate, g_3. In this example, we treat the growth in outstanding stock as the *plug* variable. That is, the growth rate in outstanding stock is chosen to make the growth rate in income statement items consistent with the growth rate in balance sheet items. Surprisingly, even if the income statement items grow at the *same* rate as the balance sheet items, consistency might be achieved only if outstanding stock grows at a different rate.

   Of course, the growth rate in outstanding stock need not be the plug variable. One could have income statement items grow at g_1, and assets, long-term debt, and outstanding stock grow at g_2. In this case, compatibility between g_1 and g_2 might be achieved by letting short-term debt grow at a rate of g_3.

6. **Economic assumptions.** The plan must explicitly state the economic environment in which the firm expects to reside over the life of the plan. Among the economic assumptions that must be made is the level of interest rates.

The Computerfield Corporation's 20X5 financial statements are as follows:

Income Statement 20X5		Balance Sheet Year-End 20X5			
Sales	$1,000	Assets	$500	Debt	$250
Costs	800			Equity	250
Net income	$ 200	Total	$500	Total	$500

In 20X5, Computerfield's profit margin is 20 percent, and it has never paid a dividend. Its debt–equity ratio is 1. This is also the firm's *target* debt–equity ratio. Unless otherwise stated, the financial planners at Computerfield assume that all variables are tied directly to sales and that current relationships are optimal.

Suppose that sales increase by 20 percent from 20X5 to 20X6. Because the planners would then also forecast a 20 percent increase in costs, the pro forma income statement would be:

Income Statement 20X6	
Sales	$1,200
Costs	960
Net income	$ 240

The assumption that all variables will grow by 20 percent will enable us to construct the pro forma balance sheet as well:

Balance Sheet
Year-End 20X6

Assets	$600	Debt	$300
		Equity	300
Total	$600	Total	$600

Now we must reconcile these two pro formas. How, for example, can net income be equal to $240 and equity increase by only $50? The answer is that Computerfield must have paid a dividend or repurchased stock equal to $190. In this case dividends are the plug variable.

Suppose Computerfield does not pay a dividend and does not repurchase its own stock. With these assumptions, Computerfield's equity will grow to $490, and debt must be retired to keep total assets equal to $600. In this case the debt-to-equity ratio is the plug variable; with $600 in total assets and $490 in equity, debt will have to be $600 − $490, or $110. Since we started with $250 in debt, Computerfield will have to retire $250 − $110, or $140 of debt. The resulting balance sheet would look like this:

Balance Sheet
Year-End 20X6

Asset	$600	Debt	$110
		Equity	490
Total	$600	Total	$600

The thing to notice in our simple example is the way the change in liabilities and equity depends on the firm's financing policy and the firm's dividend policy. The firm ensures growth in assets by having a plan in place to finance such growth.

This example shows the interaction of sales growth and financial policy. The next section focuses on the need for external funds. It identifies a six-step procedure for constructing the pro forma balance sheet.

3.3 The Percentage Sales Method

In the previous section, we described a simple planning model in which every item increased at the same rate as sales. This may be a reasonable assumption for some elements. For others, such as long-term borrowing, it probably is not, because the amount of long-term borrowing is something set by management, and it does not necessarily relate directly to the level of sales. We return to this in detail in Chapters 16 and 17.

In this section, we describe an extended version of our simple model. The basic idea is to separate the income statement and balance sheet accounts into two groups: those that do vary directly with sales, and those that do not. Given a sales forecast, we will then be able to calculate how much financing the firm will need to support the predicted sales level.

The financial planning model we describe next is based on the **percentage of sales approach.** Our goal here is to develop a quick and practical way of generating pro forma statements. We defer discussion of some possible extensions to a later section.

The Income Statement

We start out with the most recent income statement for the Rosengarten Corporation, as shown in Table 3.1. Notice we have still simplified things by including costs, depreciation, and interest in a single cost figure. We separate these out in a later section.

Rosengarten has projected a 10 percent increase in sales for the coming year, so we are anticipating sales of $20 million × 1.1 = $22 million. To generate a pro forma income statement, we assume that total costs will continue to run at $16.9697 million/$20 million = 84.85% of sales. With this assumption, Rosengarten's pro forma income statement is as shown in Table 3.2. The effect here of assuming that costs are a constant percentage of sales is to assume that the profit margin is constant. To check this, notice that the profit margin was $2 million/$20 million = 10%. In our pro forma, the profit margin is $2.2 million/$22 million = 10%; so it is unchanged.

Next, we need to project the dividend payment. This amount is up to Rosengarten's management. We will assume Rosengarten has a policy of paying out a constant fraction of net income in the form of a cash dividend. For the most recent year, the **dividend payout ratio** was:

$$\text{Dividend payout ratio} = \frac{\text{Cash dividends}}{\text{Net income}}$$

$$= \frac{\$1 \text{ million}}{\$2 \text{ million}} = 50\% \qquad (3.1)$$

We can also calculate the ratio of the addition to retained earnings to net income as:

$$\frac{\text{Addition to retained earnings}}{\text{Net income}} = \frac{\$1 \text{ million}}{\$2 \text{ million}}$$

This ratio is called the **retention ratio** or **plowback ratio,** and it is equal to 1 minus the dividend payout ratio because everything not paid out is retained. Assuming that the payout ratio is constant, the projected dividends and addition to retained earnings will be:

Projected dividends paid to shareholders = $1.1 million × ½ = $ 550 thousand

Projected addition to retained earnings = $1.1 million × ½ = $\dfrac{550 \text{ thousand}}{\$1,100 \text{ thousand}}$

TABLE 3.1	Rosengarten Corporation Income Statement

ROSENGARTEN CORPORATION
Income Statement
($ in thousands)

Sales	$20,000.00
Costs	16,969.70
Taxable income	$ 3,030.30
Taxes (34%)	1,030.30
Net income	$ 2,000.00
Dividends	$1,000.00
Addition to retained earnings	1,000.00

TABLE 3.2   Rosengarten Corporation Pro Forma Income Statement

ROSENGARTEN CORPORATION
Pro Forma Income Statement
($ in thousands)

Sales (projected)	$22,000.00
Costs (84.85% of sales)	18,666.00
Taxable income	$ 3,334.00
Taxes (34%)	1,134.00
Net income	$ 2,200.00

The Balance Sheet

To generate a pro forma balance sheet, we start with the most recent statement, as shown in the table below.

On our balance sheet, we assume that most of the items vary directly with sales. Only common stock does not. For those items that do vary with sales, we express each as a percentage of sales for the year just completed. When an item does not vary directly with sales, we write "constant."

For example, on the asset side, fixed assets are equal to 120 percent of sales ($24 million/$20 million) for the year just ended. We assume this percentage applies to the coming year, so for each $1 increase in sales, fixed assets will rise by $1.20.

	Current Balance Sheet ($ in thousands)	Pro Forma Balance Sheet ($ in thousands)	Explanation
Current assets	$ 6,000	$ 6,600	30% of sales
Fixed assets	24,000	26,400	120% of sales
Total assets	$30,000	$33,000	150% of sales
Short-term debt	$10,000	$11,000	50% of sales
Long-term debt	6,000	6,600	30% of sales
Common stock	4,000	4,000	Constant
Retained earnings	10,000	11,100	Net income
Total financing	$30,000	$32,700	
		$ 300	Funds needed (the difference between total assets and total financing)

From this information we can determine the pro forma balance sheet, which is on the right-hand side. The change in retained earnings will be

$$\text{Net income} - \text{Dividends} = \text{Change in retained earnings}$$
$$(0.10 \times \$22 \text{ million}) - (0.5 \times 0.10 \times \$22 \text{ million}) = \$1.1 \text{ million}$$

In this example the plug variable is new shares of stock. The company must issue $300,000 of new stock. The equation that can be used to determine if external funds are needed is

External Funds Needed (EFN):

$$\left(\frac{\text{Assets}}{\text{Sales}}\right) \times \Delta\text{Sales} - \frac{\text{Debt}}{\text{Sales}} \times \Delta\text{Sales} - (p \times \text{Projected sales}) \times (1 - d)$$

$$= (1.5 \times \$2 \text{ million}) - (0.80 \times \$2 \text{ million}) - (0.10 \times \$22 \text{ million} \times 0.5)$$
$$= \$1.4 \text{ million} \qquad\qquad - \$1.1 \text{ million}$$
$$= \$0.3 \text{ million}$$

where

$$\frac{\text{Assets}}{\text{Sales}} = 1.5$$

$$\frac{\text{Debt}}{\text{Sales}} = 0.8$$

$$p = \text{Net profit margin} = 0.10$$

$$d = \text{Dividend payout ratio} = 0.5$$

$$\Delta\text{Sales} = \text{Projected change in sales}$$

The steps in the estimation of the pro forma sheet for the Rosengarten Corporation and the external funds needed (EFN) are as follows:

1. Express balance sheet items that vary with sales as a percentage of sales.

2. Multiply the percentages determined in step 1 by projected sales to obtain the amount for the future period.

3. Where no percentage applies, simply insert the previous balance sheet figure in the future period.

4. Compute projected retained earnings as follows:

$$\text{Projected retained earnings} = \text{Present retained earnings}$$
$$+ \text{Projected net income} - \text{Cash dividends}$$

5. Add the asset accounts to determine projected assets. Next, add the liabilities and equity accounts to determine the total financing; any difference is the *shortfall*. This equals external funds needed (EFN).

6. Use the plug to fill EFN. In this example, new shares are the plug but debt could also be used.

Table 3.3 computes EFN for several different growth rates. For low growth rates, Rosengarten will run a surplus, and for high growth rates, it will run a deficit. The "break-even" growth rate is 7.7 percent. Figure 3.1 illustrates the relation between projected sales growth and EFN. As can be seen, the need for new assets from projected sales growth grows much faster than the additions to retained earnings plus new debt. Eventually, a deficit is created and a need for external financing becomes evident.

TABLE 3.3   Projected Sales Growth and EFN for the Rosengarten Corporation

Projected Sales Growth	Increase in Assets Required	Addition to Retained Earnings	External Financing Needed (EFN)
0 %	$ 0	$1,000,000	− $1,000,000
5	1,500,000	1,050,000	− 350,000
7.7	2,310,000	1,077,000	—
10	3,000,000	1,100,000	300,000
20	6,000,000	1,200,000	1,600,000

FIGURE 3.1

Growth and
EFN for the
Rosengarten
Corporation

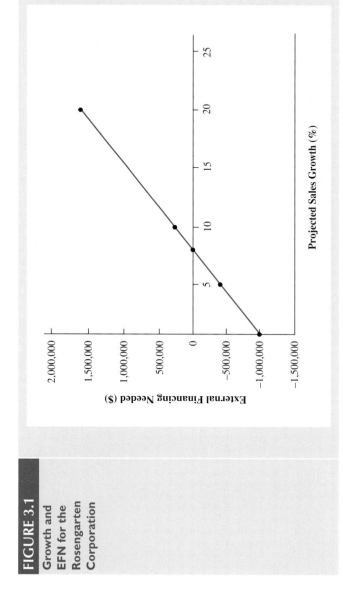

3.4 What Determines Growth?

This section furthers our discussion of a firm's growth and its accounting statements. Firms frequently make growth forecasts an explicit part of financial planning. Donaldson reports on the pervasiveness of stating corporate goals in terms of growth rates.[2] This may seem puzzling in the light of our previous emphasis on maximizing the shareholder's value as the central goal of management. One way to reconcile the difference is to think of growth as an intermediate goal that leads to higher value. Rappaport correctly points out that, in applying the shareholder value approach, growth should not be a goal but must be a consequence of decisions that maximize shareholder value.[3] In fact, if the firm is willing to accept any project just to grow in size, growth will probably make the shareholders worse off.

Donaldson also concludes that most major industrial companies are very reluctant to use external equity as a regular part of their financial planning. To illustrate the linkages between the ability of a firm to grow and its accounting statements when the firm does not issue equity, we can make some planning assumptions.

1. The firm's assets will grow in proportion to its sales.

2. Net income is a constant proportion of its sales.

3. The firm has a given dividend-payout policy and a given debt–equity ratio.

4. The firm will not change the number of outstanding shares of stock.

---

[2]G. Donaldson, *Managing Corporation Wealth: The Operations of a Comprehensive Financial Goals System* (New York: Praeger, 1984).

[3]A. Rappaport, *Creating Shareholder Value: The New Standard for Business Performance* (New York: Free Press, 1986).

There is only one growth rate that is consistent with the preceding assumptions. In effect, with these assumptions, growth has been made a plug variable. To see this, recall that a change in assets must always be equal to a change in debt plus a change in equity:

$$\begin{array}{ccc} \boxed{\begin{array}{c} \text{Change} \\ \text{in} \\ \text{assets} \end{array}} & = & \boxed{\begin{array}{c} \text{Change} \\ \text{in} \\ \text{debt} \\ + \\ \text{Change} \\ \text{in} \\ \text{equity} \end{array}} \end{array}$$

Now we can write the conditions that ensure this equality and solve for the growth rate that will give it to us.

The variables used in this demonstration are the following:

T = The ratio of total assets to sales
p = The net profit margin on sales
d = The dividend-payout ratio
L = The debt–equity ratio
S_0 = Sales this year
ΔS = The change in sales ($S_1 - S_0 = \Delta S$)
S_1 = Next year's projected sales
RE = Retained earnings = Net income × Retention ratio = $S_1 \times p \times (1 - d)$
NI = Net income = $S_1 \times p$

If the firm is to increase sales by ΔS during the year, it must increase assets by $T\Delta S$. The firm is assumed not to be able to change the number of shares of stock outstanding, so the equity financing must come from retained earnings. Retained earnings will depend on next year's sales, the payout ratio, and the profit margin. The amount of borrowing will depend on the amount of retained earnings and the debt–equity ratio.

Moving things around a little gives the following:

New equity: $S_1 \times p \times (1 - d)$
       plus
Borrowing: $[S_1 \times p \times (1 - d)] \times L$
       equals
Capital spending: $T\Delta S$

$$T\Delta S = [S_1 \times p \times (1 - d)] + [S_1 \times p \times (1 - d) \times L]$$

and

$$\frac{\Delta S}{S_0} = \frac{p \times (1 - d) \times (1 + L)}{T - [p \times (1 - d) \times (1 + L)]} = \text{Growth rate in sales} \qquad (3.2)$$

This is the growth-rate equation. Given the profit margin (p), the payout ratio (d), the debt–equity ratio (L), and the asset-requirement ratio (T), the growth rate can be determined. It is the only growth possible with the preset values for the four variables. Higgins has referred to this growth rate as the firm's **sustainable growth rate.**[4]

––––––
[4] R. C. Higgins, "Sustainable Growth Under Inflation," *Financial Management* (Autumn 1981). The definition of sustainable growth was popularized by the Boston Consulting Group and others.

EXAMPLE

Table 3.4 shows the current income statement, the sources-and-uses-of-cash statement, and the balance sheet for the Hoffman Corporation. Net income for the corporation was 16.5 percent ($1,650/$10,000) of sales revenue. The company paid out 72.4 percent ($1,195/$1,650) of its net income in dividends. The interest rate on debt was 10 percent, and the long-term debt was 50 percent ($5,000/$10,000) of assets. (Notice that, for simplicity, we use the single term *net working capital*, in Table 3.4, instead of separating current assets from current liabilities.) Hoffman's assets grew at the rate of 10 percent ($910/$9,090). In addition, sales grew at 10 percent, though this increase is not shown in Table 3.4.

TABLE 3.4	Current Financial Statements: The Hoffman Corporation (in thousands)

THE HOFFMAN CORPORATION
Income Statement

	This Year
Net sales (S)	$10,000
Cost of sales	7,000
Earnings before taxes and interest	3,000
Interest expense	500
Earnings before taxes	2,500
Taxes	850
Net income (NI)	$ 1,650

Sources and Uses of Cash

	This Year
Sources:	
Net income (NI)	$ 1,650
Depreciation	500
Operating cash flow	2,150
Borrowing	455
New stock issue	0
Total sources	$ 2,605
Uses:	
Increase in net working capital	455
Capital spending	955
Dividends	1,195
Total uses	$ 2,605

Balance Sheet

	This Year	Last Year	Change
Assets			
Net working capital	$ 5,000	$4,545	$455
Fixed assets	5,000	4,545	455
Total assets	$10,000	$9,090	$910
Liabilities and Shareholders' Equity			
Debt	$ 5,000	$4,545	$455
Equity	5,000	4,545	455
Total liabilities and shareholders' equity	$10,000	$9,090	$910

In Their Own Words
Robert C. Higgins on Sustainable Growth

Most financial officers know intuitively that it takes money to make money. Rapid sales growth requires increased assets in the form of accounts receivable, inventory, and fixed plant, which, in turn, require money to pay for assets. They also know that if their company does not have the money when needed, it can literally "grow broke." The sustainable growth equation states these intuitive truths explicitly.

Sustainable growth is often used by bankers and other external analysts to assess a company's creditworthiness. They are aided in this exercise by several sophisticated computer software packages that provide detailed analyses of the company's past financial performance, including its annual sustainable growth rate.

Bankers use this information in several ways. Quick comparison of a company's actual growth rate to its sustainable rate tells the banker what issues will be at the top of management's financial agenda. If actual growth consistently exceeds sustainable growth, management's problem will be where to get the cash to finance growth. The banker thus can anticipate interest in loan products. Conversely, if sustainable growth consistently exceeds actual, the banker had best be prepared to talk about investment products, because management's problem will be what to do with all the cash that keeps piling up in the till.

Bankers also find the sustainable growth equation useful for explaining to financially inexperienced small business owners and overly optimistic entrepreneurs that, for the long-run viability of their business, it is necessary to keep growth and profitability in proper balance.

Finally, comparison of actual to sustainable growth rates helps a banker understand why a loan applicant needs money and for how long the need might continue. In one instance, a loan applicant requested $100,000 to pay off several insistent suppliers and promised to repay in a few months when he collected some accounts receivable that were coming due. A sustainable growth analysis revealed that the firm had been growing at four to six times its sustainable growth rate and that this pattern was likely to continue in the foreseeable future. This alerted the banker that impatient suppliers were only a symptom of the much more fundamental disease of overly rapid growth, and that a $100,000 loan would likely prove to be only the down payment on a much larger, multiyear commitment.

Robert C. Higgins is Professor of Finance at the University of Washington. He pioneered the use of sustainable growth as a tool for financial analysis.

The cash flow generated by Hoffman was enough not only to pay a dividend but also to increase net working capital and fixed assets by $455 each. The company did not issue any shares of stock. A firm can do several things to increase its sustainable growth rate as seen from the Hoffman example:

1. Sell new shares of stock.
2. Increase its reliance on debt.
3. Reduce its dividend-payout ratio.
4. Increase profit margins.
5. Decrease its asset-requirement ratio.

However, suppose its desired growth rate was to be 20 percent. It is possible for Hoffman's desired growth to exceed its sustainable growth because Hoffman is able to issue new shares of stock. A firm can do several things to increase its sustainable growth rate as seen from the Hoffman example:

The sustainable growth rate for the Hoffman Corporation is 10 percent, or[5]

$$\frac{0.165 \times 0.276 \times 2}{1 - (0.165 \times 0.276 \times 2)} = 0.1$$

[5]This expression is exactly equal to the rate of return on equity (ROE) multiplied by the retention rate (RR): ROE × RR if by ROE we mean net income this year divided by equity *last year*, i.e., $1,650/$4,545 = 36.3%. In this case ROE × RR = 36.3% × 27.6% = 10% = sustainable growth in sales. On the other hand, if by ROE we mean net income this year divided by equity *this year*, i.e., $1,650/$5,000 = 33%, the sustainable growth rate in sales = ROE × RR/1 − (ROE × RR).

Now we can see the use of a financial planning model to test the feasibility of the planned growth rate. If sales are to grow at a rate higher than the sustainable growth rate, the firm must improve operating performance, increase financial leverage, decrease dividends, or sell new shares. At the other extreme, suppose the firm is losing money (has a negative profit margin) or is paying out more than 100 percent of earnings in dividends so that the retention rate $(1 - d)$ is negative. In each of these cases, the negative sustainable growth rate signals the rate at which sales and assets must shrink. Firms can achieve negative growth by selling off assets and laying off employees. Nortel is an example of a Canadian firm that has had to undergo this painful downsizing process.

Of course, either way the planned rates of growth should be the result of a complete maximization of shareholder value-based planning process.

Concept
Questions

- **When might the goals of growth and value maximization be in conflict, and when would they be aligned?**
- **What are the determinants of growth?**

3.5 Some Caveats of Financial Planning Models

Financial planning models such as sustainable growth suffer from a great deal of criticism. We present two commonly voiced attacks below.

First, financial planning models do not indicate which financial policies are the best. For example, our model could not tell us whether Hoffman's decision to issue new equity to achieve a higher growth rate raises the shareholder value of the firm.

Second, financial planning models are too simple. In reality, costs are not always proportional to sales, assets need not be a fixed percentage of sales, and capital budgeting involves a sequence of decisions over time. These assumptions are generally not incorporated into financial plans.

Financial planning models are necessary to assist in planning the future investment and financial decisions of the firm. Without some sort of long-term financial plan, the firm may find itself adrift in a sea of change without a rudder for guidance. But, because of the assumptions and the abstractions from reality necessary in the construction of the financial plan, we also think that they should carry the label: Let the user beware!

3.6 SUMMARY AND CONCLUSIONS

Financial planning forces the firm to think about and forecast the future. It involves the following:

1. Building a corporate financial model.
2. Describing different scenarios of future development from worst to best cases.
3. Using the models to construct pro forma financial statements.
4. Running the model under different scenarios (conducting sensitivity analysis).
5. Examining the financial implications of ultimate strategic plans.

Corporate financial planning should not become a purely mechanical activity. If it does, it will probably focus on the wrong things. In particular, plans are formulated all too often in terms of a growth target with an explicit linkage to creation of value. We talk about a particular financial planning model called sustainable growth. It is a very simple model. Nonetheless, the alternative to financial planning is stumbling into the future.

KEY TERMS

Aggregation 55	Plug 56
Asset requirements 56	Pro forma statements 56
Dividend payout ratio 58	Retention ratio (plowback ratio) 58
Economic assumptions 56	Sales forecast 55
Financial requirements 56	Sustainable growth rate 62
Percentage of sales approach 57	

SUGGESTED READING

Some aspects of economic growth and stock market returns are covered in:
Jay Ritter, "Economic Growth—Equity Returns." Unpublished working paper. University of Florida, March 1, 2003.

We also recommend:
John K. Campbell and Robert Shiller, "Valuation Ratios and the Long Run Stock Market Outlook: An Update." Cowles Foundation Discussion Paper, no. 1295.

Phillippe Jorion and William Goetzmann, "Global Stock Markets in the Twentieth Century." *Journal of Finance* (1995).

Lamont Owen, "Earnings and Expect Returns." *Journal of Finance* 53 (1998).

QUESTIONS & PROBLEMS

Financial Planning Models: The Ingredients

3.1   After examining patterns from recent years, management found the following regression-estimated relationships between some company balance sheets and income statement accounts and sales.

$$CA = 0.5 \text{ million} + 0.25S$$
$$FA = 1.0 \text{ million} + 0.50S$$
$$CL = 0.1 \text{ million} + 0.10S$$
$$NP = 0.0 \text{ million} + 0.02S$$

where

CA = Current assets
FA = Fixed assets
CL = Current liabilities
NP = Net profit after taxes
S = Sales

The company's sales for last year were $10 million. The year-end balance sheet is reproduced below.

Current assets	$3,000,000	Current liabilities	$1,100,000
Fixed assets	6,000,000	Bonds	2,500,000
		Common stock	2,000,000
		Retained earnings	3,400,000
Total	$9,000,000	Total	$9,000,000

Management further found that the company's sales bear a relationship to GNP. That relationship is:

$$S = 0.00001 \times GNP$$

The forecast of GNP for next year is $2.05 trillion. The firm pays out 34 percent of net profits after taxes in dividends.

Create a pro forma balance sheet for this firm.

3.2   Cheryl Colby, the CFO of Charming Florist Ltd., has created the firm's pro forma balance sheet for the next fiscal year. Sales are projected to grow at 10 percent to the level of $330 million. Current assets, fixed assets, short-term debt, and long-term debt are 25 percent, 150 percent, 40 percent, and 45 percent of the total sales, respectively.

Charming Florist pays out 40 percent of net income. The value of common stock is constant at $50 million. The profit margin on sales is 12 percent.

a. Based on Ms. Colby's forecast, how much external funding does Charming Florist need?

b. Reconstruct the current balance sheet based on the projected figures.

c. Lay out the firm's pro forma balance sheet for the next fiscal year.

What Determines Growth?

3.3   The Stieben Company has determined that the following will be true next year:

T = Ratio of total assets to sales = 1
P = Net profit margin on sales = 5%
d = Dividend-payout ratio = 50%
L = Debt–equity ratio = 1

a. What is Stieben's sustainable growth rate in sales?

b. Can Stieben's actual growth rate in sales be different from its sustainable growth rate? Why or why not?

c. How can Stieben change its sustainable growth?

3.4   The Optimal Scam Company would like to see its sales grow at 20 percent for the foreseeable future. Its financial statements for the current year are presented below.

Income Statement ($ millions)		Balance Sheet ($ millions)	
Sales	32.00	Current assets	16
Costs	28.97	Fixed assets	16
Gross profit	3.03	Total assets	32
Taxes	1.03		
Net income	2.00	Current debt	10
		Long-term debt	4
Dividends	1.40	Total debt	14
Retained earnings	0.60	Common stock	14
		Ret. earnings	4
		Total liabilities and equity	32

The current financial policy of the Optimal Scam Company includes:

Dividend-payout ratio (d) = 70%
Debt-to-equity ratio (L) = 77.78%
Net profit margin (P) = 6.25%
Assets–sales ratio (T) = 1

a. Determine Optimal Scam's need for external funds next year.

b. Construct a pro forma balance sheet for Optimal Scam.

c. Calculate the sustainable growth rate for the Optimal Scam Company.

d. How can Optimal Scam change its financial policy to achieve its growth objective?

3.5   The MBI Company does not want to grow. The company's financial management believes it has no positive NPV projects. The company's operating financial characteristics are:

Profit margin = 10%
Assets–sales ratio = 150%
Debt–equity ratio = 100%
Dividend-payout ratio = 50%

a. Calculate the sustainable growth rate for the MBI Company.

b. How can the MBI Company achieve its stated growth goal?

3.6   Starting in Chapter 1, we argue that financial managers should select positive share-holder value projects. How does this project selection criterion relate to financial planning models?

**S & P
PROBLEMS**

STANDARD
&POOR'S

3.7   Your firm recently hired a new MBA. She insists that your firm is incorrectly computing its sustainable growth rate. Your firm computes the sustainable growth rate using the following formula:

$$\frac{P \times (1 - d) \times (1 + L)}{T - P \times (1 - d) \times (1 + L)}$$

P = Net profit margin on sales
d = Dividend-payout ratio
L = Debt-equity ratio
T = Ratio of total assets to sales

Your new employee claims that the correct formula is ROE $\times (1 - d)$ where ROE is net profit divided by net worth and d is dividends divided by net profit. Is your new employee correct?

3.8   Atlantic Transportation Co. has a payout ratio of 60 percent, debt–equity ratio of 50 percent, return on equity of 16 percent, and an assets–sales ratio of 175 percent.

a.   What is its sustainable growth rate?
b.   What must its profit margin be in order to achieve its sustainable growth rate?

3.9   A firm wishes to maintain a growth rate of 12 percent per year and a debt–equity ratio of 0.40. Its profit margin is 6 percent and the ratio of total assets to sales is constant at 1.90. Is this growth rate possible? To answer, determine what the dividend payout must be and interpret the result.

Some Caveats of Financial Planning Models

3.10   What are the shortcomings of financial planning models that we should be aware of?

3.11   Use the annual income statements and balance sheets under the "Excel Analytics" link to calculate the sustainable growth rate for Molson Coors Brewing Company (TAP) each year for the past four years. Is the sustainable growth rate the same every year? What are possible reasons the sustainable growth rate may vary from year to year?

3.12   Hilton Hotels Inc. (HLT) operates over 60 hotels in 29 countries. Under the "Financial Highlights" link you can find a five-year growth rate for sales. Using this growth rate and the most recent income statement and balance sheet, compute the external funds needed for ESA next year.

Part II

Value and Capital Budgeting

Firms and individuals invest in a large variety of assets. Some are real assets such as machinery and land, and some are financial assets such as stocks and bonds. The objective of the investment is to maximize value. In the simplest terms, this means to find assets that add more value to the firm than they cost. To do this we need a theory of value. Developing such a theory is the goal of Part II.

In Chapter 4 we describe how financial markets allow us to determine the values of financial instruments. We study some stylized examples and show why financial markets and financial instruments are created. We introduce the basic principles of rational decision making and apply these principles to a two-period investment. Here, we introduce one of the most important ideas in finance: net present value (NPV). We show why net present value is useful and the conditions that make it applicable.

In Chapter 5 we extend the concept of net present value to more than one time period. The mathematics of compounding and discounting is presented. In Chapter 6 we apply present value to bonds and stocks. This is a very important chapter because present value can be used to determine the value of a wide variety of financial instruments.

Although we have made a strong case for using the NPV rule in Chapters 4 and 5, Chapter 7 presents four other rules: the payback rule, the accounting-rate-of-return rule, the internal rate of return (IRR), and the profitability index. Each of these alternatives has some redeeming features, but they are not sufficient to replace the NPV rule.

In Chapter 8 we analyze how to estimate the cash flows required for capital budgeting. We start the chapter with a discussion of the concept of incremental cash flows—the difference between the cash flows for the firm with and without the project. Chapter 9 focuses on assessing the reliability and reasonableness of estimates of NPV. The chapter introduces techniques for dealing with uncertain incremental cash flows in capital budgeting, including break-even analysis, decision trees, and sensitivity analysis.

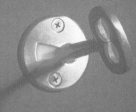

Chapter 4

Financial Markets and Net Present Value: First Principles of Finance

EXECUTIVE SUMMARY

Finance refers to the process by which special markets deal with cash flows over time. These markets are called *financial markets*. Making investment and financing decisions requires an understanding of the basic economic principles of financial markets. This introductory chapter describes a financial market as one that makes it possible for individuals and corporations to borrow and lend. As a consequence, financial markets can be used by individuals and corporations to adjust their patterns of consumption over time and by corporations to adjust their patterns of investment spending over time. The main point of this chapter is that individuals and corporations can use the financial markets to help them make investment decisions. We introduce one of the most important ideas in finance: net present value.

By far the most important economic decisions are those that involve investments in real assets. We don't mean savings decisions, which are decisions not to consume some of this year's income, but decisions regarding actual investments: building a machine or a whole factory or a Tim Hortons, for example. These decisions determine the economic future for a society. Economists use the word *capital* to describe the total stock of machines and equipment that a society possesses and uses to produce goods and services. Investment decisions are decisions about whether or not to increase this stock of capital.

The investment decisions made today determine how much additional capital the society will add to its current stock of capital. That capital then can be used in the future to produce goods and services for the society. Some of the forms that capital takes are obvious, like steel mills and computers. But many kinds of capital are things that you probably never would have considered as part of a country's capital stock. Public roads, for example, are a form of capital, and the decisions to build them are investment decisions. Perhaps most important, the decision you are making to invest in an education is no different in principle from these other investment decisions. Your decision to invest in an education is a decision to build your human capital, just as a company's decision to build a new factory is a decision to invest in physical capital.[1] The total of all the capital possessed by a society is a measure of its wealth. The purpose of this chapter is to develop the basic principles that guide rational investment decision making. We show that a particular investment decision should be made if it is superior to available alternatives in the financial markets.

---

[1] If you have any doubt about the importance of human capital as part of a country's wealth, think about the conditions of Germany and Japan at the end of World War II. The physical capital of these countries had been destroyed, and even the basic social capital like roads, sewer systems, and factories was in rubble. Even though these countries might have appeared to be economically crippled beyond repair, a look below the surface would have revealed a different picture. A huge part of the wealth of these countries consisted of the human capital inherent in their literate and skilled populations. Building on this substantial base of capital by a long-term policy of investment has brought Germany and Japan to a very high standard of living.

4.1 The Financial Market Economy

Financial markets develop to facilitate borrowing and lending between individuals. Here we talk about how this happens. Suppose we describe the economic circumstances of two people: Tom and Leslie. Both Tom and Leslie have current income of $100,000. Tom is a very patient person, and some people call him a miser. He wants to consume only $50,000 of current income and save the rest. Leslie is a very impatient person, and some people call her extravagant. She wants to consume $150,000 this year. Tom and Leslie have different intertemporal consumption preferences.

Such preferences are personal matters and have more to do with psychology than with finance. However, it seems that Tom and Leslie could strike a deal: Tom could give up some of his income this year in exchange for future income that Leslie can promise to give him. Tom can *lend* $50,000 to Leslie, and Leslie can *borrow* $50,000 from Tom. This deal illustrates the useful role of financial markets in allowing borrowing and lending.

Suppose that they do strike this deal, with Tom giving up $50,000 this year in exchange for $55,000 next year. This is illustrated in Figure 4.1 with the basic cash flow time chart, a representation of the timing and amount of the cash flows. The cash flows that are received are represented by an arrow pointing up from the point on the time line at which the cash flow occurs. The cash flows paid out are represented by an arrow pointing down. In other words, for each dollar Tom trades away or lends, he gets a commitment to get it back as well as to receive 10 percent more.

In the language of finance, 10 percent is the annual rate of interest on the loan. When a dollar is lent out, the repayment of $1.10 can be thought of as being made up of two parts. First, the lender gets the dollar back; that is the *principal repayment*. Second, the lender receives an *interest payment*, which is $0.10 in this example.

Now, not only have Tom and Leslie struck a deal, but as a by-product of their bargain they have created a financial instrument, the IOU. This piece of paper entitles whoever receives it to present it to Leslie next year and redeem it for $55,000. Financial instruments that entitle whoever possesses them to receive payment are called *bearer instruments* because whoever bears them can use them. Presumably there could be more such IOUs in the economy written by many different lenders and borrowers like Tom and Leslie.

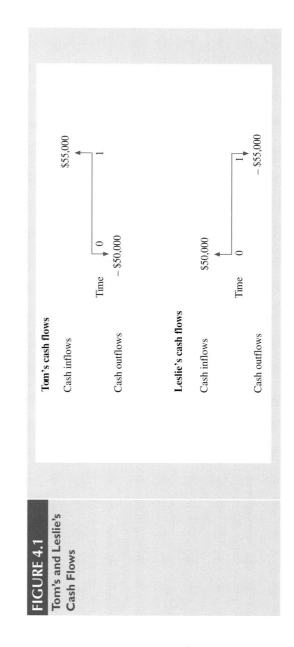

FIGURE 4.1

Tom's and Leslie's Cash Flows

The Anonymous Market

If the borrower does not care whom she has to pay back, and if the lender does not care whose IOUs he is holding, we could just as well drop Tom's and Leslie's names from their contract. All we need is a record book, in which we could record the fact that Tom has lent $50,000 and Leslie has borrowed $50,000 and that the terms of the loan, the interest rate, are 10 percent. Perhaps another person could keep the records for borrowers and lenders—for a fee, of course. In fact—and this is one of the virtues of such an arrangement—Tom and Leslie wouldn't even need to meet. Instead of needing to find and trade with each other, they could each trade with the recordkeeper. The recordkeeper could deal with thousands of such borrowers and lenders, none of whom would need to meet the other.

Institutions that perform this sort of market function, matching borrowers and lenders or traders, are called **financial intermediaries**. Chartered banks are modern examples of financial intermediaries. A bank's depositors lend the bank money, and the bank makes loans from the funds it has on deposit. In essence, the bank is an intermediary between the depositors and the ultimate borrowers. To make the market work, we must be certain that the market clears. By *market clearing* we mean that the total amount that people like Tom wish to lend to the market, say $11 million, equals the total amount that people like Leslie wish to borrow.

Market Clearing

If the lenders wish to lend more than the borrowers want to borrow, then presumably the interest rate is too high. Because there would not be enough borrowing for all of the lenders at, say, 15 percent, there are really only two ways that the market could be made to clear. One is to ration the lenders. For example, if the lenders wish to lend $20 million when interest rates are at 15 percent and the borrowers wish to borrow only $8 million, the market could take, say, 8/20 of each dollar, or $0.40, from each of the lenders and distribute it to the borrowers. This is one possible scheme for making the market clear, but it is not one that would be sustainable in a free and competitive marketplace. Why not?

To answer this important question, we return to our lender, Tom. Tom sees that interest rates are 15 percent and, not surprisingly, rather than simply lending the $50,000 that he was willing to lend when rates were 10 percent, Tom decides that at the higher rates he would like to lend more, say, $80,000. But since the lenders want to lend more money than the borrowers want to borrow, the recordkeepers tell Tom that they won't be able to take all of his $80,000; rather, they will take only 40 percent of it, or $32,000. With the interest rate at 15 percent, people are not willing to borrow enough to match up with all of the loans that are available at that rate.

Tom is not very pleased with that state of affairs, but he can do something to improve his situation. Suppose that he knows that Leslie is borrowing $20,000 in the market at the 15 percent interest rate. That means that Leslie must repay $20,000 on her loan next year plus the interest of 15 percent of $20,000, or $0.15 × $20,000 = $3,000. Suppose that Tom goes to Leslie and offers to lend her the $20,000 for 14 percent. Leslie is happy because she will save 1 percent on the deal and will need to pay back only $2,800 in interest next year. This is $200 less than if she had borrowed from the recordkeepers. Tom is happy, too, because he has found a way to lend some of the money that the recordkeepers would not take. The net result of this transaction is that the recordkeepers have lost Leslie as a customer. Why should she borrow from them when Tom will lend her the money at a lower interest rate?

Tom and Leslie are not the only ones cutting side deals in the marketplace, and it is clear that the recordkeepers will not be able to maintain the 15 percent rate. The interest rate must fall if they are to stay in business.

Suppose, then, that the market clears at the rate of 10 percent. At this rate the amount of money that the lenders wish to lend, $11 million, is exactly equal to the amount that the borrowers desire. We refer to the interest rate that clears the market, 10 percent in our example, as the **equilibrium rate of interest.**

In this section we have shown that, in the market for loans, bonds or IOUs are traded. These are *financial instruments*. The interest rate on these loans is such that the total demand for such loans by borrowers equals the total supply of loans by lenders. At a higher interest rate, lenders wish to supply more loans than are demanded, and if the interest rate is lower than this equilibrium level, borrowers demand more loans than lenders are willing to supply.

Concept
Questions

- **What is an interest rate?**
- **What do we mean when we say a market clears?**
- **What is an equilibrium rate of interest?**

4.2 Making Consumption Choices Over Time

Figure 4.2 illustrates the situation faced by an individual in the financial market. This person is assumed to have an income of $50,000 this year and an income of $60,000 next year. The market allows him not only to consume $50,000 worth of goods this year and $60,000 next year, but also to borrow and lend at the equilibrium interest rate. The line *AB* in Figure 4.2 shows all of the consumption possibilities open to the person through borrowing or lending, and the shaded area contains all of the feasible choices. Notice that the lender chooses to consume less than $50,000 and the borrower more than this amount.

We will use the letter *r* to denote the interest rate—the equilibrium rate—in this market. The rate is risk-free because we assume that no default can take place. Look at point *A* on the vertical axis of Figure 4.2. Point *A* represents consumption next year (on the vertical axis) of:

$$A = \$60{,}000 + \$50{,}000 \times (1 + r)$$

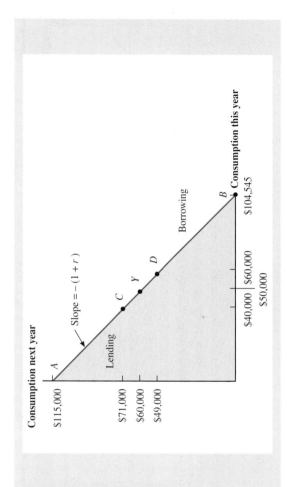

Intertemporal Consumption Opportunities

For example, if the rate of interest is 10 percent, then point A is

$$A = \$60,000 + \$50,000 \times (1 + 0.1)$$
$$= \$60,000 + \$55,000$$
$$= \$115,000.$$

Point A is the maximum amount of wealth that this person can spend in the second year. He gets to point A by lending the full income that is available this year, $50,000, and consuming none of it. In the second year, then, he will have the second year's income of $60,000 plus the proceeds from the loan that he made in the first year, $55,000, for a total of $115,000.

Following the same logic, point B is a distance of

$$B = \$50,000 + \$60,000/(1 + r)$$

along the horizontal axis. If the interest rate is 10 percent, point B will be

$$B = \$50,000 + \$60,000/(1 + 0.1)$$
$$= \$50,000 + \$54,545$$
$$= \$104,545 \text{ (rounded off to the nearest dollar)}$$

Why do we divide next year's income of $60,000 by $(1 + r)$ or 1.1 in the preceding computation? Point B represents the maximum amount available for this person to consume this year. To achieve that maximum he would borrow as much as possible and repay the loan from the income, $60,000, that he was going to receive next year. Because $60,000 will be available to repay the loan next year, we are asking how much he could borrow this year at an interest rate of r and still be able to repay the loan. The answer is

$$\$60,000/(1 + r)$$

because if he borrows this amount, he must repay it next year with interest. Thus, next year he must repay

$$[\$60,000/(1 + r)] \times (1 + r) = \$60,000$$

no matter what the interest rate, r, is. In our example we found that he could borrow $54,545 and, sure enough,

$$\$54,545 \times 1.1 = \$60,000$$

(after rounding off to the nearest dollar).

Furthermore, by borrowing and lending different amounts, the person can achieve any point on the line AB. For example, at point C he has chosen to lend $10,000 of today's income. This means that at point C he will have

Consumption this year at point C = $50,000 − $10,000 = $40,000

and

Consumption next year at point C = $60,000 + $10,000 × (1 + r) = $71,000

when the interest rate is 10 percent.

Similarly, at point D, the individual has decided to borrow $10,000 and repay the loan next year. At point D, then,

Consumption this year at point C = $50,000 + $10,000 = $60,000

and

Consumption next year at point D = $60,000 − $10,000 × (1 + r) = $49,000

at an interest rate of 10 percent.

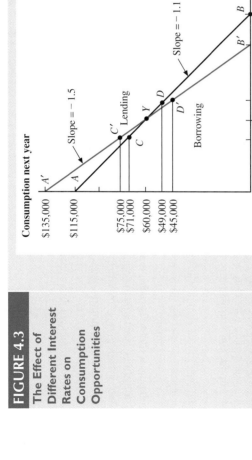

FIGURE 4.3

The Effect of Different Interest Rates on Consumption Opportunities

In fact, this person can consume at any point on the line *AB*. This line has a slope of $-(1 + r)$, which means that, for each dollar that is added to the *x*-coordinate along the line, $(1 + r)$ dollars are subtracted from the *y*-coordinate. Moving along the line from point *A*, the initial point of $50,000 this year and $60,000 next year, toward point *B* gives the person more consumption today and less next year. In other words, moving toward point *B* is borrowing. Similarly, moving up toward point *A*, he is consuming less today and more next year and he is lending. The line is a straight line because the individual has no effect on the interest rate. This is one of the assumptions of perfectly competitive financial markets.

Where in Figure 4.2 will the person actually be? The answer to that question depends on the individual's tastes and personal situation, just as it did before there was a market. If the person is impatient, he might wish to borrow money at a point such as *D*, and if he is patient, he might wish to lend some of this year's income and enjoy more consumption next year at, for example, a point such as *C*.

Notice that whether we think of someone as patient or impatient depends on the interest rate he or she faces in the market. Suppose that our individual was impatient and chose to borrow $10,000 and move to point *D*. Now suppose that we raise the interest rate to 20 percent or even 50 percent. Suddenly our impatient person may become very patient and might prefer to lend some of this year's income to take advantage of the very high interest rate. The general result is depicted in Figure 4.3. We can see that lending at point *C'* yields much greater future income and consumption possibilities than before.[2]

Concept Questions

- **How does an individual change consumption across periods through borrowing and lending?**
- **How do interest rate changes affect one's degree of impatience?**

---

[2]Those familiar with consumer theory might be aware of the surprising case where raising the interest rate actually makes people borrow more or lowering the rate makes them lend more. The latter case might occur, for example, if the decline in the interest rate made the lenders have so little consumption next year that they have no choice but to lend out even more than they did before, just to subsist. Nothing we do depends on excluding such cases, but it is much easier to ignore them, and the resulting analysis fits the real markets much more closely.

4.3 The Competitive Market

In the previous analysis we assumed the individual moves freely along the line *AB*, and we ignored—and assumed that the individual ignores—any effect his borrowing or lending decisions might have on the equilibrium interest rate itself. What would happen, though, if the total amount of loans outstanding in the market when the person was doing no borrowing or lending was $10 million, and if our person then decided to lend, say, $5 million? His lending would be half as much as the rest of the market put together, and it would not be unreasonable to think that the equilibrium interest rate would fall to induce more borrowers into the market to take his additional loans. In such a situation the person has some power in the market to influence the equilibrium rate significantly, and he would take this power into consideration in making his decisions.

In modern financial markets, however, the total amount of borrowing and lending is not $10 million; rather, as we say in Chapter 1, it is far higher. In such a huge market no one investor or even any single company can have a significant effect (although a government might). We assume, then, in all of our subsequent discussions and analyses that the financial market is perfectly competitive. By that we mean no individuals or firms think they have any effect whatsoever on the interest rates that they face no matter how much borrowing, lending, or investing they do. In the language of economics, individuals who respond to rates and prices by acting as though they have no influence on them are called *price takers*, and this assumption is sometimes called the *price-taking assumption*. It is the condition of **perfectly competitive financial markets** (or, more simply, *perfect markets*). The following conditions characterize perfect financial markets:

1. Trading is costless. Access to the financial markets is free.
2. Information about borrowing and lending opportunities is readily available.
3. There are many traders, and no single trader can have a significant impact on market prices.

In Chapter 14 we introduce the concept of efficient markets. Although efficient markets are less than perfectly competitive, available evidence suggests that most of the time, the three conditions above are a good approximation for financial markets.

How Many Interest Rates Are There in a Competitive Market?

An important point about this one-year market where no defaults can take place is that only one interest rate can be quoted in the market at any one time. Suppose that some competing recordkeepers decide to set up a rival market. To attract customers, their business plan is to offer lower interest rates, say, 9 percent, to attract borrowers away from the first market and soon have all of the business.

Their business plan will work, but it will do so beyond their wildest expectations. They will indeed attract the borrowers, all $11 million worth of them! But the matter doesn't stop there. By offering to borrow and lend at 9 percent when another market is offering 10 percent, they have created the proverbial money machine.

The world of finance is populated by sharp-eyed inhabitants who would not let this opportunity slip by them. Any one of these, whether a borrower or a lender, would go to the new market and borrow everything he could at the 9 percent rate. At the same time he was borrowing in the new market, he would also be striking a deal to lend in the old market at the 10 percent rate. If he could borrow $100 million at 9 percent and lend it at

10 percent, he could net 1 percent, or $1 million, next year. He would repay the $109 million he owed to the new market from the $110 million he would receive when the 10 percent loan he had made in the original market was repaid, pocketing $1 million.

This process of striking a deal in one market and an offsetting deal in another simultaneously and at more favourable terms is called *arbitrage*; the individuals who do it are called *arbitrageurs*. Of course, someone must be paying for all of this free money, and it must be the recordkeepers because the borrowers and the lenders are all making money. Our intrepid, entrepreneurial recordkeepers will lose their proverbial shirts and go out of business. The moral of this is clear: As soon as different interest rates are offered for essentially the same risk-free loans, arbitrageurs will take advantage of the situation by borrowing at the low rate and lending at the high rate. The gap between the two rates will be closed quickly, and for all practical purposes there will be only one rate available in the market.

Concept Questions

- What is the most important feature of a competitive financial market?
- What conditions are likely to lead to this?
- What is arbitrage and why does it result in one rate for riskless loans?

4.4 The Basic Principle

We have already shown how people use the financial markets to adjust their patterns of consumption over time to fit their particular preferences. By borrowing and lending, they can greatly expand their range of choices. They need only to have access to a market with an interest rate at which they can borrow and lend.

In the previous section we saw how these savings and consumption decisions depend on the interest rate. The financial markets also provide a benchmark against which proposed investments can be compared, and the interest rate is the basis for a test that any proposed investment must pass. The financial markets give the individual, the corporation, or even the government a standard of comparison for economic decisions. This benchmark is critical when investment decisions are being made.

The way we use the financial markets to aid us in making investment decisions is a direct consequence of our basic assumption that individuals can never be made worse off by increasing the range of choices open to them. People always can make use of the financial markets to adjust their savings and consumption by borrowing or lending. An investment project is worth undertaking only if it increases the range of choices in the financial markets. To do this, the project must be at least as desirable as what is available in the financial markets.[3] If it were not as desirable as what the financial markets have to offer, people could simply use the financial markets instead of undertaking the investment. This point will govern us in all of our investment decisions. It is the *first principle of investment decision making*, and it is the foundation on which all of our rules are built.

Concept Question

- Describe the basic financial principle of investment decision making.

[3]You might wonder what to do if an investment is exactly as desirable as an alternative in the financial markets. In principle, if there is a tie, it doesn't matter whether or not we take on the investment. In practice, we've never seen an exact tie.

4.5 Practising the Principle

Let us apply the basic principle of investment decision making to some concrete situations.

A Lending Example

Consider a person who is concerned only about this year and next. She has an income of $100,000 this year and expects to make the same amount next year. The interest rate is 10 percent. This individual is thinking about investing in a piece of land that costs $70,000. She is certain that next year the land will be worth $75,000, a sure $5,000 gain. Should she undertake the investment? This situation is described in Figure 4.4 with the cash flow time chart.

A moment's thought should be all it takes to convince her that this is not an attractive business deal. By investing $70,000 in the land, she will have $75,000 available next year. Suppose, instead, that she puts the same $70,000 into a loan in the financial market. At the 10 percent rate of interest, this $70,000 would grow to

$$(1 + 0.1) \times \$70,000 = \$77,000$$

next year.

It would be foolish to buy the land when the same $70,000 investment in the financial market would beat it by $2,000 (that is, $77,000 from the loan minus $75,000 from the land investment).

Figure 4.5 illustrates this situation. Notice that the $70,000 loan gives no less income today and $2,000 more next year. This example illustrates some amazing features of the financial markets. It is remarkable to consider all of the information that we did *not* use when arriving at the decision not to invest in the land. We did not need to know how much income the person has this year or next year. We also did not need to know whether the person preferred more income this year or next.

We did not need to know any of these other facts, and, more importantly, the person making the decision did not need to know them either. She only needed to be able to compare the investment with a relevant alternative available in the financial market. When the proposed investment fell short of that standard—by $2,000 in the previous example—regardless of what the individual wanted to do, she knew that she should not buy the land.

A Borrowing Example

Let us sweeten the deal a bit. Suppose that instead of being worth $75,000 next year, the land will be worth $80,000. What should our investor do now? This case is a bit more difficult. After all, even if the land seems like a good deal, this person's income this year is only $100,000. Does she really want to make a $70,000 investment this year? Won't that leave only $30,000 for consumption?

The answers to these questions are yes, the individual should buy the land; yes, she does want to make a $70,000 investment this year; and, most surprising of all, even though

Cash inflows

Cash outflows

Time

$75,000

0   1

−$70,000

FIGURE 4.5

Consumption Opportunities with Borrowing and Lending

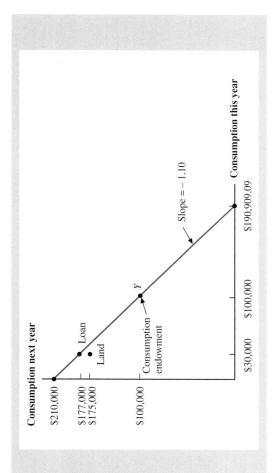

her income is $100,000, making the $70,000 investment will not leave her with $30,000 to consume this year! Now let us see how finance lets us get around the basic laws of arithmetic.

The financial markets are the key to solving our problem. First, the financial markets can be used as a standard of comparison against which any investment project must measure up. Second, they can be used as a tool to help the individual actually undertake investments. These twin features of the financial markets enable us to make the right investment decision.

Suppose that the person borrows the $70,000 initial investment that is needed to purchase the land. Next year she must repay this loan. Because the interest rate is 10 percent, she will owe the financial market $77,000 next year. This is depicted in Figure 4.6. Because the land will be worth $80,000 next year, she will be able to sell it, pay off her debt of $77,000, and have $3,000 extra cash.

If she wishes, this person can now consume an extra $3,000 worth of goods and services next year. This possibility is illustrated in Figure 4.7. In fact, even if she wants to do all of her consuming this year, she is still better off taking the investment. All she must do is take out a loan this year and repay it from the proceeds of the land next year and profit by $3,000.

Furthermore, instead of borrowing just the $70,000 that she needed to purchase the land, she could have borrowed $72,727.27. She could have used $70,000 to buy the land and consumed the remaining $2,727.27. We will call $2,727.27 the net present value of the transaction. Notice that it is equal to $3,000 × 1/1.1. How did we figure out that this was the exact amount that she could borrow? It was easy: If $72,727.27 is the amount that she borrows, then, because the interest rate is 10 percent, she must repay

$$\$72{,}727.27 \times (1 + 0.1) = \$80{,}000$$

next year, and that is exactly what the land will be worth. The line through the investment position in Figure 4.7 illustrates this borrowing possibility.

The amazing thing about both of these cases, one where the land is worth $75,000 next year and the other where it is worth $80,000 next year, is that we needed only to compare the investment with the financial markets to decide whether it was worth undertaking or

FIGURE 4.6

Cash Flows of Borrowing to Purchase the Land

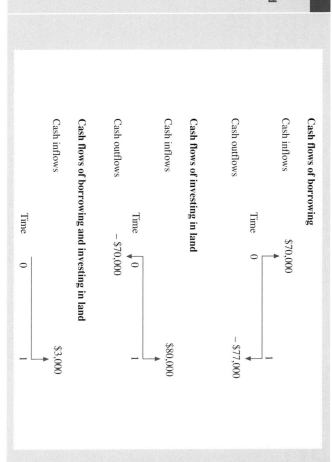

Cash flows of borrowing

Cash inflows $70,000

Time   0 ———————— 1

Cash outflows   −$77,000

Cash flows of investing in land

Cash inflows $80,000

Time   0 ———————— 1

Cash outflows   −$70,000

Cash flows of borrowing and investing in land

Cash inflows $3,000

Time   0 ———————— 1

not. This is one of the more important points in all of finance. It is true regardless of the consumption preferences of the individual. This is one of a number of *separation theorems* in finance. It states that the value of an investment to an individual is not dependent on consumption preferences. In our examples we showed that the person's decision to invest in land was not affected by consumption preferences. However, these preferences dictated whether the person borrowed or lent.

FIGURE 4.7

Consumption Opportunities with Investment Opportunity and Borrowing and Lending

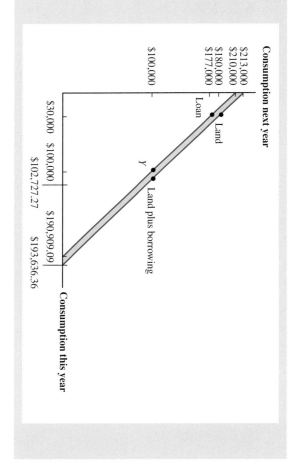

Consumption next year

$213,000
$210,000
$180,000
$177,000

$100,000

• Land

Loan

Y • Land plus borrowing

$30,000 $100,000 $190,909.09
$102,727.27 $193,636.36

Consumption this year

Concept
Questions

• Describe how the financial markets can be used to evaluate investment alternatives.
• What is the separation theorem? Why is it important?

4.6 Illustrating the Investment Decision

Figure 4.2, discussed earlier, describes the possibilities open to a person who has an income of $50,000 this year and $60,000 next year and faces a financial market in which the interest rate is 10 percent. But at that moment, the person has no investment possibilities beyond the 10 percent borrowing and lending that is available in the financial market.

Suppose that we give this person the chance to undertake an investment project that will require a $30,000 outlay of cash this year and that will return $40,000 to the investor next year. Refer to Figure 4.2 and determine how you could include this new possibility in that figure and how you could use the figure to help you decide whether to undertake the investment.

Now look at Figure 4.8. In Figure 4.8 we have labelled the original point with $50,000 this year and $60,000 next year as point A. We have also added a new point B, with $20,000 available for consumption this year and $100,000 next year. The difference between point A and point B is that at point A the person is just where we started him off, and at point B the person has also decided to undertake the investment project. As a result of this decision, the person at point B has

$$\$50,000 - \$30,000 = \$20,000$$

left for consumption this year, and

$$\$60,000 + \$40,000 = \$100,000$$

available next year. These are the coordinates of point B.

We must use our knowledge of the individual's borrowing and lending opportunities in order to decide whether to accept or reject the investment. This is illustrated in Figure 4.9. Figure 4.9 is similar to Figure 4.8, but in it we have drawn a line through point A that shows the possibilities open to the person if he stays at point A and does not take the investment. This line is exactly the same as the one in Figure 4.2. We have also drawn a parallel line through point B that shows the new possibilities that are available to the person if he undertakes the investment. The two lines are parallel because the slope of each is determined by the same interest rate, 10 percent. It does not matter whether the person takes the investment and goes to point B or does not and stays at point A; in the financial market, each dollar of lending is a dollar less available for consumption this year and moves him to the left by a dollar along the x-axis. Because the interest rate is 10 percent, the $1 loan repays $1.10 and it moves him up by $1.10 along the y-axis.

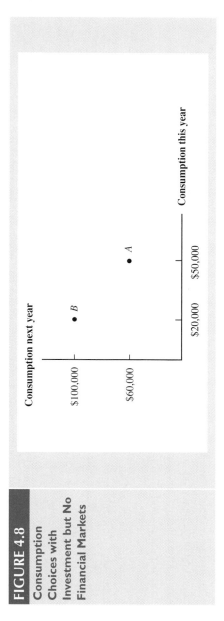

FIGURE 4.8

Consumption Choices with Investment but No Financial Markets

FIGURE 4.9
Consumption
Choices with
Investment
Opportunities and
Financial Markets

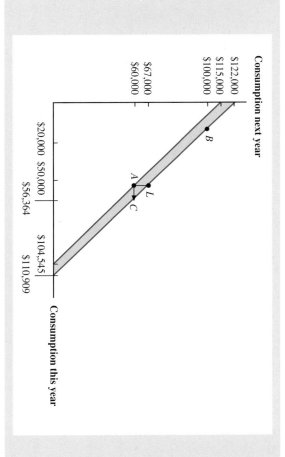

It is easy to see from Figure 4.9 that the investment has made the person better off. The line through point *B* is higher than the line through point *A*. Thus, no matter what pattern of consumption this person wanted this year and next, he could have more in each year if he undertook the investment.

For example, suppose that our individual wanted to consume everything this year. If he did not take the investment, the point where the line through point *A* intersected the *x*-axis would give the maximum amount of consumption he could enjoy this year—$104,545. To recall how we found this figure, review the analysis of Figure 4.2. But in Figure 4.9 the line that goes through point *B* intersects the *x*-axis at a higher point than the line that goes through point *A*. Along this line the person can have the $20,000 that is left after investing $30,000, plus all that he can borrow and repay with both next year's income and the proceeds from the investment. The total amount available to consume today is therefore

$$\$50,000 - \$30,000 + (\$60,000 + \$40,000)/(1 + 0.1)$$
$$= \$20,000 + \$100,000/(1.1)$$
$$= \$110,909$$

The additional consumption available this year from undertaking the investment and using the financial market is the difference on the *x*-axis between the points where these two lines intersect:

$$\$110,909 - \$104,545 = \$6,364$$

This difference is an important measure of what the investment is worth to the person. It answers a variety of questions. For example, it is the answer to the question: How much money would we need to give the investor this year to make him just as well off as he is with the investment?

Because the line through point *B* is parallel to the line through point *A* but has been moved over by $6,364, we know that if we were to add this amount to the investor's current income this year at point *A* and take away the investment, he would wind up on the line through point *B* and with the same possibilities. If we do this, the person will have

$56,364 this year and $60,000 next year, which is the situation of the point on the line through point B that lies to the right of point A in Figure 4.9. This is point C.

We could also ask a different question: How much money would we need to give the investor next year to make him just as well off as he is with the investment?

This is the same as asking how much higher the line through point B is than the line through point A. In other words, what is the difference in Figure 4.9 between the point where the line through A intercepts the y-axis and the point where the line through B intercepts the y-axis?

The point where the line through A intercepts the y-axis shows the maximum amount the person could consume next year if all of his current income were lent out and the proceeds of the loan were consumed along with next year's income.

As we showed in our analysis of Figure 4.2, this amount is $115,000. How does this compare with what the person can have next year if he takes the investment? By taking the investment we saw that the person would be at point B, where he has $20,000 left this year and would have $100,000 next year. By lending the $20,000 that is left this year and adding the proceeds of this loan to the $100,000, we find the line through B intercepts the y-axis at

$$\$20,000 \times (1.1) + \$100,000 = \$122,000$$

The difference between this amount and $115,000 is

$$\$122,000 - \$115,000 = \$7,000$$

which is the answer to the question of how much we would need to give the person next year to make him as well off as he is with the investment.

There is a simple relationship between these two numbers. If we multiply $6,364 by 1.1 we get $7,000! Consider why this must be so. The $6,364 is the amount of extra cash we must give the person this year to substitute for having the investment. In a financial market with a 10 percent rate of interest, however, $1 this year is worth exactly the same as $1.10 next year. Thus, $6,364 this year is the same as $6,364 × 1.1 next year. In other words, the person does not care whether he has the investment, $6,364, this year or $6,364 × 1.1 next year. But we already showed that the investor is equally willing to have the investment and to have $7,000 next year. This must mean that

$$\$6,364 \times 1.1 = \$7,000$$

You can also verify this relationship between these two variables by using Figure 4.9. Because the lines through A and B have the same slope of -1.1, the difference of $7,000 between where they intersect on the y-axis and $6,364 between where they intersect on the x-axis must be in the ratio of 1.1 to 1.

Now we can show you how to evaluate the investment opportunity on a stand-alone basis. Here are the relevant facts: The individual must give up $30,000 this year to get $40,000 next year. These cash flows are illustrated in Figure 4.10.

The investment rule that follows from the previous analysis is the net present value (NPV) rule. Here we convert all consumption values to the present and add them up:

$$\begin{aligned} \text{Net present value} &= -\$30,000 + \$40,000 \times (1/1.1) \\ &= -\$30,000 + \$36,364 \\ &= \$6,364 \end{aligned}$$

The future amount, $40,000, is called the *future value (FV)*.

The net present value of an investment is a simple criterion for deciding whether or not to undertake it. NPV answers the question of how much cash an investor would need

FIGURE 4.10

Cash Flows for the Investment Project

to have today as a substitute for making the investment. If the net present value is positive, the investment is worth taking on because doing so is essentially the same as receiving a cash payment equal to the net present value. If the net present value is negative, taking on the investment today is equivalent to giving up some cash today, and the investment should be rejected.

We use the term *net present value* to emphasize that we are already including the current cost of the investment in determining its value and not simply measuring what it will return. For example, if the interest rate is 10 percent and an investment of $30,000 today will produce a total cash return of $40,000 in one year's time, the *present value* of the $40,000 by itself is

$$\$40,000/1.1 = \$36,364$$

but the *net present value* of the investment is $36,364 minus the original investment:

$$\text{Net present value} = \$36,364 - \$30,000 = \$6,364$$

The present value of a future cash flow is the value of that cash flow after considering the appropriate market interest rate. The net present value of an investment is the present value of the investment's future cash flows, minus the initial cost of the investment. We have just decided that our investment is a good opportunity. It has a positive net present value because it is worth more than it costs.

In general, the above can be stated in terms of the **net present value rule:**

> An investment is worth making if it has a positive NPV. If an investment's NPV is negative, it should be rejected.

? Concept Questions

- **Give the definitions of net present value, future value, and present value.**
- **What information does a person need to compute an investment's net present value?**

4.7 Corporate Investment Decision Making

Up to now, everything we have done has been from the perspective of the individual investor. How do corporations and firms make investment decisions? Are their decisions governed by a much more complicated set of rules and principles than the simple NPV rule that we have developed for individuals?

We discussed corporate decision making, corporate governance, and stakeholder issues in Chapter 1 and will return to these issues later in the book. Still, it is remarkable how well our central ideas and the NPV rule hold up even when applied to corporations.

We may view firms as means by which many investors can pool their resources to make large-scale business decisions. Suppose, for example, that you own 1 percent of some firm. Now suppose further that this firm is considering whether or not to undertake some investment. If that investment passes the NPV rule, that is, if it has a positive NPV, then 1 percent of the NPV belongs to you. If the firm takes on this investment, the value of the whole firm will rise by the NPV and your investment in the firm will rise by 1 percent of the NPV of the investment. Similarly, the other shareholders in the firm will profit by having the firm take on the positive NPV project because the value of their shares in the firm will also increase. This means that the shareholders in the firm will be unanimous in wanting the firm to increase its value by taking on the positive NPV project. If you follow this line of reasoning, you will also be able to see why the shareholders would oppose the firm's taking on any projects with a negative NPV because this would lower the value of their shares.

One difference between the firm and the individual is that the firm has no consumption endowment. In terms of our one-period consumption diagram, the firm starts at the origin. Figure 4.11 illustrates the situation of a firm with investment opportunity *B*. *B* is an investment that has a future value of $33,000 and will cost $25,000 now. If the interest rate is 10 percent, the NPV of *B* can be determined using the NPV rule. This is marked as point *C* in Figure 4.11. The cash flows of this investment are depicted in Figure 4.12.

One common objection to this line of reasoning is that people differ in their tastes and that they won't necessarily agree to take on or reject investments by the NPV rule. For instance, suppose that you and we each own some shares in a company. Further suppose that we are older than you and might be anxious to spend our money. Being younger, you might be more patient than we are and more willing to wait for a good long-term investment to pay off.

Because of the financial markets we all agree that the company should take on investments with positive NPVs and reject those with negative NPVs. If there were no financial markets, then, being impatient, we might want the company to do little or no investing so that we could have as much money as possible to consume now, and, being patient, you might prefer the company to make some investments. With financial markets, we are both satisfied by having the company follow the NPV rule.

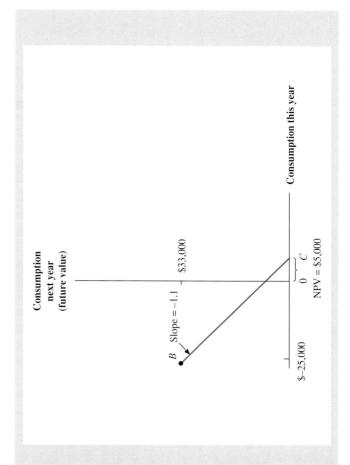

FIGURE 4.11

Consumption Choices, the NPV Rule, and the Corporation

FIGURE 4.12
Corporate Investment Cash Flows

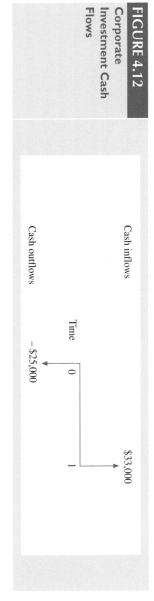

Cash inflows

$33,000

Time

0   1

Cash outflows   –$25,000

To see why this is so, suppose that the company takes on a positive NPV investment. Let us assume that this investment has a net payoff of $1 million next year. That means that the value of the company will increase by $1 million next year; consequently, if you own 1 percent of the company's shares, the value of your shares will increase by 1 percent of $1 million, or $10,000, next year. Because you are patient, you might be prepared to wait for your $10,000 until next year. Being impatient, we do not want to wait—and with financial markets, we do not need to wait. We can simply borrow against the extra $10,000 we will have tomorrow and use the loan to consume more today.

In fact, if there is also a market for the firm's shares, we do not even need to borrow. After the company takes on a positive NPV investment, our shares in the company increase in value today. This is because owning the shares today entitles investors to their portion of the extra $1 million the company will have next year. This means that the shares would rise in value today by the present value of $1 million. Because you want to delay your consumption, you could wait until next year and sell your shares then to have extra consumption next year. Being impatient, we might sell our shares now and use the money to consume more today. If we owned 1 percent of the company's shares, we could sell our shares for an extra amount equal to the present value of $10,000.

In reality, shareholders in big companies do not vote on every investment decision, and their managers must have rules to follow. We have seen that all shareholders in a company will be made better off—no matter what their levels of patience or impatience—if managers follow the NPV rule. This is a marvellous result because it makes it possible for many different owners to delegate decision-making powers to the managers. They need only to tell the managers to follow the NPV rule, and if the managers do so, they will be doing exactly what the shareholders want them to do. Sometimes this form of the NPV rule is stated as having the managers maximize the value of the company. As we argued, the current value of the shares of the company will increase by the NPV of any investments that the company undertakes. This means that the managers of the company can make the shareholders as well off as possible by taking on all positive NPV projects and rejecting projects with negative NPVs.

Separating investment decision making from the owners is a basic requirement of the modern large firm. An important **separation theorem** in financial markets says that all investors will want to accept or reject the same investment projects by using the NPV rule, regardless of their personal preferences. Investors can delegate the operations of the firm and require that managers use the NPV rule. Of course, much remains for us to discuss about this topic. For example, what ensures that managers will actually do what is best for their shareholders?

We discussed this interesting topic in Chapter 1, and we take it up again later in the book. For now, though, we will no longer consider our perspective to be that of the lone investor. Instead, thanks to the separation theorem, we will use the NPV rule for companies as well as for investors. Our justification of the NPV rule depends on the conditions necessary to derive the separation theorem. These conditions are the ones that result in competitive financial markets. The analysis we have presented has been restricted to risk-free cash flows in one time period. However, the separation theorem also can be derived for risky cash flows that extend beyond one period.

For the reader interested in studying further about the separation theorem, we include several suggested readings at the end of this chapter that build on the material we have presented.

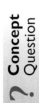

Concept Question

- In terms of the net present value rule, what is the essential difference between the individual and the corporation?

4.8 SUMMARY AND CONCLUSIONS

Finance is a subject that builds understanding from the ground up. Whenever you encounter a new problem or issue in finance, you can always return to the basic principles of this chapter for guidance.

1. Financial markets exist because people want to adjust their consumption over time. They do so by borrowing and lending.

2. Financial markets provide the key test for investment decision making. Whether a particular investment decision should or should not be taken depends only on this test: If there is a superior alternative in the financial markets, the investment should be rejected; if not, the investment is worth taking. The most important thing about this principle is that the investor need not use his preferences to decide whether the investment should be taken. Regardless of the individual's preference for consumption this year versus next, regardless of how patient or impatient the individual is, making the proper investment decision depends only on comparing it with the alternatives in the financial markets.

3. The net present value of an investment helps us make the comparison between the investment and the financial market. If the NPV is positive, our rule tells us to undertake the investment. This illustrates the second major feature of the financial markets and investment. Not only does the NPV rule tell us which investments to accept and which to reject, but the financial markets also provide us with the tools for acquiring the funds to make the investments. In short, we use the financial markets to decide both what to do and how to do it.

4. The NPV rule can be applied to corporations as well as to individuals. The separation theorem developed in this chapter says that all of the owners of the firm would agree that the firm should use the NPV rule even though each might differ in personal tastes for consumption and savings.

In the next chapter we learn more about the NPV rule by using it to examine a wide array of problems in finance.

KEY TERMS

Equilibrium rate of interest 73
Financial intermediaries 72
Net present value rule 84
Perfectly competitive financial
    market 76
Separation theorem 86

SUGGESTED READING

Two books that have good discussions of the consumption and savings decisions of individuals and the beginnings of financial markets are:
E. F. Fama and M. H. Miller. *The Theory of Finance.* Chap. 1. New York: Holt, Rinehart & Winston, 1971.

J. Hirshleifer. *Investment, Interest and Capital.* Chap. 1. Englewood Cliffs, N.J.: Prentice Hall, 1970.

The seminal work on the net present value rule is:

J. G. Fisher. *The Theory of Interest.* New York: Augustus M. Kelly, 1965. (This is a reprint of the 1930 edition.)

A rigorous treatment of the net present value rule along the lines of Irving Fisher can be found in:

J. Hirshleifer. "On the Theory of Optimal Investment Decision." *Journal of Political Economy* 66 (August 1958).

QUESTIONS & PROBLEMS

Making Consumption Choices

4.1 Currently, Jim Morris makes $100,000. Next year his income will be $120,000. Jim is a big spender and he wants to consume $150,000 this year. The equilibrium interest rate is 10 percent. What will be Jim's consumption potential next year if he consumes $150,000 this year?

4.2 Rich Pettit is a miser. His current income is $50,000; next year he will earn $40,000. He plans to consume only $20,000 this year. The current interest rate is 12 percent. What will Rich's consumption potential be next year?

The Competitive Finance Market

4.3 What is the basic reason that financial markets develop?

4.4 Suppose that the equilibrium interest rate is 6 percent. What would happen in the market if a group of financial intermediaries attempted to control interest rates at 4 percent?

Illustrating the Investment Decision

4.5 The following figure depicts the financial situation of Ms. J. Fawn. In period 0 her labour income and current consumption are $40; later, in period 1, her labour income and consumption will be $22. She has an opportunity to make the investment represented by point D. By borrowing and lending, she will be able to reach any point along the line FDE.

a. What is the market rate of interest? (Hint: The new market interest rate line EF is parallel to AH.)

b. What is the NPV of point D?

c. If Ms. Fawn wishes to consume the same quantity in each period, how much should she consume in period 0?

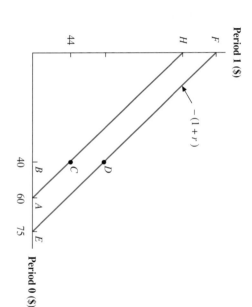

4.6   Harry Hernandez has $60,000 this year. He faces the investment opportunities represented by point B in the following figure. He wants to consume $20,000 this year and $67,500 next year. This pattern of consumption is represented by point F.

a. What is the market interest rate?

b. How much must Harry invest in financial assets and productive assets today if he follows an optimum strategy?

c. What is the NPV of his investment in nonfinancial assets?

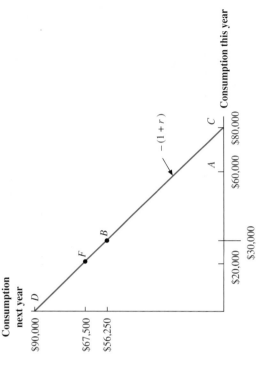

4.7   To answer this question, refer to the figure below. The Badvest Corporation is an all-equity firm with BD in cash on hand. It has an investment opportunity at point C, and it plans to invest AD in real assets today. Thus, the firm will need to raise AB by a new issue of equity.

a. What is the present value of the investment?

b. What is the rate of return on the old equity? Measure this rate of return from before the investment plans are announced to afterwards.

c. What is the rate of return on the new equity?

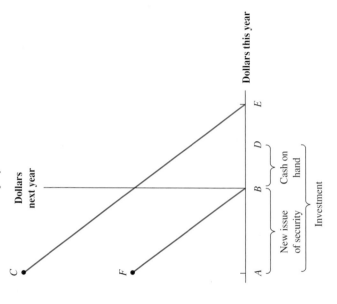

Chapter 5

The Time Value of Money

EXECUTIVE SUMMARY

We now examine one of the most important concepts in all of corporate finance: the relationship between $1 today and $1 in the future. Consider the following example: A firm is contemplating investing $1 million in a project that is expected to pay out $200,000 per year for nine years. Should the firm accept the project? One might say yes at first glance, since the total inflows of $1.8 million ($= \$200,000 \times 9$) are greater than the $1 million outflow. However, the $1 million is paid out *immediately*, whereas the $200,000 per year is received in the future. Also, the immediate payment is known with certainty, whereas the later inflows can only be estimated. Thus, we need to know the relationship between a dollar today and a (possibly uncertain) dollar in the future before deciding on the project.

This relationship is called the *time value of money* concept. It is important in such areas as capital budgeting, lease-versus-buy decisions, accounts receivable analysis, financing arrangements, mergers, and pension funding.

The basics are presented in this chapter. We begin by discussing two fundamental concepts: future value and present value. Next, we treat simplifying formulas such as perpetuities and annuities.

5.1 The One-Period Case

Antony Robart is trying to sell a piece of raw land in Saskatchewan. Yesterday, he was offered $10,000 for the property. He was ready to accept the offer when another individual offered him $11,424. However, the second offer was to be paid a year from now. Antony has satisfied himself that both buyers are honest, so he has no fear that the offer he selects will fall through. These two offers are pictured as cash flows in Figure 5.1. Which offer should Mr. Robart choose?

FIGURE 5.1
Cash Flow for Mr. Robart's Sale

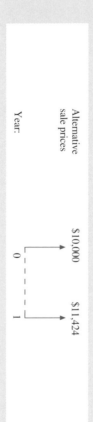

	Alternative sale prices	
	$10,000	$11,424
Year:	0	1

Cynthia Titos, Antony's financial adviser, points out that if Antony takes the first offer, he could invest the $10,000 in the bank at 12 percent. At the end of one year, he would have:

$$\$10,000 + (0.12 \times \$10,000) = \$10,000 \times 1.12 = \$11,200$$

$$\underset{\text{principal}}{\underbrace{\text{Return of}}} \qquad \underset{}{\underbrace{\text{Interest}}}$$

Because this is less than the $11,424 Antony could receive from the second offer, Ms. Titos recommends that he take the latter. This analysis uses the concept of **future value** or **compound value,** which is the value of a sum after investing over one or more periods. Here the compound or future value of $10,000 is $11,200.

An alternative method employs the concept of **present value (PV).** One can determine present value by asking the following question: How much money must Antony put in the bank today so that he will have $11,424 next year? We can write this algebraically as:

$$PV \times 1.12 = \$11,424 \qquad (5.1)$$

We want to solve for present value (PV), the amount of money that yields $11,424 if invested at 12 percent today. Solving for PV, we have

$$PV = \frac{\$11,424}{1.12} = \$10,200$$

The formula for PV can be written as

Present Value of Investment:

$$PV = \frac{C_1}{1 + r}$$

where C_1 is cash flow at date 1 and r is the interest rate.

Present value analysis tells us that a payment of $11,424 to be received next year has a present value of $10,200 today. In other words, at a 12 percent interest rate, Mr. Robart should be indifferent to whether you give him $10,200 today or $11,424 next year. If you give him $10,200 today, he can put it in the bank and receive $11,424 next year.

Because the second offer has a present value of $10,200, whereas the first offer is for only $10,000, present value analysis also indicates that Mr. Robart should take the second offer. In other words, both future value analysis and present value analysis lead to the same decision. As it turns out, present value analysis and future value analysis must always lead to the same decision.

As simple as this example is, it contains the basic principles that we will be working with over the next few chapters. We now use another example to develop the concept of net present value.

EXAMPLE

Geneviève Gagnon is thinking about investing in a piece of land that costs $85,000. She is certain that next year the land will be worth $91,000, a sure $6,000 gain. Given that the interest rate in the bank is 10 percent, should she undertake the investment in land? Ms. Gagnon's choice is described in Figure 5.2 with the cash flow time chart.

FIGURE 5.2

Cash Flows for Land Investment

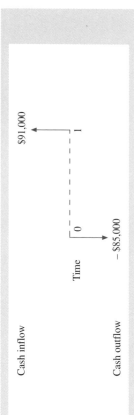

A moment's thought should be all it takes to convince her that this is not an attractive business deal. By investing $85,000 in the land, she will have $91,000 available next year. Suppose, instead, that she puts the same $85,000 into the bank. At the interest rate of 10 percent, this $85,000 would grow to

$$(1 + 0.10) \times \$85,000 = \$93,500$$

next year.

It would be foolish to buy the land when investing the same $85,000 in the financial market would produce an extra $2,500 (that is, $93,500 from the bank minus $91,000 from the land investment). This is a future-value calculation. Alternatively, she could calculate the present value of the sale price next year as

$$\text{Present value} = \frac{\$91,000}{1.10} = \$82,727.27$$

Since the present value of next year's sale price is less than this year's purchase price of $85,000, present value analysis also indicates that she should not purchase the property.

Frequently, businesspeople want to determine the exact *cost* or *benefit* of a decision. The decision to buy this year and sell next year can be evaluated as

Net Present Value of Investment:

$$-\$2.273 = -\$85,000 + \frac{\$91,000}{1.10} \qquad (5.2)$$

Cost of	Present value of
land today	next year's sales price

Equation (5.2) says that the value of the investment is $-\$2.273$, after stating all the benefits and all the costs as of date 0. We say that $-\$2.273$ is the **net present value (NPV)** of the investment. That is, NPV is the present value of future cash flows minus the present value of the cost of the investment. Because the net present value is negative, Geneviève Gagnon should not purchase the land.

Both the Robart and the Gagnon examples deal with perfect certainty. That is, Antony Robart knows with perfect certainty that he could sell his land for $11,424 next year. Similarly, Geneviève Gagnon knows with perfect certainty that she could receive $91,000 for selling her land. Unfortunately, businesspeople frequently do not know future cash flows. This uncertainty is treated in the next example.

Atkinson Art, Inc., is a firm that speculates in modern paintings. The manager is thinking of buying an original Picasso for $400,000 with the intention of selling it at the end of one year. The manager expects that the painting will be worth $480,000 in one year. The relevant cash flows are depicted in Figure 5.3.

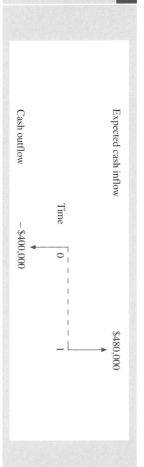

FIGURE 5.3
Cash Flows for
Investment in
Painting

Expected cash inflow $480,000

Time

0   1

Cash outflow   −$400,000

Of course, this is only an expectation—the painting could be worth more or less than $480,000. Suppose the interest rate granted by banks is 10 percent. Should the firm purchase the piece of art?

Our first thought might be to discount at the interest rate, yielding

$$\frac{\$480,000}{1.10} = \$436,364$$

Because $436,364 is greater than $400,000, it looks at first glance as if the painting should be purchased. However, 10 percent is the return one can earn on a riskless investment. Because the painting is quite risky, a higher *discount rate* is called for. The manager chooses a rate of 25 percent to reflect this risk. In other words, he argues that a 25 percent expected return is fair compensation for an investment as risky as this painting.

The present value of the painting becomes

$$\frac{\$480,000}{1.25} = \$384,000$$

Thus, the manager believes that the painting is currently overpriced at $400,000 and does not make the purchase.

The above analysis is typical of decision making in today's corporations, though real-world examples are, of course, much more complex. Unfortunately, any example with risk poses a problem not faced by a riskless example. In an example with riskless cash flows, the appropriate interest rate can be determined by simply checking with a few banks.[1] The selection of the discount rate for a risky investment is quite a difficult task. We simply do not know at this point whether the discount rate on the painting should be 11 percent, 25 percent, 52 percent, or some other percentage.

Because the choice of a discount rate is so difficult, we merely wanted to broach the subject here. The rest of the chapter will revert back to examples under perfect certainty. We must wait until the specific material on risk and return is covered in later chapters before a risk-adjusted analysis can be presented.

Concept Questions

· **Define future value and present value.**
· **How does one use net present value when making an investment decision?**

5.2 The Multiperiod Case

The previous section presented the calculation of future value and present value for one period only. We will now perform the calculations for the multiperiod case.

---

[1]In Chapter 9, we discuss estimation of the riskless rate in more detail.

Future Value and Compounding

Suppose an individual were to make a loan of $1. At the end of the first year, the borrower would owe the lender the principal amount of $1 plus the interest on the loan at the interest rate of r. For the specific case where the interest rate is, say, 9 percent, the borrower owes the lender

$$\$1 \times (1 + r) = \$1 \times 1.09 = \$1.09$$

At the end of the year, though, the lender has two choices. He or she can either take the $1.09—or, more generally, $(1 + r)$—out of the capital market, or leave it in and lend it again for a second year as shown in Figure 5.4. The process of leaving the money in the capital market and lending it for another year is called **compounding**.

Suppose that the lender decides to compound the loan for another year by taking the proceeds from the first one-year loan, $1.09, and lending this amount for the next year. At the end of next year, then, the borrower will owe

$$\$1 \times (1 + r) \times (1 + r) = \$1 \times (1 + r)^2 = 1 + 2r + r^2$$
$$\$1 \times (1.09) \times (1.09) = \$1 + \$0.18 + \$0.0081 = \$1.1881$$

This is the total the lender will receive two years from now by compounding the loan.

In other words, by providing a ready opportunity for lending, the capital market enables the investor to transform $1 today into $1.1881 at the end of two years. At the end of three years, the cash will be $1 \times (1.09)^3 = \$1.2950$. The shaded area indicates the difference between compound and simple interest. The difference is substantial over a period of many years or decades, as shown in Figure 5.4.

The most important point to notice is that the total amount that the lender receives is not just the $1 lent out plus two years' worth of interest on $1:

$$2 \times r = 2 \times \$0.09 = \$0.18$$

The lender also gets back an amount r^2, which is the interest in the second year on the interest that was earned in the first year. The term, $2 \times r$, represents **simple interest** over the two years, and the term, r^2, is referred to as the *interest on interest*. In our example this latter amount is exactly

$$r^2 = (\$0.09)^2 = \$0.0081$$

When cash is invested at **compound interest**, each interest payment is reinvested. With simple interest, the interest is not reinvested. Benjamin Franklin's statement, "Money makes money and the money that money makes makes more money," is a colourful way of explaining compound interest. The difference between compound interest and simple interest is also illustrated in Figure 5.4. In this example the difference does not amount to much because the loan is for $1. If the loan were for $1 million, the lender would receive $1,188,100 in two years' time. Of this amount, $8,100 is interest on interest. The lesson is that those small numbers beyond the decimal point can add up to significant dollar amounts when the transactions are for large amounts. In addition, the longer-lasting the loan, the more important interest on interest becomes.

The general formula for an investment over many periods can be written as

Future Value of an Investment:
$$FV = C_0 \times (1 + r)^T$$

where C_0 is the cash to be invested at date 0, r is the interest rate, and T is the number of periods over which the cash is invested.

95

FIGURE 5.4
Simple and Compound Interest

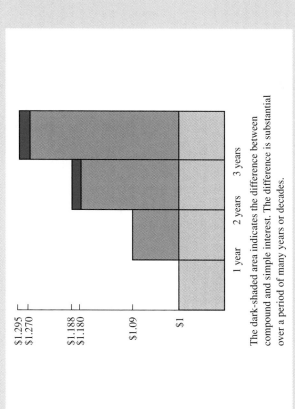

$1.295
$1.270

$1.188
$1.180

$1.09

$1

1 year   2 years   3 years

The dark-shaded area indicates the difference between compound and simple interest. The difference is substantial over a period of many years or decades.

EXAMPLE

Irene Lau has put **$500** in a savings account at the Home Bank of Canada. The account earns 7 percent, compounded annually. How much will Ms. Lau have at the end of three years?

$$\$500 \times 1.07 \times 1.07 \times 1.07 = \$500 \times (1.07)^3 = \$612.52$$

Figure 5.5 illustrates the growth of Ms. Lau's account.

FIGURE 5.5
Ms. Lau's Savings Account

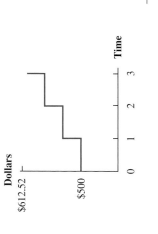

Dollars

$612.52

$500

0   1   2   3   Time

$612.52

0   1   2   3   Time

−$500

EXAMPLE

Heather Courtney invested **$1,000** in the stock of the BMH Company. The company pays a current dividend of $2 per share, which is expected to grow by 20 percent per year for the next two years. What will the dividend of the BMH Company be after two years?

$$\$2 \times (1.20)^2 = \$2.88$$

Figure 5.6 illustrates the increasing value of BMH's dividends.

FIGURE 5.6
The Growth of
Dividends

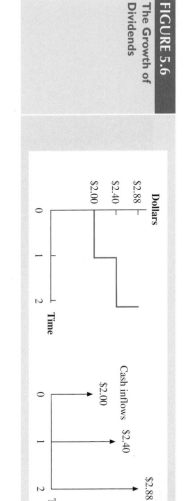

The two previous examples can be calculated in any one of three ways: by hand, by calculator, or with the help of a table.[2] The appropriate table is Table A.3, which appears in Appendix A. This table presents *future values of $1 at the end of T periods*. The table is used by locating the appropriate interest rate on the horizontal and the appropriate number of periods on the vertical.

For example, Irene Lau would look at the following portion of Table A.3:

	Interest Rate		
Period	6%	7%	8%
1	1.0600	1.0700	1.0800
2	1.1236	1.1449	1.1664
3	1.1910	1.2250	1.2597
4	1.2625	1.3108	1.3605

She could calculate the future value of her $500 as

$$\begin{array}{ccc} \$500 & \times & 1.2250 \\ \text{Initial} & & \text{Future value} \\ \text{investment} & & \text{of \$1} \end{array} = \$612.50$$

In the example concerning Irene Lau, we gave you both the initial investment and the interest rate and then asked you to calculate the future value. Alternatively, the interest rate could have been unknown, as shown in the following example.

Raghu Venugopal, who recently won $10,000 in a lottery, wants to buy a car in five years. Raghu estimates that the car will cost $16,105 at that time. His cash flows are displayed in Figure 5.7.

What interest rate must he earn to be able to afford the car? The ratio of purchase price to initial cash is

$$\frac{\$16,105}{\$10,000} = 1.6105$$

___
[2] To solve this problem on a financial calculator (here we use the order of inputs for a Sharp calculator; it may vary for other brands):

1. Clear the calculator.
2. Enter the number of periods as 2 and press *n*.
3. Enter the interest rate of 20 percent as 20 (not 0.20) and press *I* (on some calculators it is *r*).
4. Enter the present value of −2.00 and press *PV*.
5. Ask the calculator for the future value by pressing *COMP FV*.

FIGURE 5.7

Cash Flows for Future Purchase of a Car

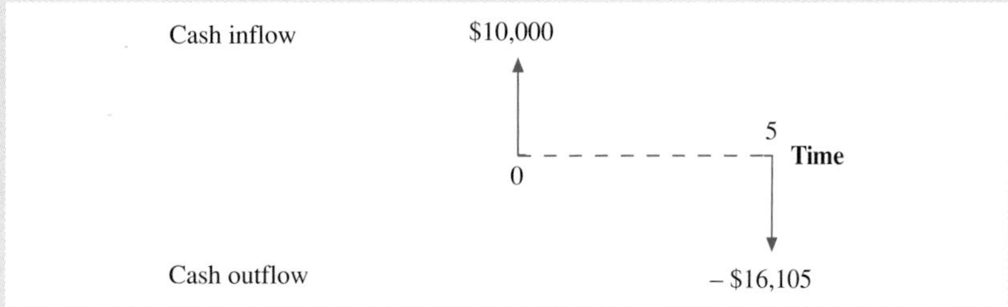

Cash inflow $10,000

```
        0          5   Time
```

Cash outflow   −$16,105

Thus, he must earn an interest rate that allows $1 to become $1.6105 in five years. Table A.3 tells us that an interest rate of 10 percent will allow him to purchase the car. One can express the problem algebraically as

$$\$10,000 \times (1 + r)^5 = \$16,105$$

where *r* is the interest rate needed to purchase the car. Because $16,105/$10,000 = 1.6105, we have

$$(1 + r)^5 = 1.6105$$

Either the table or any sophisticated hand calculator solves[3] for *r* = 10%.

The Power of Compounding: A Digression

Most people who have had any experience with compounding are impressed with its power over long periods of time. Take the stock market, for example. In Chapter 10, we use data collected by William M. Mercer Ltd. to calculate that the average Canadian common stock had approximately an 11 percent rate of return per year from 1957 through 2003. A return of this magnitude may not appear to be anything special over, say, a one-year period. However, $1 placed in these stocks at the beginning of 1957 would have been worth $134.95 at the end of 2003.

The example illustrates the great difference between compound and simple interest. At 11 percent, simple interest on $1 is 11 cents a year. Simple interest over 47 years is $5.17 (47 × $0.11). That is, an individual withdrawing 11 cents every year would have withdrawn $5.17 over 47 years. This is quite a bit below the $134.95 that was obtained by reinvestment of all principal and interest.

The results are more impressive over even longer periods of time. A person with no experience in compounding might think that the value of $1 at the end of 94 years would be twice the value of $1 at the end of 47 years, if the yearly rate of return stayed the same. Actually the value of $1 at the end of 94 years would be the *square* of the value of $1 at the end of 47 years. That is, if the annual rate of return remained the same, a $1 investment in common stocks should be worth $18,211.50 (or $134.95 × 134.95).

---

[3] Conceptually, we are taking the fifth roots of both sides of the equation. That is,

$$r = \sqrt[5]{1.6105} - 1$$

To solve this problem on a financial calculator:

1. Clear the calculator.
2. Enter the number of periods as 5 and press *n*.
3. Enter the present value of −10,000 and press *PV*.
4. Enter the future value of $16,105 and press *FV*.
5. Ask the calculator for the interest rate by pressing *COMP I*.

A few years ago an archaeologist unearthed a relic stating that Julius Caesar lent the Roman equivalent of one penny to someone. Since there was no record of the penny ever being repaid, the archaeologist wondered what the interest and principal would be if a descendant of Caesar tried to collect from a descendant of the borrower in the twentieth century. The archaeologist felt that a rate of 6 percent might be appropriate. To his surprise, the principal and interest due after more than 2,000 years was far greater than the entire wealth on Earth.

The power of compounding can explain one reason why the parents of well-to-do families frequently bequeath wealth to their grandchildren rather than to their children. That is, they skip a generation. The parents would rather make the grandchildren very rich than make the children moderately rich. We have found that in these families the grandchildren have a more positive view of the power of compounding than do the children.

Present Value and Discounting

We now know that an annual interest rate of 9 percent enables the investor to transform $1 today into $1.1881 two years from now. In addition, we would like to know:

> How much would an investor need to lend today to make it possible to receive $1 two years from today?

Algebraically, we can write this as

$$PV \times (1.09)^2 = \$1 \qquad (5.3)$$

In (5.3), PV stands for present value, the amount of money we must lend today in order to receive $1 in two years' time. Solving for PV in (5.3), we have

$$PV = \frac{\$1}{1.1881} = \$0.84$$

This process of calculating the present value of a future cash flow is called **discounting.** It is the opposite of compounding. The difference between compounding and discounting is illustrated in Figure 5.8.

To be certain that $0.84 is in fact the present value of $1 to be received in two years, we must check whether or not, if we lent out $0.84 and rolled the loan over for two years,

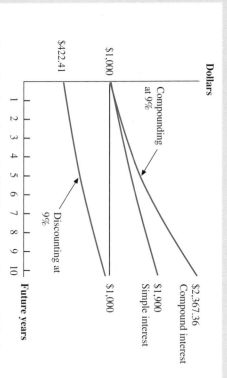

Dollars

Compounding
at 9%

$2,367.36
Compound interest

$1,900
Simple interest

$1,000

$1,000

$422.41

Discounting at
9%

$1,000

Future years
1 2 3 4 5 6 7 8 9 10

The top line shows the growth of $1,000 at compound interest with the funds invested at 9 percent: $1,000 × $(1.09)^{10}$ = $2,367.36. Simple interest is shown on the next line. It is $1,000 + 10 × ($1,000 × 0.09) = $1,900. The bottom line shows the discounted value of $1,000 if the interest rate is 9 percent.

we would get exactly $1 back. If this were the case, the capital markets would be saying that $1 received in two years' time is equivalent to having $0.84 today. Checking with the exact numbers, we get

$$\$0.84168 \times 1.09 \times 1.09 = \$1$$

In other words, when we have capital markets with a sure interest rate of 9 percent, we are indifferent between receiving $0.84 today or $1 in two years. We have no reason to treat these two choices differently from each other, because if we had $0.84 today and lent it out for two years, it would return $1 to us at the end of that time. The value 0.84 $[1/(1.09)^2]$ is called the **present value factor.** It is the factor used to calculate the present value of a future cash flow.

EXAMPLE

Pat Song will receive $10,000 three years from now. Pat can earn 8 percent on his investments. What is the present value of his future cash flow?

$$PV = \$10,000 \times (1/1.08)^3$$
$$= \$10,000 \times 0.7938$$
$$= \$7,938$$

Figure 5.9 illustrates the application of the present value factor to Pat's investment.

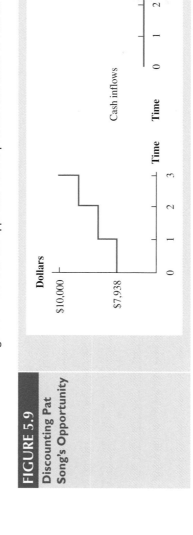

FIGURE 5.9
Discounting Pat Song's Opportunity

When his investments grow at an 8 percent rate of interest, Pat Song is equally inclined toward receiving $7,938 now or receiving $10,000 in three years' time. After all, he could convert the $7,938 he receives today into $10,000 in three years by lending it at an interest rate of 8 percent.

Pat Song could have reached his present value calculation in one of three ways. The computation could have been done by hand, by calculator, or with the help of Table A.1 in Appendix A. This table presents *present value of $1 to be received after T periods*. The table is used by locating the appropriate interest rate on the horizontal and the appropriate number of periods on the vertical. For example, Pat Song would look at the following portion of Table A.1:

	Interest Rate		
Period	7%	8%	9%
1	0.9346	0.9259	0.9174
2	0.8734	0.8573	0.8417
3	0.8163	0.7938	0.7722
4	0.7629	0.7350	0.7084

The appropriate present value factor is 0.7938.

EXAMPLE

In the above example, we gave both the interest rate and the future cash flow.
Alternatively, the interest rate could have been unknown.

A customer of the Cristall Corp. wants to buy a tugboat today. Rather than paying immediately,
he will pay $50,000 in three years. It will cost the Cristall Corp. $38,610 to build the tugboat
immediately. The relevant cash flows to Cristall Corp. are displayed in Figure 5.10. By charging
what interest rate would the Cristall Corp. neither gain nor lose on the sale?

FIGURE 5.10

Cash Flows for Tugboat

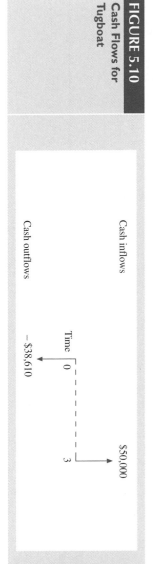

The ratio of construction cost to sale price is

$$\frac{\$36,810}{\$50,000} = 0.7722$$

We must determine the interest rate that allows $1 to be received in three years to have a
present value of $0.7722. Table A.1 tells us that 9 percent is that interest rate. [4]

Frequently, an investor or a business will receive more than one cash flow. The present value of the set of cash flows is simply the sum of the present values of the individual
cash flows. This is illustrated in the following example.

EXAMPLE

While on vacation in the U.S., Terence Chiu won a lottery and will receive the following set of
cash flows over the next two years:

Year	Cash Flow
1	$2,000
2	$5,000

Terence can currently earn 6 percent in his savings account. The present value of the cash flows is

Year	Cash flow × Present value factor		= Present value
1	$2,000	× 1/1.06 = 0.943	= $1,887
2	$5,000	× 1/(1.06)² = 0.890	= $4,450
		Total	$6,337

In other words, Terence is equally inclined toward receiving $6,337 today and receiving $2,000
and $5,000 over the next two years.

---

[4] Algebraically, we are solving for r in the equation

$$\frac{\$50,000}{(1+r)^3} = \$38,610$$

or, equivalently,

$$\frac{\$1}{(1+r)^3} = \$0.7722$$

EXAMPLE

Finance.com has an opportunity to invest in a new high-speed computer that costs $50,000. The computer will generate cash flows (from cost savings) of $25,000 one year from now, $20,000 two years from now, and $15,000 three years from now. The computer will be worthless after three years, and no additional cash flows will occur. Finance.com has determined that the appropriate discount rate is 7 percent for this investment. Should Finance.com make this investment in a new high-speed computer? What is the present value of the investment?

The cash flows and present value factors of the proposed computer are as follows.

	Cash Flows	Present Value Factor
Year 0	−$50,000	$1 = 1$
1	$25,000	$\dfrac{1}{1.07} = 0.9346$
2	$20,000	$\left(\dfrac{1}{1.07}\right)^2 = 0.8734$
3	$15,000	$\left(\dfrac{1}{1.07}\right)^3 = 0.8163$

The present values of the cash flows are:

$$\text{Cash flows} \times \text{Present value factor} = \text{Present value}$$

Year 0	−$50,000 × 1	= −$50,000
1	$25,000 × 0.9346	= $23,365
2	$20,000 × 0.8734	= $17,468
3	$15,000 × 0.8163	= $12,244.5
	Total:	$ 3,077.5

Finance.com should invest in a new high-speed computer because the present value of its future cash flows is greater than its cost. The NPV is $3,077.5.

The Algebraic Formula

To derive an algebraic formula for net present value of a cash flow, recall that the PV of receiving a cash flow one year from now is

$$PV = C_1/(1 + r)$$

and the PV of receiving a cash flow two years from now is

$$PV = C_2/(1 + r)^2$$

We can write the NPV of a T-period project as

$$NPV = -C_0 + \frac{C_1}{1 + r} + \frac{C_2}{(1 + r)^2} + \ldots + \frac{C_T}{(1 + r)^T} = -C_0 + \sum_{t=1}^{T} \frac{C_t}{(1 + r)^t}$$

The initial flow, $-C_0$, is assumed to be negative because it represents an investment. The term Σ is shorthand for the sum of the series.[5]

? Concept Questions

- **What is the difference between simple interest and compound interest?**
- **What is the formula for the net present value of a project?**

---

[5]In Chapter 6 we apply the NPV formula to investments that have a cash inflow in year 0 and outflows in later years. For these investments, the term $-C_0$ is replaced by $-PV$ (outflows).

5.3 Compounding Periods

So far we have assumed that compounding and discounting occur yearly. Sometimes compounding may occur more frequently than just once a year. For example, imagine that a bank pays a 10 percent interest rate "compounded semiannually." This means that a $1,000 deposit in the bank would be worth $1,000 × 1.05 = $1,050 after six months, and $1,050 × 1.05 = $1,102.50 at the end of the year. The end-of-the-year wealth can be written as[6]

$$\$1,000 \left(1 + \frac{0.10}{2}\right)^2 = \$1,000 \times (1.05)^2 = \$1,102.50$$

Of course, a $1,000 deposit would be worth $1,100 (or $1,000 × 1.10) with yearly compounding. Note that the future value at the end of one year is greater with semiannual compounding than with yearly compounding. With yearly compounding, the original $1,000 remains the investment base for the full year. The original $1,000 is the investment base only for the first six months with semiannual compounding. The base over the second six months is $1,050. Hence, one gets *interest on interest* with semiannual compounding.

Because $1,000 × 1.1025 = $1,102.50, 10 percent compounded semiannually is the same as 10.25 percent compounded annually. In other words, a rational investor will be indifferent between a rate of 10 percent compounded semiannually, or a rate of 10.25 percent compounded annually.

Quarterly compounding at 10 percent yields wealth at the end of one year of

$$\$1,000 \left(1 + \frac{0.10}{4}\right)^4 = \$1,103.81$$

More generally, compounding an investment m times a year provides end-of-year wealth of

$$C_0 \left(1 + \frac{r}{m}\right)^m \tag{5.4}$$

where C_0 is one's initial investment and r is the **stated annual interest rate**. The stated annual interest rate is the annual interest rate without consideration of compounding. Banks and other financial institutions may use other names for the stated annual interest rate. **Annual percentage rate** is perhaps the most common synonym.

What is the end-of-year wealth if Julie Andrew receives a 24 percent rate of interest compounded monthly on a $1 investment? Using (5.4), her wealth is

$$\$1\left(1 + \frac{0.24}{12}\right)^{12} = \$1 \times (1.02)^{12}$$
$$= \$1.2682$$

The annual rate of return is 26.82 percent. This annual rate of return is called the **effective annual interest rate**. Due to compounding, the effective annual interest rate is greater than the stated annual interest rate of 24 percent. Algebraically, we can rewrite the effective annual interest rate as

Effective Annual Interest Rate:

$$\left(1 + \frac{r}{m}\right)^m - 1 \tag{5.5}$$

Students are often bothered by the subtraction of 1 in (5.5). Note that end-of-year wealth is composed of both the interest earned over the year and the original principal. We remove the original principal by subtracting 1 in (5.5).

---

[6]In addition to using a calculator, one can still use Table A.3 when the compounding period is less than a year. Here, one sets the interest rate at 5 percent and the number of periods at two.

EXAMPLE

If the stated annual rate of interest, 8 percent, is compounded quarterly, what is the effective annual rate of interest? Using (5.5), we have

$$(1 + r/m)^m - 1 = (1 + 0.08/4)^4 - 1 = 0.0824 = 8.24\%$$

Referring back to our original example where $C_0 = \$1,000$ and $r = 10\%$, we can generate the following table:

C_0	Compounding Frequency (m)	C_1	Effective Annual Interest Rate = $(1 + r/m)^m - 1$
$1,000	Yearly ($m = 1$)	$1,100.00	0.10
1,000	Semiannually ($m = 2$)	1,102.50	0.1025
1,000	Quarterly ($m = 4$)	1,103.81	0.10381
1,000	Daily ($m = 365$)	1,105.16	0.10516

As this example shows, the formula converts any stated annual rate into an effective annual rate.

Compounding Over Many Years

Equation (5.4) applies for an investment over one year. For an investment over one or more (T) years, the formula becomes

Future Value with Compounding:

$$FV = C_0 (1 + r/m)^{mT} \qquad (5.6)$$

EXAMPLE

Margaret Cortes is investing $5,000 at 4 percent per year, compounded quarterly for five years. What is her wealth at the end of five years? Using (5.6), her wealth is

$$\$5,000 \times (1 + 0.04/4)^{4 \times 5} = \$5,000 \times (1.01)^{20}$$
$$= \$5,000 \times 1.2202 = \$6,101.00$$

Cost of Borrowing Disclosure regulations (part of the *Bank Act*) in Canada require that lenders disclose an annual percentage rate on virtually all consumer loans. This rate must be displayed on a loan document in a prominent and unambiguous way. Unfortunately, this does not tell the borrower the effective annual rate on the loan.

EXAMPLE

Suppose that a credit card agreement quotes an annual percentage rate of 18 percent. Monthly payments are required. Based on our discussion, an annual percentage rate of 18 percent with monthly payments is really 0.18/12 = 0.015 or 1.5 percent per month. The effective annual rate is thus

$$\begin{aligned} \text{Effective annual rate} &= [1 + 0.18/12]^{12} - 1 \\ &= 1.015^{12} - 1 \\ &= 1.1956 - 1 \\ &= 19.56\% \end{aligned}$$

The difference between an annual percentage rate and an effective annual rate probably will not be great, but it is somewhat ironic that cost-of-borrowing disclosure regulations sometimes require lenders to be untruthful about the actual rate on a loan.

The Alberta Treasury Branch offers one-year Guaranteed Investment Certificates (GICs) at 4 percent per year compounded semiannually, TD Canada Trust offers one-year GICs at 4.25 percent compounded annually. Which would you prefer?

The effective annual rate at TD Canada Trust is 4.25 percent since the compounding is annual. To find the effective annual rate offered by the Alberta Treasury Branch, use Equation 5.5:

$$\text{Effective annual interest rate} = (1 + r/m)^m - 1$$
$$= (1 + 0.04/2)^2 - 1$$
$$= 4.04\%$$

You would prefer the TD Canada Trust GIC since it offers a higher effective annual rate.

Concept Questions

- What is a stated annual interest rate?
- What is an effective annual interest rate?
- What is the relationship between the stated annual interest rate and the effective annual interest rate?

Continuous Compounding (Advanced)

The previous discussion shows that one can compound much more frequently than once a year. One could compound semiannually, quarterly, monthly, daily, hourly, each minute, or even more often. The limiting case would be to compound every infinitesimal instant, which is commonly called **continuous compounding**.

Though the idea of compounding this rapidly may boggle the mind, a simple formula is involved.[7] With continuous compounding, the value at the end of T years is expressed as

$$C_0 \times e^{rT} \qquad (5.7)$$

where C_0 is the initial investment, r is the stated annual interest rate, and T is the number of years over which the investment runs. The number e is a constant and is approximately equal to 2.718. It is not an unknown like C_0, r, and T.

John MacDonald invested $1,000 at a continuously compounded rate of 10 percent for one year. What is the value of his wealth at the end of one year?

From Equation (5.7) we have

$$\$1,000 \times e^{0.10} = \$1,000 \times 1.1052 = \$1,105.20$$

This number can easily be read from our Table A.5 in Appendix A. One merely sets r, the value on the horizontal dimension, to 10 percent and sets T, the value on the vertical dimension, to 1.

---

[7] Readers familiar with introductory calculus will recognize the expression:

$$\lim_{m \to \infty} (1 + r/m)^m = e^r$$

For this problem, the relevant portion of the table is

Period	Continuously Compounded Rate (r)			
	9%	10%	11%	
1	1.0942	1.1052	1.1163	
2	1.1972	1.2214	1.2461	
3	1.3100	1.3499	1.3910	

Note that a continuously compounded rate of 10 percent is equivalent to an annually compounded rate of 10.52 percent. In other words, John MacDonald would not care whether his bank quoted a continuously compounded rate of 10 percent or a 10.52 percent rate, compounded annually.

EXAMPLE

John MacDonald's brother, Robert, invested $1,000 at a continuously compounded rate of 10 percent for two years.

The appropriate formula here is

$$\$1,000 \times e^{0.10 \times 2} = \$1,000 \times e^{0.20} = \$1,221.40$$

Using the portion of the table of continuously compounded rates reproduced above, we find the value to be 1.2214.

Figure 5.11 illustrates the relationship among annual, semiannual, and continuous compounding. Semiannual compounding gives rise to both a smoother curve and a higher ending value than does annual compounding. Continuous compounding has both the smoothest curve and the highest ending value of all.

EXAMPLE

An investment is going to pay you $1,000 at the end of four years. If the annual continuously compounded rate of interest is 8 percent, what is the present value of this payment?

$$\$1,000 \times \frac{1}{e^{0.08 \times 4}} = \$1,000 \times \frac{1}{1.3771} = \$726.16$$

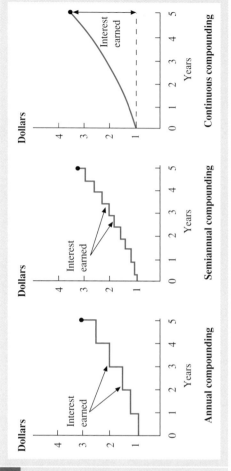

FIGURE 5.11

Annual, Semiannual, and Continuous Compounding

5.4 Simplifications

The first part of this chapter has examined the concepts of future value and present value. Although these concepts allow one to answer a host of problems concerning the time value of money, the human effort involved can frequently be excessive. For example, consider a bank calculating the present value on a 20-year mortgage with monthly payments. Because this mortgage has 240 (or 20 × 12) payments, a lot of time is needed to perform a conceptually simple task.

Because many basic finance problems are potentially so time-consuming, we search out simplifications in this section. We provide simplifying formulas for four classes of cash flow streams:

• Perpetuity
• Growing perpetuity
• Annuity
• Growing annuity

Perpetuity

A **perpetuity** is a constant stream of cash flows without end. If you are thinking that perpetuities have no relevance to reality, it will surprise you that there is a well-known case of an unending cash flow stream: the British bonds called *consols*. An investor purchasing a consol is entitled to receive yearly interest from the British government forever.

How can the price of a consol be determined? Consider a consol that pays a coupon of C dollars each year and will do so forever. Simply applying the PV formula gives us

$$PV = \frac{C}{1+r} + \frac{C}{(1+r)^2} + \frac{C}{(1+r)^3} + \cdots$$

where the dots at the end of the formula stand for the infinite string of terms that continues the formula. Series like the preceding one are called *geometric series*. It is well known that even though they have an infinite number of terms, the whole series has a finite sum because each term is only a fraction of the preceding term. Before turning to a calculus book, though, it is worth going back to our original principles to see if a bit of financial intuition can help us find the PV.

The present value of the consol is the present value of all of its future coupons. In other words, it is an amount of money that, if an investor had it today, would make it possible to achieve the same pattern of expenditures that the consol and its coupons would. Suppose that an investor wanted to spend exactly C dollars each year. If our investor owned the consol, this spending pattern would be possible. How much money must the investor have today to spend the same amount? Clearly the investor would need exactly enough so that the interest on the money would be C dollars per year. If the investor had any more, spending could be more than C dollars each year. If the amount were any less, the investor would eventually run out of money spending C dollars per year.

The amount that will give the investor C dollars each year, and therefore the present value of the consol, is simply

$$PV = \frac{C}{r} \tag{5.8}$$

To confirm that this is the right answer, notice that if we lend the amount C/r, the interest it earns each year will be

$$\text{Interest} = \frac{C}{r} \times r = C$$

which is exactly the consol payment.[8] To sum up, we have shown that for a consol

Formula for Present Value of Perpetuity:

$$PV = \frac{C}{1+r} + \frac{C}{(1+r)^2} + \frac{C}{(1+r)^3} + \cdots$$
$$= C/r$$

It is comforting to know how easily we can use a bit of financial intuition to solve this mathematical problem.

EXAMPLE

Consider a perpetuity paying $100 a year. If the interest rate is 8 percent, what is the value of the consol? Using (5.8), we have

$$PV = \frac{\$100}{0.08} = \$1,250$$

Now suppose that the interest rate falls to 6 percent. Using (5.8), the value of the perpetuity is

$$PV = \frac{\$100}{0.06} = \$1,666.67$$

Note that the value of the perpetuity rises with a drop in the interest rate. Conversely, the value of the perpetuity falls with a rise in the interest rate.

Growing Perpetuity

Imagine an apartment building where cash flows to the landlord after expenses will be $100,000 next year. These cash flows are expected to rise at 5 percent per year. If one assumes that this rise will continue indefinitely, the cash flow stream is termed a **growing perpetuity.** Positing an 11 percent discount rate, the present value of the cash flows can be represented as

$$PV = \frac{\$100,000}{1.11} + \frac{\$100,000(1.05)}{(1.11)^2} + \frac{\$100,000(1.05)^2}{(1.11)^3} + \cdots + \frac{\$100,000(1.05)^{N-1}}{(1.11)^N} + \cdots$$

---

[8] We can prove this by looking at the PV equation:

$$PV = C/(1+r) + C/(1+r)^2 + \cdots$$

Let $C/(1+r) = a$ and $1/(1+r) = x$. We now have

$$PV = a(1 + x + x^2 \ldots) \tag{1}$$

Next we can multiply by x:

$$xPV = ax + ax^2 + \cdots \tag{2}$$

Subtracting (2) from (1) gives

$$PV(1-x) = a$$

Now we substitute for a and x and rearrange:

$$PV = C/r$$

Algebraically, we can write the formula as

$$PV = \frac{C}{1+r} + \frac{C \times (1+g)}{(1+r)^2} + \frac{C \times (1+g)^2}{(1+r)^3} + \cdots + \frac{C \times (1+g)^{N-1}}{(1+r)^N} + \cdots \quad (5.9)$$

where C is the cash flow to be received one period hence, g is the rate of growth per period, expressed as a percentage, and r is the interest rate.

Fortunately, (5.9) reduces to the following simplification:[9]

Formula for Present Value of Growing Perpetuity:

$$PV = \frac{C}{r-g} \quad (5.10)$$

From (5.10), the present value of the cash flows from the apartment building is

$$\frac{\$100,000}{0.11 - 0.05} = \$1,666,667$$

There are three important points concerning the growing perpetuity formula:

1. *The Numerator.* The numerator in (5.10) is the cash flow one period hence, not at date 0. Consider the following example.

EXAMPLE

Hoffstein Corporation paid a dividend of \$3.00 per share last year. Investors anticipate that the annual dividend will rise by 6 percent a year forever. The applicable interest rate is 11 percent. What is the price of the stock today?

The numerator in Equation (5.10) is the cash flow to be received next period. Since the growth rate is 6 percent, the dividend next year is \$3.18 (or \$3.00 × 1.06). The price of the stock today is

$$\$63.60 = \frac{\$3.18}{0.11 - 0.06}$$

Present value
of all dividends
beginning a year
from now

The price of \$63.60 represents the present value of all dividends beginning a year from now. Equation (5.10) only makes it possible to calculate the present value of all dividends beginning a year from now. Be sure you understand this example; test questions on this subject always seem to trip up a few of our students.

---

[9]PV is the sum of an infinite geometric series:

$$PV = a(1 + x + x^2 + \cdots)$$

where $a = C/(1+r)$ and $x = (1+g)/(1+r)$. Previously we showed that the sum of an infinite geometric series is $a/(1-x)$. Using this result and substituting for a and x, we find

$$PV = C/(r-g)$$

Note that this geometric series converges to a finite sum only when x is less than 1. This implies that the growth rate, g, must be less than the interest rate, r.

2. *The Interest Rate and the Growth Rate.* The interest rate r must be greater than the growth rate g for the growing perpetuity formula to work. Consider the case in which the growth rate approaches the interest rate in magnitude. Then the denominator in the growing perpetuity formula gets infinitesimally small and the present value grows infinitely large. The present value is in fact undefined when r is less than g.

3. *The Timing Assumption.* Cash generally flows into and out of real-world firms both randomly and nearly continuously. However, Equation (5.10) assumes that cash flows are received and disbursed at regular and discrete points in time. In the example of the apartment, we assumed that the net cash flows of $100,000 only occurred once a year. In reality, rent cheques are commonly received every month. Payments for maintenance and other expenses may occur anytime within the year.

The growing perpetuity formula of (5.10) can be applied only by assuming a regular and discrete pattern of cash flow. Although this assumption is sensible because the formula saves so much time, the user should never forget that it is an assumption. This point will be mentioned again in the chapters ahead.

A few words should be said about terminology. Authors of financial textbooks generally use one of two conventions to refer to time. A minority of financial writers treat cash flows as being received on exact *dates*, for example date 0, date 1, and so forth. Under this convention, date 0 represents the present time. However, because a year is an interval, not a specific moment in time, the great majority of authors refer to cash flows that occur at the end of a year (or, alternatively, at the end of a period). Under this *end-of-the-year* convention, the end of year 0 is the present, the end of year 1 occurs one period hence, and so on.[10] (The beginning of year 0 has already passed and is not generally referred to.)

The interchangability of the two conventions can be seen from the following chart:

Date 0	Date 1	Date 2	Date 3	⋯
= Now				
End of year 0	End of year 1	End of year 2	End of year 3	⋯
= Now				

We strongly believe that the *dates convention* reduces ambiguity. However, we use both conventions because you are likely to see the *end-of-year convention* in later courses. In fact, both conventions may appear in the same example for the sake of practice.

Annuity

An **annuity** is a level stream of regular payments that lasts for a fixed number of periods. Not surprisingly, annuities are among the most common kinds of financial instruments. The pensions that people receive when they retire are often in the form of an annuity. Leases, mortgages, and pension plans are also annuities.

To figure out the present value of an annuity we need to evaluate the following equation:

$$\frac{C}{1+r} + \frac{C}{(1+r)^2} + \frac{C}{(1+r)^3} + \cdots + \frac{C}{(1+r)^T}$$

---

[10] Sometimes financial writers merely speak of a cash flow in year x. Although this terminology is ambiguous, such writers generally mean the *end of year x*.

The present value of receiving only the coupons for T periods must be less than the present value of a consol, but how much less? To answer this we have to look at consols a bit more closely. Consider the following time chart:

	Now							
Date (or end of year)	0	1	2	3	T	$(T+1)$	$(T+2)$	
Consol 1		C	C	$C \dots$	C			
Consol 2						C	$C \dots$	
Annuity		C	C	$C \dots$	C			

Consol 1 is a normal consol with its first payment at date 1. The first payment of consol 2 occurs at date $T + 1$.

The present value of having a cash flow of C at each of T dates is equal to the present value of consol 1 minus the present value of consol 2. The present value of consol 1 is given by

$$PV = \frac{C}{r}$$

(5.11)

Consol 2 is just a consol with its first payment at date $T + 1$. From the perpetuity formula, this consol will be worth C/r at date T.[11] However, we do not want the value at date T. We want the value now (in other words, the present value at date 0). We must discount C/r back by T periods. Therefore, the present value of consol 2 is

$$PV = C/r \times 1/(1 + r)^T$$

(5.12)

The present value of having cash flows for T years is the present value of a consol with its first payment at date 1 minus the present value of a consol with its first payment at date $T + 1$. Thus, the present value of an annuity is Equation (5.11) minus Equation (5.12). This can be written as

$$C/r - C/r[1/(1 + r)^T]$$

This simplifies to

Formula for Present Value of Annuity:[12,13]

$$PV = C\left[\frac{1}{r} - \frac{1}{r(1 + r)^T}\right]$$

(5.13)

---

[11] Students frequently think that C/r is the present value at date $T + 1$ because the consol's first payment is at date $T + 1$. However, the formula values the annuity as of one period prior to the first payment.

[12] This can also be written as $C[1 - 1/(1 + r)^T]/r$.

[13] We can also provide a formula for the future value of an annuity:

$$FV = C[(1 + r)^T/r - 1/r]$$

EXAMPLE

Andrea Mullings has just won a lottery in the U.S., paying $50,000 a year for 20 years. She is to receive her first payment a year from now. The lottery advertisements bill this as the Million Dollar Lottery because $1,000,000 = $50,000 × 20. If the interest rate is 8 percent, what is the true value of the prize?

Equation (5.13) yields

Present value of Million Dollar Lottery = $50,000 × [1/0.08 − 1/0.08(1.08)^{20}]

$$\begin{array}{ccc} \text{Periodic payment} & & \text{Annuity factor} \\ = \$\ 50,000 & \times & 9.8181 \\ = \$490,905 & & \end{array}$$

Rather than being overjoyed at winning, Ms. Mullings sues the lottery authorities for misrepresentation and fraud. Her legal brief states that she was promised $1 million but received only $490,905.[14]

The term we use to compute the value of the stream of level payments, C, for T years is called an **annuity factor.** The annuity factor in the current example is 9.8181. Because the annuity factor is used so often in PV calculations, we have included it in Table A.2 in Appendix A. The table gives the values of these factors for a range of interest rates, r, and maturity dates, T.

The annuity factor as expressed in the brackets of (5.13) is a complex formula. For simplification, we may from time to time refer to the annuity factor as

$$A_r^T \tag{5.14}$$

that is, expression (5.14) stands for the present value of $1 a year for T years at an interest rate of r.

Mortgages

Mortgages are a common example of an annuity with monthly payments. To understand mortgage calculations, you need to keep in mind two institutional arrangements. First, although payments are monthly, regulations for Canadian financial institutions require that mortgage rates be quoted with semiannual compounding. Further, payments on conventional mortgages are calculated to maturity (usually after 25 years) although rate adjustments after the initial locked-in period will cause payments to change subsequently.

---

[14]To solve this problem on a common type HP19B II financial calculator, you should do the following:

1. Press *FIN* and *TVM*.
2. Enter the payment 50,000 and press *PMT*.
3. Enter the interest rate 8 and press *I% YR*.
4. Enter the number of periods 20 and press *N*.
5. Finally, press *PV* to solve.

Notice your answer is $490,907.370372. The calculator uses 11 digits for the annuity factor and the answer, whereas the example uses only four digits in the annuity factor and rounds the final answer to the nearest dollar. That is why the answer in the text example differs from the one using the calculator. In practice, the answer using the calculator is the best because it is more precise.

EXAMPLE

A financial institution is offering a $100,000 mortgage at a stated rate of 6 percent. To find the payments we first need to find the effective *monthly* rate. To do this we convert the stated semi-annual rate to an equivalent annual rate. [15]

$$\text{Effective annual interest rate} = [1 + r/m]^m - 1$$
$$= [1 + 0.06/2]^2 - 1$$
$$= 1.0609 - 1$$
$$= 6.09\%$$

Then we find the effective monthly rate used to calculate the payments.

$$\text{Stated rate}/m = (\text{Effective annual rate} + 1)^{1/m} - 1$$
$$\text{Stated rate}/12 = (1.0609)^{1/12} - 1$$
$$= 1.0049 - 1 = 0.49\%$$

The effective monthly rate is 0.49 percent and there are $12 \times 25 = 300$ payments so we need to find $A_{0.0049}^{300}$. Since this in not in Table A.2, we use (5.13) as rearranged in footnote 13 to solve for C, the monthly payment.

$$PV = \$100,000 = C \times (1 - \text{Present value factor})/r$$
$$\$100,000 = C \times (1 - 1/1.0049^{300})/0.0049$$
$$C = \$636.99$$

The monthly mortgage payments will be $636.99.

Using Annuity Formulas

Our experience is that annuity formulas are not hard, but can be tricky for the beginning student. Here we present four tricks.

Trick 1: A Delayed Annuity. One of the tricks in working with annuities or perpetuities is getting the timing exactly right. This is particularly useful when an annuity or perpetuity begins at a date many periods in the future. Consider the following example.

EXAMPLE

Earlier, we pointed out that, while mortgages are amortized over 300 months, the rate is fixed for a shorter period usually no longer than five years. Suppose the rate of 6 percent in the previous example is fixed for five years and you are wondering whether to lock in this rate or to take a lower rate of 5 percent fixed for only one year. If you choose the one-year rate, how much lower will your payments be for the first year?

The payments at 5 percent are $579.94, a reduction of $57.05 per month. If you choose to take the shorter-term mortgage with lower payments, you are betting that rates will not take a big jump over the next year leaving you with a new rate after one year much higher than 6 percent. While the mortgage formula cannot make this decision for you (it depends on risk and return discussed in Chapter 9), it does give you the risk you are facing in terms of higher monthly payments. In 1981, mortgage rates were around 20 percent!

---

[15] Chartered banks use 10 decimal places for all calculations. This may result in some rounding error in using this formula to check the payments on an outstanding mortgage.

EXAMPLE

Fauzia Mohammed will receive a four-year annuity of $500 per year beginning at date 6. If the interest rate is 10 percent, what is the present value of her annuity?

This situation can be graphed as

The analysis involves two steps:

1. Calculate the present value of the annuity using (5.13). This is

Present Value of Annuity at Date 5:

$$\$500\left[\frac{1}{0.10} - \frac{1}{0.10(1.10)^4}\right] = \$500 \times A_{0.10}^4$$
$$= \$500 \times 3.1699$$
$$= \$1,584.95$$

Note that $1,584.95 represents the present value at date 5.

Students frequently think that $1,584.95 is the present value at date 6, because the annuity begins at date 6. However, our formula values the annuity as of one period prior to the first payment. This can be seen in the most typical case where the first payment occurs at date 1. The formula values the annuity as of date 0 here.

2. Discount the present value of the annuity back to date 0. That is

Present Value at Date 0:

$$\frac{\$1,584.95}{(1.10)^5} = \$984.13$$

Again, it is worthwhile mentioning that, because the annuity formula brings Fauzia's annuity back to date 5, the second calculation must discount over the remaining five periods. The two-step procedure is graphed in Figure 5.12.

Trick 2: Annuity in Advance. The annuity formula of (5.12) assumes that the first annuity payment begins a full period hence. This type of annuity is frequently called an *annuity in arrears*. What happens if the annuity begins today, in other words, at date 0?

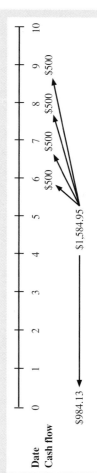

Step One: Discount the four payments back to date 5 by using the annuity formula.
Step Two: Discount the present value at date 5 ($1,584.95) back to present value at date 0.

EXAMPLE

In a previous example, Andrea Mullings received $50,000 a year for 20 years as a prize in a U.S. lottery. In that example, she was to receive the first payment a year from the winning date. Let us now assume that the first payment occurs immediately. The total number of payments remains 20. Under this new assumption, we have a 19-date annuity with the first payment occurring at date 1—plus an extra payment at date 0. The present value is

$$\underset{\text{Payment at date 0}}{\$50,000} \quad + \quad \underset{\text{19-year annuity}}{\$50,000 \times A_{0.08}^{19}}$$

$$= \$50,000 + \$50,000 \times 9.6036$$

$$= \$530,180$$

The present value in this example is greater than $490,905, the present value in the earlier lottery example. This is to be expected because the annuity of the current example begins earlier. An annuity with an immediate initial payment is called an *annuity in advance*. Always remember that both Equation (5.13) and Table A.2 refer to an *annuity in arrears*.

A second way to find the present value of our annuity in advance is to compute the present value of a 20-year annuity in arrears and compound the result for one period. This gives the same present value (except for a small rounding error):

$$\$50,000 \times A_{0.08}^{20} = \$50,000 \times 9.8181 = \$490,905$$
$$\$490,905 \, (1.08) = \$530,177$$

Trick 3: The Infrequent Annuity. The following example deals with an annuity with payments occurring less frequently than once a year.

EXAMPLE

Alex Bourne receives an annuity of $450 payable once every two years. The annuity stretches out over 20 years. The first payment occurs at date 2, that is, two years from today. The annual interest rate is 6 percent.

The trick is to determine the interest rate over a two-year period. The interest rate over two years is

$$1.06 \times 1.06 - 1 = 12.36\%$$

That is, $100 invested over two years will yield $112.36.

What we want is the present value of a $450 annuity over 10 periods, with an interest rate of 12.36 percent per period. This is

$$\$450 \left[\frac{1}{0.1236} - \frac{1}{0.1236 \times (1.1236)^{10}} \right] = \$450 \times A_{0.1236}^{10} = \$2,505.57$$

---

[16] To solve this problem on a financial calculator:

1. Clear the calculator.
2. Set the calculator for an annuity in advance. On some calculators you must press the BGN key.
3. Enter the number of periods as 19 and press N.
4. Enter the payment as 50,000 and press PMT.
5. Enter the interest rate of 8 percent and press i.
6. Ask the calculator for the present value by pressing COMP PV.

Trick 4: Equating Present Value of Two Annuities.

The following example equates the present value of inflows with the present value of outflows.

Jon Rabinowitz and Gila Messeri are saving for the university education of their newborn daughter, Gabrielle. They estimate that expenses will run $30,000 per year when their daughter enters university in 18 years. The annual return on their university investment account over the next few decades will be 14 percent. How much money must they deposit in the bank each year so that their daughter will be completely supported through four years of university?

To simplify the calculations, we assume that Gabrielle is born today. Her parents will make the first of her four annual tuition payments on her 18th birthday. They will make equal deposits on each of her first 17 birthdays, but no deposit at date 0. This is illustrated as

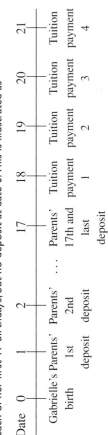

Date	0	1	2	...	17	18	19	20	21
	Gabrielle's birth	Parents' 1st deposit	Parents' 2nd deposit	...	Parents' 17th and last deposit	Tuition payment 1	Tuition payment 2	Tuition payment 3	Tuition payment 4

Jon and Gila will be making deposits over the next 17 years. They will be withdrawing $30,000 per year over the following four years. We can be sure they will be able to withdraw fully $30,000 per year if the present value of the deposits equals the present value of the four $30,000 withdrawals.

This calculation requires three steps. The first two determine the present value of the withdrawals. The final step determines yearly deposits that will have a present value equal to that of the withdrawals.

1. We calculate the present value of the four years at university using the annuity formula:

$$\$30,000 \times \left[\frac{1}{0.14} - \frac{1}{0.14 \times (1.14)^4} \right] = \$30,000 \times A_{0.14}^4$$

$$= \$30,000 \times 2.9137 = \$87,411$$

We assume that Gabrielle enters university on her 18th birthday.

Given our discussion in trick 1 above, $87,411 represents the present value at date 17.

2. We calculate the present value of a university education at date 0 as

$$\frac{\$87,411}{(1.14)^{17}} = \$9,422.91$$

3. Assuming that Gila Messeri and Jon Rabinowitz make deposits to the bank at the end of each of the 17 years, we calculate the annual deposit that will yield a present value of all deposits of $9,422.91 as

$$C \times A_{0.14}^{17} = \$9,422.91$$

Since

$$A_{0.14}^{17} = 6.3729$$

we find that

$$C = \frac{\$9,422.91}{6.3729} = \$1,478.59$$

Thus, deposits of **$1,478.59** made at the end of each of the first 17 years and invested at 14 percent will provide enough money to make tuition payments of **$30,000** over the following four years.

An alternative method would be: (1) calculate the present value of the tuition payments at Gabrielle's 18th birthday and (2) calculate annual deposits such that the future value of the deposits at her 18th birthday equals the present value of the tuition payments at that date. Although this technique can also provide the right answer, we have found that it is more likely to lead to errors. Therefore, we only equate present values in our presentation.

Growing Annuity

Cash flows in business are very likely to grow over time, due either to real growth or to inflation. The growing perpetuity, which assumes an infinite number of cash flows, provides one formula to handle this growth. We now consider a **growing annuity**, which is a *finite* number of growing cash flows. Because perpetuities of any kind are rare, a formula for a growing annuity would be useful indeed. The formula is[17]

Formula for Present Value of Growing Annuity:

$$PV = C\left[\frac{1}{r-g} - \frac{1}{r-g} \times \left(\frac{1+g}{1+r}\right)^T\right] \qquad (5.15)$$

where, as before, C is the payment to occur at the end of the first period, r is the interest rate, g is the rate of growth per period, expressed as a percentage, and T is the number of periods for the annuity.

EXAMPLE

Gilles Lebouder, a second-year MBA student, has just been offered a job at $50,000 a year. He anticipates his salary increasing by 9 percent a year until his retirement in 40 years. Given an interest rate of 20 percent, what is the present value of his lifetime salary?

We simplify by assuming he will be paid his $50,000 salary exactly one year from now, and that his salary will continue to be paid in annual installments. From (5.15), the calculation is

Present value
of Gilles' = $50,000 × {[1/(0.20 − 0.09)] − [1/(0.20 − 0.09) (1.09/1.20)⁴⁰]}
lifetime salary

= $444,832

---

[17]This can be proved as follows. A growing annuity can be viewed as the difference between two growing perpetuities. Consider a growing perpetuity A, where the first payment of C occurs at date 1. Next, consider a growing perpetuity B, where the first payment of $C(1 + g)^T$ is made at date $T + 1$. Both perpetuities grow at rate g. The growing annuity over T periods is the difference between annuity A and annuity B. This can be represented as:

Date	0	1	2	3	...	T	T+1	T+2	T+3
Perpetuity A		C	$C \times (1+g)$	$C \times (1+g)^2$	...	$C \times (1+g)^{T-1}$	$C \times (1+g)^T$	$C \times (1+g)^{T+1}$	$C \times (1+g)^{T+2}$ ...
Perpetuity B							$C \times (1+g)^T$	$C \times (1+g)^{T+1}$	$C \times (1+g)^{T+2}$ ...
Annuity		C	$C \times (1+g)$	$C \times (1+g)^2$	...	$C \times (1+g)^{T-1}$			

The value of perpetuity A is $\dfrac{C}{r-g}$.

The value of perpetuity B is $\dfrac{C \times (1+g)^T}{r-g} \times \dfrac{1}{(1+r)^T}$.

The difference between the two perpetuities is given by (5.15).

EXAMPLE

In a previous example, Jon Rabinowitz and Gila Messeri planned to make 17 identical payments to fund the university education of their daughter, Gabrielle. Alternatively, imagine that they planned to increase their payments at 4 percent per year. What would their first payment be?

The first two steps of the previous Messeri–Rabinowitz example showed that the present value of the university costs was $9,422.91. These two steps would be the same here. However, the third step must be altered. Now we must ask, How much should their first payment be so that, if payments increase by 4 percent per year, the present value of all payments will be $9,422.91?

We set the growing annuity formula equal to $9,422.91 and solve for C:

$$C[1/r - g - (1/r - g)(1 + g/1 + r)^T]$$
$$= C[1/0.14 - 0.04 - (1/0.14 - 0.04)(1.04/1.14)^{17}]$$
$$= \$9,422.91$$

Here, $C = \$1,192.78$. Thus, the deposit on their daughter's first birthday is $1,192.78, the deposit on the second birthday is $1,240.49 (or $1.04 \times \$1,192.78$), and so on.

? Concept Questions

· What are the formulas for a perpetuity, growing perpetuity, annuity, and growing annuity?
· What are three important points concerning the growing perpetuity formula?
· What are four tricks concerning annuities?

Making the Decision to Convert Lottery Prize Winnings: The Case of the Singer Asset Finance Company

In 1987, Rosalind Setchfield won more than $1.3 million in the Arizona state lottery. The winnings were to be paid in 20 yearly installments of $65,276.79. Eight years later, in 1995, Mrs. Setchfield received a phone call from a salesman for the Singer Asset Finance Company of West Palm Beach, Florida. The Singer company offered to give her $140,000 immediately for one-half of the next nine lottery cheques (i.e., $140,000 now for $32,638.39 × 9 = $293,745.51 over nine years). Singer is a prize broker with many employees whose main job is to track down million-dollar-lottery prizewinners like Mrs. Setchfield. Singer knows that many people are eager to trade all or part of their promised winnings for a discounted lump sum immediately. Singer is part of a growing $700 million prize-broker business. Singer and Woodbridge Sterling Capital currently account for about 80 percent of the market for lottery prize conversions. Prize brokers like Singer resell their rights to receive future payouts (called structured payouts) to institutional investors such as SunAmerica, Inc., or the John Hancock Mutual Life Insurance Co. In the case of Mrs. Setchfield, the investor was the Enhance Financial Service Group, a New York municipal bond reinsurer. Singer had arranged to sell its stake in Mrs. Setchfield's lottery prize to Enhance for $196,000 and would make a quick $56,000 profit if she accepted the offer. Mrs. Setchfield accepted Singer's offer and the deal was made.

How was Singer able to structure a deal that resulted in a $56,000 profit? The answer is that individuals and institutions have different intertemporal consumption preferences. Mrs. Setchfield's family had experienced some financial difficulties and was in need of some immediate cash. She didn't want to wait nine years for her prize winnings. On the other hand, the Enhance Group had some excess cash and was very willing to make a $196,000 investment in order to receive the rights to obtain half of Mrs. Setchfield's prize winnings, or $32,638.39 a year for nine years. The discount rate that Enhance Group applied to the future payouts was about 8.96 percent (i.e., the discount rate that equates the present value of $196,000 with Singer's right to receive their equal payments of $32,638.39).

The discount rate that Mrs. Setchfield used was 18.1 percent, reflecting her aversion to deferred cash flows.

Source: Vanessa Williams, "How Major Players Turn Lottery Jackpots into Guaranteed Bet," *The Wall Street Journal*, September 23, 1997.

5.5 What Is a Firm Worth?

Suppose you are a business appraiser who determines the value of small companies. The lesson you learn from this chapter is that the present value of a firm depends upon its future cash flows.

Let us consider the example of a firm that is expected to generate net cash flows (cash inflows minus cash outflows) of $5,000 in the first year and $2,000 for each of the next five years. The firm can be sold for $10,000 seven years from now. The owners of the firm would like to be able to make 10 percent on their investment.

The value of the firm is found by multiplying the net cash flow by the appropriate present value factor. The value of the firm is simply the sum of the present values of the individual net cash flows.

The present value of the net cash flows is given below:

The Present Value of the Firm

End of Year	Net Cash Flow of the Firm	Present Value Factor (10%)	Present Value of Net Cash Flows
1	$ 5,000	0.90909	$ 4,545.45
2	2,000	0.82645	1,652.90
3	2,000	0.75131	1,502.62
4	2,000	0.68301	1,366.02
5	2,000	0.62092	1,241.84
6	2,000	0.56447	1,128.94
7	10,000	0.51315	5,131.58
		Present value of firm	$16,569.35

We can also use the simplifying formula for an annuity to give us

$$\frac{\$5,000}{1.1} + \frac{\$2,000}{1.1} \times A_{0.10}^5 + \frac{10,000}{(1.1)^7} = \$16,569.35$$

Suppose you have the opportunity to acquire the firm for $12,000. Should you make this investment? The answer is yes because the NPV is positive.

$$\text{NPV} = \text{PV} - \text{Cost}$$
$$\$4,569.35 = \$16,569.35 - \$12,000$$

The incremental value (NPV) of acquiring the firm is $4,569.35.

EXAMPLE

The Napoli Pizza Company is contemplating investing $1 million in four new outlets in Calgary. Matthew Lee, the firm's chief financial officer (CFO), has estimated that the investments will pay out cash flows of $200,000 per year for nine years and nothing thereafter. (The cash flows will occur at the end of each year and there will be no cash flow after year 9.) Mr. Lee has determined that the relevant discount rate for this investment is 15 percent. This is the rate of return that the firm can earn for comparable projects. Should the Napoli Pizza Company make the investments in the new outlets?

The decision can be evaluated as:

$$\text{NPV} = -\$1,000,000 + \frac{\$200,000}{1.15} + \frac{\$200,000}{(1.15)^2} + \ldots + \frac{\$200,000}{(1.15)^9}$$

$$= -\$1,000,000 + \$200,000 \times A_{0.15}^9$$

$$= -\$1,000,000 + \$954,316.78$$

$$= -\$45,683.22$$

The present value of the four new outlets is only $954,316.78. The outlets are worth less than they cost. The Napoli Pizza Company should not make the investment because the NPV is −$45,683.22. If the Napoli Pizza Company requires a 15 percent rate of return, the new outlets are not a good investment.

5.6 SUMMARY AND CONCLUSIONS

1. Two basic concepts, *future value* and *present value*, were introduced in the beginning of this chapter. With a 10 percent interest rate, an investor with $1 today can generate a future value of $1.10 in a year, $1.21 [$1 × $(1.10)^2$] in two years, and so on. Conversely, present value analysis places a current value on a later cash flow. With the same 10 percent interest rate, a dollar to be received in one year has a present value of $0.909($1/1.10) in year 0. A dollar to be received in two years has a present value of $0.826 [$1/$(1.10)^2$].

2. One commonly expresses the interest rate as, say, 12 percent per year. However, one can speak of the interest rate as 3 percent per quarter. Although the stated annual interest rate remains 12 percent (3 percent × 4), the effective annual interest rate is 12.55 percent [$(1.03)^4 - 1$]. In other words, the compounding process increases the future value of an investment. The limiting case is continuous compounding, where funds are assumed to be reinvested every infinitesimal instant.

3. A basic quantitative technique for financial decision making is net present value analysis. The net present value formula for an investment that generates cash flows (C_t) in future periods is

$$\text{NPV} = -C_0 + \frac{C_1}{1+r} + \frac{C_2}{(1+r)^2} + \ldots + \frac{C_T}{(1+r)^T} = -C_0 + \sum_{t=1}^{T}\frac{C_t}{(1+r)^t}$$

The formula assumes that the cash flow at date 0 is the initial investment (a cash outflow).

4. Frequently, the actual calculation of present value is long and tedious. The computation of the present value of a long-term mortgage with monthly payments is a good example of this. We presented four simplifying formulas:

$$\text{Perpetuity: PV} = \frac{C}{r}$$

$$\text{Growing perpetuity: PV} = \frac{C}{r-g}$$

$$\text{Annuity: PV} = C\left[\frac{1}{r} - \frac{1}{r(1+r)^T}\right]$$

$$\text{Growing annuity: PV} = C\left[\frac{1}{r-g} - \frac{1}{r-g}\times\left(\frac{1+g}{1+r}\right)^T\right]$$

5. We stressed a few practical considerations in the application of these formulas:
   a. The numerator in each of the formulas, C, is the cash flow to be received *one full period* hence.
   b. Cash flows are generally irregular in practice. To avoid unwieldy problems, assumptions to create more regular cash flows are made both in this textbook and in practice.
   c. A number of present value problems involve annuities (or perpetuities) beginning a few periods hence. Students should practise combining the annuity (or perpetuity) formula with the discounting formula to solve these problems.
   d. Annuities and perpetuities may have periods of every two or every n years, rather than once a year. They may also have shorter periods like one month or one quarter. The annuity and perpetuity formulas can easily handle such circumstances.
   e. One frequently encounters problems where the present value of one annuity must be equated with the present value of another annuity.

KEY TERMS

Annual percentage rate 102		Future value 90	
Annuity 109		Growing annuity 116	
Annuity factor 111		Growing perpetuity 107	
Compounding 94		Net present value (NPV) 92	
Compound interest 94		Perpetuity 106	
Compound value 90		Present value (PV) 91	
Continuous compounding 104		Present value factor 99	
Discounting 98		Simple interest 94	
Effective annual interest rate 102		Stated annual interest rate 102	

SUGGESTED READING

To learn how to perform the mathematics of present value, we encourage you to see the handbooks that come with the Hewlett-Packard HP 19BII calculator.

We also recommend:

M. White, *Financial Analysis with a Calculator*, 5th ed. Burr Ridge, Ill.: McGraw-Hill/Irwin, 2004.

QUESTIONS & PROBLEMS[18]

Annual Compounding

5.1 Compute the future value of $1,000 compounded annually for
   a. 10 years at 5 percent
   b. 10 years at 7 percent
   c. 20 years at 5 percent
   d. Why is the interest earned in part (c) not twice the amount earned in part (a)?

5.2 Calculate the present value of the following cash flows discounted at 10 percent.
   a. $1,000 received seven years from today.
   b. $2,000 received one year from today.
   c. $500 received eight years from today.

5.3 Would you rather receive $1,000 today or $2,000 in 10 years? Assume a discount rate of 8 percent.

---

[18]The following conventions are used in the questions and problems for this chapter.

If more frequent compounding than once a year is indicated, the problem will either state: (1) both a stated annual interest rate and a compounding period, or (2) an effective annual interest rate.

If annual compounding is indicated, the problem will provide an annual interest rate. Since the stated annual interest rate and the effective annual interest rate are the same here, we use the simpler annual interest rate.

Chapter 5   The Time Value of Money

5.4   The government has issued a bond that will pay $1,000 in 25 years. The bond will pay no interim coupon payments. What is the present value of the bond if the discount rate is 10 percent?

5.5   A firm has an estimated pension liability of $1.5 million due 27 years from today. If the firm can invest in a risk-free security with an interest rate of 4 percent, how much must the firm invest today to be able to make the $1.5 million payment?

5.6   You have won the Florida state lottery. Lottery officials offer you the choice of the following alternative payouts:

Alternative 1: $10,000,000 one year from now.

Alternative 2: $20,000,000 five years from now.

Which alternative should you choose if the discount rate is:

a. 0 percent?

b. 10 percent?

c. 20 percent?

d. What discount rate makes the two alternatives equally attractive to you?

5.7   You are selling your house. The Smiths have offered you $115,000. They will pay you immediately. The Joneses have offered you $150,000, but they cannot pay you until three years from today. The interest rate is 10 percent. Which offer should you choose?

5.8   Suppose you bought a bond that will pay $1,000 in 20 years. No intermediate coupon payments will be made. If the appropriate interest rate is 8 percent,

a. what is the current price of the bond?

b. what will the price be 10 years from today?

c. what will the price be 15 years from today?

Assume the interest rate does not change over the life of the bond.

5.9   Ann Woodhouse wants to invest in raw land. She expects to own the property for 10 years and to sell it at the end of the 10th year for $5 million. There are no other cash flows. What is the most she would be willing to pay for the property if the appropriate discount rate is 12 percent?

5.10   You have the opportunity to make an investment of $900,000. If you make this investment now, you will receive $120,000, $250,000 and $800,000 one, two, and three years from today, respectively. The appropriate discount rate for this investment is 12 percent.

a. Should you make the investment?

b. What is the net present value (NPV) of this opportunity?

c. If the discount rate is 11 percent, should you invest? Compute the NPV to support your answer.

5.11   You have the opportunity to invest in a machine that costs $340,000. The machine generates revenues of $100,000 at the end of each year and requires maintenance costs of $10,000 at the beginning of each year. The machine incurs a maintenance cost today because of start-up expenses. If the economic life of the machine is five years and the relevant discount rate is 10 percent, should you buy the machine? What if the relevant discount rate is 9 percent?

5.12   Today a firm signed a contract to sell a capital asset for $90,000. The firm will receive the payment five years from today. The asset costs $60,000 to produce, payable immediately.

a. If the appropriate discount rate is 10 percent, what is the NPV of the contract?

b. At what discount rate will the firm break even on the sale of the asset?

5.13   Your aunt owns an auto dealership. She promised to pay you $3,000 for your car when you graduate one year from now. However, your roommate offered you $3,500 for the car now. The prevailing interest rate is 12 percent. If the future value of the benefit from owning the car for one additional year is $1,000, should you accept your aunt's offer? You are not planning to buy another car and will not need the car after you graduate.

5.14 You wish to purchase a new convertible 12 years from today. At that time, the car will cost $80,000. You currently have $10,000 to invest. What rate must your investment earn so that you can pay for the car?

5.15 Suppose you deposit $1,000 in an account at the end of each of the next four years. If the account earns 12 percent annually, how much will be in the account at the end of seven years?

Compounding Periods

5.16 What is the future value three years hence of $1,000 invested in an account with a stated annual interest rate of 8 percent,
   a. compounded annually?
   b. compounded semiannually?
   c. compounded monthly?
   d. compounded continuously?
   e. Why does the future value increase as the compounding period shortens?

5.17 Compute the future value of $1,000 continuously compounded for
   a. five years at a stated annual interest rate of 12 percent.
   b. three years at a stated annual interest rate of 10 percent.
   c. 10 years at a stated annual interest rate of 5 percent.
   d. eight years at a stated annual interest rate of 7 percent.

5.18 Calculate the present value of $5,000 received 12 years from today. Assume a stated annual interest rate of 10 percent, compounded quarterly.

5.19 First Canadian Bank offers a stated annual interest rate of 4.1 percent, compounded quarterly, while the Home Bank offers a stated annual interest rate of 4.05 percent, compounded monthly. In which bank should you deposit your money?

Perpetuities and Growing Perpetuities

5.20 An investor purchasing a British consol is entitled to receive annual payments from the British government forever. What is the price of a consol that pays £120 annually if the next payment occurs one year from today? The market interest rate is 15 percent.

Annual compounding

5.21 Assuming an interest rate of 10 percent, calculate the present value of the following streams of yearly payments:
   a. $1,000 per year, forever, with the first payment one year from today.
   b. $500 per year, forever, with the first payment two years from today.
   c. $2,420 per year, forever, with the first payment three years from today.

5.22 Given an interest rate of 10 percent per year, what is the value at the end of year 5 of a perpetual stream of $120 annual payments starting at the end of year 9?

5.23 Harris, Inc., paid a $3 dividend yesterday. If the firm raises its dividend 5 percent every year and the appropriate discount rate is 12 percent, what is the price of Harris stock?

5.24 In its most recent corporate report, Williams, Inc., apologized to its shareholders for not paying a dividend. The report states that management will pay a $1 dividend next year. That dividend will grow at 4 percent every year thereafter. If the discount rate is 10 percent, how much are you willing to pay for a share of Williams, Inc.?

5.25 Mark Weinstein has been working on an advanced technology in laser eye surgery. His technology will be available in the near term. He anticipates his first annual cash flow from the technology to be $200,000, received two years from today. Subsequent annual cash flows will grow at 5 percent, in perpetuity. What is the present value of the technology if the discount rate is 10 percent?

5.26 Barrett Pharmaceuticals is considering a drug project that costs $100,000 today and is expected to generate end-of-year annual cash flow of $50,000, forever. At what discount rate would Barrett be indifferent between accepting or rejecting the project?

Compounding Periods

5.27 A prestigious investment bank designed a new security that pays a quarterly dividend of $10 in perpetuity. The first dividend occurs one quarter from today. What is the price of the security if the stated annual interest rate is 12 percent, compounded quarterly?

5.28 World Transportation, Inc., is expected to wait five years and then to initiate its quarterly dividend of $1 at the end of the following quarter, and the dividend is expected to remain constant, forever. What is the price of World Transportation stock if the stated annual interest rate is 15 percent, compounded quarterly?

Annuities and Growing Annuities

5.29 Should you buy an asset that will generate income of $1,200 at the end of each year for eight years? The price of the asset is $6,200 and the annual interest rate is 10 percent.

Annual Compounding

5.30 What is the present value of an annuity of $2,000 per year, with the first cash flow received three years from today and the last one received 22 years from today? Use a discount rate of 8 percent.

5.31 What is the value today of a 15-year annuity that pays $500 a year? The annuity's first payment occurs at the end of year 6. The annual interest rate is 12 percent for years 1 through 5, and 15 percent thereafter.

5.32 You are offered the opportunity to buy a note for $12,800. The note will pay $2,000 at the end of each of the next 10 years. If you buy the note, what rate of interest will you receive?

EXCEL

5.33 You need $25,000 to buy a car five years from now.

  a. In order to buy the car, you plan to make equal payments at the end of every year into an account yielding 7 percent per year. What are these annual payments?

  b. Your rich uncle died and left you $20,000. How much of it must you put into the same account as a lump sum today to meet your goal if you do not want to make any of the annual payments calculated in part (a)?

5.34 Nancy Ferris bought a building for $120,000. She paid 15 percent down and agreed to pay the balance in 20 equal, end-of-year, installments. What are the equal installments if the annual interest rate is 10 percent?

5.35 You have recently won the super jackpot in the Washington state lottery. On reading the fine print, you discover that you have the following two options:

  a. You receive 31 annual payments of $160,000, with the first payment being delivered today. The income will be taxed at a rate of 28 percent. Taxes are withheld when the cheques are issued.

  b. You receive $446,000 now, and you will not have to pay taxes on this amount. In addition, beginning one year from today, you will receive $101,055 each year for 30 years. The cash flows from this annuity will be taxed at 28 percent.

  Using a discount rate of 10 percent, which option should you select?

EXCEL

5.36 You are saving for the university education of your two children. They are two years apart in age; one will begin university 15 years from today and the other will begin 17 years from today. You estimate your children's university expenses to be $21,000 per year per child, payable at the end of each school year. The annual interest rate is 15 percent. How much money must you deposit in an account each year to fund your children's education? Your deposits begin one year from today. You will make your last deposit when your oldest child enters university.

5.37 A well-known insurance company offers a policy known as the "Estate Creator Six Pay." Typically, a parent or grandparent buys a policy for a child at the child's birth. The details of the policy are as follows.

EXCEL

The purchaser (say, the parent) makes the following six payments to the insurance company.

First birthday	$750	Fourth birthday	$800
Second birthday	$750	Fifth birthday	$800
Third birthday	$750	Sixth birthday	$800

No more payments are made after the child's sixth birthday. When the child reaches the age of 65, he or she receives $250,000. If the relevant interest rate is 6 percent for the first six years and 7 percent for all subsequent years, is the policy worth buying?

5.38 Your company is considering either buying or leasing a $120,000 piece of equipment for the next 10 years. The company plans to use the equipment indefinitely. The annual lease payments of $15,000 begin today. The lease includes an option for your company to buy the equipment for $25,000 at the end of the leasing period (i.e., 10 years). Assume that, if the company decides to lease, the company will exercise the option to buy the equipment at the end of the 10-year lease. Should your company accept the lease offer if the appropriate discount rate is 8 percent per year?

5.39 Your job pays you only once a year, for all the work you did over the previous 12 months. Today, December 31, you just received your salary of $50,000 and you plan to spend all of it. However, you want to start saving for retirement beginning next year. You have decided that one year from today you will begin depositing 2 percent of your annual salary in an account that will earn 8 percent per year. Your salary will increase at 4 percent per year throughout your career. How much money will you have on the date of your retirement 40 years from today?

5.40 You must decide whether or not to purchase new capital equipment. The cost of the machine is $5,000. It will produce the following cash flows.

Year	Cash Flow
1	$ 700
2	900
3	1,000
4	1,000
5	1,000
6	1,000
7	1,250
8	1,375

The appropriate discount rate is 10 percent. Should you purchase the equipment?

5.41 Your younger brother has come to you for advice. He is about to enter university and has two options open to him. His first option is to study engineering. If he does this, his undergraduate degree would cost him $12,000 a year for four years. Having obtained his undergraduate degree, he would need to gain two years of practical experience. He would earn $20,000 in the first year and he would earn $25,000 in the second year. He would then need to obtain his master's degree, which will cost $15,000 a year for two years. After completion of his master's degree, he will be fully qualified as an engineer and can earn $40,000 per year for 25 years.

His other alternative is to study accounting. If he does this, he would pay $13,000 a year for four years and then he would earn $31,000 per year for 30 years.

The effort involved in the two careers is the same, so he is only interested in the earnings that the jobs provide. All earnings and costs are paid at the end of the year.

a. What advice would you give him if the market interest rate is 5 percent?

b. A day later he comes back and says that he took your advice, but in fact, the market interest rate was 6 percent. Has your brother made the right choice?

5.42 Tom Adams has received a job offer from a large investment bank as a clerk to an associate banker. His base salary will be $35,000. He will receive his first annual salary payment one year from the day he begins to work. In addition, he will get an immediate

$10,000 bonus for joining the company. His salary will grow at 4 percent each year. Each year he will receive a bonus equal to 10 percent of his salary. Mr. Adams is expected to work for 25 years. What is the present value of the offer if the discount rate is 12 percent?

5.43 Great White North Publishing Company is trying to decide whether or not to revise its popular textbook, *Financial Psychoanalysis Made Simple*. It has estimated that the revision will cost $40,000. Cash flows from increased sales will be $10,000 the first year. These cash flows will increase by 7 percent per year. The book will go out of print five years from now. Assume that the initial cost is paid now and revenues are received at the end of each year. If the company requires a 10 percent return for such an investment, should it undertake the revision?

5.44 Ian Krassner wants to save money to meet two objectives. First, he wants to retire 31 years from today with a retirement income of $300,000 per year for 20 years. The first retirement payment will occur 31 years from today. Second, he would like to purchase a cabin in the mountains 10 years from today at an estimated cost of $350,000. He can afford to save only $40,000 at the end of each year for the first 10 years. He expects to earn 7 percent per year on his savings. Assuming he saves the same amount each year, what must Ian save annually at the end of year 11 through year 30 to meet his objectives?

Compounding Periods

5.45 On January 1, Jack Ferguson signed a three-year contract to work for a computer software company. He will be paid $5,000 at the end of each month and will receive a bonus of $10,000 at each year-end. What is the present value of the contract if the stated annual interest rate, compounded monthly, is 12 percent?

5.46 Sarah Buchwalter bought a $15,000 Honda Civic with 20 percent down and financed the rest with a four-year loan at an 8 percent stated annual interest rate, compounded monthly. What is her monthly payment if she makes the first payment one month after the purchase?

5.47 On September 1, 2003, Susan Chao bought a motorcycle for $10,000. She paid $1,000 down and financed the balance with a five-year loan at a stated annual interest rate of 9.6 percent, compounded monthly. She started the monthly payments exactly one month after the purchase, i.e., October 1, 2003. Two years later, at the end of October, 2005, Susan got a new job and decided to pay off the loan. If the bank charges her a 1 percent prepayment penalty based on the loan balance, how much must she pay the bank on November 1, 2005?

5.48 When Marilyn Monroe died, ex-husband Joe DiMaggio vowed to place fresh flowers on her grave every Sunday as long as he lived. The week after she died in 1962, a bunch of fresh flowers that the former baseball player thought appropriate for the star cost about $5. Based on actuarial tables, "Joltin' Joe" could expect to live for 30 years after the actress died. Assume that the stated annual interest rate, compounded weekly, is 10.4 percent. Also, assume that the price of the flowers will increase at 3.9 percent per year, when expressed as a stated annual growth rate, compounded weekly. Assuming that each year has exactly 52 weeks, what is the present value of this commitment? Joe began purchasing flowers the week after Marilyn died.

5.49 In January 1984, Richard "Goose" Gossage signed a contract to play for the San Diego Padres that guaranteed him a minimum of $9,955,000 (undiscounted). The guaranteed payments were $875,000 in 1984, $650,000 in 1985, $800,000 in 1986, $1 million in 1987, $1 million in 1988, and $300,000 in 1989. In addition, the contract called for $5,330,000 (undiscounted) in deferred money payable at the rate of $240,000 per year from 1990 through 2006 and then $125,000 a year from 2007 through 2016. If the annual interest rate is 9 percent and all payments are made on July 1 of each year, what would the present value of these guaranteed payments be on January 1, 1984? Assume an interest rate of 4.4 percent per six months. If he were to receive an equal annual salary at the end of each of the five years from 1984 through 1988, what would his equivalent annual salary be? Ignore taxes throughout this problem.

126

Part II   Value and Capital Budgeting

5.50 Mike Bayles has just arranged to purchase a $400,000 vacation home in the Bahamas with a 20 percent down payment. The mortgage has an 8 percent stated annual interest rate, compounded monthly, and calls for equal monthly payments over the next 30 years. His first payment will be due one month from now. However, the mortgage has an eight-year balloon payment, meaning that the balance of the loan must be paid off at the end of year 8. There were no other transaction costs or finance charges. How much will Mike's balloon payment be in eight years?

5.51 You want to lease a set of golf clubs from Pings Ltd. The lease contract is in the form of 24 equal monthly payments at a 12 percent stated annual interest rate, compounded monthly. Since the clubs cost $4,000 retail, Pings wants the PV of the lease payments to equal $4,000. Suppose that your first payment is due immediately. What will your monthly lease payments be?

5.52 A 10-year annuity pays $900 per year. The first $900 will be paid five years from now. If the stated interest rate is 8 percent, compounded quarterly, what is the present value of this annuity?

5.53 Larry Harris, CFO of MakeMyDecision, is evaluating the financial viability of a new production line for graphite electrodes. His research team has provided him with the following information:

Investment required to set up the production line: $1.8 million

Cash flow projections:

First year of production (production begins 3 years after initial investment): $60,000

Cash flow grows at 4% annually for first five years and then at a constant rate forever

Required rate of return: 10%

For Larry to accept the project, what should the growth rate be after the first five years of operation?

5.54 Paul Adams owns a health club in downtown Toronto. He charges his customers an annual fee of $400 and has an existing customer base of 500. Paul plans to raise the annual fee by 10 percent every year and expects the club membership to grow at a constant rate of 3 percent for the next five years. The overall expenses of running the health club are $80,000 a year and are expected to grow at the inflation rate of 2 percent annually. After five years, Paul plans to buy a luxury boat for $500,000, close the health club, and travel the world in his boat for the rest of his life. What is the annual amount that Paul can spend while on his world tour if he will have no money left in the bank when he dies? Assume Paul has a remaining life of 15 years and earns 8 percent on his savings.

5.55 A real estate investor in Vancouver is considering buying a condominium. The condo is priced at $450,000 and a bank is offering a mortgage of $337,500 for 25 years at 5.5 percent APR compounded semiannually. Find the monthly mortgage payment and calculate the amortization schedule for the first five years.

S & P
PROBLEM
STANDARD
&POOR'S

5.56 Under the "Excel Analytics" link find the "Mthly. Adj. Price" for BCE stock. What was your annual return over the last four years assuming you purchased the stock at the close price four years ago? (Assume no dividends were paid.) Using this same return, what price will BCE stock sell for five years from now? ten years from now? What if the stock prices increases at 11 percent per year?

Chapter 6

How to Value Bonds and Stocks

EXECUTIVE SUMMARY

The previous chapter discussed the mathematics of compounding, discounting, and present value. We now use the mathematics of compounding and discounting to determine the present values of financial instruments, beginning with a discussion of how bonds are valued. Since the future cash flows of bonds are known (at least for government bonds and issues of high-quality corporations with minimal default risk), application of net present value techniques is fairly straightforward. The uncertainty of future cash flows makes the pricing of stocks more difficult.

6.1 Definition and Example of a Bond

A *bond* is a certificate showing that a borrower owes a specified sum. In order to repay the money, the borrower has agreed to make interest and principal payments on designated dates. For example, imagine that Kreuger Enterprises just issued 100,000 bonds for $1,000 each carrying a coupon rate of 5 percent and a maturity of two years. Interest on the bonds is to be paid yearly. This means that

1. $100 million (or 100,000 × $1,000) has been borrowed by the firm.
2. The firm must pay interest of $5 million (or 5% × $100 million) at the end of one year.
3. The firm must pay both $5 million of interest and $100 million of principal at the end of two years.

We now consider how to value a few different types of bonds.

6.2 How to Value Bonds

Pure Discount Bonds

The **pure discount bond** is perhaps the simplest kind of bond. It promises a single payment, say $1, at a fixed future date. If the payment is one year from now, it is called a *one-year discount bond*; if it is two years from now, it is called a *two-year discount bond*, and so on. The date when the issuer of the bond makes the last payment is called the **maturity date** of the bond, or just its *maturity* for short. The bond is said to mature or *expire* on the date of its final payment. The payment at maturity ($1 in this example) is termed the bond's **face value**.

Pure discount bonds are often called *zero-coupon bonds* or *zeros* to emphasize the fact that the holder receives no cash payments until maturity. We will use the terms *zero*, *bullet*, and *discount* interchangeably to refer to bonds that pay no coupons.

The first row of Figure 6.1 shows the pattern of cash flows from a four-year pure discount bond. Note that the face value, F, is paid when the bond expires in the 48th month. There are no payments of either interest or principal prior to this date.

In Chapter 5, we indicated that one discounts a future cash flow to determine its present value. The present value of a pure discount bond can easily be determined by the techniques of the previous chapter. For short, we sometimes speak of the *value* of a bond instead of its present value.

Consider a pure discount bond that pays a face value of F in T years, where the interest rate is r in each of the T years. (We also refer to this rate as the *market interest rate*.) Because the face value is the only cash flow that the bond pays, the present value of this face amount is

Value of a Pure Discount Bond:

$$PV = \frac{F}{(1 + r)^T}$$

The present value formula can produce some surprising results. Suppose that the interest rate is 10 percent. Consider a bond with a face value of $1 million that matures in 20 years. Applying the formula to this bond, its PV is given by

$$PV = \frac{\$1 \text{ million}}{(1.1)^{20}}$$
$$= 148,644$$

or only about 15 percent of the face value.

Level-Coupon Bonds

Many bonds, however, are not of the simple, pure discount variety. Typical bonds issued by either governments or corporations offer cash payments not just at maturity, but also at regular times in between. For example, payments on Canadian government issues and Canadian corporate bonds are made every six months until the bond matures. These payments are called the **coupons** of the bond. The middle row of Figure 6.1 illustrates the case of a four-year, *level-coupon* bond: The coupon, C, is paid every six months and is the same throughout the life of the bond.

Note that the face value of the bond, F, is paid at maturity (end of year 4). F is sometimes called the *principal* or the *denomination*. Bonds issued in Canada typically have face values of $1,000, though this can vary with the type of bond.

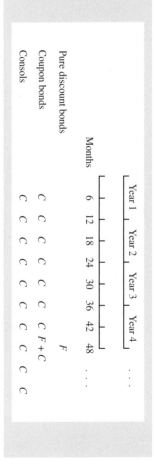

FIGURE 6.1

Different Types of Bonds: C, Coupon Paid Every Six Months; F, Face Value at Year 4 (maturity for pure discount and coupon bonds)

	Year 1		Year 2		Year 3		Year 4		
Months	6	12	18	24	30	36	42	48	…
Pure discount bonds								F	
Coupon bonds	C	C	C	C	C	C	C	F + C	…
Consols	C	C	C	C	C	C	C	C	C

As we mentioned above, the value of a bond is simply the present value of its cash flows. Therefore, the value of a level-coupon bond is merely the present value of its stream of coupon payments plus the present value of its repayment of principal. Because a level-coupon bond is just an annuity of C each period, together with a payment at maturity of $1,000, the value of a level-coupon bond is

Value of a Level-Coupon Bond:

$$PV = \frac{C}{1+r} + \frac{C}{(1+r)^2} + \cdots + \frac{C}{(1+r)^T} + \frac{\$1,000}{(1+r)^T}$$

where C is the coupon and the face value, F, is $1,000. The value of the bond can be rewritten as

Value of a Level-Coupon Bond:

$$PV = C \times A_r^T + \frac{\$1,000}{(1+r)^T}$$

As mentioned in the previous chapter, A_r^T is the present value of an annuity of $1 per period for T periods at an interest rate per period of r.

EXAMPLE

Selected bond trading figures for April 27, 2004 appear in Figure 6.2. Suppose an investor was interested in the EDC 5.000 May 04/06. This is jargon that means the bond was issued by Export Development Corporation, a federal Crown corporation, and the annual coupon rate is 5.00 percent.[1] The face value is $1,000, implying that the yearly coupon is $50.00 (5% × $1,000). Interest is paid each November and May, implying that the coupon every six months is $25 ($50/2). The face value will be paid out in May 2006, two years later. By this we mean that the purchaser obtains claims to the following cash flows:

11/04	05/05	11/05	05/06
$25	$25	$25	$25 + $1,000

If the stated annual interest rate in the market is 2.86 percent per year, what is the present value of the bond?

The standard North American method of expressing both bond coupons and bond yields is as a stated rate per year, compounded semiannually. Our work on compounding in the previous chapter showed that the interest rate over any six-month interval is one-half of the stated annual interest rate. In the current example, this semiannual rate is 1.43 percent (2.86%/2). Since the coupon payment in each period is $25, and there are four of these payment dates, the present value of the bond is

$$PV = \frac{\$25}{(1.043)} + \frac{\$25}{(1.043)^2} + \cdots + \frac{\$25}{(1.043)^4} + \frac{\$25}{(1.043)^4} + \frac{\$1,000}{(1.043)^4}$$

$$= \$25 \times A_{0.0143}^4 + \$1,000/(1.043)^4$$

$$= \$96.52 + \$944.79$$

$$= \$1,041.31$$

Traders will generally quote the bond as 104.13, indicating that it is selling at 104.13 percent of the face value of $1,000. This can be seen in Figure 6.2 in the "Bid $" column for our bond. (The small difference in price ($0.03) between our price calculations and the newspaper listing reflects accrued interest arising from the few days between April 27 and May 4 and rounding differences.)

---

[1] The coupon rate is specific to the bond and indicates what cash flow should appear in the numerator of the NPV equation. The coupon rate does not appear in the denominator of the NPV equation.

FIGURE 6.2
Sample of a Bond Quotation

BONDS

INDEXES

RBC CM Index	Index level	Total ret	Price ret	MTD tot.ret
Market	449.42	0.03	0.01	-1.64
Short	374.59	0.06	0.02	-0.89
Intermed	463.60	0.05	0.03	-1.89
Long	562.15	0.02	-0.03	-2.62
Govts	443.63	0.05	0.01	-1.70
Canadas	428.34	0.06	0.01	-1.60
Prov	482.75	0.06	0.01	-1.90
Munis	169.66	0.04	0.01	-2.04
Corps	487.03	0.06	0.01	-1.45

FEDERAL

	Coupon	Mat. Date	Bid $	Yld%
Canada	3.500	Jun 01/05	101.29	2.30
Canada	6.000	Sep 01/05	104.65	2.46
Canada	12.250	Sep 01/05	112.85	2.46
Canada	8.750	Sep 01/05	109.52	2.61
Canada	12.500	Mar 01/06	117.30	2.80
Canada	5.750	Sep 01/06	106.26	2.96
Canada	14.000	Oct 01/06	125.55	3.00
Canada	7.000	Dec 01/06	109.71	3.07
Canada	7.250	Jun 01/07	111.49	3.31
Canada	4.500	Sep 01/07	103.38	3.42
Canada	13.000	Oct 01/07	130.55	3.46
Canada	10.000	Jun 01/08	123.92	3.65
Canada	6.000	Sep 01/08	108.69	3.69
Canada	4.250	Sep 01/08	101.84	3.79
Canada	5.500	Jun 01/09	135.88	3.99
Canada	11.000	Jun 01/09	132.28	3.94
Canada	4.50	Sep 01/09	100.89	4.06
Canada	10.750	Mar 01/10	132.31	4.05
Canada	9.750	Mar 01/10	128.61	4.18
Canada	5.500	Jun 01/10	106.77	4.23
Canada	9.500	Jun 01/10	128.36	4.18
Canada	9.000	Mar 01/11	127.25	4.35
Canada	6.000	Jun 01/11	109.50	4.42
Canada	8.500	Jun 01/11	124.81	4.39
Canada	8.000	Jun 01/11	121.24	4.57
Canada	4.750	Jun 01/14	104.54	4.68
Canada	5.250	Jun 01/13	104.14	4.68
Canada	11.250	Jun 01/15	156.26	4.69
Canada	5.750	Jun 01/22	162.54	4.98
Canada	9.250	Jun 01/22	153.63	5.03
Canada	8.000	Jun 01/23	149.28	5.06
Canada	9.000	Jun 01/25	147.41	5.19
Canada	8.000	Jun 01/27	133.79	5.25
CHT	5.750	Dec 01/06	106.53	5.28
CHT	5.527	Jun 15/96	107.39	5.25
CHT	4.750	Mar 15/08	105.35	2.92
CMHC	4.400	Mar 15/08	103.98	3.29
CMHC	5.750	Dec 01/04	102.41	3.75
CMHC	5.750	Dec 01/05	102.17	2.34
CMHC	5.250	Dec 01/06	105.57	2.66
CMHC	5.750	Dec 03/07	105.21	3.14
CMHC	5.300	Jun 01/33	105.66	3.61
EDC	5.500	Jun 18/04	100.47	2.02
EDC	5.000	May 04/06	104.16	2.36
EDC	5.000	Feb 09/09	104.29	4.02

CORPORATE

	Coupon	Mat. Date	Bid $	Yld%
AGT Lt	8.800	Sep 22/25	126.52	6.49
BCTT	3.838	Mar 17/09	98.35	4.24
BCE	6.750	Oct 30/07	108.84	4.02
BCE	7.350	Oct 30/09	112.81	4.68
Bell	7.500	May 09/05	104.07	2.46
Bell	6.550	<ar 31/09	101.77	6.41
BMO	4.660	<ar 31/09	101.82	4.31
BMO	6.903	Jun 30/10	111.07	4.93
BMO	6.647	Dec 31/10	109.59	5.15
BNS	6.685	Dec 31/11	109.59	5.15
BNS	4.515	Nov 19/08	101.56	4.14
BNS	7.310	Dec 31/10	113.46	4.92
CDP	4.950	Oct 14/08	100.79	4.01
CIBC	4.950	Jan 23/14	98.21	5.18
DimrCCF	5.940	Apr 22/10	103.23	2.59
Domtar	10.800	May 15/11	123.94	5.77
Ford C	6.650	Jun 20/05	103.66	3.35
GE CAP	4.350	Dec 01/08	102.56	2.86
GE CAP	5.300	Apr 26/06	105.20	2.96
GE CAP	5.000	Jun 03/05	105.03	3.64
GE CAP	5.150	Jul 24/07	103.83	3.95
GE CAP	5.700	Jun 06/13	100.00	5.14
GE CAP	4.440	Aug 15/06	105.67	3.12
GldCrl	4.159	Dec 05/07	100.38	4.07
GldCrl	5.950	Oct 15/08	106.10	4.02
GrfAA	6.450	Dec 03/07	97.54	6.66
GrfAQA	6.200	Jun 01/07	104.68	4.36
GTC Yr	6.450	Gulf C	104.68	4.39
Gulf C	5.995	Jan 01/07	100.75	4.39
GWLife	6.140	Aug 10/10	111.03	4.70
GWLife	6.995	Dec 31/12	106.75	5.31
GWLife	6.740	Aug 10/10	105.11	5.60
GWLife	6.670	Nov 24/31	106.96	6.21
GWLife	%.672	Mar 21/43	106.01	6.22
HoRec	7.780	Apr 26/06	105.20	2.96
HSBC	6.940	Dec 31/10	115.13	5.08
HydOne	7.150	Jun 03/05	104.88	2.40
HydOne	6.400	Jun 03/05	113.72	4.55
HydOne	5.770	Dec 01/11	109.78	4.84
HydOne	7.350	Nov 15/12	105.28	5.00
HydOne	6.930	Jun 01/32	117.72	6.00
IPL	8.200	Jun 01/32	112.59	6.00
Loblaw	6.650	Nov 08/27	125.02	6.02
Loblaw	5.730	Jun 30/19	104.17	6.31
MLI	5.700	Feb 16/06	104.82	2.93
MLI	6.240	Feb 16/11	106.12	4.82
MLI	5.700	Jun 30/12	108.44	5.26

PROVINCIAL

	Coupon	Mat. Date	Bid $	Yld%
Alberta	6.375	Jun 01/04	100.38	2.01
B C	5.250	Jun 09/06	105.10	3.18
B C	6.000	Jun 09/08	108.12	3.85
B C	6.375	Aug 23/10	110.44	4.46
B C	5.750	Jan 09/12	106.62	4.71
B C	6.150	Nov 19/27	106.83	5.62
B C MF	5.700	Dec 01/29	100.75	5.64
B C MF	7.750	Jun 01/03	107.81	2.70
B C MF	5.900	Mar 24/08	107.94	2.74
HydQue	5.777	Jan 01/09	106.63	3.79
HydQue	5.500	Feb 01/05	107.45	4.65
HydQue	5.600	Jul 16/12	111.02	4.59
HydQue	9.625	Jul 15/22	146.48	5.54
HydQue	6.000	Aug 15/35	159.14	5.47
HydQue	5.750	Dec 15/35	103.20	5.77
Manit	7.750	Dec 22/25	126.35	5.63
NewBr	5.700	Jun 27/17	106.88	3.87
NewBr	6.000	Jun 27/17	106.34	5.34
Newfld	6.150	Apr 17/28	103.76	5.86
NovaSc	6.600	Jun 01/27	102.60	5.76
Ontario	9.00	Jan 19/06	107.94	2.74
Ontario	7.500	Sep 15/04	102.60	2.00
Ontario	6.200	Jun 02/31	110.37	5.71
Ontario	4.750	Mar 08/06	110.63	5.72
Ontario	5.900	Mar 08/33	100.54	2.78
Ontario	5.200	Jun 02/08	105.09	3.32
Ontario	6.125	Sep 12/07	105.69	3.54
Ontario	5.700	Dec 01/08	106.97	4.02
Ontario	3.210	Aug 19/09	98.73	3.47
Ontario	6.100	Nov 19/09	109.28	4.30
Ontario	6.200	Nov 19/09	108.87	4.52
Ontario	5.375	Dec 02/11	108.71	4.72
Ontario	4.750	Dec 22/12	98.30	4.91
Ontario	5.000	Mar 08/14	99.34	4.98
Ontario	8.109	Sep 08/23	129.47	5.08
Ontario	7.500	Mar 08/27	324.63	5.67
Ontario	9.00	Jun 02/27	110.37	5.71
Omthyd	5.850	Nov 03/05	100.50	3.38
Omthyd	7.750	Nov 03/05	101.80	5.72
Omthyd	5.600	Sep 02/08	105.56	3.85
Omthyd	8.250	Jun 22/26	132.33	5.67
Quebec	6.500	Dec 01/05	105.88	2.69
Quebec	7.750	Mar 30/06	109.14	2.82
Quebec	6.500	Jun 01/07	109.36	3.57
Quebec	5.500	Jun 01/09	105.98	4.18
Quebec	6.250	Dec 01/10	109.56	4.55
Quebec	6.000	Oct 01/12	107.32	4.93
Quebec	5.250	Jan 16/23	101.26	5.08
Quebec	9.375	Jan 16/23	143.73	5.58
Quebec	8.500	Apr 01/26	135.02	5.69
Quebec	6.000	Jun 01/32	106.60	5.77
Quebec	6.250	Jun 01/32	103.15	5.77
Saskat	5.500	May 30/25	138.25	5.63
Saskat	8.750	Aug 15/07	107.84	3.56
Toronto	6.100	Dec 12/17	106.71	5.40

INTERNATIONAL

	Coupon	Mat. Date	Bid $	Yld%
Australia	7.50	15 Se 04	102.51	5.32
Australia	8.75	15 Oc 07	111.63	5.60
Australia	15 My 13	110.44	5.63	
Britain	5.08	07 Jn 04	106.05	4.56
Britain	8.50	07 De 07	96.23	4.88
Britain	5.60	07 Ma 12	100.08	4.99
France	5.00	12 Jn 04	104.23	2.44
France	3.50	12 Jl 07	100.50	3.38
France	4.00	25 Ap 12	99.32	4.26
Germany	2.000	12 Ma 04	99.21	2.44
Germany	3.25	16 Fb 07	99.21	3.42
Germany	4.25	04 Ja 12	100.45	4.19
Italy	2.75	15 Jl 05	99.85	2.83
Italy	3.50	01 Ma 07	100.63	3.37
Italy	4.25	01 Fe 12	99.05	4.41
Japan	3.30	20 Se 04	106.72	0.15

One final note concerning level-coupon bonds: Although our example uses government bonds, corporate bonds are identical in form. For example, BMO has a 6.903 percent bond maturing in 2010. This means that BMO will make semiannual payments of $34.52 (6.903%/2 × $1000) between now and 2010 for each face value of $1,000.

Consols

Not all bonds have a final maturity date. As we mentioned in the previous chapter, consols are bonds that never stop paying a coupon, have no final maturity date, and therefore never mature. Thus, a consol is a perpetuity. In the eighteenth century the Bank of England issued such bonds, called *English consols*. These were bonds that the Bank of

England guaranteed would pay the holder a cash flow forever! Through wars and depressions, the Bank of England continued to honour this commitment, and you can still buy such bonds in London today. The Government of Canada also once sold consols. Even though these Canadian bonds were supposed to last forever and to pay their coupons forever, don't go looking for any. There was a special clause in the bond contract that gave the government the right to buy them back from the holders, and that is what the government did. Clauses like that are *call provisions*; we'll study them later.

An important current Canadian example of a consol is fixed-rate preferred stock that provides the holder a fixed dividend in perpetuity. If there were never any question that the firm would actually pay the dividend on the preferred stock, such stock would in fact be a consol.

These instruments can be valued by the perpetuity formula of the previous chapter. For example, if the marketwide interest rate is 10 percent, a consol with a yearly interest payment of $50 is valued at

$$\frac{\$50}{0.10} = \$500$$

? Concept
Questions
- Define pure discount bonds, level-coupon bonds, and consols.
- Contrast the stated interest rate and the effective annual interest rate for bonds paying semiannual interest.

6.3 Bond Concepts

We complete our discussion on bonds by considering three important concepts: the relationship between interest rates and bond prices, the concept of yield to maturity, and the idea of holding-period return.

Interest Rates and Bond Prices

The above discussion on level-coupon bonds allows us to relate bond prices to interest rates. Consider the following example.

EXAMPLE

The interest rate is 10 percent. A two-year bond with a 10 percent coupon pays interest of $100 (or $1,000 × 10%). For simplicity, we assume that the interest is paid annually. The bond is priced at its face value of $1,000:

$$\$1,000 = \frac{\$100}{1.1} + \frac{\$1,000 + \$100}{(1.1)^2}$$

If the interest rate unexpectedly rises to 12 percent, the bond sells at

$$\$966.20 = \frac{\$100}{1.12} + \frac{\$1,000 + \$100}{(1.12)^2}$$

Because $966.20 is below $1,000, the bond is said to sell at a **discount.** This is a sensible result. Now that the interest rate is 12 percent, a newly issued bond with a 12 percent coupon rate will sell at $1,000. This newly issued bond will have coupon payments of $120 (or 0.12 × $1,000).

Because our bond has interest payments of only $100, investors will pay less than $1,000 for it.

If the interest rate fell to 8 percent, the bond would sell at

$$\$1,035.67 = \frac{\$100}{1.08} + \frac{\$1,000 + \$100}{(1.08)^2}$$

Because $1,035.67 is above $1,000, the bond is said to sell at a **premium.**

Thus, we find that bond prices fall with a rise in interest rates and rise with a fall in interest rates. Furthermore, the general principle is that a level-coupon bond trades in the following ways:

1. At the face value of $1,000 if the coupon rate is equal to the marketwide interest rate.
2. At a discount if the coupon rate is below the marketwide interest rate.
3. At a premium if the coupon rate is above the marketwide interest rate.

Yield to Maturity

Let us now consider the previous example in reverse. If our bond is selling at $1,035.67, what return is a bondholder receiving? This can be answered by considering the following equation:

$$\$1,035.67 = \frac{\$100}{1 + y} + \frac{\$1,000 + \$100}{(1 + y)^2}$$

The unknown, y, is the rate of return that the holder is earning on the bond.[2] Our earlier work implies that $y = 8\%$. Thus, traders state that the bond is yielding an 8 percent return. Equivalently, they say that the bond has a **yield to maturity** of 8 percent. The yield to maturity is frequently called the bond's yield for short. So we would say the bond with its 10 percent coupon is priced to yield 8 percent at $1,035.67.

Holding-Period Return

Our example of interest rates and bond prices showed how the price of a two-year bond with a 10 percent coupon varied as market yields changed. Suppose that a bond trader bought the bond when its market yield was 12 percent and sold a month later when the yield was 8 percent. This means that the trader succeeded in buying low ($966.20) and selling high ($1,035.67). In this example the trader earned a **holding-period return** of 7.19 percent:

$$\text{Holding-period return} = (\text{Ending price} - \text{Beginning price})/\text{Beginning price}$$
$$= (\$1,035.67 - \$966.20)/\$966.20 = 7.19\%$$

This annualizes to an effective rate of $(1.0719)^{11} - 1 = 2.1463$ or 215 percent! While this is a bit extreme it does illustrate how a bond trader who could correctly anticipate shifts in market yields could make large profits. By working the example backwards we can also see how such a strategy has potentially large risks.

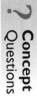

Concept Questions

- **What is the relationship between interest rates and bond prices?**
- **How does one calculate the yield to maturity on a bond?**

---

[2]Technically, the yield to maturity calculation assumes that the bond is held to maturity and all coupons are reinvested at y.

The Present Value Formulas for Bonds

Pure Discount Bonds

$$PV = \frac{F}{(1+r)^T}$$

Level-Coupon Bonds

$$PV = C\left[\frac{1}{r} - \frac{1}{r \times (1+r)^T}\right] + \frac{F}{(1+r)^T} = C \times A_r^T + \frac{F}{(1+r)^T}$$

where F is typically $1,000 for a level-coupon bond.

Consols

$$PV = \frac{C}{r}$$

6.4 The Present Value of Common Stocks

Dividends Versus Capital Gains

Our goal in this section is to value common stocks. We learned in the previous chapter that an asset's value is determined by the present value of its future cash flows. A stock provides two kinds of cash flows. First, most stocks pay dividends on a regular basis. Second, the shareholder receives the sale price when the stock is sold. Thus, in order to value common stocks, we need to answer an interesting question: Is the value of a stock equal to

1. The discounted present value of the sum of next period's dividend plus next period's stock price, or
2. The discounted present value of all future dividends?

This is the kind of question that students would love to see on a multiple-choice exam because both (1) and (2) are correct.

To see that (1) and (2) are the same, we start with an individual who will buy the stock and hold it for one year. In other words, this investor has a one-year *holding period*. In addition, the investor is willing to pay P_0 for the stock today.

$$P_0 = \frac{\text{Div}_1}{1+r} + \frac{P_1}{1+r} \qquad (6.1)$$

Div_1 is the dividend paid at year-end and P_1 is the price at year-end. P_0 is the PV of the common stock investment. The term r in the denominator is the discount rate for the stock. It is the required rate of return for investments of similar risk.

That seems easy enough, but where does P_1 come from? P_1 is not pulled out of thin air. Rather, there must be a buyer at the end of year 1 who is willing to purchase the stock for P_1. This buyer determines price by

$$P_1 = \frac{\text{Div}_2}{1+r} + \frac{P_2}{1+r} \qquad (6.2)$$

Substituting the value of P_1 from (6.2) into Equation (6.1) yields

$$P_0 = \frac{1}{1+r}\left[\text{Div}_1 + \left(\frac{\text{Div}_2 + P_2}{1+r}\right)\right] \qquad (6.3)$$

We can ask a similar question for (6.3): Where does P_2 come from? An investor at the end of year 2 is willing to pay P_2 because of the dividend and stock price at year 3. This process can be repeated ad nauseam.[3] At the end, we are left with

$$P_0 = \frac{\text{Div}_1}{1+r} + \frac{\text{Div}_2}{(1+r)^2} + \frac{\text{Div}_3}{(1+r)^3} + \cdots = \sum_{t=1}^{\infty}\frac{\text{Div}_t}{(1+r)^t} \qquad (6.4)$$

Thus, the value of a firm's common stock to the investor is equal to the present value of all of the expected future dividends.[4]

This is a very useful result. A common objection to applying present value analysis to stocks is that investors are too shortsighted to care about the long-run stream of dividends. Critics argue that an investor will generally not look past his or her time horizon. Thus, prices in a market dominated by short-term investors will reflect only near-term dividends. However, our discussion shows that a long-run dividend discount model holds even when investors have short-term time horizons. Although an investor may want to cash out early, he or she must find another investor who is willing to buy. The price this second investor pays is dependent on dividends *after* the date of purchase.

Valuation of Different Types of Stocks

The discussion to this point shows that the value of the firm is the present value of its future dividends. How do we apply this idea in practice? Equation (6.4) represents a very general model and is applicable regardless of whether the level of expected dividends is growing, fluctuating, or constant. The general model can be simplified if the firm's dividends are expected to follow any of three basic patterns: (1) zero growth, (2) constant growth, and (3) differential growth. These cases are illustrated in Figure 6.3.

Case 1 (Zero Growth)   The value of a stock with a constant dividend is given by

$$P_0 = \frac{\text{Div}_1}{1+r} + \frac{\text{Div}_2}{(1+r)^2} + \cdots = \frac{\text{Div}}{r}$$

Here it is assumed that $\text{Div}_1 = \text{Div}_2 = \cdots = \text{Div}$. This is just an application of the perpetuity formula of the previous chapter.

Case 2 (Constant Growth)   Dividends grow at rate g, as follows:

End of Year	1	2	3	4	...
Dividend	Div	$\text{Div}(1+g)$	$\text{Div}(1+g)^2$	$\text{Div}(1+g)^3$	...

Note that Div is the dividend at the end of the first period.

---

[3] This procedure reminds us of the physicist lecturing on the origins of the universe. He was approached by an elderly gentleman in the audience who disagreed with the lecture. The attendee said that the universe rests on the back of a huge turtle. When the physicist asked what the turtle rested on, the gentleman said another turtle. Anticipating the physicist's objections, the attendee said, "Don't tire yourself out, young fellow. It's turtles all the way down."

[4] The dividend valuation model is often called the Gordon model in honour of Professor Myron Gordon of the University of Toronto, its best-known developer.

FIGURE 6.3

Zero-Growth, Constant-Growth, and Differential-Growth Patterns

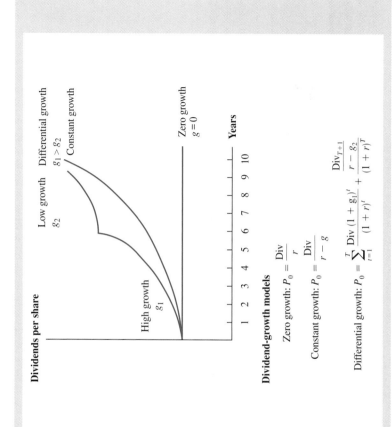

Dividends per share

High growth g_1

Low growth g_2

Differential growth $g_1 > g_2$

Constant growth

Zero growth $g = 0$

Years

1 2 3 4 5 6 7 8 9 10

Dividend-growth models

Zero growth: $P_0 = \dfrac{\text{Div}}{r}$

Constant growth: $P_0 = \dfrac{\text{Div}}{r-g}$

Differential growth: $P_0 = \displaystyle\sum_{t=1}^{T} \dfrac{\text{Div}(1+g_1)^t}{(1+r)^t} + \dfrac{\dfrac{\text{Div}_{T+1}}{r-g_2}}{(1+r)^T}$

EXAMPLE

Canadian Products will pay a dividend of $4 per share a year from now. Financial analysts believe that dividends will rise at 6 percent per year for the foreseeable future. What is the dividend per share at the end of each of the first five years?

End of Year	1	2	3	4	5
Dividend	$4.00	$4 × (1.06) = $4.24	$4 × (1.06)² = $4.4944	$4 × (1.06)³ = $4.7641	$4 × (1.06)⁴ = $5.0499

The value of a common stock with dividends growing at a constant rate is

$$P_0 = \frac{\text{Div}}{1+r} + \frac{\text{Div}(1+g)}{(1+r)^2} + \frac{\text{Div}(1+g)^2}{(1+r)^3} + \frac{\text{Div}(1+g)^3}{(1+r)^4} + \cdots = \frac{\text{Div}}{r-g}$$

where g is the growth rate. Div is the dividend on the stock at the end of the first period. This is the formula for the present value of a growing perpetuity, which we derived in the previous chapter.

EXAMPLE

Suppose an investor is considering the purchase of a share of the Saskatchewan Mining Company. The stock will pay a $3 dividend a year from today. This dividend is expected to grow at 10 percent per year ($g = 10\%$) for the foreseeable future. The investor thinks that the required return (r) on this stock is 15 percent, given her assessment of Saskatchewan Mining's risk. (We also refer to r as the discount rate of the stock.) What is the value of a share of Saskatchewan Mining Company's stock?

Using the constant growth formula of case 2, we assess the value to be $60:

$$\$60 = \frac{\$3}{0.15 - 0.10}$$

P_0 is quite dependent on the value of g. If g had been estimated to be 12½ percent, the value of the share would have been

$$\$120 = \frac{\$3}{0.15 - 0.125}$$

The stock price doubles (from $60 to $120) when g increases only 25 percent (from 10 percent to 12.5 percent). Because of P_0's dependency on g, one must maintain a healthy sense of skepticism when using this constant growth version of the dividend valuation model.

Furthermore, note that P_0 is equal to infinity when the growth rate, g, equals or exceeds the discount rate, r. Because stock prices do not grow infinitely, an estimate of g greater than r implies an error in estimation. More will be said about this later.

Case 3 (Differential Growth)   In this case, an algebraic formula would be too unwieldy. Instead, we present examples.

Consider the stock of Elixir Drug Company, which has a new back-rub ointment and is enjoying rapid growth. The dividend a year from today will be $1.15. During the next four years, the dividend will grow at 15 percent per year ($g_1 = 15\%$). After that, growth (g_2) will be equal to 10 percent per year. What is the present value of the stock if the required return (r) is 15 percent?

Figure 6.4 displays the growth in the dividends. We need to apply a two-step process to discount these dividends. We first calculate the net present value of the dividends growing at

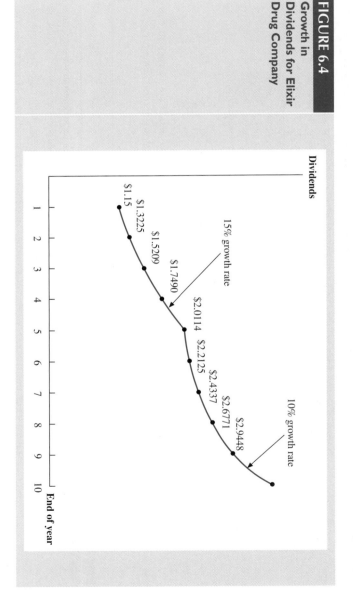

FIGURE 6.4

Growth in Dividends for Elixir Drug Company

Dividends

$1.15
$1.3225
$1.5209
$1.7490

15% growth rate

$2.0114
$2.2125
$2.4337
$2.6771
$2.9448

10% growth rate

1   2   3   4   5   6   7   8   9   10

End of year

15 percent per annum. That is, we first calculate the present value of the dividends at the end of each of the first five years. Second, we calculate the present value of the dividends beginning at the end of year 6.

Calculate Present Value of First Five Dividends   The present values of dividend payments in years 1 through 5 are

Future Year	Growth Rate (g_1)	Expected Dividend	Present Value
1	0.15	$1.15	$1
2	0.15	1.3225	$1
3	0.15	1.5209	$1
4	0.15	1.7490	$1
5	0.15	2.0114	$1
Years 1–5		The present value of dividends =	$5

The growing-annuity formula of the previous chapter could normally be used in this step. However, note that dividends grow at 15 percent, which is also the discount rate. Since $g = r$, the growing-annuity formula cannot be used in this example.

Calculate Present Value of Dividends Beginning at End of Year 6   This is the procedure for deferred perpetuities and deferred annuities that we mentioned in the previous chapter. The dividends beginning at the end of year 6 are

End of Year	6	7	8	9
Dividend	$\text{Div}_5 \times (1 + g_2)$ $\$2.0114 \times 1.10$ $= \$2.2125$	$\text{Div}_5 \times (1 + g_2)^2$ $2.0114 \times (1.10)^2$ $= \$2.4337$	$\text{Div}_5 \times (1 + g_2)^3$ $2.0114 \times (1.10)^3$ $= \$2.6771$	$\text{Div}_5 \times (1 + g_2)^4$ $2.0114 \times (1.10)^4$ $= \$2.9448$

As stated in the previous chapter, the growing-perpetuity formula calculates present value as of one year prior to the first payment. Because the payment begins at the end of year 6, the present value formula calculates present value as of the end of year 5. The price at the end of year 5 is given by

$$P_5 = \frac{\text{Div}_6}{r - g_2} = \frac{\$2.2125}{0.15 - 0.10}$$

$$= \$44.25$$

The present value of P_5 at the end of year 0 is

$$\frac{P_5}{(1 + r)^5} = \frac{\$44.25}{(1.15)^5} = \$22$$

The present value of all dividends as of the end of year 0 is $27 (or $22 + $5).

6.5 Estimates of Parameters in the Dividend Discount Model

The value of the firm is a function of its growth rate, g, and its discount rate, r. How does one estimate these variables?

Where Does g Come From?

The previous discussion on stocks assumed that dividends grow at the rate g. We now want to estimate this rate of growth. Consider a business whose earnings next year are expected to be the same as earnings this year unless a *net investment* is made. This situation is likely to occur, because net investment is equal to gross, or total, investment less depreciation. A net investment of zero occurs when *total investment* equals depreciation. If total investment is equal to depreciation, the firm's physical plant is maintained, consistent with no growth in earnings.

Net investment will be positive only if some earnings are not paid out as dividends, that is, only if some earnings are retained.[5] This leads to the following equation:

Earnings next year	=	Earnings this year	+	Retained earnings this year	×	Return on retained earnings	(6.5)

$$\underbrace{\phantom{\text{Retained earnings this year} \times \text{Return on retained earnings}}}_{\text{Increase in earnings}}$$

As explained in Chapter 3, the increase in earnings is a function of both the *retained earnings* and the return on the retained earnings.

We now divide both sides of (6.5) by earnings this year, yielding

$$\frac{\text{Earnings next year}}{\text{Earnings this year}} = \frac{\text{Earnings this year}}{\text{Earnings this year}} + \left(\frac{\text{Retained earnings this year}}{\text{Earnings this year}}\right) \times \frac{\text{Return on retained earnings}}{} \quad (6.6)$$

The left-hand side of (6.6) is simply 1 plus the growth rate in earnings, which we write as $1 + g$.[6] The ratio of retained earnings to earnings is called the retention ratio. Thus, we can write

$$1 + g = 1 + \text{Retention ratio} \times \text{Return on retained earnings} \quad (6.7)$$

It is difficult for a financial analyst to determine the return to be expected on currently retained earnings, because the details on forthcoming projects are not generally public information. However, it is frequently assumed that the projects selected in the current year have an anticipated return equal to returns from projects in other years. Here, we can estimate the anticipated return on current retained earnings by the historical **return on equity (ROE)**. After all, ROE is simply the return on the firm's entire equity, which is the return on the cumulation of all the firm's past projects.[7]

From (6.7), we have a simple way to estimate growth:

Formula for Firm's Growth Rate:

$$g = \text{Retention ratio} \times \text{Return on retained earnings} \quad (6.8)$$

---

[5] We ignore the possibility of the issuance of stocks or bonds in order to raise capital. These possibilities are considered in later chapters.

[6] Previously g referred to growth in dividends. However, the growth rate in earnings is equal to the growth rate in dividends in this context because, as we will presently see, the ratio of dividends to earnings is held constant.

[7] Students frequently wonder whether return on equity (ROE) or return on assets (ROA) should be used here. ROA and ROE are identical in our model because debt financing is ignored. However, most real-world firms have debt. Because debt is treated in later chapters, we are not yet able to treat this issue in depth now. Suffice it to say that ROE is the appropriate rate, because both ROE for the firm as a whole and the return to equityholders from a future project are calculated after interest has been deducted.

EXAMPLE

Trent Enterprises just reported earnings of $2 million. It plans to retain 40 percent of its earnings. The historical return on equity (ROE) was 0.16, a figure that is expected to continue into the future. How much will earnings grow over the coming year?

We first perform the calculation without reference to (6.8). Then we use (6.8) as a check.

Calculation Without Reference to Equation (6.8)   The firm will retain $800,000 (or 40% × $2 million). Assuming that historical ROE is an appropriate estimate for future returns, the anticipated increase in earnings is

$$800,000 \times 0.16 = \$128,000$$

The percentage growth in earnings is

$$\frac{\text{Change in earnings}}{\text{Total earnings}} = \frac{\$128,000}{\$2 \text{ million}} = 0.064$$

This implies that earnings in one year will be $2,128,000 (or $2,000,000 × 1.064).

Check Using Equation (6.8)   We use g = Retention ratio × ROE. We have

$$g = 0.4 \times 0.16 = 0.064$$

Where Does *r* Come From?

In this section, we want to estimate *r*, the rate used to discount the cash flows of a particular stock. There are two methods developed by academics. We present one method below but must defer the second until we give it extensive treatment in later chapters.

The first method begins with the concept that the value of a growing perpetuity is

$$P_0 = \frac{\text{Div}}{r - g}$$

Solving for *r*, we have

$$r = \frac{\text{Div}}{P_0} + g \tag{6.9}$$

As stated earlier, Div refers to the dividend to be received one year hence.

Thus, the discount rate can be broken into two parts. The ratio, Div/P_0, places the dividend return on a percentage basis, frequently called the *dividend yield*. The second term, *g*, is the growth rate of dividends.

Because information on both dividends and stock price is publicly available, the first term on the right-hand side of (6.9) can be easily calculated. The second term on the right-hand side, *g*, can be estimated from (6.8).

EXAMPLE

Trent Enterprises, the company examined in the previous example, has 1,000,000 shares of stock outstanding. The stock is selling at $10. What is the required return on the stock?

Because the retention ratio is 40 percent, the payout ratio is 60 percent (1 − Retention ratio). The **payout ratio** is the ratio of dividends/earnings. Because earnings one year from now will be $2,128,000 (or $2,000,000 × 1.064), dividends will be $1,276,800 (or 0.60 × $2,128,000). Dividends per share will be $1.28 (or $1,276,800/1,000,000). Given our previous result that g = 0.064, we calculate *r* from (6.9) as follows:

$$0.192 = \frac{\$1.28}{\$10.00} + 0.064$$

A Healthy Sense of Skepticism

It is important to emphasize that our approach merely *estimates* g; it does not determine g precisely. We mentioned earlier that our estimate of g is based on a number of assumptions. For example, we assume that the return on reinvestment of future retained earnings is equal to the firm's past ROE. We assume that the future retention ratio is equal to the past retention ratio. Our estimate for g will be off if these assumptions prove to be wrong.

Unfortunately, the determination of r is highly dependent on g. In our example, if g is estimated to be 0, r equals 12.8 percent ($1.28/$10.00). If g is estimated to be 12 percent, r equals 24.8 percent ($1.28/$10.00 + 12%). Thus, one should view estimates of r with a healthy sense of skepticism.

For this reason, some financial economists generally argue that the estimation error for r for a single security is too large to be practical. Therefore, they suggest calculating the average r for an entire industry. This r would then be used to discount the dividends of a particular stock in the same industry.

One should be particularly skeptical of two polar cases when estimating r for individual securities. First, consider a firm currently paying no dividend. The stock price will be above zero because investors believe that the firm may initiate a dividend at some point or the firm may be acquired at some point. However, when a firm goes from no dividend to a positive number of dividends, the implied growth rate is *infinite*. Thus, Equation (6.9) must be used with extreme caution here, if at all—a point we emphasize later in this chapter.

Second, we mentioned earlier that the value of the firm is infinite when g is equal to r. Because prices for stocks do not grow infinitely, an analyst whose estimate of g for a particular firm is equal to or above r must have made a mistake. Most likely, the analyst's high estimate for g is correct for the next few years. However, firms simply cannot maintain an abnormally high growth rate *forever*. The analyst's error was to use a short-run estimate of g in a model requiring a perpetual growth rate.

In brief, there are a number of difficulties with using the dividend discount model to determine r. In practice, analysts use a number of models including the capital asset pricing model, which we present in Chapters 11 and 13.

6.6 Growth Opportunities

We previously spoke of the growth rate of dividends. We now want to address the related concept of growth opportunities. Imagine a company with a level stream of earnings per share in perpetuity. The company pays all of these earnings out to shareholders as dividends. Hence,

$$EPS = Div$$

where EPS is *earnings per share* and Div is dividend per share. A company of this type is frequently called a *cash cow*.

From the perpetuity formula of the previous chapter, the value of a share of stock is

Value of a Share of Stock When Firm Acts as a Cash Cow:

$$\frac{EPS}{r} = \frac{Div}{r}$$

where r is the discount rate on the firm's stock.

The above policy of paying out all earnings as dividends may not be the optimal one. Many firms have *growth* opportunities, that is, opportunities to invest in profitable projects. Because these projects can represent a significant fraction of the firm's value, it would be foolish to forgo them in order to pay out all earnings as dividends.

While firms frequently think in terms of a *set* of growth opportunities, we focus here on only one opportunity, that is, the opportunity to invest in a single project. Suppose the firm retains the entire dividend at date 1 in order to invest in a particular capital budgeting project. The net present value *per share* of the project as of date 0 is *NPVGO*, which stands for the *net present value (per share) of the growth opportunity.*

What is the price of a share of stock at date 0 if the firm decides to take on the project at date 1? Because the per share value of the project is added to the original stock price, the stock price must now be

Stock Price After Firm Commits to New Project:

$$\frac{\text{EPS}}{r} + \text{NPVGO} \qquad (6.10)$$

Equation (6.10) indicates that the price of a share of stock can be viewed as the sum of two different items. The first term (EPS/r) is the value of the firm if it rested on its laurels, that is, if it simply distributed all earnings to the shareholders. The second term is the *additional* value if the firm retains earnings in order to fund new projects.

Nova Scotia Shipping, Ltd., expects to earn $1 million per year in perpetuity if it undertakes no new investment opportunities. There are 100,000 shares outstanding, so earnings per share equal $10 (or $1,000,000/100,000). The firm will have an opportunity at date 1 to spend $1,000,000 in a new marketing campaign. The new campaign will increase earnings in every subsequent period by $210,000 (or $2.10 per share). This is a 21 percent return per year on the project. The firm's discount rate is 10 percent. What is the value per share before and after deciding to accept the marketing campaign?

The value of a share of Nova Scotia Shipping before the campaign is

Value of a Share of Nova Scotia Shipping When Firm Acts as a Cash Cow:

$$\frac{\text{EPS}}{r} = \frac{\$10}{0.1} = \$100$$

The value of the marketing campaign as of date 1 is

Value of Marketing Campaign at Date 1:

$$-\$1,000,000 + \frac{\$210,000}{0.1} = \$1,100,000 \qquad (6.11)$$

Because the investment is made at date 1 and the first cash inflow occurs at date 2, Equation (6.11) represents the value of the marketing campaign as of date 1. We determine the value at date 0 by discounting back one period as follows:

Value of Marketing Campaign at Date 0:

$$\frac{\$1,100,000}{1.1} = \$1,000,000$$

Because the investment is made at date 1 and the first cash inflow occurs at date 2, Equation (6.11) represents the value of the marketing campaign as of date 1. We determine the value at date 0 by discounting back one period as follows:

Thus, NPVGO per share is $10 (or $1,000,000/100,000).

The price per share is

$$\text{EPS}/r + \text{NPVGO} = \$100 + \$10 = \$110$$

The calculation can also be made on a straight net present value basis. Because all the earnings at date 1 are spent on the marketing effort, no dividends are paid to shareholders at that date. Dividends in all subsequent periods are $1,210,000 (or $1,000,000 + $210,000). In this case, $1,000,000 is the annual dividend when Nova Scotia Shipping is a cash cow. The additional contribution to the dividend from the marketing effort is $210,000. Dividends per share are $12.10 (or $1,210,000/100,000). Because these dividends start at date 2, the price per share at date 1 is $121 (or $12.10/0.1). The price per share at date 0 is $110 (or $121/1.1).

Note that value is created in this example because the project earned a 21 percent rate of return when the discount rate was only 10 percent. No value would have been created had the project earned a 10 percent rate of return—the NPVGO would have been zero. Value would have been negative had the project earned a percentage return below 10 percent—the NPVGO would be negative in that case.

Two conditions must be met in order to increase value:

1. Earnings must be retained so that projects can be funded.[8]
2. The projects must have positive net present value.

Surprisingly, a number of companies seem to invest in projects known to have *negative* net present values. For example, Jensen has pointed out that, in the late 1970s, oil companies and tobacco companies were flush with cash.[9] Due to declining markets in both industries, high dividends and low investment would have been the rational action. Unfortunately, a number of companies in both industries reinvested heavily in what were widely perceived to be negative-NPVGO projects. A study by McConnell and Muscarella documents this perception.[10] They find that, during the 1970s, the stock prices of oil companies generally decreased on the days that announcements of increases in exploration and development were made.

Canada is not immune to the practice of investing in negative-NPV projects. For example, Nortel lost money for investors large and small. Many technology companies have made acquisitions that have subsequently been written down or written off, and therefore have lowered the value of the companies.

Given that NPV analysis (such as that presented in the previous chapter) is common knowledge in business, why would managers choose projects with negative NPVs? Bad judgment and bad luck are two reasons. Another is that some managers enjoy controlling a large company. Because paying dividends in lieu of reinvesting earnings reduces the size of the firm, some managers find it emotionally difficult to pay high dividends.

Growth in Earnings and Dividends Versus Growth Opportunities

As mentioned earlier, a firm's value increases when it invests in growth opportunities with positive NPVGOs. A firm's value falls when it selects opportunities with negative NPVGOs. However, dividends grow whether projects with positive NPVs or negative NPVs are selected. This surprising result can be explained by the following example.

[8] Later in the text we discuss issuing stock or debt in order to fund projects.

[9] M. C. Jensen, "Agency Costs of Free Cash Flows, Corporate Finance and Takeovers," *American Economic Review* (May 1986).

[10] J. J. McConnell and C. J. Muscarella, "Corporate Capital Expenditure Decisions and the Market Value of the Firm," *Journal of Financial Economics* 14 (1985).

EXAMPLE

Lane Supermarkets, a new firm, will earn $100,000 a year in perpetuity if it pays out all its earnings as dividends. However, the firm plans to invest 20 percent of its earnings in projects that earn 10 percent per year. The discount rate is 18 percent. An earlier formula tells us that the growth rate of dividends is

$$g = \text{Retention ratio} \times \text{Return on retained earnings} = 0.2 \times 0.10 = 2\%$$

For example, in this first year of the new policy, dividends are $80,000, calculated from $(1 - 0.2) \times \$100,000$. Dividends next year are $81,600 (or $80,000 × 1.02). Dividends the following year are $83,232 or $80,000 × $(1.02)^2$ and so on. Because dividends represent a fixed percentage of earnings, earnings must grow at 2 percent a year as well.

However, note that the policy reduces value because the rate of return on the projects of 10 percent is less than the discount rate of 18 percent. That is, the firm would have had a higher value at date 0 if it had a policy of paying all its earnings out as dividends. Thus, a policy of investing in projects with negative NPVs rather than paying out earnings as dividends will lead to growth in dividends and earnings, but will reduce value.

Dividends or Earnings: Which to Discount?

As mentioned earlier, this chapter applied the growing-perpetuity formula to the valuation of stocks. In our application, we discounted dividends, not earnings. This is sensible since investors select a stock for the cash flows they can get out of it. They only get two things out of a stock: dividends and the ultimate sales price, which is determined by what future investors expect to receive in dividends.

The calculated stock price would be too high were earnings to be discounted instead of dividends. As we saw in our estimation of a firm's growth rate, only a portion of earnings goes to the shareholders as dividends. The remainder is retained to generate future dividends. In our model, retained earnings are equal to the firm's investment. To discount earnings instead of dividends would be to ignore the investment that a firm must make today in order to generate future returns.

The No-Dividend Firm

Students frequently ask the following question: If the dividend discount model is correct, why are no-dividend stocks not selling at zero? This is a good question that addresses the goals of the firm. A firm with many growth opportunities is faced with a dilemma: The firm can pay out dividends now, or it can forgo current dividends in order to make investments that will generate even greater dividends in the future.[11] This is often a painful choice, because a strategy of dividend deferment may be optimal yet unpopular among certain shareholders.

Many firms choose to pay no dividends—and these firms sell at positive prices.[12] Rational shareholders believe that they will either receive dividends at some point or they will receive something just as good. That is, the firm will be acquired in a merger, with the shareholders receiving either cash or shares in the acquiring firm.

Of course, the actual application of the dividend discount model is difficult for firms of this type. Clearly, the model for constant growth of dividends does not apply. Though the differential growth model can work in theory, the difficulties of estimating the date of first dividend, the growth rate of dividends after that date, and the ultimate merger price make application of the model quite difficult in reality.

Empirical evidence suggests that firms with high growth rates are likely to pay lower dividends, a result consistent with the above analysis. For example, consider Rogers Communications, Inc. The company started in the 1960s and grew rapidly throughout the decades thereafter. It paid its first dividend in history in July of 2003, though it was a multimillion dollar company prior to that date. Why did it wait so long to pay a dividend? It likely waited because it had so many positive growth opportunities, largely in the form of acquisitions.

Utilities are an interesting contrast because, as a group, historically they have had few growth opportunities. As a result, they pay out a large fraction of their earnings in dividends. For example, Canadian Utilities Limited, Utilicorp United, and Nova Scotia Power have had payout ratios of over 70 percent in many recent years. Today, the utility business is getting more exciting as deregulation allows companies to diversify into new businesses. This suggests utility payout ratios may fall.

6.7 The Dividend Growth Model and the NPVGO Model (Advanced)

This chapter has revealed that the price of a share of stock is the sum of its price as a cash cow plus the per share value of its growth opportunities. The Nova Scotia Shipping example illustrated this formula using only one growth opportunity. We also used the growing perpetuity formula to price a stock with a steady growth in dividends. When the formula is applied to stocks, it is typically called the *dividend growth model*. A steady growth in dividends results from a continual investment in growth opportunities, not just investment in a single opportunity. Therefore, it is worthwhile to compare the dividend growth model with the *NPVGO model* when growth occurs through continual investing.

Prairie Book Publishers has EPS of **$10** at the end of the first year, a dividend payout ratio of 40 percent, a discount rate of 16 percent, and a return on its retained earnings of 20 percent. Because the firm retains some of its earnings each year, it is selecting growth opportunities each year. This is different from Nova Scotia Shipping, which had a growth opportunity in only one year. We wish to calculate the price per share using both the dividend growth model and the NPVGO model.

The Dividend Growth Model

The dividends at date 1 are $0.40 \times \$10 = \$4$ per share. The retention ratio is 0.60 (or $1 - 0.40$), implying a growth rate in dividends of 0.12 (or 0.60×0.20).

From the dividend growth model, the price of a share of stock is

$$\frac{Div}{r - g} = \frac{\$4}{0.16 - 0.12} = \$100$$

The NPVGO Model

Using the NPVGO model, it is more difficult to value a firm with growth opportunities each year (like Prairie) than a firm with growth opportunities in only one year (like Nova Scotia Shipping). In order to value according to the NPVGO model, we need to calculate on a per share basis (1) the net present value of a single growth opportunity, (2) the net present value of all growth opportunities, and (3) the stock price if the firm acts as a cash cow, that is, the value of the firm without these growth opportunities. The value of the firm is the sum of (2) + (3).

1. *Value Per Share of a Single Growth Opportunity.* Out of the earnings per share of $10 at date 1, the firm retains $6 (or $0.6 \times \$10$) at that date. The firm earns $1.20 (or $\$6 \times 0.20$) per year in perpetuity on that $6 investment. The NPV from the investment is

Per Share NPV Generated from Investment at Date 1:

$$-\$6 + \frac{\$1.20}{0.16} = \$1.50 \qquad (6.12)$$

That is, the firm invests $6 in order to reap $1.20 per year on the investment. The earnings are discounted at 0.16, implying a value per share from the project of $1.50. Because the investment occurs at date 1 and the first cash flow occurs at date 2, $1.50 is the value of the investment at *date 1*. In other words, the NPV from the date 1 investment has *not yet* been brought back to date 0.

2. *Value Per Share of All Opportunities.* As pointed out earlier, the growth rate of earnings and dividends is 12 percent. Because retained earnings are a fixed percentage of total earnings, retained earnings must also grow at 12 percent a year. That is, retained earnings at date 2 are $6.72 (or $\$6 \times 1.12$), retained earnings at date 3 are $7.5264 [or $\$6 \times (1.12)^2$], and so on.

Let's analyze the retained earnings at date 2 in more detail. Because projects will always earn 20 percent per year, the firm earns $1.344 (or $\$6.72 \times 0.20$) in each future year on the $6.72 investment at date 2.

The NPV from the investment is

NPV Per Share Generated from Investment at Date 2:

$$-\$6.72 + \frac{\$1.344}{0.16} = \$1.68 \qquad (6.13)$$

$1.68 is the NPV as of date 2 of the investment made at date 2. The NPV from the date 2 investment has *not yet* been brought back to date 0.

Now consider the retained earnings at date 3 in more detail. The firm earns $1.5053 (or $\$7.5264 \times 0.20$) per year on the investment of $7.5264 at date 3. The NPV from the investment is

NPV Per Share Generated from Investment at Date 3:

$$-\$7.5264 + \frac{\$1.5053}{0.16} = \$1.882 \qquad (6.14)$$

From (6.12), (6.13), and (6.14), the NPV per share of all of the growth opportunities, discounted back to date 0, is

$$\frac{\$1.50}{1.16} + \frac{\$1.68}{(1.16)^2} + \frac{\$1.882}{(1.16)^3} + \cdots \qquad (6.15)$$

Because it has an infinite number of terms, this expression looks quite difficult to compute. However, there is an easy simplification. Note that retained earnings are growing at 12 percent per year. Because all projects earn the same rate of return per year, the NPVs in (6.12), (6.13), and (6.14) are also growing at 12 percent per year. Hence, we can rewrite (6.15) as

$$\frac{\$1.50}{1.16} + \frac{\$1.50 \times 1.12}{(1.16)^2} + \frac{\$1.50 \times (1.12)^2}{(1.16)^3} + \cdots$$

This is a growing perpetuity whose value is

$$\text{NPVGO} = \frac{\$1.50}{0.16 - 0.12} = \$37.50$$

Because the first NPV of $1.50 occurs at date 1, the NPVGO is $37.50 as of date 0. In other words, the firm's policy of investing in new projects from retained earnings has an NPV of $37.50.

3. *Value Per Share If Firm Is a Cash Cow.* We now assume that the firm pays out all of its earnings as dividends. The dividends would be $10 per year in this case. Since there would be no growth, the value per share would be evaluated by the perpetuity formula:

$$\frac{\text{Div}}{r} = \frac{\$10}{0.16} = \$62.50$$

Summation

Equation (6.10) states that value per share is the value of a cash cow plus the value of the growth opportunities. This is

$$\$100 = \$62.50 + \$37.50$$

Hence, value is the same whether calculated by a discounted-dividend approach or a growth opportunities approach. The share prices from the two approaches must be equal, because the approaches are different yet equivalent methods of applying concepts of present value.

6.8 Price–Earnings Ratio

We argued earlier that one should not discount earnings in order to determine price per share. Nevertheless, financial analysts frequently relate earnings and price per share, as made evident by their heavy reliance on the price–earnings (or P/E) ratio. Their logic is that earnings provide the basis for dividends and capital gains.

Our previous discussion stated that

$$\text{Price per share} = \frac{\text{EPS}}{r} + \text{NPVGO}$$

Dividing by EPS yields

$$\frac{\text{Price per share}}{\text{EPS}} = \frac{1}{r} + \frac{\text{NPVGO}}{\text{EPS}}$$

The left-hand side is the formula for the price–earnings ratio. The equation shows that the P/E ratio is related to the net present value of growth opportunities. As an example, consider two firms, each having just reported earnings per share of $1. However, one firm has many valuable growth opportunities while the other firm has no growth opportunities at all. The firm with growth opportunities should sell at a higher price, because an investor is buying both current income of $1 and growth opportunities. Suppose that the firm with growth opportunities sells for $16 and the other firm sells for $8. The $1 earnings per share number appears in the denominator of the P/E ratio for both firms. Thus, the P/E ratio is 16 for the firm with growth opportunities, but only 8 for the firm without the opportunities.

This explanation seems to hold fairly well in the real world. Biotech and other high-tech stocks generally sell at very high P/E ratios (or *multiples*, as they are often called) because they are perceived to have high growth rates. For example, in April 2004, Research in Motion traded at a P/E of 167. In fact, some technology stocks sell at high prices even though the companies have never earned a profit. The P/E ratios of these companies are infinite. Conversely, utilities and financial services companies sell at lower multiples because of the prospects of lower growth.

Of course, the market is merely pricing *perceptions* of the future, not the future itself. We will argue later in the text that the stock market generally has realistic perceptions of a firm's prospects. However, this is not always true. In the late 1960s, many electronics firms were selling at multiples of 200 times earnings. The high perceived growth rates did not materialize, causing great declines in stock prices during the early 1970s. In earlier decades, fortunes were made in stocks like IBM and Xerox because the high growth rates were not anticipated by investors.

There are two additional factors explaining the P/E ratio. The first is the discount rate, r. The above formula shows that the P/E ratio is *negatively* related to the firm's discount rate. We have already suggested that the discount rate is positively linked to the stock's risk or variability. Thus, the P/E ratio is negatively related to the stock's risk. To see that this is a sensible result, consider two firms, A and B, behaving as cash cows. The stock market *expects* both firms to have annual earnings of $1 per share forever. However, the earnings of firm A are known with certainty while the earnings of firm B are quite variable. A rational shareholder is likely to pay more for a share of firm A because of the absence of risk. If a share of firm A sells at a higher price and both firms have the same EPS, the P/E ratio of firm A must be higher.

The second additional factor concerns the firm's choice of accounting methods. Under current accounting rules, companies are given a fair amount of leeway. For example, consider depreciation accounting where many different methods may be used. A firm's choice of depreciation method can increase or decrease its earnings in different years. Similar accounting leeway exists for construction costs (completed-contracts versus percentage-of-completion methods).

As an example, consider two identical firms: C and D. Firm C uses straight-line depreciation and reports earnings of $2 per share. Firm D uses declining-balance depreciation and reports earnings of $3 per share. The market knows that the two firms are identical and prices both at $18 per share. This price–earnings ratio is 9 (or $18/$2) for firm C and 6 (or $18/$3) for firm D. Thus, the firm with the more conservative principles has a higher P/E ratio.

This last example depends on the assumption that the market sees through differences in accounting treatments. A significant portion of the academic community believes this, adhering to the hypothesis of *efficient capital markets*, a theory that we explore in great detail later in the text. Though many financial people might be more moderate in their beliefs regarding this issue, the consensus view is certainly that many of the accounting differences are seen through. Thus, the proposition that firms with conservative accountants have high P/E ratios is widely accepted.

In Their Own Words

Matthew Ingram on the New Tally for Tech Stocks

At the annual meeting of his holding company, Berkshire Hathaway, last May, legendary value investor and billionaire Warren Buffett told his audience that if he were a business professor, he would ask his students to pick an Internet company and try to determine how much it was worth. "And anybody who turned in an answer would fail," he quipped.

Mr. Buffett is just one of the many traditional value-oriented investors who have given up trying to explain why technology shares have been trading the way they have. Who can blame them? Some of these tiny companies were worth billions of dollars not long ago, and now they are worth a fraction of that — and yet some feel they are still overvalued.

It's easy enough for Mr. Buffett to avoid investing in tech stocks, since he's made billions by buying insurance companies, shoe stocks, and shares in Coca-Cola. But plenty of people believe they have to be invested in technology stocks, despite the recent turmoil, and they are trying to figure out how to separate the winners from the losers.

Looking at a stock's price compared to its earnings is one way of doing so, but it's only a broad measure — like using binoculars instead of a magnifying glass. It doesn't really tell you whether a stock that was $250 and is now $75 is cheap or not.

Instead of just relying on one such measure, analysts say investors should try to use as many tools as possible. That includes old standbys such as the price-earnings ratio, newer ones such as the PEG (price-earnings-growth) ratio, price-to-cash-flow multiples, and various measures of how a company is spending its money — including its "customer-acquisition" costs, or its sales per customer or per registered user.

The investor's task is made even more difficult by the fact that, during the tech stock runup last year, even some industry analysts apparently gave up trying to figure out what stocks were worth.

Last fall, for example, analysts expected Research In Motion Ltd. to reach $150 (Canadian) in a year. The stock hit that level in just a few months, and peaked at $220, giving it a market value of $15-billion.

"Valuing tech stocks became a very difficult process in the past 18 months or so," says one analyst, who didn't want to be named. "As casino-style investing took over ... valuation became nearly irrelevant."

Two Kinds of Tech Stocks

Despite the recent pullback in some share prices, arriving at a value for a high-flying tech stock hasn't gotten

any easier. For example, Research In Motion has fallen by 70 per cent from its peak, but it is still trading at 250 times its earnings per share. Yahoo Inc. (540 times earnings), eBay Inc. (1,600 times) and Nortel Networks Corp. (105 times) are also still at lofty levels. Of course, those multiples are based on last year's earnings, and most analysts look at next year's — but even that doesn't reduce the multiple very much.

Broadly speaking, there are two kinds of tech stocks: those that have earnings, and those that don't. If they do, you have to decide how much you're willing to pay for those earnings. But arriving at a value for a company like Amazon.com Inc. — which lost $720-million last year — is a lot more difficult, to the point where some professional money managers advise ordinary investors not to buy these kinds of stocks at all.

One way to try and value such a company is to look at its revenue per share, and compare that to similar companies. Analysts say this should always be used in combination with other measures, such as how much the company spends per customer and its revenue per user — as well as its gross profit margin, since having sales isn't worth much if a company is losing money with each sale. Many retailing stocks, on-line or not, are valued this way because such companies live or die on their customer base.

One point analysts make is that for most tech stocks, the current level of earnings isn't what is really important: growth is. For that reason, an increasingly popular valuation method combines the price-earnings multiple with a company's earnings growth rate, to get something called the PEG ratio, for price-earnings-growth.

If a stock is trading at 40 times earnings, and earnings are expected to grow at 40 per cent a year, that stock has a PEG ratio of 1 to 1. A stock trading at 20 times earnings may look a lot cheaper than one at 50 times earnings

---

—but if the first company is only growing at 10 per cent a year, and the second is growing at 50 per cent, the first has a PEG of 2 to 1 and the second 1 to 1. If you want growth, the second is the better buy....

Coming up with a company's PEG ratio is far from an exact science, mind you. For one thing, analysts often use projected earnings in their calculations, which leaves plenty of room for error. It also used to be assumed that a company's price–earnings multiple should be the same as its growth rate—but some analysts say firms growing at high rates deserve premiums of up to three or four times their growth rate.

None of these valuation methods is a one-size-fits-all tool, and that's why investors should use as many as possible to try and separate the wheat from the chaff. It's harder than buying a stock knowing it will double without you lifting a finger, but those days appear to be gone.

Matthew Ingram writes for *The Globe and Mail*. His comments are reproduced with permission from the May 4, 2000, edition.

In summary, our discussion argued that the P/E ratio is a function of three different factors. A company's ratio or multiple is likely to be high if (1) it has many growth opportunities, (2) it has low risk (reflected in a low discount rate), and (3) its accounting is conservative. While each of the three factors is important, it is our opinion that the first factor is the most important. Thus, our discussion of growth is quite relevant in understanding price–earnings multiples.

During the tech "bubble" of 1999 and early 2000, Internet stocks like Yahoo and Research in Motion were trading at P/Es over 1,000! Clearly the P/E analysis we present could never explain these prices in terms of growth opportunities. As covered in the In Their Own Words box above, some analysts who recommended buying these stocks developed a new measure called the PEG ratio to justify their recommendation. Although it is not based on any theory, the PEG ratio became popular among proponents of Internet stocks. On the other side, many analysts believed that the market had lost touch with reality. To these analysts, Internet stock prices were the result of speculative fever.

By 2001, it was clear the pessimists were correct that tech stocks were overvalued. Investment dealers on Wall Street and Bay Street were establishing rules to curb possible conflicts of interest on the part of overenthusiastic analysts. Around the same time, a New York investor brought a lawsuit against Merrill Lynch and its star Internet analyst. Merrill Lynch settled out of court without admitting any wrongdoing. The claim criticized PEG ratios and the like as "newly minted 'valuation criteria' [that] justify widely inflated price targets and 'buy' recommendations for Internet and technology companies with no profits expected for years."

Concept Questions

- What are the three factors determining a firm's P/E ratio?
- How does each affect the P/E and why?

6.9 Stock Market Reporting

Financial newspapers publish information on a large number of stocks in several different markets. Figure 6.5 produces sample stock listings for the Toronto Stock Exchange (TSX) for April 27, 2004. In Figure 6.5, locate the line for Telus Corporation (TELUS). The first two numbers, 28.52 and 19.25, are the high and low prices for the last 52 weeks. Stock prices are quoted in decimals.

The number 0.60 is the annual dividend rate. Since Telus, like most companies, pays dividends quarterly, this $0.60 is actually the last quarterly dividend multiplied by 4. So

FIGURE 6.5

Sample Stock Market Quotation

52W high	52W low	Stock	Ticker	Div	Yield %	P/E	Vol 00s	High	Low	Close	Net chg
108.42	102.51	TD Mtg.ab …TDB	64.60	61.2	-	e90	105.50	105.50	105.50	+1.44
35.00	25.50	TD TSX Cap …TCF	p0.41	1.2		4	33.81	33.78	33.78	+0.05
30.50	22.00	TD TSX Cmp …TTF	p0.34	1.2		13	29.19	29.00	29.00	+0.06
8.60	5.90	TDCdnGrwth …TAG		-		11	8.21	8.07	8.21	-0.03
21.25	15.20	TDCdnValue …TAV		1.7		21	19.83	19.64	19.70	-0.08
32.90	18.51	TDSpltCap …TDS	p0.33	0.09		51	29.25	28.99	28.99	+0.28
15.68	14.96	TDSplt.pf …TDS	p0.26	5.8		32	15.49	15.31	15.31	-0.01
2.98	1.01	TECSYS …TCS	0.88			29	2.00	2.00	2.00	-0.03
26.50	19.25	TELUS Epf …BT	1.21	4.7		5	25.98	25.98	25.98	
106.00	82.00	TELUS Gpf	5.75	5.5		4	104.00	104.00	104.00	+0.42
28.52	19.25	TELUS …T	0.60	2.5	25.8	2177	23.95	23.50	23.70	+0.15
26.79	18.02	TELUS nv	0.60	2.7	24.0	7161	22.44	22.03	22.05	-0.40
17.84	2.37	TLC Vision …TLC		-		2163	17.65	17.00	17.10	-0.40
4.10	1.50	TS03 …TOS		-		441	1.62	1.55	1.59	+0.04
60.75	21.10	TSX Group …X	1.00	1.8	24.3	262	55.25	54.95	54.96	+0.11
4.60	2.81	TUSK Eng …TKE		-		1026	4.23	4.13	4.20	+0.02
25.24	16.00	TVA.B …TVA	0.20	0.9	14.1	151	23.95	22.09	23.23	+0.75
0.39	0.06	TVI Pac …TVI		-	45.0	11548	0.23	0.215	0.225	+0.01
0.69	0.105	Tahera …TAH		-		7685	0.36	0.35	0.355	
†84.36	56.16	TalismnEn …TLM	p0.80	1.0	10.9	4503	84.36	82.75	83.33	+0.58
2.10	1.14	TanRange …TNX		-		576	1.35	1.31	1.35	+0.20
n 11.00	9.70	TxOptdinc …TO	1.10	10.3		45	10.65	10.40	10.65	-0.49
27.46	11.25	TeckCmA. …TEK	0.20	0.9	29/1	21	23.95	23.01	23.01	-0.10
26.33	10.10	TeckComB …TEK	0.20	0.9	27.7	7275	23.01	21.60	21.90	+0.08
c 20.65	2.40	Telesys …TIW		-	54.1	1440	15.73	15.10	15.32	+0.08
11.25	6.20	Tembec …TBC		-	8.8	1115	10.90	10.70	10.78	+0.20
6.13	4.65	TempstEngA …TMY		-	33.1	150	5.30	5.19	5.30	-0.18
3.48	0.85	TenkeMng …TNK		-		1819	3.10	2.90	2.90	+0.64
50.00	38.50	Terasen …TER	1.68	3.5	17.7	823	48.00	47.45	47.50	-0.05
15.25	8.15	Tesco …TEO		-		60	10.35	10.19	10.21	-0.06
34.00	25.00	Tesma A. …TSM	p0.64	2.0	10.3	457	31.46	31.46	31.76	-0.01
0.245	0.065	TesoroEnrg …TOG		-	31.7	10383	0.195	0.185	0.19	+0.02
46.00	43.52	Texac Cpf …TXC		-		20	45.90	45.90	45.90	+0.04
6.50	3.04	Theratech …TH		-		393	3.42	3.27	3.31	-0.21
25.50	14.00	3rdCdnGen …THD	0.30	1.3	2.9	12	23.50	23.50	23.50	-0.51
24.93	13.25	35Split …TFS		-		6	22.76	22.25	22.25	
26.26	25.16	35SplitApf	1.27	5.0			25.60	25.60	25.60	+0.01
0.75	0.26	ThistleMn …THT		-		2512	0.29	0.28	0.29	+0.01
47.99	39.86	Thomson …TOC	u0.74	2.4	23.3	2718	41.99	41.00	41.12	-0.67

the last cash dividend was $0.60/4 = $0.15. Jumping ahead a bit, the column labelled "Yield %" gives the dividend yield based on the current dividend and the closing price. For Telus this is $0.60/23.70 = 2.5% as shown.

The High, Low, and Close figures are the high, low, and closing prices during the day. The "Net Chg" of +0.15 tells us that the closing price of $23.70 per share is $0.15 higher than the closing price the day before.

The column labelled P/E (short for price/earnings or P/E ratio), is the closing price of $23.70 divided by annual earnings per share (based on the most recent full fiscal year). In the jargon of Bay Street, we might say that Telus "sells for 25.8 times earnings."

The remaining column, "Vol 00s," tells how many shares traded during the reported day (in hundreds). For example, the 2177 for Telus tells us that 217,700 shares changed hands. The dollar volume of transactions was on the order of $23.70 × 217,700 = $5,159,490 worth of Telus stock.

6.10   SUMMARY AND CONCLUSIONS

In this chapter we use general present-value formulas from the previous chapter to price bonds and stock.

Chapter 6   How to Value Bonds and Stocks

151

1. Pure discount bonds and perpetuities are the polar cases of bonds. The value of a pure discount bond (also called a *zero-coupon bond* or simply a *zero*) is

$$PV = \frac{F}{(1 + r)^T}$$

The value of a perpetuity (also called a *consol*) is

$$PV = \frac{C}{r}$$

2. Level-payment bonds represent an intermediate case. The coupon payments form an annuity and the principal repayment is a lump sum. The value of this type of bond is simply the sum of the values of its two parts.

3. The yield to maturity on a bond is that single rate that discounts the payments on the bond to its purchase price.

4. A stock can be valued by discounting its dividends. We mention three types of situations:
   a. The case of zero growth of dividends.
   b. The case of constant growth of dividends.
   c. The case of differential growth.

5. An estimate of the growth rate of a stock is needed for cases (4*b*) or (4*c*) above. A useful estimate of the growth rate is

$$g = \text{Retention ratio} \times \text{Return on retained earnings}$$

6. It is worthwhile to view a share of stock as the sum of its worth if the company behaves as a cash cow (the company does no investing) and the value per share of its growth opportunities. We write the value of a share as

$$\frac{EPS}{r} + NPVGO$$

We show that, in theory, share price must be the same whether the dividend growth model or the above formula is used.

7. From accounting, we know that earnings are divided into two parts: dividends and retained earnings. Most firms continually retain earnings in order to create future dividends. One should not discount earnings to obtain price per share since part of earnings must be reinvested. Only dividends reach the shareholders and only they should be discounted to obtain share price.

8. We suggested that a firm's price–earnings ratio is a function of three factors:
   a. The per share amount of the firm's valuable growth opportunities.
   b. The risk of the stock.
   c. The conservatism of the accounting methods used by the firm.

KEY TERMS

Coupons 128
Discount 131
Face value 127
Holding-period return 132
Maturity date 127

Payout ratio 139
Premium 132
Pure discount bond 127
Return on equity (ROE) 138
Yield to maturity 132

SUGGESTED READING

The best place to look for additional information is in investment textbooks. Some good ones are:

Z. Bodie, A. Kane, A. Marcus, S. Perrakis, and P. J. Ryan. *Investments.* 4th Canadian ed. Whitby, Ontario: McGraw-Hill Ryerson, 2003.

W. F. Sharpe, G. J. Alexander, J. W. Bailey, D. J. Fowler and D. Domian. *Investments.* 3rd Canadian ed. Scarborough, Ont.: Prentice-Hall, 1999.

For more on tech stock stocks, see:

G. Athanassakos, "Valuation of Internet Stocks," *Canadian Investment Review* (Summer 2000).

QUESTIONS & PROBLEMS

How to Value Bonds

6.1   What is the present value of a 10-year, pure discount bond paying $1,000 at maturity if the appropriate interest rate is:

a.   5 percent

b.   10 percent

c.   15 percent

6.2   Microhard has issued a bond with the following characteristics:

Principal: $1,000

Time to maturity: 20 years

Coupon rate: 8 percent, compounded semiannually

Semiannual payments

Calculate the price of this bond if the stated annual interest rate, compounded semiannually, is:

a.   8 percent

b.   10 percent

c.   6 percent

6.3   Consider a bond with a face value of $1,000. The coupon payment is made semiannually and the yield on the bond is 12 percent (effective annual yield). How much would you pay for the bond if:

a.   The coupon rate is 8 percent and the remaining time to maturity is 20 years?

b.   The coupon rate is 10 percent and the remaining time to maturity is 15 years?

6.4   Jay's Trucking, Inc., has issued an 8 percent, 20-year bond paying interest semiannually. The bond has a face value of $1,000. If the yield on the bond is 10 percent (effective annual yield), what is the price of the bond?

6.5   A bond is sold at $923.14 (below its face value of $1,000). The bond matures in 15 years and has a 10 percent yield, expressed as a stated annual interest rate, compounded semiannually. What is the coupon rate on the bond if the coupon is paid semiannually? The next payment occurs six months from today.

6.6   You have just purchased a newly issued $1,000 five-year Vanguard Company bond at par. This five-year bond pays $60 in interest semiannually. You are also considering the purchase of another Vanguard Company bond that pays $30 in semiannual interest payments and has six years remaining before maturity. This bond has a face value of $1,000.

a.   What is the yield on the five-year bond (expressed as an effective annual yield)?

b.   Assume that the five-year bond and the six-year bond have the same yield. What should you be willing to pay for the six-year bond?

c.   How will your answer in part (b) change if the five-year bond pays $40 in semiannual interest instead of $60? Assume that the five-year bond paying $40 semiannually is purchased at par.

Bond Concepts

6.7   Consider two bonds, A and B. The coupon rates are 10 percent and the face values are $1,000 for both bonds. Both bonds have annual coupons. Bond A has 20 years to maturity while bond B has 10 years to maturity.

a.   What are the prices of the two bonds if the relevant market interest rate for both bonds is 10 percent?

b.   If the market interest rate increases to 12 percent, what will be the prices of the two bonds?

c.   If the market interest rate decreases to 8 percent, what will be the prices of the two bonds?

6.8   *a.* If the market interest rate unexpectedly increases, what would be the effect on the prices of long-term bonds? Why?

    b. How would a rise in the interest rate affect the general level of stock prices? Why?

6.9   Consider a bond paying an annual coupon of $80 with a face value of $1,000. Calculate the yield to maturity if the bond has:

    a. 20 years remaining to maturity and is priced at $1,200.

    b. 10 years remaining to maturity and is priced at $950.

6.10 HexCorp Inc. has two different bonds currently outstanding. Bond *A* has a face value of $40,000 and matures in 20 years. The bond makes no payments for the first six years, pays $2,000 semiannually for the subsequent eight years, and finally pays $2,500 semi-annually for the last six years. Bond *B* also has a face value of $40,000 and matures in 20 years. However, it makes no coupon payments over the life of the bond. If the stated annual interest rate is 12 percent, compounded semiannually,

    a. What is the current price of Bond *A*?

    b. What is the current price of Bond *B*?

EXCEL

6.11 Referring back to the bond quotes in Figure 6.2, calculate the price of the Newfoundland 6.150 Apr 17/28 to prove that it was approximately 103.76 as shown.

6.12 In 2004 Quebec provincial bonds carried a yield roughly the same as comparable Ontario bonds because investors appeared to be unconcerned about Quebec's political future. Suppose that you were an investment manager who thought that the market was under-playing these fears. In particular, suppose that you thought that yields on Quebec bonds would rise by 50 basis points. Which bonds in Figure 6.2 would you buy or sell? Explain in words. Illustrate with a numerical example showing your potential profit.

The Present Value of Common Stocks

6.13 A common stock just paid an annual dividend of $2 yesterday. The dividend is expected to grow at 8 percent annually for the next three years, after which it will grow at 4 percent in perpetuity. The appropriate discount rate is 12 percent. What is the price of the stock?

6.14 You own $100,000 worth of Smart Money stock. One year from now, you will receive a dividend of $2 per share. You will receive a $4 dividend two years from now. You will sell the stock for $50 per share three years from now. Dividends are taxed at the rate of 28 percent. Assume there is no capital gains tax. The required rate of return is 15 percent. How many shares of stock do you own?

6.15 Consider the stock of Davidson Company, which will pay an annual dividend of $2 one year from today. The dividend will grow at a constant annual rate of 5 percent, forever. The market requires a 12 percent return on the company's stock.

    a. What is the current price of a share of the stock?

    b. What will the stock price be 10 years from today?

6.16 Scubaland, Inc., is experiencing a period of rapid growth. Earnings and dividends per share are expected to grow at a rate of 18 percent during the next two years, 15 percent in the third year, and 6 percent thereafter. Yesterday, Scubaland paid a dividend of $1.15. If the required rate of return on the stock is 12 percent, what is the price of a share of the stock today?

EXCEL

6.17 Calamity Mining Company's iron ore reserves are being depleted, and its costs of recov-ering a declining quantity of ore are rising each year. As a result, the company's earnings are declining at a rate of 10 percent per year. If the dividend per share to be paid tomor-row is $5 and the required rate of return is 14 percent, what is the value of the firm's stock? Assume that the dividend payments are based on a fixed percentage of the firm's earnings.

6.18 Pasqually Mineral Water, Inc., will pay a quarterly dividend per share of $1 at the end of each of the next 12 quarters. Thereafter, the dividend will grow at a quarterly rate of 0.5 percent, forever. The appropriate rate of return on the stock is 10 percent, compounded quarterly. What is the current stock price?

EXCEL

6.19 Suppose Amsterdam Foods, Inc., has just paid a dividend of $1.40 per share. Its dividend is expected to grow at 5 percent per year in perpetuity. If the required return is 10 percent, what is the value of a share of Amsterdam Foods?

6.20 In order to buy back its own shares, Pennzoil Co. has decided to suspend its dividends for the next two years. It will resume its annual cash dividend of $2.00 in year 3 and year 4. Thereafter, its dividend payments will grow at an annual growth rate of 6 percent, forever. The required rate of return on Pennzoil's stock is 16 percent. According to the discounted dividend model, what should Pennzoil's current share price be?

6.21 The Webster Co. has just paid a dividend of $5.25 per share. The company will increase its dividend by 14 percent next year. The company will then reduce its dividend growth rate by 3 percent each year until the dividend reaches the industry average of 5 percent growth. The company will maintain that dividend growth rate, forever. The required rate of return for the Webster Co. is 14 percent. What is the price of the stock?

Estimates of Parameters in the Dividend Discount Model

6.22 Malik, Inc., is expected to pay equal dividends at the end of each of the next two years. Thereafter, the dividend will grow at a constant annual rate of 4 percent, forever. The current stock price is $30. What is next year's dividend payment if the required rate of return is 12 percent?

6.23 The newspaper reported last week that Bradley Enterprises earned $20 million this year. The report also stated that the firm's return on equity is 14 percent. Bradley retains 60 percent of its earnings.
 a. What is the firm's earnings growth rate?
 b. What will next year's earnings be?

6.24 Juggernaut Satellite Corporation earned $10 million for the fiscal year ending yesterday. The firm also paid out 25 percent of its earnings as dividends yesterday. The firm will continue to pay out 25 percent of its earnings as annual, end-of-year dividends. The remaining 75 percent of earnings is retained by the company for use in projects. The company has 1.25 million shares of common stock outstanding. The current stock price is $30. The historical return on equity (ROE) of 12 percent is expected to continue in the future. What is the required rate of return on the stock?

6.25 Four years ago, Bling Diamond, Inc., paid a dividend of $0.80 per share. Bling paid a dividend of $1.66 per share yesterday. Dividends will grow over the next five years at the same rate they grew over the last four years. Thereafter, dividends will grow at 8 percent per year. The required return on the stock is 18 percent. What will Bling Diamond's cash dividend be in seven years?

Growth Opportunities

6.26 Rite Bite Enterprises sells toothpicks. Gross revenues last year were $3 million, and total costs were $1.5 million. Rite Bite has 1 million shares of common stock outstanding. Gross revenues and costs are expected to grow at 5 percent per year. Rite Bite pays no income taxes. All earnings are paid out as dividends.
 a. If the appropriate discount rate is 15 percent and all cash flows are received at year's end, what is the price per share of Rite Bite stock?
 b. Rite Bite has decided to produce toothbrushes. The project requires an immediate outlay of $15 million. In one year, another outlay of $5 million will be needed. The year after that, net cash inflows will be $6 million. That profit level will be maintained in perpetuity. What effect will undertaking this project have on the price per share of the stock?

6.27 Frump Real Estate, Inc., expects to earn $100 million per year in perpetuity if it does not undertake any new projects. The firm has an opportunity to invest $15 million today and $5 million in one year in real estate. The new investment will generate annual earnings of $10 million in perpetuity, beginning two years from today. The firm has 20 million

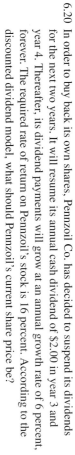

shares of common stock outstanding, and the required rate of return on the stock is 15 percent. Land investments are not depreciable. Ignore taxes.

a. What is the price of a share of stock if the firm does not undertake the new investment?

b. What is the value of the investment?

c. What is the per-share stock price if the firm undertakes the investment?

6.28 The annual earnings of Avalanche Skis Inc. will be $4 per share in perpetuity if the firm makes no new investments. Under such a situation, the firm would pay out all of its earnings as dividends. Assume the first dividend will be received exactly one year from now. Alternatively, assume that three years from now, and in every subsequent year in perpetuity, the company can invest 25 percent of its earnings in new projects. Each project will earn 40 percent at year-end, in perpetuity. The firm's discount rate is 14 percent.

a. What is the price per share of Avalanche Skis Inc. stock today without the company making the new investment?

b. If Avalanche announces that the new investment will be made, what will the per-share stock price be today?

Price–Earnings Ratio

6.29 Consider Pacific Energy Company and Canadian Bluechips, Inc., both of which reported cash flows of $800,000 and have 500,000 shares of common stock outstanding. Without new projects, both firms will continue to generate cash flows of $800,000 in perpetuity. Assume that the cash flows are equal to earnings. Assume both firms require a 15 percent rate of return.

a. Pacific Energy Company has a new project that will generate additional cash flows of $100,000 each year in perpetuity. Calculate the P/E ratio of the company.

b. Canadian Bluechips has a new project that will increase cash flows by $200,000 in perpetuity. Calculate the P/E ratio of the firm.

6.30 (Challenge Question) Lewin Skis Inc. (today) expects to earn $4 per share for each of the future operating periods (beginning at time 1) if the firm makes no new investments (and returns the earnings as dividends to the shareholders). However, Clint Williams, president and CEO, has discovered an opportunity to retain (and invest) 25 percent of the earnings beginning three years from today (starting at time 3). This opportunity to invest will continue (for each period) indefinitely. He expects to earn 40 percent (per year) on this new equity investment (ROE of 40), the return beginning one year after each investment is made. The firm's equity discount rate is 14 percent throughout.

a. What is the price per share (now at time 0) of Lewin Skis Inc. stock *without* making the new investment?

b. If the new investment is expected to be made, per the preceding information, what would the value of the stock (per share) be now (at time 0)?

c. What is the expected capital gain yield for the second period, assuming the proposed investment is made? What is the expected capital gain yield for the second period if the proposed investment is *not* made?

d. What is the expected dividend yield for the second period if the new investment is made? What is the expected dividend yield for the second period if the new investment is *not* made?

Valuation of Stocks

6.31 ABC Inc. has a P/E ratio of 12 and maintains a dividend payout ratio of 40 percent. The stock price of ABC Inc. on January 1 is $32. What would the value of stock be if the dividend payout ratio was 60 percent?

6.32 XYZ Inc. has earnings of $10 million and is projected to grow at a constant rate of 5 percent forever because of the benefits gained from the learning curve. Currently all earnings are paid out as dividends. The company plans to launch a new project two years from now which would be completely internally funded and require 20 percent of the

Part II   Value and Capital Budgeting

earnings that year. The project would start generating revenues one year after the launch of the project and the earnings from the new project in any year are estimated to be constant at $0.5 million. The company has 10 million shares of stock outstanding. Estimate the value of XYZ stock. The discount rate is 10 percent.

6.33 Enter the ticker symbol "FD" for Federal Department Stores. Using the most recent balance sheet and income statement under the "Excel Analytics" link, calculate the sustainable growth rate for Sears. Now download the "Mthly. Adj. Price" and find the closing stock price for the same month as the balance sheet and income statement you used. What is the implied required return on Sears according to the dividend growth model? Does this number make sense? Why or why not?

6.34 Assume that investors require an 11 percent return on ATI Technologies Inc. (ATYT) stock. Under the "Excel Analytics" link find the "Mthly. Adj. Price" and find the closing price for the month of the most recent fiscal year-end for ATY. Using this stock price and the EPS for the most recent year, calculate the NPVGO for ATI Technologies Inc. What is the appropriate P/E ratio for ATI Technologies Inc. using these calculations?

Appendix 6A

The Term Structure of Interest Rates

Spot Rates and Yield to Maturity

In the main body of this chapter, we have assumed that the interest rate is constant over all future periods. In reality, interest rates vary through time. This occurs primarily because inflation rates are expected to differ through time.

To illustrate, we consider two zero-coupon bonds. Bond A is a one-year bond and bond B is a two-year bond. Both have face values of $1,000. The one-year interest rate, r_1, is 8 percent. The two-year interest rate, r_2, is 10 percent. These two rates of interest are examples of spot rates. Perhaps this inequality in interest rates occurs because inflation is expected to be higher over the second year than over the first year. The two bonds are depicted in the following time chart:

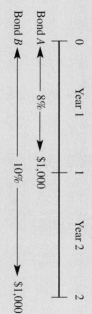

We can easily calculate the present values for bond A and bond B as

$$PV_A = \$925.93 = \frac{\$1,000}{1.08}$$

and

$$PV_B = \$826.45 = \frac{\$1,000}{(1.10)^2}$$

Of course, if PV_A and PV_B were observable and the spot rates were not, we could determine the spot rates using the PV formula, because

$$PV_A = \$925.93 = \frac{\$1,000}{(1 + r_1)} \rightarrow r_1 = 8\%$$

and

$$PV_B = \$826.45 = \frac{\$1,000}{(1 + r_2)^2} \rightarrow r_2 = 10\%$$

Now we can see how the prices of more complicated bonds are determined. Try to do the next example. It illustrates the difference between spot rates and yields to maturity.

EXAMPLE

Given the spot rates, r_1 equals 8 percent and r_2 equals 10 percent, what should a 5 percent coupon, two-year bond cost? The cash flows C_1 and C_2 are illustrated in the following time chart:

The bond can be viewed as a portfolio of zero-coupon bonds with one- and two-year maturities. Therefore

$$PV = \frac{\$50}{1 + 0.08} + \frac{\$1,050}{(1 + 0.10)^2} = \$914.06 \qquad (6A.1)$$

We now want to calculate a single rate for the bond. We do this by solving for y in the following equation:

$$\$914.06 = \frac{\$50}{1 + y} + \frac{\$1,050}{(1 + y)^2} \qquad (6A.2)$$

In (6A.2), y equals 9.95 percent. As mentioned in the chapter, we call y the *yield to maturity* on the bond. Solving for y for a multiyear bond is generally done by means of trial and error.[13] While this can take much time with paper and pencil, it is virtually instantaneous on a hand-held calculator.

It is worthwhile to contrast Equation (6A.1) and Equation (6A.2). In (6A.1), we use the marketwide spot rates to determine the price of the bond. Once we get the bond price, we use (6A.2) to calculate its yield to maturity. Because Equation (6A.1) employs two spot rates whereas only one appears in (6A.2), we can think of yield to maturity as some sort of average of the two spot rates.[14]

Using the above spot rates, the yield to maturity of a two-year coupon bond whose coupon rate is 12 percent and PV equals \$1,036.73 can be determined by

$$\$1,036.73 = \frac{\$120}{1 + r} + \frac{\$1,120}{(1 + r)^2} \rightarrow r = 9.89\%$$

As these calculations show, two bonds with the same maturity will usually have different yields to maturity if the coupons differ.

[13]The quadratic formula may be used to solve for y for a two-year bond. However, formulas generally do not apply for longer-term bonds.

[14]Yield to maturity is not a simple average of r_1 and r_2. Rather, financial economists speak of it as a time-weighted average of r_1 and r_2.

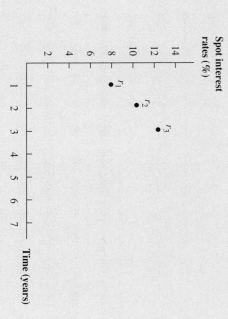

FIGURE 6A.1

The Term
Structure of
Interest Rates

Graphing the Term Structure

The *term structure* describes the relationship of spot rates with different maturities. Figure 6A.1 graphs a particular term structure. In Figure 6A.1 the spot rates are increasing with longer maturities, that is, $r_3 > r_2 > r_1$. Graphing the term structure is easy if we can observe spot rates. Unfortunately, this can be done only if there are enough zero-coupon government bonds.

A given term structure, such as that in Figure 6A.1, exists for only a moment in time, say, 10:00 AM, July 30, 2005. Interest rates are likely to change in the next minute, so that a different (though quite similar) term structure would exist at 10:01.

Concept Question

• What is the difference between a spot interest rate and the yield to maturity?

Explanations of the Term Structure

Figure 6A.1 showed one of many possible relationships between the spot rate and maturity. We now want to explore the relationship in more detail. We begin by defining a new term, the *forward rate*, and relate it to future interest rates. We also consider alternative theories of the term structure.

Definition of Forward Rate

Earlier in this appendix, we developed a two-year example where the spot rate over the first year is 8 percent and the spot rate over the two years is 10 percent. Here, an individual investing \$1 in a two-year zero-coupon bond would have \$1 × (1.10)^2 in two years.

In order to pursue our discussion, it is worthwhile to rewrite[15]

$$\$1 \times (1.10)^2 = \$1 \times 1.08 \times 1.1204 \qquad (6A.3)$$

---

[15] 12.04 percent is equal to

$$\frac{(1.10)^2}{1.08} - 1$$

when rounding is performed after four digits.

Equation (6A.3) tells us something important about the relationship between one- and two-year rates. When an individual invests in a two-year zero-coupon bond yielding 10 percent, his wealth at the end of two years is the same as if he received an 8 percent return over the first year and a 12.04 percent return over the second year. This hypothetical rate over the second year, 12.04 percent, is called the *forward rate*. Thus, we can think of an investor with a two-year zero-coupon bond as getting the one-year spot rate of 8 percent and locking in 12.04 percent over the second year. This relationship is presented in Figure 6A.2.

More generally, if we are given spot rates r_1 and r_2, we can always determine the forward rate, f_2, such that

$$(1 + r_2)^2 = (1 + r_1) \times (1 + f_2) \qquad (6A.4)$$

We solve for f_2, yielding

$$f_2 = \frac{(1 + r_2)^2}{1 + r_1} - 1 \qquad (6A.5)$$

If the one-year spot rate is 7 percent and the two-year spot rate is 12 percent, what is f_2? We plug in (6A.5), yielding

$$f_2 = \frac{(1.12)^2}{1.07} - 1 = 17.23\%$$

Consider an individual investing in a two-year zero-coupon bond yielding 12 percent. We say it is as if he receives 7 percent over the first year and simultaneously locks in 17.23 percent over the second year. Note that both the one-year spot rate and the two-year spot rate are known at date 0. Because the forward rate is calculated from the one-year and two-year spot rates, it can be calculated at date 0 as well.

Forward rates can be calculated over later years as well. The general formula is

$$f_n = \frac{(1 + r_n)^n}{(1 + r_{n-1})^{n-1}} - 1 \qquad (6A.6)$$

where f_n is the forward rate over the nth year, r_n is the n-year spot rate, and r_{n-1} is the spot rate for $n - 1$ years.

FIGURE 6A.2

Breakdown of a Two-Year Spot Rate Into a One-Year Spot Rate and Forward Rate Over the Second Year

Date 0	Year 1	Date 1	Year 2	Date 2

$1 —————————— 10% —————————— $1 × (1.10)² = $1.21

With a two-year spot rate of 10 percent, investor in two-year bond receives $1.21 at date 2.

This is the same return *as if* investor received the spot rate of 8 percent over the first year and 12.04 percent return over the second year.

$1 —— 8% —— $1.08 —— 12.04% —— $1 × 1.08 × 1.1204 = $1.21

Because both the one-year spot rate and the two-year spot rate are known at date 0, the forward rate over the second year can be calculated at date 0.

EXAMPLE

Assume the following set of rates:

Year	Spot Rate
1	5%
2	6%
3	7%
4	6%

What are the forward rates over each of the four years?

The forward rate over the first year is, by definition, equal to the one-year spot rate. Thus, we do not generally speak of the forward rate over the first year. The forward rates over the later years are

$$f_2 = \frac{(1.06)^2}{1.05} - 1 = 7.01\%$$

$$f_3 = \frac{(1.07)^3}{(1.06)^2} - 1 = 9.03\%$$

$$f_4 = \frac{(1.06)^4}{(1.07)^3} - 1 = 3.06\%$$

An individual investing \$1 in the two-year zero-coupon bond receives \$1.1236 [or \$1 × (1.06)²] at date 2. He can be viewed as receiving the one-year spot rate of 5 percent over the first year and receiving the forward rate of 7.01 percent over the second year. Another individual investing \$1 in a three-year zero-coupon bond receives \$1.2250 [or \$1 × (1.07)³] at date 3. She can be viewed as receiving the two-year spot rate of 6 percent over the first two years and receiving the forward rate of 9.03 percent over the third year. An individual investing \$1 in a four-year zero-coupon bond receives \$1.2625 [or \$1 × (1.06)⁴] at date 4. He can be viewed as receiving the three-year spot rate of 7 percent over the first three years and receiving the forward rate of 3.06 percent over the fourth year.

Note that all of the four spot rates in this problem are known at date 0. Because the forward rates are calculated from the spot rates, they can be determined at date 0 as well.

The material in this appendix is likely to be difficult for a student exposed to term structure for the first time. In brief, here is what the student should know at this point. Given Equations (6A.5) and (6A.6), a student should be able to calculate a set of forward rates given a set of spot rates. This can simply be viewed as a mechanical computation. In addition to the calculations, a student should understand the intuition of Figure 6A.2.

We now turn to the relationship between the forward rate and the expected spot rates in the future.

Estimating the Price of a Bond at a Future Date

In the example from the body of this chapter, we considered zero-coupon bonds paying \$1,000 at maturity and selling at a discount prior to maturity. We now wish to change the example slightly. Now, each bond initially sells for \$1,000 so that its payment at maturity is above \$1,000.[16] Keeping the spot rates at 8 percent and 10 percent, we have

---
[16] This change in assumptions simplifies our presentation but does not alter any of our conclusions.

Chapter 6   How to Value Bonds and Stocks

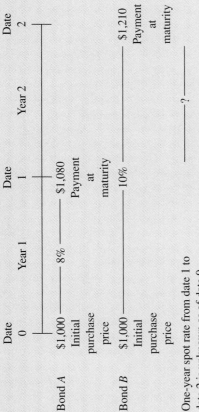

One-year spot rate from date 1 to date 2 is unknown as of date 0.

The payments at maturity are $1,080 and $1,210 for the one- and two-year zero-coupon bonds, respectively. The initial purchase price of $1,000 for each bond is determined as

$$\$1,000 = \frac{\$1,080}{1.08}$$

$$\$1,000 = \frac{\$1,210}{(1.10)^2}$$

We refer to the one-year bond as bond A and the two-year bond as bond B.

There will be a different one-year spot rate when date 1 arrives. This will be the spot rate from date 1 to date 2. We can also call it the spot rate over year 2. This spot rate is not known as of date 0. For example, should the rate of inflation rise between date 0 and date 1, the spot rate over year 2 would likely be high. Should the rate of inflation fall between date 0 and date 1, the spot rate over year 2 would likely be low.

Now that we have determined the price of each bond at date 0, we want to determine what the price of each bond will be at date 1. The price of the one-year bond (bond A) must be $1,080 at date 1, because the payment at maturity is made then. The hard part is determining what the price of the two-year bond (bond B) will be at that time.

Suppose we find that, on date 1, the one-year spot rate from date 1 to date 2 is 6 percent. We state that this is the one-year spot rate over year 2. This means that one can invest $1,000 at date 1 and receive $1,060 (or $1,000 × 1.06) at date 2. Because one year has already passed for bond B, the bond has only one year left. Because bond B pays $1,210 at date 2, its value at date 1 is

$$\$1,141.51 = \frac{\$1,210}{1.06} \qquad (6A.7)$$

Note that no one knew ahead of time the price that bond B would sell for on date 1, because no one knew that the one-year spot rate over year 2 would be 6 percent.

Suppose the one-year spot rate beginning at date 1 turned out not to be 6 percent, but to be 7 percent instead. This means that one can invest $1,000 at date 1 and receive $1,070 (or $1,000 × 1.07) at date 2. In this case, the value of bond B at date 1 would be

$$\$1,130.84 = \frac{\$1,210}{1.07} \qquad (6A.8)$$

Part II   Value and Capital Budgeting

Finally, suppose that the one-year spot rate at date 1 turned out to be neither 6 percent nor 7 percent, but 14 percent instead. This means that one can invest $1,000 at date 1 and receive $1,140 (or $1,000 × 1.14) at date 2. In this case, the value of bond *B* at date 1 would be

$$\$1,061.40 = \frac{\$1,210}{1.14}$$

The above possible bond prices are represented in Table 6A.1. The price that bond *B* will sell for on date 1 is not known before date 1 since the one-year spot rate prevailing over year 2 is not known until date 1.

<table>
<tr><td colspan="2">TABLE 6A.1   Price of Bond *B* at Date 1 as a Function of Spot Rate Over Year 2</td></tr>
<tr><td>Price of Bond *B* at Date 1</td><td>Spot Rate Over Year 2</td></tr>
<tr><td>$1,141.51 = $\frac{\$1,210}{1.06}$</td><td>6%</td></tr>
<tr><td>$1,130.84 = $\frac{\$1,210}{1.07}$</td><td>7%</td></tr>
<tr><td>$1,061.40 = $\frac{\$1,210}{1.14}$</td><td>14%</td></tr>
</table>

It is important to re-emphasize that, although the forward rate is known at date 0, the one-year spot rate beginning at date 1 is *unknown* ahead of time. Thus, the price of bond *B* at date 1 is unknown ahead of time. Prior to date 1, we can speak only of the amount that bond *B* is *expected* to sell for on date 1. We write this as[17]

The Amount That Bond *B* Is Expected to Sell for on Date 1:

$$\frac{\$1,210}{1 + \text{Spot rate expected over year 2}}$$ (6A.9)

Making two points is worthwhile now. First, because all individuals are different, the expected value of bond *B* differs across individuals. Later we will speak of a consensus expected value across investors. Second, Equation (6A.9) represents one's forecast of the price that the bond will be selling for on date 1. The forecast is made ahead of time, that is, on date 0.

The Relationship Between Forward Rate over Second Year and Spot Rate Expected Over Second Year

Given a forecast of bond *B*'s price, an investor can choose one of two strategies at date 0:

1. Buy a one-year bond. Proceeds at date 1 would be

$$\$1,080 = \$1,000 \times 1.08$$

---

[17]Technically, Equation (6A.9) is only an approximation due to *Jensen's inequality*. That is, expected values of

$$\frac{\$1,210}{1 + \text{Spot rate}} > \frac{\$1,210}{1 + \text{Spot rate expected over year 2}}$$

However, we ignore this very minor issue in the rest of the analysis.

Chapter 6   How to Value Bonds and Stocks

2. Buy a two-year bond but sell at date 1. His *expected* proceeds would be

$$\frac{1,000 \times (1.10)^2}{1 + \text{Spot rate expected over year 2}} \quad (6A.11)$$

Given our discussion of forward rates, we can rewrite (6A.11) as

$$\frac{1,000 \times 1.08 \times 1.1204}{1 + \text{Spot rate expected over year 2}} \quad (6A.12)$$

(Remember that 12.04 percent was the forward rate over year 2, f_2.)

Under what condition will the return from strategy 1 equal the expected return from strategy 2? In other words, under what condition will formula (6A.10) equal formula (6A.12)?

The two strategies will yield the same expected return only when

$$12.04\% = \text{Spot rate expected over year 2} \quad (6A.13)$$

In other words, if the forward rate equals the expected spot rate, one would expect to earn the same return over the first year whether one invested in a one-year bond, or invested in a two-year bond but sold after one year.

The Expectations Hypothesis

Equation (6A.13) seems fairly reasonable. That is, it is reasonable that investors would set interest rates in such a way that the forward rate would equal the spot rate expected by the marketplace a year from now.[18] For example, imagine that individuals in the marketplace do not concern themselves with risk. If the forward rate, f_2, is less than the spot rate expected over year 2, individuals desiring to invest for one year would always buy a one-year bond. That is, our work above shows that an individual investing in a two-year bond but planning to sell at the end of one year would expect to earn less than if he simply bought a one-year bond.

Equation (6A.13) was stated for the specific case where the forward rate was 12.04 percent. We can generalize this to

Expectations Hypothesis:

$$f_2 = \text{Spot rate expected over year 2} \quad (6A.14)$$

Equation (6A.14) says that the forward rate over the second year is set to the spot rate that people expect to prevail over the second year. This is called the *expectations hypothesis*. It states that investors will set interest rates such that the forward rate over the second year is equal to the one-year spot rate expected over the second year.

Liquidity-Preference Hypothesis

At this point, many students think that Equation (6A.14) *must* hold. However, note that we developed (6A.14) by assuming that investors were risk-neutral. Suppose, alternatively, that investors are averse to risk.

---

[18] Of course, all individuals will have different expectations, so Equation (6A.13) cannot hold for all individuals. However, financial economists generally speak of a consensus expectation. This is the expectation of the market as a whole.

Part II   *Value and Capital Budgeting*

Which of the following strategies would appear more risky for an individual who wants to invest for one year?

1. Invest in a one-year bond.
2. Invest in a two-year bond but sell at the end of one year.

Strategy 1 has no risk because the investor knows that the rate of return must be r_1. Conversely, strategy 2 has much risk; the final return is dependent on what happens to interest rates.

Because strategy 2 has more risk than strategy 1, no risk-averse investor will choose strategy 2 if both strategies have the same expected return. Risk-averse investors can have no preference for one strategy over the other only when the expected return on strategy 2 is *above* the return on strategy 1. Because the two strategies have the same expected return when f_2 equals the spot rate expected over year 2, strategy 2 can only have a higher rate of return when

Liquidity-Preference Hypothesis:

$$f_2 > \text{Spot rate expected over year 2} \qquad (6\text{A}.15)$$

That is, in order to induce investors to hold the riskier two-year bonds, the market sets the forward rate over the second year to be above the spot rate expected over the second year. Equation (6A.15) is called the *liquidity-preference hypothesis*.

We developed the entire discussion by assuming that individuals are planning to invest over one year. We pointed out that for such individuals, a two-year bond has extra risk because it must be sold prematurely. What about those individuals who want to invest for two years? (We call these people investors with a *two-year time horizon*.)

They could choose one of the following strategies:

3. Buy a two-year zero-coupon bond.
4. Buy a one-year bond. When the bond matures, they immediately buy another one-year bond.

Strategy 3 has no risk for an investor with a two-year time horizon, because the proceeds to be received at date 2 are known as of date 0. However, strategy 4 has risk since the spot rate over year 2 is unknown at date 0. It can be shown that risk-averse investors will prefer neither strategy 3 nor strategy 4 over the other when

$$f_2 < \text{Spot rate expected over year 2} \qquad (6\text{A}.16)$$

Note that introducing risk aversion gives contrary predictions. Relationship (6A.15) holds for a market dominated by investors with a one-year time horizon. Relationship (6A.16) holds for a market dominated by investors with a two-year time horizon. Financial economists have generally argued that the time horizon of the typical investor is generally much shorter than the maturity of typical bonds in the marketplace. Thus, economists view (6A.15) as the better depiction of equilibrium in the bond market with *risk-averse* investors.

However, do we have a market of risk-neutral investors or risk-averse investors? In other words, can the expectations hypothesis of Equation (6A.14) or the liquidity-preference hypothesis of Equation (6A.15) be expected to hold? As we will learn later in this book, economists view investors as being risk-averse for the most part. Yet economists are never satisfied with a casual examination of a theory's assumptions. To them, empirical evidence of a theory's predictions must be the final arbiter.

There has been a great deal of empirical evidence on the term structure of interest rates. Unfortunately (perhaps fortunately for some students), we will not be able to present the evidence in any detail. Suffice it to say that, in our opinion, the evidence supports the liquidity-preference hypothesis over the expectations hypothesis. One simple result might give students the flavour of this research. Consider an individual choosing between one of the following two strategies:

1. Invest in a one-year bond.
2.′ Invest in a 20-year bond but sell at the end of one year.

(Strategy 2′ is identical to strategy 2 except that a 20-year bond is substituted for a two-year bond.)

The expectations hypothesis states that the expected returns on both strategies are identical. The liquidity-preference hypothesis states that the expected return on strategy 2′ should be above the expected return on strategy 1. Though no one knows what returns are actually expected over a particular time period, actual returns from the past may allow us to infer expectations. The results from January 1926 to December 1999 are illuminating. Over this time period the average yearly return on strategy 1 is 3.8 percent; it is 5.5 percent on strategy 2′.[19] This evidence is generally considered to be consistent with the liquidity-preference hypothesis and inconsistent with the expectations hypothesis.

Application of Term Structure Theory

In explaining term structure theory, it was convenient to use examples of zero-coupon bonds and spot and forward rates. To see the application, we go back to coupon bonds and yields to maturity the way that actual bond data is presented in the financial press.

Figure 6A.3 shows a yield curve for Government of Canada bonds, a plot of bond yields to maturity against time to maturity. Yield curves are observed at a particular date and change shape over time. This yield curve is for April 2004.

FIGURE 6A.3

Government of Canada Yield Curve

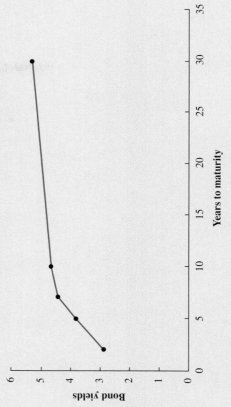

Source: *The National Post,* April 28, 2004, page IN9.

---

[19]Taken from *Stocks, Bonds, Bills, and Inflation 2000 Yearbook* (Chicago: Ibbotson Associates).

It is important to note that strategy 2′ does not involve buying a 20-year bond and holding it to maturity. Rather, it consists of buying a 20-year bond and selling it one year later, that is, when it has become a 19-year bond. This round-trip transaction occurs 63 times in the 63-year sample from January 1926 to December 1999.

Part II   Value and Capital Budgeting

Notice that the yield curve is ascending, with the long rates above the short rates. Term structure theory gives us two reasons why the observed yield curve is ascending. Investors expect that rates will rise in the future and that there is a liquidity premium.

Now suppose you were advising a friend who was renewing a home mortgage. Suppose further that the alternatives were a one-year mortgage at 8.5 percent and a two-year mortgage at 10 percent. We know that on average, over the life of a mortgage, rolling over one-year rates will probably be cheaper because the borrower will avoid paying the liquidity premium. But we also know that this approach is riskier because the ascending yield curve for bond and mortgages suggests that investors believe that rates will rise.

Appendix Questions and Problems

6.A1 Define the forward rate.

6.A2 What is the relationship between the one-year spot rate, the two-year spot rate, and the forward rate over the second year?

6.A3 What is the expectations hypothesis?

6.A4 What is the liquidity-preference hypothesis?

6.A5 What is the difference between a spot interest rate and the yield to maturity?

6.A6 Assume that the five-year spot rate is 7 percent.
   a. If the forward rate over the sixth year is currently at 5.21 percent, what is the six-year spot rate?
   b. If the forward rate over the fifth year is currently at 6.80 percent, what is the four-year spot rate?

6.A7 The appropriate discount rate for cash flows received one year from today is 9 percent. The appropriate annual discount rate for cash flows received two years from today is 10 percent.
   a. What is the price of a two-year bond that pays an annual coupon of 6 percent?
   b. What is the yield to maturity of this bond?

6.A8 The one-year spot rate equals 9 percent and the two-year spot rate equals 7 percent. What should a 5 percent coupon two-year bond cost?

6.A9 If the one-year spot rate is 8 percent and the two-year spot rate is 9 percent, what is the forward rate?

6.A10 Assume the following spot rates:

Maturity	Spot Rates (%)
1	4
2	6
3	10

What are the forward rates over each of the 3 years?

6.A11 Consider the following three zero-coupon bonds:

Bond	Face Value	Time to Maturity	Market Price
1	$1,000	one year	$900.00
2	1,000	two years	812.00
3	1,000	three years	693.18

   a. Calculate the one-, two-, and three-year spot rates.
   b. Calculate the forward rate over the second year, and the one corresponding to the third year.
   c. Is the forward rate over the third year the same as the one-year spot rate investors expect to prevail at the end of the second year? Discuss.

Chapter 6   How to Value Bonds and Stocks 167

6.A12 Consider the bonds from problem 6.A11.

a. What is the price of the third bond that risk-neutral investors expect to prevail at the end of the second year?

b. Now assume that investors are risk-averse with a two-year investment horizon. Further assume that for every year at maturity beyond two years, investors demand a 1 percent liquidity premium. What is the price of the third bond that the risk-averse investors expect to prevail at the end of the second year?

Chapter 7

Some Alternative Investment Rules

EXECUTIVE SUMMARY

Chapter 5 examined the relationship between $1 today and $1 in the future. For example, a corporate project generating a set of cash flows can be valued by discounting these flows, an approach called the *net present value* (NPV) approach. While we believe that the NPV approach is the best one for evaluating capital budgeting projects, our treatment would be incomplete if we ignored alternative methods. This chapter examines these alternative methods. We first consider the NPV approach as a benchmark. Next we examine four alternatives: payback, accounting rate of return, internal rate of return, and the profitability index.

7.1 Why Use Net Present Value?

This chapter, as well as the next two, focuses on *capital budgeting*, the decision-making process for accepting or rejecting projects. This chapter develops the basic capital budgeting methods, leaving much of the practical application to Chapters 8 and 9. But we don't have to develop these methods from scratch. In Chapter 5, we pointed out that a dollar received in the future is worth less than a dollar received today. The reason, of course, is that today's dollar can be reinvested, yielding a greater amount in the future. And we showed in Chapter 5 that the exact worth of a dollar to be received in the future is its present value. Furthermore, Section 5.1 suggested calculating the *net present value* of any project. That is, the section suggested calculating the difference between the sum of the present values of the project's future cash flows and the initial cost of the project.

The net present value (NPV) method is the first one to be considered in this chapter. We begin by reviewing the approach with a simple example. Next we ask why the method leads to good decisions.

The Alpha Corporation is considering investing in a riskless project costing $100. The project receives $107 in one year and has no other cash flows. The interest rate is 6 percent.

The NPV of the project can easily be calculated as:

$$\$0.94 = -\$100 + \frac{\$107}{1.06} \qquad (7.1)$$

From Chapter 5, we know that the project should be accepted since its NPV is positive. Had the NPV of the project been negative, as would have been the case with an interest rate greater than 7 percent, the project should be rejected.

The basic investment rule can be generalized to:

Accept a project if the NPV is greater than zero.

Reject a project if NPV is less than zero.

We refer to this as the NPV rule.

Now why does the NPV rule lead to good decisions? Consider the following two strategies available to the managers of Alpha Corporation:

1. Use $100 of corporate cash to invest in the project. The $107 will be paid as a dividend in one year.

2. Forgo the project and pay the $100 of corporate cash as a dividend today.

If strategy 2 is employed, the shareholder might deposit the dividend in his bank for one year. With an interest rate of 6 percent, strategy 2 would produce cash of $106 ($100 × 1.06) at the end of the year. The shareholder would prefer strategy 1, since strategy 2 produces less than $107 at the end of the year.

Thus, our basic point is:

Accepting positive NPV projects benefits the shareholders.

How do we interpret the exact NPV of $0.94? This is the increase in the value of the firm from the project. For example, imagine that the firm today has productive assets worth $V and has $100 of cash. If the firm forgoes the project, the value of the firm today would simply be:

$$\$V + \$100 \qquad (7.2)$$

If the firm accepts the project, the firm will receive $107 in one year but will have no cash today. Thus, the firm's value today would be:

$$\$V + \frac{\$107}{1.06} \qquad (7.3)$$

The difference between Equation (7.2) and Equation (7.3) is just $0.94, the present value of Equation (7.1). Thus:

The value of the firm rises by the NPV of the project.

Note that the value of the firm is merely the sum of the values of the different projects, divisions, or other entities within the firm. This property, called **value additivity,** is quite important. It implies that the contribution of any project to a firm's value is simply the NPV of the project. As we will see later, alternative methods discussed in this chapter do not generally have this nice property.

One detail remains. We assumed that the project was riskless, a rather implausible assumption. Future cash flows of real-world projects are invariably risky. In other words, cash flows can only be estimated, rather than known. Imagine that the managers of Alpha *expect* the cash flow of the project to be $107 next year. That is, the cash flow could be higher, say $117, or lower, say $97. With this slight change, the project is risky. Suppose the project is about as risky as the stock market as a whole, where the expected return this year is, say 10 percent. Well, 10 percent becomes the discount rate, implying that the NPV of the project would be:

$$-\$2.73 = -\$100 + \frac{\$107}{1.10}$$

Since the NPV is negative, the project should be rejected. This makes sense since a shareholder of Alpha receiving a $100 dividend today could invest it in the stock market, expecting a 10 percent return. Why accept a project with the same risk as the market but with an expected return of only 7 percent?

Conceptually, the discount rate is the return that one can expect to earn on a financial asset of comparable risk. This discount rate is often referred to as an *opportunity cost*, since corporate investment in the project takes away the shareholder's opportunity to invest the dividend in a financial asset. If the actual calculation of the discount rate strikes you as extremely difficult in the real world, you are probably right. While you can call a bank to find out the interest rate, whom do you call to find the expected return on the market this year? And, if the risk of the project differs from that of the market, how do you make the adjustment? However, the calculation is by no means impossible. While we forgo the calculation in this chapter, we present it in later chapters of the text.

Having shown that NPV is a sensible approach, how can we tell whether alternative methods are as good as NPV? The key to NPV is its three attributes:

1. *NPV Uses Cash Flows.* Cash flows from a project can be used for other corporate purposes (e.g., dividend payments, other capital-budgeting projects, or payments of corporate interest). By contrast, earnings are an artificial construct. While earnings are useful to accountants, they should not be used in capital budgeting because they do not represent cash.

2. *NPV Uses All the Cash Flows of the Project.* Other approaches ignore cash flows beyond a particular date; beware of these approaches.

3. *NPV Discounts the Cash Flows Properly.* Other approaches may ignore the time value of money when handling cash flows. Beware of these approaches as well.

? Concept
  Questions

- **What is the NPV rule?**
- **Why does this rule lead to good investment decisions?**

7.2   The Payback Period Rule

Defining the Rule

One of the most popular alternatives to NPV is the **payback period rule.** Here is how the payback period rule works.

Consider a project with an initial investment of $50,000 (ie., an initial cash outflow of $50,000). Cash flows are $30,000, $20,000, and $10,000 in the first three years, respectively. These flows are illustrated in Figure 7.1. A useful way of writing down investments like the preceding is with the notation

$$(-\$50,000, \$30,000, \$20,000, \$10,000)$$

The minus sign in front of the $50,000 reminds us that this is a cash outflow for the investor, and the commas between the different numbers indicate that they are received—or if they are cash outflows, that they are paid out—at different times. In this example we are assuming that the cash flows occur one year apart, with the first one occurring the moment we decide to take on the investment.

The firm receives cash flows of $30,000 and $20,000 in the first two years, which add up to the $50,000 original investment. This means that the firm has recovered its investment within two years. In this case two years is the *payback period* of the investment.

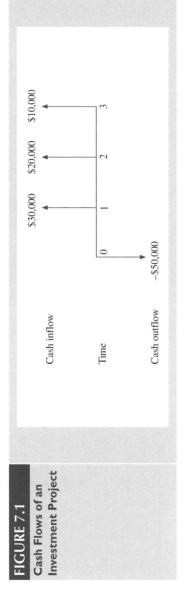

FIGURE 7.1

Cash Flows of an Investment Project

The payback period rule for making investment decisions is simple. A particular cut-off time, say two years, is selected. All investment projects that have payback periods of two years or less are accepted and all of those that pay off in more than two years, if at all, are rejected.

Problems With the Payback Method

There are at least three problems with the payback method. To illustrate the first two problems, we consider the three projects in Table 7.1. All three projects have the same three-year payback period, so they should all be equally attractive—right?

Actually, they are not equally attractive, as can be seen by a comparison of different *pairs* of projects.

Problem 1: Timing of Cash Flows Within the Payback Period Let us compare project *A* with project *B*. In years 1 through 3, the cash flows of project *A* rise from $20 to $50 while the cash flows of project *B* fall from $50 to $20. Because the large cash flow of $50 comes earlier with project *B*, its net present value must be higher. Nevertheless, we saw above that the payback periods of the two projects are identical. Thus, a problem with the payback period is that it does not consider the timing of the cash flows within the payback period. This shows that the payback method is inferior to NPV because, as we pointed out earlier, the NPV approach *discounts the cash flows properly*.

Problem 2: Payments After the Payback Period Now consider projects *B* and *C*, which have identical cash flows within the payback period. However, project *C* is clearly preferred because it has the cash flow of $60,000 in the fourth year. Thus, another problem with the payback method is that it ignores all cash flows occurring after the payback period. This flaw is not present with the NPV approach because, as we pointed out earlier, the NPV approach *uses all the cash flows of the project*. The payback method forces managers to have an artificially short-term orientation, which may lead to decisions not in the shareholders' best interests.

Problem 3: Arbitrary Standard for Payback Period We do not need to refer to Table 7.1 when considering a third problem with the payback approach. Capital markets help us estimate the discount rate used in the NPV method. The riskless rate, perhaps proxied by the yield on a Treasury instrument, would be the appropriate rate for a riskless investment.

Later chapters of this textbook show how to use historical returns in the capital markets in order to estimate the discount rate for a risky project. However, there is no comparable guide for choosing the payback cutoff date, so the choice is somewhat arbitrary.

TABLE 7.1	Expected Cash Flows for Projects A through C		
Year	A	B	C
0	−$100	−$100	−$100
1	20	50	50
2	30	30	30
3	50	20	20
4	60	60	60,000
Payback period (years)	3	3	3

Managerial Perspective

Despite its shortcomings, the payback method can be acceptable when making relatively small decisions. The decision to build a small warehouse, for example, or to pay for a tune-up for a truck is the sort of decision that is often made by lower-level management. Typically a manager might reason that a tune-up would cost, say, $200, and if it saved $120 each year in reduced fuel costs, it would pay for itself in less than two years. On such a basis the decision would be made.

Although the treasurer of the company might not have made the decision in the same way, the company endorses such decision making. Why would upper management condone or even encourage such retrograde activity in its employees? One answer would be that it is easy to make decisions using payback. Multiply the tune-up decision into 50 such decisions a month, and the appeal of this simple method becomes clearer.

The payback method also has some desirable features for managerial control. Just as important as the investment decision itself is the company's ability to evaluate the manager's decision-making ability. Under the NPV method, a long time may pass before one decides whether or not a decision was correct. With the payback method we know in two years whether the manager's assessment of the cash flows was correct.

It has also been suggested that firms with good investment opportunities but no available cash may justifiably use payback. For example, the payback method could be used by small, privately held firms with good growth prospects but limited access to the capital markets. Quick cash recovery enhances the reinvestment possibilities for such firms.

Finally, practitioners often argue that standard academic criticisms of payback overstate any real-world problems with the method. For example, textbooks typically make fun of payback by positing a project with low cash inflows in the early years but a huge cash inflow right after the payback cutoff date. This project is likely to be rejected under the payback method, though its acceptance would, in truth, benefit the firm. Project C in our Table 7.1 is an example of such a project. Practitioners point out that the pattern of cash flows in these textbook examples is much too stylized to mirror the real world. In fact, a number of executives have told us that, for the overwhelming majority of real-world projects, both payback and NPV lead to the same decision. In addition, these executives indicate that, if an investment like project C were encountered in the real world, decision makers would almost certainly make *ad hoc* adjustments to the payback rule so that the project would be accepted.

Notwithstanding all of the preceding rationale, it is not surprising to discover that as the decision grows in importance, which is to say when firms look at bigger projects, NPV becomes the order of the day. When questions of controlling and evaluating the manager become less important than making the right investment decision, payback is used less frequently. For big-ticket decisions, such as whether or not to buy a machine, build a factory, or acquire a company, the payback method is seldom used.

Summary of Payback

The payback method differs from NPV and is therefore conceptually wrong. With its arbitrary cutoff date and its blindness to cash flows after that date, it can lead to some flagrantly foolish decisions if it is used too literally. Nevertheless, because of its simplicity, as well as its other advantages mentioned above, companies often use it as a screen for making the myriad of minor investment decisions they continually face.

Although this means that you should be wary of trying to change approaches such as the payback method when you encounter them in companies, you should probably be careful not to accept the sloppy financial thinking they represent. After this course, you would do your company a disservice if you used payback instead of NPV when you had a choice.

Concept
Questions

- List the problems of the payback method.
- What are some advantages?

7.3 The Discounted Payback Period Rule

Aware of the pitfalls of the payback approach, some decision makers use a variant called the **discounted payback period rule**. Under this approach, we first discount the cash flows. Then we ask how long it takes for the discounted cash flows to equal the initial investment.

For example, suppose that the discount rate is 10 percent and the cash flows on a project are given by

$$(-\$100, \$50, \$50, \$20)$$

This investment has a payback period of two years, because the investment is paid back in that time.

To compute the project's discounted payback period, we first discount each of the cash flows at the 10 percent rate. In discounted terms, then, the cash flows look like

$$[-\$100, \$50/1.1, \$50/(1.1)^2, \$20/(1.1)^3] = (-\$100, \$45.45, \$41.32, \$15.03)$$

The discounted payback period of the original investment is simply the payback period for these discounted cash flows. The payback period for the discounted cash flows is slightly less than three years since the discounted cash flows over the three years are $101.80 (or $45.45 + $41.32 + $15.03). As long as the cash flows are positive, the discounted payback period will never be smaller than the payback period, because discounting will lower the cash flows.

At first glance the discounted payback may seem like an attractive alternative, but on closer inspection we see that it has some of the same major flaws as the payback. Like payback, discounted payback first requires us to make a somewhat magical choice of an arbitrary cutoff period, and then it ignores all of the cash flows after that date.

If we have already gone to the trouble of discounting the cash flows, any small appeal to simplicity or to managerial control that payback may have has been lost. We might just as well add up the discounted cash flows and use the NPV to make the decision. Although discounted payback looks a bit like the NPV, it is just a poor compromise between the payback method and the NPV.

7.4 The Average Accounting Return (AAR)

Defining the Rule

Another attractive and fatally flawed approach to making financial decisions is the **average accounting return (AAR)**. The average accounting return is the average project earnings after taxes and depreciation, divided by the average book value of the investment during its life. In spite of its flaws, the average accounting return method is worth examining because it is still used in business.

Consider a company that is evaluating whether or not to buy a store in a newly built mall. The purchase price is $500,000. We will assume that the store has an estimated life of five years and will need to be completely scrapped or rebuilt at the end of that time. The projected yearly sales and expense figures are shown in Table 7.2.

It is worth looking carefully at this table. In fact, the first step in any project assessment is a careful look at the projected cash flows. When the store starts up, it is estimated that first-year sales will be $433,333 and that, after expenses, the before-tax cash flow will be $233,333. After the first year, sales are expected to rise and expenses are expected to fall, resulting in a before-tax cash flow of $300,000. After that, competition from other stores and the loss in novelty will drop before-tax cash flow to $166,667, $100,000, and $33,333, respectively, in the next three years.

To compute the average accounting return on the project, we divide the average net income by the average amount invested. This can be done in three steps.

TABLE 7.2	Projected Yearly Revenue and Costs for Average Accounting Return				
	Year 1	Year 2	Year 3	Year 4	Year 5
Revenue	$433,333	$450,000	$266,667	$200,000	$133,333
Expenses	200,000	150,000	100,000	100,000	100,000
Before-tax cash flow	233,333	300,000	166,667	100,000	33,333
Depreciation	100,000	100,000	100,000	100,000	100,000
Earnings before taxes	133,333	200,000	66,667	0	−66,667
Taxes ($T_c = 0.25$)*	33,333	50,000	16,667	0	−16,667
Net income	100,000	150,000	50,000	0	−50,000

$$\text{Average net income} = \frac{(\$100,000 + 150,000 + 50,000 + 0 - 50,000)}{5} = \$50,000$$

$$\text{Average investment} = \frac{\$500,000 + 0}{2} = \$250,000$$

$$\text{AAR} = \frac{\$50,000}{\$250,000} = 20\%$$

*Corporate tax rate = T_c. The tax rebate in year 5 of −$16,667 occurs if the rest of the firm is profitable. Here, the loss in the project reduces the taxes of the entire firm.

Step 1: Determining Average Net Income   The net income in any year is the net cash flow minus depreciation and taxes. Depreciation is not a cash outflow.[1] Rather, it is a charge reflecting the fact that the investment in the store becomes less valuable every year.

We assume the project has a useful life of five years, at which time it will be worthless. Because the initial investment is $500,000 and because it will be worthless in five years, we will assume that it loses value at the rate of $100,000 each year. This steady loss in value of $100,000 is called *straight-line depreciation*. We subtract both depreciation and taxes from before-tax cash flow to derive the net income, as shown in Table 7.2. The net income over the five years is $100,000 in the first year, $150,000 in year 2, $50,000 in year 3, zero in year 4, and −$50,000 in the last year. The average net income over the life of the project is therefore

Average Net Income:

[$100,000 + $150,000 + $50,000 + $0 + (−$50,000)]/5 = $50,000

Step 2: Determining Average Investment   We stated earlier that, due to depreciation, the investment in the store becomes less valuable every year. Because depreciation is $100,000 per year, the value at the end of year zero is $500,000, the value at the end of year 1 is $400,000, and so on. What is the average value of the investment over the life of the investment?

The mechanical calculation is

Average Investment:

($500,000 + $400,000 + $300,000 + $200,000 + $100,000 + $0)/6 = $250,000   (7.4)

We divide by 6 and not 5, because $500,000 is what the investment is worth at the beginning of the five years and $0 is what it is worth at the beginning of the sixth year. In other words, there are six terms in the parentheses of Equation (7.4). Note that Table 7.2 arrives at the same answer for average investment by averaging the initial investment and ending value. This works here because we assume straight-line depreciation and zero salvage.

Step 3: Determining AAR   The average return is simply

$$AAR = \frac{\$50,000}{\$250,000} = 20\%$$

If the firm had a targeted accounting rate of return greater than 20 percent, the project would be rejected, and if its targeted return were less than 20 percent, it would be accepted.

Analyzing the Average Accounting Return Method

By now you should be able to see what is wrong with the AAR method.

The most important flaw with AAR is that it does not work with the right raw materials. It uses net income and book value of the investment, both of which come from the accounting books. Accounting numbers are somewhat arbitrary. For example, certain cash outflows, such as the cost of a building, are depreciated under current accounting rules. Other flows, such as maintenance, are expensed. In real-world situations, the decision to depreciate or expense an item involves judgment. Thus, the basic inputs of the AAR

---

[1]The rates of depreciation and tax used in this example are chosen for simplicity. Leasehold improvements are one of the few asset classes for which tax depreciation in Canada is straight-line. We discuss these topics in detail in Appendix 1A and in Chapter 8. Recall from Chapter 2 that depreciation is the special case of amortization applicable to capital assets.

method, income and average investment, are affected by the accountant's judgment. Conversely, the NPV method *uses cash flows*. Accounting judgments do not affect cash flow.

Second, AAR takes no account of timing. In the previous example, the AAR would have been the same if the $100,000 net income in the first year had occurred in the last year. However, delaying an inflow for five years would have lowered the NPV of the investment. As mentioned earlier in this chapter, the NPV approach *discounts properly*.

Third, just as payback requires an arbitrary choice of the cutoff date, the AAR method offers no guidance on what the right targeted rate of return should be. It could be the discount rate in the market. But then again, because the AAR method is not the same as the present value method, it is not obvious that this would be the right choice.

Given these problems, is the AAR method employed in practice? Like the payback method, the AAR (and variations of it) is frequently used as a "backup" to discounted cash flow methods. Perhaps this is so because it is easy to calculate and uses accounting numbers readily available from the firm's accounting system. In addition, both shareholders and the media pay a lot of attention to the overall profitability of a firm. Thus, some managers may feel pressured to select projects that are profitable in the near term, even if the projects come up short in terms of NPV. These managers may focus on the AAR of individual projects more than they should.

7.5 The Internal Rate of Return (IRR)

Now we come to the most important alternative to the NPV approach: the internal rate of return, universally known as the IRR. The IRR is about as close as you can get to the NPV without actually being the NPV. The basic rationale behind the IRR is that it tries to find a single number that summarizes the merits of a project. That number does not depend on the interest rate that prevails in the capital market. That is why it is called the internal rate of return; the number is internal or intrinsic to the project and does not depend on anything except the cash flows of the project.

For example, consider the simple project (−$100, $110) in Figure 7.2. For a given rate, the net present value of this project can be described as

$$NPV = -\$100 + \frac{\$110}{1+r} \qquad (7.5)$$

where *r* is the discount rate.

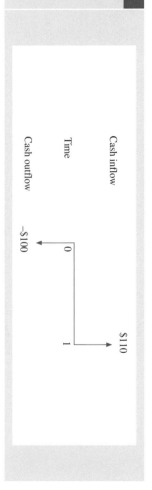

Cash inflow $110

Time   0 ————————→ 1

Cash outflow   −$100

What must the discount rate be to make the NPV of the project equal to zero? We begin by using an arbitrary discount rate of 0.08, which yields

$$\$1.85 = \$100 + \frac{\$110}{1.08} \qquad (7.6)$$

Since the NPV in Equation (7.6) is positive, we now try a higher discount rate, say, 0.12. This yields

$$-\$1.79 = \$100 + \frac{\$110}{1.12} \qquad (7.7)$$

Since the NPV in Equation (7.7) is negative, we lower the discount rate to, say, 0.10. This yields

$$0 = -\$100 + \frac{\$110}{1.10} \qquad (7.8)$$

This trial-and-error procedure tells us that the NPV of the project is zero when r equals 10 percent.[2] Thus, we say that 10 percent is the project's **internal rate of return (IRR)**. In general, the IRR is the rate that causes the NPV of the project to be zero. The implication of this exercise is very simple. The firm should be equally willing to accept or reject the project if the discount rate is 10 percent. The firm should accept the project if the discount rate is below 10 percent. The firm should reject the project if the discount rate is above 10 percent.

The general investment rule is clear:

Accept the project if IRR is greater than the discount rate.
Reject the project if IRR is less than the discount rate.

We refer to this as the **basic IRR rule.** Having mastered the basics of the IRR rule, you should recognize that we used the IRR (without defining it) when we calculated the yield to maturity of a bond in Chapter 6. In fact, the yield to maturity is the bond's IRR.[3] Now we can try the more complicated example in Figure 7.3. As we did in Equations (7.6) to (7.8), we use trial and error to calculate the internal rate of return.

[2]Of course, we could have directly solved for r in Equation (7.5) after setting NPV equal to zero. However, with a long series of cash flows, one cannot generally directly solve for r. Instead, one is forced to use a trial-and-error method similar to that in Equations (7.6), (7.7), and (7.8).

[3]Strictly speaking, this is true for bonds with annual coupons. Typically, bonds carry semiannual coupons so yield to maturity is the six-month IRR expressed as a stated rate per year.

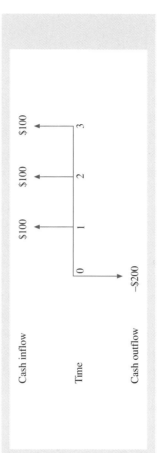

FIGURE 7.3

Cash Flows for a More Complex Project

Cash inflow   \$100   \$100   \$100   \$100

Time   0   1   2   3

Cash outflow   −\$200

We try 20 percent and 30 percent, yielding

Discount Rate	NPV
20%	$10.65
30%	−18.39

After much more trial and error, we find that the NPV of the project is zero when the discount rate is 23.37 percent. Thus, the IRR is 23.37 percent. With a 20 percent discount rate the NPV is positive and we accept it. However, if the discount rate is 30 percent, we reject it.

Algebraically, IRR is the unknown in the following equation:[4]

$$0 = -\$200 + \frac{\$100}{1 + \text{IRR}} + \frac{\$100}{(1 + \text{IRR})^2} + \frac{\$100}{(1 + \text{IRR})^3}$$

Figure 7.4 illustrates what it means to find the IRR for a project. The figure plots the NPV as a function of the discount rate. The curve crosses the horizontal axis at the IRR of 23.37 percent because this is where the NPV equals zero.

It should also be clear that the NPV is positive for discount rates below the IRR and negative for discount rates above the IRR. This means that if we accept projects like this one when the discount rate is less than the IRR, we will be accepting positive NPV projects. Thus, the IRR rule will coincide exactly with the NPV rule.

If this were all there was to it, the IRR rule would always coincide with the NPV rule. This would be a wonderful discovery because it would mean that just by computing the IRR for a project we would be able to tell where it ranks among all of the projects we are

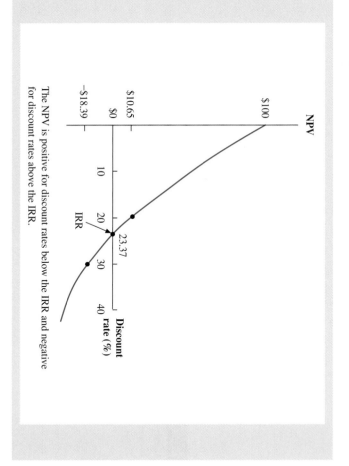

FIGURE 7.4
Net Present Value
(NPV) and
Discount Rates for
a Relatively
Complex Project

NPV

$100

$10.65

$0

−$18.39

10   20   30   40   **Discount rate (%)**

IRR

23.37

The NPV is positive for discount rates below the IRR and negative for discount rates above the IRR.

[4] One can derive the IRR directly for a problem with an initial outflow and either one or two subsequent inflows. In the case of two subsequent inflows, the quadratic formula is needed. In general, however, only trial and error will work for an outflow and three or more subsequent inflows. Hand calculators calculate IRR by trial and error, though at lightning speed.

considering. For example, if the IRR rule really works, a project with an IRR of 20 percent will always be at least as good as one with an IRR of 15 percent.

But the world of finance is not so kind. Unfortunately, the IRR rule and the NPV rule are the same only for simple examples like the ones above. Several problems with the IRR occur in more complicated situations.

Concept Question

• How does one calculate the IRR of a project?

7.6 Problems with the IRR Approach

Definition of Independent and Mutually Exclusive Projects

An **independent project** is one whose acceptance or rejection is independent of the acceptance or rejection of other projects. For example, imagine that McDonald's is considering putting another hamburger outlet in Beijing to get ready for the 2008 Olympics. Acceptance or rejection of this unit is likely to be unrelated to the acceptance or rejection of any other restaurant in its system. The remoteness of the outlet in question ensures that it will not pull sales away from other outlets.

Now consider the other extreme, **mutually exclusive investments.** What does it mean for two projects, *A* and *B*, to be mutually exclusive? You can accept *A* or you can accept *B* or you can reject both of them, but you cannot accept both of them. For example, *A* might be a decision to build an apartment building on a corner lot that you own, and *B* might be a decision to build a movie theatre on the same lot.

We now present two general problems with the IRR approach that affect both independent and mutually exclusive projects. Next, we deal with two problems affecting mutually exclusive projects only.

Two General Problems Affecting Both Independent and Mutually Exclusive Projects

We begin our discussion with project *A*, which has the following cash flows:

$$(-\$100, \$130)$$

The IRR for project *A* is 30 percent. Table 7.3 provides other relevant information on the project. The relationship between NPV and the discount rate is shown for this project in Figure 7.5. As you can see, the NPV declines as the discount rate rises.

TABLE 7.3	The Internal Rate of Return and Net Present Value								
	Project A			Project B			Project C		
Dates:	0	1	2	0	1	2	0	1	2
Cash flows	−$100	$130		$100	−$130		−$100	$230	−$132
IRR	30%			30%			10%	20%	
NPV @ 10%	$18.2			−$18.2			>10%		<20%
Accept if market rate	<30%			>30%					
Financing or investing	Investing			Financing			Mixture		

FIGURE 7.5   Net Present Value and Discount Rates for Projects A, B, and C

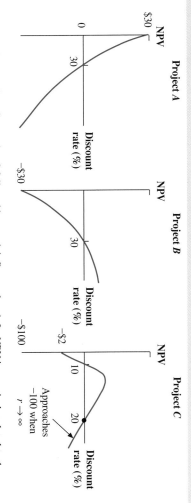

Project A has a cash outflow at date 0 followed by a cash inflow at date 1. Its NPV is negatively related to the discount rate.

Project B has a cash inflow at date 0 followed by a cash outflow at date 1. Its NPV is positively related to the discount rate.

Project C has two changes of sign in its cash flows. It has an outflow at date 0, an inflow at date 1, and an outflow at date 2. Projects with more than one change of sign can have multiple rates of return.

These cash flows are exactly the reverse of the flows for project A. In project B, the firm receives funds first and then pays out funds later. While unusual, projects of this type do exist. For example, consider a corporation conducting a seminar where the participants pay in advance. Because large expenses are frequently incurred at the seminar date, cash inflows precede cash outflows.

Consider our trial-and-error method to calculate IRR:

$$-\$4 = +\$100 - \frac{\$130}{1.25}$$

$$\$0 = +\$100 - \frac{\$130}{1.30}$$

$$\$3.70 = +\$100 - \frac{\$130}{1.35}$$

As with project A, the internal rate of return is 30 percent. However, notice that the net present value is *negative* when the discount rate is *below* 30 percent. Conversely, the net present value is positive when the discount rate is above 30 percent. The decision rule is exactly the opposite of our previous result. For this type of a project, the rule is:

Accept the project when IRR is less than the discount rate.

Reject the project when IRR is greater than the discount rate.

This unusual decision rule follows from the graph of project B in Figure 7.5. The curve is upward sloping, implying that NPV is *positively* related to the discount rate.

The graph makes intuitive sense. Suppose that the firm wants to obtain $100 immediately. It can either (1) conduct project B or (2) borrow $100 from a bank. Thus, the project is actually a substitute for borrowing. In fact, because the IRR is 30 percent, taking on

Problem 1: Investing or Financing?

Now consider project B, with cash flows of

$$(\$100, -\$130)$$

project *B* is tantamount to borrowing at 30 percent. If the firm can borrow from a bank at, say, only 25 percent, it should reject the project. However, if a firm can only borrow from a bank at, say, 35 percent, it should accept the project. Thus, project *B* will be accepted if and only if the discount rate is *above* the IRR.[5]

This should be contrasted with project *A*. If the firm has $100 of cash to invest, it can either (1) conduct project *A* or (2) lend $100 to the bank. The project is actually a substitute for lending. In fact, because the IRR is 30 percent, taking on project *A* is tantamount to lending at 30 percent. The firm should accept project *A* if the lending rate is below 30 percent. Conversely, the firm should reject project *A* if the lending rate is above 30 percent.

Because the firm initially pays out money with project *A* but initially receives money with project *B*, we refer to project *A* as an investing-type project and project *B* as a financing-type project. Investing-type projects are the norm. Because the IRR rule is reversed for a financing-type project, we view this type of project as a problem—unless it is understood properly.

Problem 2: Multiple Rates of Return   Suppose the cash flows from a project are

$$(-\$100, \$230, -\$132)$$

Because this project has a negative cash flow, a positive cash flow, and another negative cash flow, the project's cash flows exhibit two changes of sign, or "flip-flops." While this pattern of cash flows might look a bit strange at first, many projects require outflows of cash after receiving some inflows. An example would be a strip-mining project. The first stage in such a project is the initial investment in excavating the mine. Profits from operating the mine are received in the second stage. The third stage involves a further investment to reclaim the land and satisfy the requirements of environmental protection legislation. Cash flows are negative at this stage.

Projects financed by lease arrangements also produce negative cash flows followed by positive ones. We study leasing carefully in a later chapter, but for now we will give you a hint. Using leases for financing can sometimes bring substantial tax advantages. These advantages are often sufficient to make an otherwise bad investment have positive cash flows following an initial outlay. But after a while the tax advantages decline or run out. The cash flows turn negative when this occurs.

It is easy to verify that this project has not one but two IRRs: 10 percent and 20 percent.[6] In a case like this, the IRR does not make any sense. What IRR are we to use: 10 percent or 20 percent? Because there is no good reason to use one over the other, IRR simply cannot be used here.

---

[5]This paragraph implicitly assumes that the cash flows of the project are risk-free. In this way, we can treat the borrowing rate as the discount rate for a firm needing $100. With risky cash flows, another discount rate would be chosen. However, the intuition behind the decision to accept when IRR is less than the discount rate would still apply.

[6]The calculations are

$$0 = -\$100 + \frac{\$230}{1.1} - \frac{\$132}{(1.1)^2}$$

$$= -\$100 + \$209.09 - \$109.09$$

and

$$0 = -\$100 + \frac{\$230}{1.2} - \frac{\$132}{(1.2)^2}$$

$$= -\$100 + \$191.67 - \$91.67$$

Thus, we have multiple rates of return.

Why does this project have multiple rates of return? Project *C* generates multiple internal rates of return because both an inflow and an outflow occur after the initial investment. In general, these flip-flops or changes in sign produce multiple IRRs. In theory, a cash flow stream with *K* changes in sign can have up to *K* sensible internal rates of return (IRRs above −100%).[7] Therefore, since project *C* has two changes in sign, it can have as many as two IRRs. As we pointed out, projects whose cash flows change sign repeatedly can occur in the real world.

NPV Rule   Of course, we should not be too worried about multiple rates of return. After all, we can always fall back on the NPV rule. Figure 7.5 plots the NPV of project *C* (−$100, $230, −$132) as a function of the discount rate. As the figure shows, the NPV is zero at both 10 percent and 20 percent and negative outside the range. Thus, the NPV rule tells us to accept the project if the appropriate discount rate is between 10 percent and 20 percent. The project should be rejected if the discount rate lies outside of this range.

Modified IRR   As an alternative to NPV, we now introduce the **modified IRR (MIRR)** method, which handles the multiple-IRR problem by combining cash flows until only one change in sign remains. To see how it works, consider project *C* again. With a discount rate of, say, 14 percent, the value of the last cash flow, −$132, is:

$$-\$132/1.14 = -\$115.79$$

as of date 1. Since $230 is already received at that time, the "adjusted" cash flow at date 1 is $114.21 (230 − 115.79). Thus, the MIRR approach produces the following two cash flows for the project:

$$(-\$100, \$114.21)$$

Note that, by discounting and then combining cash flows, we are left with only one change in sign. The IRR rule can now be applied. The IRR of these two cash flows is 14.21 percent, implying that the project should be accepted given our assumed discount rate of 14 percent.

Of course, project *C* is relatively simple to begin with, since it has only three cash flows and two changes in sign. However, the same procedure can easily be applied to more

---

[7] Those of you who are steeped in algebra might have recognized that finding the IRR is like finding the root of a polynomial equation. For a project with cash flows of $(C_0, \ldots, C_T)$, the formula for computing the IRR requires us to find the interest rate, *r*, that makes

$$NPV = C_0 + C_1/(1 + r) + \ldots + C_T/(1 + r)^T = 0$$

If we let the symbol *x* stand for the discount factor,

$$x = 1/(1 + r)$$

then the formula for the IRR becomes

$$NPV = C_0 + C_1 x + C_2 x^2 + \ldots + C_T x^T = 0$$

Finding the IRR, then, is the same as finding the roots of this polynomial equation. If a particular value x^* is a root of the equation, then, because

$$x = 1/(1 + r)$$

it follows that there is an associated IRR:

$$r^* = (1/x^*) - 1$$

From the theory of polynomials, it is well known that an *n*th-order polynomial has *n* roots. Generally, an IRR above −100 percent is considered sensible. Since each root that is positive generates an IRR above −100 percent, any positive root can have a sensible IRR associated with it. Applying Descartes' rule of signs gives the result that a stream of *n* cash flows can have up to *K* IRRs above −100 percent, where *K* is the number of changes in sign for the cash flows.

complex projects; that is, just keep discounting and combining the later cash flows until only one change of sign remains.

While this adjustment does correct for multiple IRRs, it appears, at least to us, to violate the "spirit" of the IRR approach. As stated earlier, the basic rationale behind the IRR method is that it provides a single number summarizing the merits of a project. That number does not depend on the discount rate. In fact, that is why it is called the internal rate of return; the number is *internal*, or intrinsic, to the project and does not depend on anything except the cash flows of the project. By contrast, MIRR is clearly a function of the discount rate. However, this point is not meant to be a criticism of MIRR. A firm using this adjustment will avoid the multiple-IRR problem, just as a firm using the NPV rule will avoid it.

Are We Ever Safe from the Multiple-IRR Problem?   If the first cash flow for a project is negative—because it is the initial investment—and if all of the remaining flows are positive, there can be only a single, unique IRR, no matter how many periods the project lasts. This is easy to understand by using the concept of the time value of money. For example, it is easy to verify that project A in Table 7.3 has an IRR of 30 percent, because using a 30 percent discount rate gives

$$NPV = -\$100 + \$130/(1.3)$$
$$= 0$$

How do we know that this is the only IRR? Suppose that we were to try a discount rate greater than 30 percent. In computing the NPV, changing the discount rate does not change the value of the initial cash flow of $-\$100$ because that cash flow is not discounted. But raising the discount rate can only lower the present value of the future cash flows. In other words, because the NPV is zero at 30 percent, any increase in the rate will push the NPV into the negative range. Similarly, if we try a discount rate of less than 30 percent, the overall NPV of the project will be positive. Though this example has only one positive flow, the above reasoning still implies a single, unique IRR if there are many inflows (but no outflows) after the initial investment.

If the initial cash flow is positive—and if all of the remaining flows are negative—there can only be a single, unique IRR. This result follows from reasoning similar to that above. Both these cases have only one change of sign or flip-flop in the cash flows. Thus, we are safe from multiple IRRs whenever there is only one sign change in the cash flows.

General Rules   The following chart summarizes our rules:

Flows	Number of IRRs	IRR Criterion	NPV Criterion
First cash flow is negative and all remaining cash flows are positive.	1	Accept if IRR $> r$ Reject if IRR $< r$	Accept if NPV > 0 Reject if NPV < 0
First cash flow is positive and all remaining cash flows are negative.	1	Accept if IRR $< r$ Reject if IRR $> r$	Accept if NVP > 0 Reject if NVP < 0
Some cash flows after first are positive and some cash flows after first are negative.	May be more than 1	No valid IRR	Accept if NPV > 0 Reject if NPV < 0

Note: IRR = Internal rate of return; r = Discount rate; and NPV = Net present value.

Note that the NPV criterion is the same for each of the three cases. In other words, NPV analysis is always appropriate. Conversely, the IRR can be used only in certain cases.

Problems Specific to Mutually Exclusive Projects

As mentioned earlier, two or more projects are mutually exclusive if the firm can, at most, accept only one of them. We now present two problems dealing with the application of the IRR approach to mutually exclusive projects. These two problems are quite similar, though logically distinct. [8]

The Scale Problem   A professor we know motivates class discussions on this topic with the statement: "Students, I am prepared to let one of you choose between two mutually exclusive 'business' propositions. Opportunity 1—You give me $1 now and I'll give you $1.50 back at the end of the class period. Opportunity 2—You give me $10 and I'll give you $11 back at the end of the class period. You can only choose one of the two opportunities. And you cannot choose either opportunity more than once. I'll pick the first volunteer."

Which would you choose? The correct answer is opportunity 2. [9] To see this, look at the following chart:

	Cash Flow at Beginning of Class	Cash Flow at End of Class (90 minutes later)	NPV*	IRR
Opportunity 1	−$1	+$1.50	$0.50	50%
Opportunity 2	−10	+11.00	1.00	10

*We assume a zero rate of interest because the class lasted only 90 minutes. It just seemed like a lot longer.

As we have stressed earlier in the text, one should choose the opportunity with the higher NPV. This is opportunity 2 in the example. Or, as one of the professor's students explained it: "I trust the professor, so I know I'll get my money back. And I have $10 in my pocket right now so I can choose either opportunity. At the end of the class, I'll be able to play two rounds of my favourite electronic game with opportunity 2 and still have my original investment, safe and sound. The profit on opportunity 1 buys only one round.

This business proposition illustrates a defect with the internal rate of return criterion. The basic IRR rule says take opportunity 1, because the IRR is 50 percent. The IRR is only 10 percent for opportunity 2.

Where does IRR go wrong? The problem with IRR is that it ignores issues of scale. While opportunity 1 has a greater IRR, the investment is much smaller. In other words, the high percentage return on opportunity 1 is more than offset by the ability to earn at least a decent return on a much bigger investment under opportunity 2. [10]

Since IRR seems to be misguided here, can we adjust or correct it? We illustrate how in the next example.

---

[8] Another problem with IRR occurs either when long-term interest rates differ from short-term rates (that is, when the term structure of interest rates, presented in Appendix 6A, is not flat) or when the riskiness of the cash flows changes over time. In these circumstances, using IRR is inappropriate because no one discount rate is applicable to all the cash flows

[9] The professor uses real money here. Though many students have done poorly on the professor's exams over the years, no student ever chose opportunity 1. The professor claims that his students are "money players."

[10] A 10 percent return is more than decent over a 90-minute interval!

EXAMPLE

Jack and Ramona have just purchased the rights to *Corporate Finance: The Motion Picture*. They will produce this major motion picture on either a small budget or a big budget. The estimated cash flows are

	Cash Flow at Date 0	Cash Flow at Date 1	NPV @ 25%	IRR
Small budget	–$10 million	$40 million	$22 million	300%
Large budget	– 25 million	65 million	27 million	160%

Because of high risk, a 25 percent discount rate is considered appropriate. Ramona wants to adopt the large budget because the NPV is higher. Jack wants to adopt the small budget because the IRR is higher. Who is right?

For the reasons espoused in the classroom example above, NPV is correct. Hence, Ramona is right. However, Jack is very stubborn where IRR is concerned. How can Ramona justify the large budget to Jack using the IRR approach?

This is where incremental IRR comes in. She calculates the incremental cash flows from choosing the large budget instead of the small budget as

	Cash Flow at Date 0 (in $ millions)	Cash Flow at Date 1 (in $ millions)
Incremental cash flows from choosing large budget instead of small budget	–25 – (–10) = –15	65 – 40 = 25

This chart shows that the incremental cash flows are –$15 million at date 0 and $25 million at date 1. Ramona calculates incremental IRR as

Formula for Calculating the Incremental IRR:

$$0 = -\$15 \text{ million} + \frac{\$25 \text{ million}}{1 + IRR}$$

IRR equals 66.67 percent in this equation. Ramona says that the **incremental IRR** is 66.67 percent. Incremental IRR is the IRR on the incremental investment from choosing the large project instead of the small project.

In addition, we can calculate the NPV of the incremental cash flows:

NPV of Incremental Cash Flows:

$$-\$15 \text{ million} + \frac{\$25 \text{ million}}{1.25} = \$5 \text{ million}$$

We know the small-budget picture would be acceptable as an independent project since its NPV is positive. We want to know whether it is beneficial to invest an additional $15 million in order to make the large-budget picture instead. In other words, is it beneficial to invest an additional $15 million in order to receive an additional $25 million next year? First, the calculations above show the NPV of the incremental investment to be positive. Second, the incremental IRR of 66.67 percent is higher than the discount rate of 25 percent. For both reasons, the incremental investment can be justified. The second reason is what Jack needed to hear to be convinced. Hence, the large-budget movie should be made.

Part II   Value and Capital Budgeting

In review, we can handle this example (or any mutually exclusive example) in one of three ways:

1. *Compare the NPVs of the two choices.* The NPV of the large-budget picture is greater than the NPV of the small-budget picture; that is, $27 million is greater than $22 million.

2. *Compare the incremental NPV from making the large-budget picture instead of the small-budget picture.* Because incremental NPV equals $5 million, we choose the large-budget picture.

3. *Compare the incremental IRR to the discount rate.* Because the incremental IRR is 66.67 percent and the discount rate is 25 percent, we take the large-budget picture.

All three approaches always give the same decision. However, we must not compare the IRRs of the two pictures. If we did we would make the wrong choice; that is, we would accept the small-budget picture.

While students frequently think that problems of scale are relatively unimportant, the truth is just the opposite. No real-world project comes in one clear-cut size. Rather, the firm has to *determine* the best size for the project. The movie budget of $25 million is not fixed in stone. Perhaps an extra $1 million to hire a bigger star or to film at a better location will increase the movie's gross. Similarly, an industrial firm must decide whether it wants a warehouse of, say, 500,000 square feet or 600,000 square feet. And, earlier in the chapter we imagined McDonald's opening an outlet in Beijing. If it does this, it must decide how big the outlet should be. For almost any project, someone in the firm has to decide on its size, implying that problems of scale abound in the real world.

One final note here. Students ask which project should be subtracted from the other in calculating incremental flows. Notice that we are subtracting the smaller project's cash flows from the bigger project's cash flows. This leaves an *outflow* at date 0. We then use the basic IRR rule on the incremental flows.[11]

The Timing Problem   Below we illustrate another very similar problem with using the IRR approach to evaluate mutually exclusive projects.

Suppose that the Kaufold Corporation has two alternative uses for a warehouse. It can store toxic waste containers (investment A) or electronic equipment (investment B). The cash flows are as follows:

	Year				NPV			
	0	1	2	3	@ 0%	@ 10%	@ 15%	IRR
Investment A	−$10,000	$10,000	$1,000	$ 1,000	$2,000	$669	$109	16.04%
Investment B	− 10,000	1,000	1,000	12,000	4,000	751	−484	12.94

We find that the NPV of investment B is higher with low discount rates, and the NPV of investment A is higher with high discount rates. This is not surprising if you look closely at the cash flow patterns. The cash flows of A occur early, whereas the cash flows of B occur later. If we

---

[11] Alternatively, we could have subtracted the larger project's cash flows from the smaller project's cash flows. This would have left an *inflow* at date 0, making it necessary to use the IRR rule for financing situations. This would work but we find it more confusing.

assume a high discount rate, we favour investment *A* because we are implicitly assuming that the early cash flow (for example, $10,000 in year 1) can be reinvested at that rate. Because most of investment *B*'s cash flows occur in year 3, *B*'s value is relatively high with low discount rates.[12]

    The NPVs and IRRs for both projects appear in Figure 7.6. Project *A* has an NPV of $2,000 at a discount rate of zero. This is calculated by simply adding up the cash flows without discounting them. Project *B* has an NPV of $4,000 at the zero rate. However, the NPV of project *B* declines more rapidly as the discount rate increases than does the NPV of project *A*. As stated above, this is because *B*'s cash flows occur later. Both projects have the same NPV at a discount rate of 10.55 percent. The IRR for a project is the rate at which the NPV equals zero. Because the NPV of *B* declines more rapidly, *B* actually has a lower IRR.

    As with the movie example presented above, we can select the better project with one of three different methods:

1. *Compare NPVs of the two projects.* Figure 7.6 aids our decision. If the discount rate is below 10.55 percent, one should choose project *B* because *B* has a higher NPV. If the rate is above 10.55 percent, one should choose project *A* because *A* has a higher NPV.

2. *Compare incremental IRR to discount rate.* Another way of determining that *B* is a better project is to subtract the cash flows of *A* from the cash flows of *B* and then to calculate the IRR. This is the incremental IRR approach we spoke of earlier.

    The incremental cash flows are as follows:

					NPV of Incremental Cash Flows				
Year:	0	1	2	3	@ 0%	@ 10%	@ 15%	IRR
B − A	0	−$9,000	0	$11,000	$2,000	$83	−$593	10.55%

This chart shows that the incremental IRR is 10.55 percent. In other words, the NPV on the incremental investment is zero when the discount rate is 10.55 percent. Thus, if

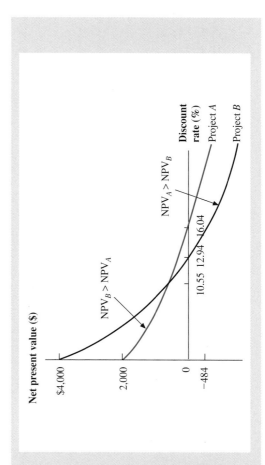

FIGURE 7.6

Net Present Value and the Internal Rate of Return for Mutually Exclusive Projects

the relevant discount rate is below 10.55 percent, project *B* is preferred to project *A*. If the relevant discount rate is above 10.55 percent, project *A* is preferred to project *B*.[13]

3. *Calculate NPV on incremental cash flows*. Finally, one could calculate the NPV on the incremental cash flows. The chart that appears with the previous method displays these NPVs. We find that the incremental NPV is positive when the discount rate is either 0 percent or 10 percent. The incremental NPV is negative if the discount rate is 15 percent. If the NPV is positive on the incremental flows, one should choose *B*. If the NPV is negative, one should choose *A*.

In summary, the same decision is reached whether one compares the NPVs of the two projects, compares the incremental IRR to the relevant discount rate, or examines the NPV of the incremental cash flows. However, as shown earlier, one should not compare the IRR of project *A* with the IRR of project *B*.

We suggested earlier that one should subtract the cash flows of the smaller project from the cash flows of the bigger project. What do we do here since the two projects have the same initial investment? Our suggestion in this case is to perform the subtraction so that the first nonzero cash flow is negative. In the Kaufold Corporation example, we achieved this by subtracting *A* from *B*. In this way, we can still use the basic IRR rule for evaluating cash flows.

These examples illustrate problems with the IRR approach in evaluating mutually exclusive projects. Both the professor–student example and the motion picture example illustrate the problem that arises when mutually exclusive projects have different initial investments. The Kaufold Corp. example illustrates the problem that arises when mutually exclusive projects have different cash flow timings. When working with mutually exclusive projects, it is not necessary to determine whether it is the scale problem or the timing problem that exists. Very likely both occur in any real world situation. Instead, the practitioner should simply use either an incremental IRR or an NPV approach.

Redeeming Qualities of the IRR

The IRR probably survives because it fills a need that the NPV does not. People seem to want a rule that summarizes the information about a project in a single rate of return. This single rate provides people with a simple way of discussing projects. For example, one manager in a firm might say to another, "Remodelling the north wing has a 20 percent IRR."

To their credit, however, companies that employ the IRR approach seem to understand its deficiencies. For example, companies frequently restrict managerial projections of cash flows to be negative at the beginning and strictly positive later. Perhaps, then, the ability of the IRR approach to capture a complex investment project in a single number and the ease of communicating that number explain the survival of the IRR.

A Test

To test your knowledge, consider the following two statements:

1. You must know the discount rate to compute the NPV of a project but you compute the IRR without referring to the discount rate.

2. Hence, the IRR rule is easier to apply than the NPV rule because you don't use the discount rate when applying IRR.

[13] In this example, we first showed that the NPVs of the two projects are equal when the discount rate is 10.55 percent. We next showed that the incremental IRR is also 10.55 percent. This is not a coincidence; this equality must always hold. The incremental IRR is the rate that causes the incremental cash flows to have zero NPV. The incremental cash flows have zero NPV when the two projects have the same NPV.

The first statement is true. The discount rate is needed to *compute* NPV. The IRR is *computed* by solving for the rate where the NPV is zero. No mention is made of the discount rate in the mere computation. However, the second statement is false. In order to *apply* IRR, you must compare the internal rate of return with the discount rate. Thus, the discount rate is needed for making a decision under either the NPV or IRR approach.

- What is the difference between independent projects and mutually exclusive projects?
- What are two problems with the IRR approach that apply to both independent and mutually exclusive projects?
- What is the MIRR?
- What are two additional problems applying only to mutually exclusive projects?

7.7 The Profitability Index (PI)

Another method that is used to evaluate projects is called the **profitability index (PI)**. It is the ratio of the present value of the future expected cash flows *after* initial investment divided by the amount of the initial investment. The profitability index can be represented as

$$\text{Profitability index (PI)} = \frac{\text{PV of cash flows subsequent to initial investment}}{\text{Initial investment}}$$

EXAMPLE

Hiram Finnegan, Inc., applies a 12 percent cost of capital to two investment opportunities.

Project	Cash Flows ($000,000)			PV @ 12% of Cash Flows Subsequent to Initial Investment ($000,000)	Profitability Index	NPV @ 12% ($000,000)
	C_0	C_1	C_2			
1	−20	70	10	70.5	3.53	50.5
2	−10	15	40	45.3	4.53	35.3

For example, the profitability index is calculated for project 1 as follows. The present value of the cash flows *after* the initial investment are

$$\$70.5 = \frac{\$70}{1.12} + \frac{\$10}{(1.12)^2} \tag{7.9}$$

The profitability index is calculated by dividing the result of Equation (7.9) by the initial investment of $20.[14] This yields

$$3.53 = \frac{\$70.5}{\$20}$$

---

[14]For a "borrowing" type of investment the initial cash flow is an inflow rather than an outlay. In this case, we restate the PI as the present value of the inflows divided by the present value of the outflows.

We consider three possibilities:

1. *Independent projects.* We first assume that we have two independent projects. According to the NPV criterion, both projects should be accepted since NPV is positive in each case. The NPV is positive whenever the profitability index is greater than 1. Thus, the *PI decision rule* is

   Accept an independent project if PI > 1.
   Reject if PI < 1.

2. *Mutually exclusive projects.* Let us assume that you can now only accept one project. NPV analysis says accept project 1 because this project has the bigger NPV. Because project 2 has the higher PI, the profitability index leads us to the wrong selection.

   The problem with the profitability index for mutually exclusive projects is the same as the scale problem with the IRR that we mentioned earlier. Project 2 is smaller than project 1. Because the PI is a ratio, this index misses the fact that project 1 has a larger investment than project 2 has. Thus, like IRR, PI ignores differences of scale for mutually exclusive projects.

   However, as with IRR, the flaw with the PI approach can be corrected using incremental analysis. We write the incremental cash flows after subtracting project 2 from project 1 as follows:

Project	Cash Flows ($000,000)			PV @ 12% of Cash Flows Subsequent to Initial Investment ($000,000)	Profitability Index	NPV @ 12% ($000,000)
	C_0	C_1	C_2			
1 − 2	−10	55	−30	25.2	2.52	15.2

   Because the profitability index on the incremental cash flows is greater than 1.0, we should choose the bigger project, that is, project 1. This is the same decision we get with the NPV approach.

3. *Capital rationing.* The two cases above implicitly assumed that the firm could always attract enough capital to make any profitable investments. Now we consider the case when a firm does not have enough capital to fund all positive NPV projects. This is the case of **capital rationing.**

   Imagine that the firm has a third project, as well as the first two. Project 3 has the following cash flows:

Project	Cash Flows ($000,000)			PV @ 12% of Cash Flows Subsequent to Initial Investment ($000,000)	Profitability Index	NPV @ 12% ($000,000)
	C_0	C_1	C_2			
3	−10	−5	60	43.4	4.34	33.4

   Further, imagine that the projects of Hiram Finnegan, Inc., are independent, but the firm has only $20 million to invest. Because project 1 has an initial investment of $20 million, the firm cannot select both this project and another one. Conversely, because projects 2 and 3 have initial investments of $10 million each, both these projects can be chosen. In other words, the cash constraint forces the firm to choose either project 1 or projects 2 and 3.

   What should the firm do? Individually, projects 2 and 3 have lower NPVs than project 1 has. However, when the NPVs of projects 2 and 3 are added together, they are higher than the NPV of project 1. Thus, common sense dictates that projects 2 and 3 shall be accepted.

What does our conclusion have to say about the NPV rule or the PI rule? In the case of limited funds, we cannot rank projects according to their NPVs. Instead, we should rank them according to the ratio of present value to initial investment. This is the PI rule. Both project 2 and project 3 have higher PI ratios than does project 1. Thus, they should be ranked ahead of project 1 when capital is rationed.[15]

The usefulness of the profitability index under capital rationing can be explained in terms of the expression "bang for the buck." In capital budgeting, the profitability index measures the bang (the dollar return) for the buck invested. Hence, it is useful for capital rationing.

It should be noted that the profitability index does not work if funds are also limited beyond the initial time period. For example, if heavy cash outflows elsewhere in the firm were to occur at date 1, project 3 might need to be rejected. In other words, the profitability index cannot handle capital rationing over multiple time periods.

Concept Questions

- How does one calculate a project's profitability index?
- How is the profitability index applied to independent projects, mutually exclusive projects, and situations of capital rationing?

7.8 The Practice of Capital Budgeting

So far, this chapter has asked the question: Which capital budgeting methods should companies be using? An equally important question is: Which methods *are* companies using? Table 7.4 goes a long way toward answering this question. As can be seen from the table, approximately three-quarters of large U.S. and Canadian companies use the IRR and NPV methods. An exclusively Canadian study by Jog and Srivastava reached a similar conclusion.[16] This is not surprising, given the theoretical advantages of these approaches.

TABLE 7.4	Percent of CFOs Who Always or Almost Always Use a Given Technique	
		% Always or Almost Always
Internal rate of return (IRR)		75.6%
Net present value (NPV)		74.9
Payback method		56.7
Discounted payback		29.5
Accounting rate of return		30.3
Profitability index		11.9

Source: Figure 2 from John R. Graham and Campbell R. Harvey, "The Theory and Practice of Corporate Finance: Evidence from the Field," *Journal of Financial Economics* 60 (2001). Based on a survey of 392 CFOs.

---

[15]Our approach to PI ranking under capital rationing worked because the initial outlays on the two higher-ranked projects exactly used up the budget of $20 million. If some funds were left over, the PI ranking method could break down. In this case, the solution would be to consider all feasible combinations of projects within the budget and to choose the combination with the highest total NPV.

[16]V. M. Jog and A. K. Srivastava, "Capital Budgeting Practices in Corporate Canada," *Financial Practice and Education* 5 (Fall/Winter 1995), pp. 37–43.

Part II   Value and Capital Budgeting

Over one-half of these companies use the payback method, a rather surprising result given the conceptual problems with this approach. And while discounted payback represents a theoretical improvement over regular payback, the usage here is far less. Perhaps companies are attracted to the user-friendly nature of payback. In addition, the flaws of this approach, as mentioned in the current chapter, may be relatively easy to correct. For example, while the payback method ignores all cash flows after the payback period, an alert manager can make ad hoc adjustments for a project with back-loaded cash flows.

One might expect the capital budgeting methods of large firms to be more sophisticated than the methods of small firms. After all, large firms have the financial resources to hire more sophisticated employees. Table 7.5 provides some support for this idea. Here, firms indicate frequency of use of the various capital budgeting methods on a scale of 0 (never) to 4 (always). Both the IRR and NPV methods are used more frequently, and payback less frequently, in large firms than in small firms. Conversely, large and small firms employ the last three approaches about equally.

The use of quantitative techniques in capital budgeting varies with the industry. As one would imagine, firms that are better able to estimate cash flows precisely are more likely to use NPV. For example, estimation of cash flow in certain aspects of the oil business is quite feasible. Because of this, energy-related firms were among the first to use NPV analysis. Conversely, the flows in the motion picture business are very hard to project. The grosses of great hits like *Titanic*, *Star Wars*, *ET*, and *Fatal Attraction* were far, far greater than anyone imagined. The big failures like *Waterworld* were unexpected as well. Consequently, NPV analysis is frowned upon in the movie business.

Non-cash-flow factors may occasionally play a role in capital budgeting decisions. Ego is a good example of such a factor (see the In Their Own Words box on p. 193).

TABLE 7.5	Frequency of Use of Various Capital Budgeting Methods	
	Large Firms	Small Firms
Internal rate of return (IRR)	3.41	2.87
Net present value (NPV)	3.42	2.83
Payback method	2.25	2.72
Discounted payback	1.55	1.58
Accounting rate of return	1.25	1.41
Profitability index	0.75	0.78

Firms indicate frequency of use on a scale from 0 (never) to 4 (always). Numbers in table are averages across respondents.

Source: Table 2 from J. R. Graham and C. R. Harvey, "The Theory and Practice of Corporate Finance: Evidence From the Field," *Journal of Financial Economics* 60 (May 2001).

In Their Own Words

Michael Frisconlanti on Tall Buildings: After 65 Storeys, It's All About Ego

The race to be the planet's tallest is playing out in four cities around the world, proving that ego — and not economics or architecture — is the engine of a world-class project.

"Most notable projects aren't done without the developer, the owner or the president having a really large ego," laughs David Klages, the principal planner on the Kuala Lumpur, Malaysia, site that now houses the Petronas Twin Towers, the world's tallest office buildings.

"It's a case of 'Mine is bigger than yours.'"

Recently, Donald Trump announced a partnership with Hollinger International Inc. to erect a building on the Chicago waterfront that could surpass Petronas. And on the weekend, the Russian government began discussions to add a few metres to its Ostankino telecommunications tower ... just to make it a tad higher than Toronto's CN Tower.

Experts suggest a tower's economic potential peaks at about 65 storeys, mainly because things such as maintenance and elevator costs begin to outweigh sources of revenue.

"Really, the economics between 80 storeys and 112 storeys is probably against economics," Hollinger president David Radler said. "But the one thing we're doing is making a statement."

"We have a building that's world famous and that creates added economic value," Mr. Radler said.

Not to mention bragging rights.

"We're going to build the biggest tower in the world," he said. "We'll see what happens."

Dubbed the Chicago Trump Tower, the project is likely to exceed US$1-billion and 80 storeys. It is to be constructed on the site where Hollinger's *Chicago Sun-Times* currently sits (Hollinger is a half-owner of the *National Post*). The skyscraper is to house at least 2.4 million square feet of office space, posh stores, luxurious condominiums and perhaps even a hotel.

A final decision has not been made, but there is a good

chance the edifice will stand slightly taller than Malaysia's 452-metre Petronas Twin Towers — restoring phallic bragging rights to Chicago. Its Sears Tower was the world's tallest until Petronas stole the title four years ago.

"We are looking at different versions of different buildings," Mr. Trump said in an interview. "I think it would be exciting, but we have to look into the practicality of it."

Despite his pragmatism, few people think he will settle for anything less than the biggest.

"You're talking about a building that Donald Trump wants to do," Mr. Klages said. "And I'm not sure anybody in the entire world has a bigger ego than Donald Trump."

When Mr. Klages was working on the Kuala Lumpur site during the 1990s, he said the Malaysian government's "mine is bigger than yours" attitude was at the heart of the development, and Mr. Trump probably has the same vision.

"They want to make a statement," he said.

The Council on Tall Buildings and Urban Habitat considers Malaysia's Twin Towers to be the world's tallest buildings. But that is only because a "building" in the council's eyes must be designed for residential, business, or manufacturing purposes.

That leaves the CN Tower, which stands at a little more than 553 metres, out of running.

It is still the world's tallest free-standing structure, but even that title is in jeopardy now that the Russian government plans to stretch the Ostankino tower in Moscow to 562 m (an extra 30 metres was added to the CN Tower during construction in 1976 just to make it higher than Ostankino).

"It's more about the fame than anything else," said William Code, director of the urban development program at the University of Western Ontario and a longtime member of the Council on Tall Buildings and Urban Habitat.

National Post, Monday, July 23, 2001, pp. A1–2. Used with permission.

7.9 SUMMARY AND CONCLUSIONS

1. In this chapter we cover different investment decision rules. We evaluate the most popular alternatives to the NPV: the payback period, the accounting rate of return, the internal rate of return, and the profitability index. In doing so, we learn more about the NPV.

2. While we find that the alternatives have some redeeming qualities, when all is said and done, they are not the NPV rule; for those of us in finance, that makes them decidedly second-rate.

3. Of the competitors to NPV, IRR must be ranked above either payback or accounting rate of return. In fact, IRR always reaches the same decision as NPV in the normal case where the initial outflows of an independent investment project are only followed by a series of inflows.

4. We classified the flaws of IRR into two types. First, we considered the general case applying to both independent and mutually exclusive projects. There appeared to be two problems here:
   a. Some projects have cash inflows followed by one or more outflows. The IRR rule is inverted here: One should accept when the IRR is *below* the discount rate.
   b. Some projects have a number of changes of sign in their cash flows. Here, there are likely to be multiple internal rates of return. The practitioner must use either NPV or modified IRR here.

5. Next, we considered the specific problems with the IRR for mutually exclusive projects. We showed that, due to differences in either size or timing, the project with the highest IRR need not have the highest NPV. Hence, the IRR rule should not be applied. (Of course, NPV can still be applied.)

   However, we then calculated incremental cash flows. For ease of calculation, we suggested subtracting the cash flows of the smaller project from the cash flows of the larger project. In that way, the incremental initial cash flow is negative.

   One can correctly pick the better of two mutually exclusive projects in three other ways:
   a. Choose the project with the higher NPV.
   b. If the incremental IRR is greater than the discount rate, choose the bigger project.
   c. If the incremental NPV is positive, choose the bigger project.

6. We describe the capital rationing as a case where funds are limited to a fixed dollar amount. With capital rationing the profitability index can be a useful method. Of course, a manager can never go wrong by maximizing the total NPV of all company projects.

KEY TERMS

Average accounting return (AAR)	174	Internal rate of return (IRR)	177
Basic IRR rule	177	Modified IRR (MIRR)	182
Capital rationing	190	Mutually exclusive investments	179
Discounted payback period rule	173	Payback period rule	170
Incremental IRR	185	Profitability index (PI)	189
Independent project	179	Value additivity	169

SUGGESTED READING

For a discussion of what capital budgeting techniques are used by large firms, see:

Vijay M. Jog and Ashwani K. Srivastava. "Capital Budgeting Practice in Corporate Canada." *Financial Practice and Education 5* (Fall/Winter 1995), pp. 37–43.

J. R. Graham and C. R. Harvey. "The Theory and Practice of Corporate Finance: Evidence from the Field." *Journal of Financial Economics 60* (May 2001).

QUESTIONS & PROBLEMS

The Payback Period Rule

7.1   Fuji Software, Inc., has the following mutually exclusive projects.

Year	Project A	Project B
0	–$7,500	–$5,000
1	4,000	2,500
2	3,500	1,200
3	1,500	3,000

   a. Suppose Fuji's payback period cutoff is two years. Which of these two projects should be chosen?
   b. Suppose Fuji uses the NPV rule to rank these two projects. Which project should be chosen if the appropriate discount rate is 15 percent?

7.2 Suppose Peach Paving, Inc., invests $1 million today on a new construction project. The project will generate annual cash flows of $150,000 in perpetuity. The appropriate annual discount rate for the project is 10 percent.

a. What is the payback period for the project? If Peach Paving, Inc.'s, cutoff is 10 years, should the project be accepted?

b. What is the discounted payback period for the project?

c. What is the NPV of the project?

The Average Accounting Return

7.3 Your firm is considering purchasing a machine with the following annual, end-of-year, book-investment accounts.

	Purchase Date	Year 1	Year 2	Year 3	Year 4
Gross investment	$16,000	$16,000	$16,000	$16,000	$16,000
Less: Accumulated depreciation	0	4,000	8,000	12,000	16,000
Net investment	$16,000	$12,000	$8,000	$4,000	$0

The machine generates, on average, $4,500 per year in additional net income.

a. What is the average accounting return for this machine?

b. What three flaws are inherent in this decision rule?

7.4 Western Printing Co. has an opportunity to purchase a $2 million printing machine. The machine has an economic life of five years and will be worthless after that time. It will generate net income of $100,000 one year from today and the income stream will grow at 6 percent per year thereafter. The company uses straight-line depreciation (i.e., equal depreciation each year). What is the average accounting return of the investment? Should the machine be purchased if Western Printing's average accounting return cutoff is 20 percent?

7.5 The Bluerock Group has invested $8,000 in a high-tech project lasting three years. Depreciation is $4,000, $2,500, and $1,500 in years 1, 2, and 3, respectively. The project generates pretax income of $2,000 each year. The pretax income already includes the depreciation expense. If the tax rate is 25 percent, what is the project's average accounting return (AAR)?

The Internal Rate of Return

7.6 Compute the internal rate of return on projects with the following cash flows.

Year	Cash Flows ($)	
	Project A	Project B
0	−3,000	−6,000
1	2,500	5,000
2	1,000	2,000

EXCEL

7.7 Teddy Bear Planet, Inc., has a project with the following cash flows.

Year	Cash Flows ($)
0	−8,000
1	4,500
2	3,500
3	2,500

a. Compute the internal rate of return on the project.

b. Suppose the appropriate discount rate is 8 percent. Should the project be accepted?

7.8   Compute the internal rate of return for the cash flows of the following two projects.

	Cash Flows ($)	
Year	Project A	Project B
0	−2,000	−1,500
1	2,000	500
2	8,000	1,000
3	8,000	1,500

EXCEL

7.9   Suppose you are offered $5,000 today but must make the following payments.

Year	Cash Flows ($)
0	5,000
1	−2,500
2	−2,000
3	−1,000
4	−1,000

   a.   What is the IRR of this offer?
   b.   If the appropriate discount rate is 10 percent, should you accept this offer?
   c.   If the appropriate discount rate is 20 percent, should you accept this offer?
   d.   What is the NPV of the offer if the appropriate discount rate is 10 percent?
          20 percent?
   e.   Are the decisions under the NPV rule in part (*d*) consistent with those of the IRR
          rule?

7.10   As the chief financial officer of the Orient Express, you are offered the following two
       mutually exclusive projects.

	Cash Flows ($)	
Year	Project A	Project B
0	−5,000	−100,000
1	3,500	65,000
2	3,500	65,000

   a.   What are the IRRs of these two projects?
   b.   If you were told only the IRRs of the projects, which would you choose?
   c.   What did you ignore when you made your decision in part (*b*)?
   d.   How can the problem be remedied? Perform the appropriate calculation.
   e.   Based on your answer to part (*d*), which project should you choose? The appropriate
          discount rate is 15 percent.
   f.   According to the NPV rule, which of these two projects should be pursued? Again,
          assume a 15 percent discount rate.

7.11   Consider two streams of cash flows, *A* and *B*. Stream *A*'s first cash flow is $5,000 and
       is received three years from today. Future cash flows in stream *A* grow by 4 percent in
       perpetuity. Stream *B*'s first cash flow is −$6,000 and is received two years from today
       and will continue in perpetuity. Assume that the appropriate discount rate is
       12 percent.
   a.   What is the present value of each stream?
   b.   Suppose that the two streams are combined into one project, called *C*. What is the
          IRR of project *C*?
   c.   What is the correct IRR rule for project *C*?

7.12 The investment in project A is $1 million, and the investment in project B is $2 million. Both projects have a unique internal rate of return of 20 percent. Is the following statement true or false?

For any discount rate from zero percent to 20 percent, project B has an NPV twice as great as that of project A.

Explain your answer.

The Profitability Index

7.13 Suppose the following two independent investment opportunities are available to Greenplain, Inc. The appropriate discount rate is 10 percent.

Year	Project Alpha	Project Beta
0	−$500	−$2,000
1	300	300
2	700	1,800
3	600	1,700

a. Compute the profitability index for each of the two projects.

b. Which project(s) should Greenplain accept based on the profitability index rule?

7.14 Consider the following two mutually exclusive projects available to Global Investments, Inc.

EXCEL

	C_0	C_1	C_2	Profitability Index	NPV
A	−$1,000	$1,000	$500	1.32	$322
B	−500	500	400	1.57	285

The appropriate discount rate for the projects is 10 percent. Global Investments chose to undertake project A. At a luncheon for shareholders, the manager of a pension fund that owns a substantial amount of the firm's stock asks you why the firm chose project A instead of project B when project B has a higher profitability index.

How would you, the CFO, justify your firm's action? Are there any circumstances under which Global Investments should choose project B?

7.15 The treasurer of Amaro Canned Fruits, Inc., has projected the cash flows of projects A, B, and C as follows.

Year	Project A	Project B	Project C
0	−$100,000	−$200,000	−$100,000
1	70,000	130,000	75,000
2	70,000	130,000	60,000

Suppose the relevant discount rate is 12 percent a year.

a. Compute the profitability index for each of the three projects.

b. Compute the NPV for each of the three projects.

c. Suppose these three projects are independent. Which project(s) should Amaro accept based on the profitability index rule?

d. Suppose these three projects are mutually exclusive. Which project(s) should Amaro accept based on the profitability index rule?

e. Suppose Amaro's budget for these projects is $300,000. The projects are not divisible. Which project(s) should Amaro accept?

7.16 Bill plans to open a self-serve grooming centre in a storefront. The grooming equipment will cost $150,000, paid immediately. Bill expects after-tax cash inflows of $40,000 annually for seven years, after which he plans to scrap the equipment and retire to the beaches of Nevis. The first cash inflow occurs at the end of the first year. Assume the required return is 15 percent. What is the project's PI? Should it be accepted?

Part II   Value and Capital Budgeting

Comparison of Investment Rules

7.17 Define each of the following investment rules. In your definition, state the criteria for accepting or rejecting independent projects under each rule.

a. Payback period

b. Average accounting return

c. Internal rate of return

d. Profitability index

e. Net present value

EXCEL

7.18 Consider the following after-tax cash flows of two mutually exclusive projects for the *China Daily News*.

Year	New Sunday Early Edition	New Saturday Late Edition
0	−$1,200	−$2,100
1	600	1,000
2	550	900
3	450	800

a. Based on the payback period rule, which project should be chosen?

b. Which project has the greater IRR?

c. Based on the incremental IRR rule, which project should be chosen? The appropriate discount rate is 12 percent.

d. Now imagine that for the same cash flows, the annual earnings for the New Sunday Early Edition are $400, $350, and $300. The annual earnings for the New Saturday Late Edition are $800, $700, and $600. Suppose there is no corporate tax and the earnings represent income after depreciation. The firm uses straight-line depreciation (i.e., equal amounts of depreciation in each year). What is the average accounting return for each of these two projects?

7.19 Consider the following cash flows on two mutually exclusive projects for the Bahamas Recreation Corporation (BRC). Both projects require an annual return of 15 percent.

Year	Deepwater Fishing	New Submarine Ride
0	−$600,000	−$1,800,000
1	270,000	1,000,000
2	350,000	700,000
3	300,000	900,000

As a financial analyst for BRC, you are asked the following questions.

a. Based on the discounted payback period rule, which project should be chosen?

b. If your decision rule is to accept the project with the greater IRR, which project should you choose?

c. Since you are fully aware of the IRR rule's scale problem, you calculate the incremental IRR for the cash flows. Based on your computation, which project should you choose?

d. To be prudent, you compute the NPV for both projects. Which project should you choose? Is it consistent with the incremental IRR rule?

7.20 The Carrick Mining Corporation is set to open a gold mine in Northern Ontario. According to the treasurer, Monty Goldstein, "This is a golden opportunity." The mine will cost $600,000 to open and will have an economic life of 11 years. It will generate a cash inflow of $100,000 at the end of the first year and the cash inflows are projected to grow at 8 percent per year for the next 10 years. After 11 years, the mine will be abandoned. Abandonment costs will be $50,000 at the end of year 11.

a. What is the IRR for the gold mine?

b. The Carrick Mining Corporation requires a 10 percent return on such undertakings. Should the mine be opened?

7.21 An investment under consideration has a payback of five years, a cost of $250,000, and the required rate of return is 12 percent.

a. What is the worst case NPV? Explain.

b. What is the best case NPV? Explain.

7.22 Consider the following cash flows of two mutually exclusive projects for Totally Electric Inc. Assume the discount rate for Totally Electric is 10 percent and the minimum acceptable IRR is 20 percent.

Year	Project A	Project B
0	−$150,000	−$80,000
1	15,000	60,000
2	35,000	40,000
3	50,000	20,000
4	200,000	13,000

a. Based on the payback period rule, which project would you choose? Why?

b. Based on the average accounting return, which project would you choose? Why? (Assume there is no corporate tax, and the cash flows above are income before depreciation. The firm uses a straight-line depreciation method.)

c. Based on the NPV, which project would you choose? Why?

d. Based on the IRR, which project would you choose? Why?

7.23 Pinnacle Electronics, a TV manufacturer, needs to decide the future of its company. It can invest its R&D in either standard HDTV technology, or the new plasma technology, but not both. Consider the following cash flows of the two mutually exclusive projects for Pinnacle. Assume the discount rate for Pinnacle is 10 percent and the minimum acceptable IRR is 25 percent.

Year	HDTV	Plasma
0	−$1,000	−$2,200
1	1,000	700
2	600	1,100
3	300	2,200

a. Based on the profitability index decision rule, in which project should the firm invest?

b. Based on the NPV, in which project should the firm invest?

c. Based on your findings in (a) and (b), what would you recommend to the CEO of Pinnacle and why?

7.24 Mario Brothers, a game manufacturer, has a new idea for an adventure game. It can market the game as either a traditional board game or an interactive CD-ROM, but not both. Consider the following cash flows of the two mutually exclusive projects for Mario Brothers. Assume the discount rate for Mario Brothers is 10 percent and the minimum acceptable IRR is 20 percent.

Year	Board Game	CD-ROM
0	−$300	−$1,500
1	400	1,100
2	100	800
3	100	400

a. Based on the payback period rule, which project should be chosen?

b. Based on the NPV, which project should be chosen?

c. Based on the IRR, which project should be chosen?

d. Based on the incremental IRR, which project should be chosen?

Part II   Value and Capital Budgeting

7.25 Hanmi Group, a consumer electronics conglomerate, is reviewing its annual budget in wireless technology. It is considering investments in three different technologies to develop wireless communication devices. Consider the following cash flows of the three independent projects for Hanmi. Assume the discount rate for Hanmi is 10 percent. Further, Hanmi Group only has $30 million to invest in new projects this year.

	Cash Flows (in millions)			
Year	CDMA	G4	Wi-Fi	
0	−$10	−$20	−$ 30	
1	25	20	20	
2	15	50	40	
3	5	40	100	

a. Based on the profitability index decision rule, rank these investments.

b. Based on the NPV, rank these investments.

c. Based on your findings in (*a*) and (*b*), what would you recommend to the CEO of Hanmi Group and why?

7.26 Consider the following cash flows of two mutually exclusive projects for AZ-Motorcars. Assume the discount rate for AZ-Motorcars is 10 percent and the minimum acceptable IRR is 30 percent.

Year	AZM Mini-SUV	AZF Full-SUV
0	−$200,000	−$500,000
1	200,000	200,000
2	150,000	300,000
3	150,000	300,000
SUM	$300,000	$300,000

a. Based on the payback period, which project should be taken?

b. Based on the NPV, which project should be taken?

c. Based on the IRR, which project should be taken?

d. Based on the above analysis, is incremental IRR analysis necessary? If yes, please conduct the analysis.

7.27 Consider the following cash flows of two mutually exclusive projects for Tokyo Rubber Company. Assume the discount rate for Tokyo Rubber Company is 10 percent and the minimum acceptable IRR is 30 percent.

Year	Dry Prepreg	Solvent Prepreg
0	−$1,000,000	−$500,000
1	600,000	500,000
2	400,000	300,000
3	1,000,000	100,000
SUM	$1,000,000	$400,000

a. Based on the payback period, which project should be taken?

b. Based on the NPV, which project should be taken?

c. Based on the IRR, which project should be taken?

d. Based on the above analysis, is incremental IRR analysis necessary? If yes, please conduct the analysis.

EXCEL

7.28 Consider two mutually exclusive new product launch projects that Nagano Golf is considering. Assume the discount rate for Nagano Golf is 15 percent and the minimum acceptable IRR is 40 percent.

Project A: Nagano NP-30
Professional clubs that will take an initial investment of $100,000 at time 0.
Next five years (years 1–5) of sales will generate a consistent cash profit of $40,000 per year.
Introduction of new product at year 6 terminates further cash flows from this project.

Project B: Nagano NX-20
High-end amateur clubs that will take an initial investment of $30,000 at time 0.
Cash profit at year 1 is $20,000. In each subsequent year cash profit will grow at 15 percent per year.
Introduction of new product at year 6 terminates further cash flows from this project.

Year	NP-30	NX-20
0	−$100,000	−$ 30,000
1	40,000	20,000
2	40,000	23,000
3	40,000	26,450
4	40,000	30,418
5	40,000	34,980
SUM	$100,000	$104,848

Please fill in the following table:

	NP-30	NX-20	Implications
NPV			
IRR			
Incremental IRR			
PI			

7.29 Consider two mutually exclusive R&D projects that ADM is considering. Assume the discount rate for ADM is 15 percent and the minimum acceptable IRR is 25 percent.

Project A: Server CPU 0.13 micron processing project
By shrinking the die size to 0.13 micron, ADM will be able to offer server CPU chips with lower power consumption and heat generation, meaning faster CPUs.

Project B: New telecom chip project
Entry into this industry will require introduction of a new chip for cell phones. The know-how will require large upfront capital, but success of the project will lead to large cash flows later on.

Year	A	B
0	−$100,000	−$200,000
1	50,000	60,000
2	50,000	60,000
3	40,000	60,000
4	30,000	100,000
5	20,000	200,000
SUM	$ 90,000	$280,000

Please fill in the following table:

	A	B	Implications
NPV			
IRR			
Incremental IRR			
PI			

7.30 You are a senior manager at Poeing Aircrafts and have been authorized to spend up to $200,000 for projects. The three projects that you are considering have the following characteristics:

Project A: Initial investment of $150,000. Cash flow of $50,000 at year 1 and $100,000 at year 2.
This is a plant expansion project, in which the required rate of return is 10 percent.

Project B: Initial investment of $200,000. Cash flow of $200,000 at year 1 and $111,000 at year 2.
This is a new product development project, in which the required rate of return is 20 percent.

Project C: Initial investment of $100,000. Cash flow of $100,000 at year 1 and $100,000 at year 2.
This is a market expansion project, in which the required rate of return is 20 percent.

Assume the corporate discount rate is 10 percent.
Please offer your recommendations, backed by your analysis.

Year	B	C
0	−$200,000	−$100,000
1	200,000	100,000
2	111,000	100,000
SUM	$111,000	$100,000

	B	C	Implications
NPV			
IRR			
Incremental IRR			
PI			
Payback			

Some Alternative Investment Rules

7.31 Darin Clay, the CFO of MakeMoney.com, has to decide between the following two projects:

Year	Project Million	Project Billion
0	−1,500	−I_o
1	$I_o + 200$	$I_o + 500$
2	1,200	1,500
3	1,500	2,000

The expected rate of return for either of the two projects is 12 percent. What is the range of initial investment (I_o) for which Project Billion is more financially attractive than Project Million?

7.32 Projects *A* and *B* have the following cash flows:

Year	Project A	Project B
0	−1,000	−2,000
1	C1A	C1B
2	C2A	C2B
3	C3A	C3B

a. Which of the two projects would have a higher IRR? Why?

b. A student claims $IRR_A = 2IRR_B$. Is it true or false? Why?

c. If $C1B = 2C1A$, $C2B = 2C2A$, and $C3B = 2C3A$, then is $IRR_A = IRR_B$?

d. To be prudent, you compute the NPV for both projects. Which project should you choose? Is it consistent with the incremental IRR rule?

7.33 Atlantic Megaprojects has a contract to build a tunnel connecting two Atlantic provinces. The contract calls for the firm to complete the tunnel in three years with an annual cash outlay of $200 million at the end of years 1 and 2. At the end of the third year, governments will pay Atlantic Megaprojects $520 million. If it wishes, the firm can exercise an option to build the tunnel in just two years by subcontracting part of the work to a government-sponsored entity designed to create employment in the region. Under this option, Atlantic Megaprojects will make a cash payment of $440 million at the end of the first year and will receive $520 million after the second year.

a. Suppose that Atlantic Megaprojects has a cost of capital of 15 percent. Should the firm subcontract the work?

b. Now suppose that Atlantic Megaprojects can estimate its cost of capital only up to a range. Over what range of discount rates is subcontracting attractive?

Chapter 8

Net Present Value and Capital Budgeting

EXECUTIVE SUMMARY

In late 1990, the Boeing Company announced its intention to build the Boeing 777, a new commercial airplane that would be able to carry up to 390 passengers and fly 12,160 kilometres without refuelling. This was expected to be an enormous undertaking. Analysts believed the up-front investment and research and development expenditures necessary to manufacture the Boeing 777 would be as much as $8 billion. Delivery of the first planes was expected to take place in 1995 and to continue for at least 35 years. Was the Boeing 777 a good project for Boeing? In 1990, was the NPV for the Boeing 777 positive? This chapter attempts to answer these important questions. The Boeing 777 is an example of capital budgeting decision making at the Boeing Company.

Previous chapters discussed the basics of capital budgeting and the net present value approach. We now want to move beyond these basics into the real-world application of these techniques. We want to show you how to use discounted cash flow (DCF) analysis and net present value (NPV) in capital budgeting decisions.

In this chapter, we show how to identify the relevant cash flows of a project, including initial investment outlays, requirements for working capital, and operating cash flows. We look at the effects of depreciation and taxes. We examine the impact of inflation on interest rates and on a project's discount rate, and we show why inflation must be handled consistently in NPV analysis.

8.1 Incremental Cash Flows

Cash Flows—Not Accounting Income

You may not have thought about it, but there is a big difference between corporate finance courses and financial accounting courses. Techniques in corporate finance generally use cash flows, whereas financial accounting generally stresses income or earnings numbers. Certainly, our text has followed this tradition since our net present value techniques discounted cash flows, not earnings. When considering a single project, we discounted the cash flows that the firm receives from the project. When valuing the firm as a whole, we discounted dividends—not earnings—because dividends are the cash flows that an investor receives.

There are many differences between earnings and cash flows. For example, consider a firm buying a building for $100,000 today. The entire $100,000 is an immediate cash outflow. However, assuming straight-line depreciation over 20 years, only $5,000 (or $100,000/20) is considered an accounting expense in the current year.[1] Current earnings

---

[1] Recall from Chapter 2 that accountants use the term *amortization* to refer to depreciation and depletion.

are thereby reduced by only $95,000. The remaining $95,000 is expensed over the following 19 years.

Because the seller of the property demands immediate payment, the cost of the project to the firm at date 0 is $100,000. Thus, the full $100,000 figure should be viewed as an immediate outflow for capital budgeting purposes.

In addition, it is not enough to use cash flows. In calculating the NPV of a project, only cash flows that are *incremental* to the project should be used. **Incremental cash flows** are the changes in the firm's cash flows that occur as a direct consequence of accepting the project. That is, we are interested in the difference between the cash flows of the firm with and without the project.

The use of incremental cash flows sounds easy enough, but pitfalls abound in the real world. In this section we describe how to avoid some of the pitfalls of determining incremental cash flows.

Sunk Costs

A **sunk cost** is a cost that has already occurred. Because sunk costs are in the past, they cannot be changed by the decision to accept or reject the project. Just as we "let bygones be bygones," we should ignore such costs. Sunk costs are not incremental cash outflows.

EXAMPLE

The General Milk Company is currently evaluating the NPV of establishing a line of chocolate milk. As part of the evaluation, the company had paid a consulting firm $100,000 to perform a test marketing analysis. The expenditure was made last year. Is this cost relevant for the capital budgeting decision now confronting the management of General Milk Company?

The answer is no. The $100,000 is not recoverable, so the $100,000 expenditure is a sunk cost, or "spilled milk." Of course, the decision to spend $100,000 for a marketing analysis was a capital budgeting decision itself and was perfectly relevant *before* it was sunk. Our point is that once the company incurred the expense, the cost became irrelevant for any future decision.

Opportunity Costs

Your firm may have an asset that it is considering selling, leasing, or employing elsewhere in the business. If the asset is used in a new project, potential revenues from alternative uses are lost. These lost revenues can meaningfully be viewed as costs. They are called **opportunity costs** because, by taking the project, the firm forgoes other opportunities for using the assets.

EXAMPLE

Suppose the Pacific Trading Company has an empty warehouse in Vancouver that can be used to store a new line of electronic pinball machines. The company hopes to market the machines to affluent West Coast consumers. Should the cost of the warehouse and land be included in the costs associated with introducing a new line of electronic pinball machines?

The answer is yes. The use of a warehouse is not free; it has an opportunity cost. The cost is the cash that could be raised by the company if the decision to market the electronic pinball machines were rejected and the warehouse and land were put to some other use (or sold). If so, the NPV of the alternative uses becomes an opportunity cost of the decision to sell electronic pinball machines.

Side Effects

Another difficulty in determining incremental cash flows comes from the side effects of the proposed project on other parts of the firm. A side effect is classified as either **erosion** or **synergy**. Erosion occurs when a new product reduces the sales and, hence, the cash flows, of existing products. Synergy occurs when a new project increases the cash flows of existing projects.

Suppose the Innovative Motors Corporation (IMC) is determining the NPV of a new convertible sports car. Some of the customers who would purchase the car are owners of IMC's compact sedan. Are all sales and profits from the new convertible sports car incremental?

The answer is no because some of the cash flow represents transfers from other elements of IMC's product line. This is erosion, which must be included in the NPV calculation. Without taking erosion into account, IMC might erroneously calculate the NPV of the sports car to be, say, $100 million. If half the customers are transfers from the sedan and lost sedan sales have an NPV of −$150 million, the true NPV is −$50 million ($100 million − $150 million).

IMC is also contemplating the formation of a racing team. The team is forecasted to lose money for the foreseeable future, with perhaps the best projection showing an NPV of −$35 million for the operation. However, IMC's managers are aware that the team will likely generate great publicity for all of IMC's products. A consultant estimates that the increase in cash flows elsewhere in the firm has a present value of $65 million. Assuming that the consultant's estimates of synergy are trustworthy, the net present value of the team is $30 million ($65 million − $35 million). The managers should form the team.

Allocated Costs

Frequently a particular expenditure benefits a number of projects. Accountants allocate this cost across the different projects when determining income. However, for capital budgeting purposes, this **allocated cost** should be viewed as a cash outflow of a project only if it is an incremental cost of the project.

The Voetmann Consulting Corp. devotes one wing of its suite of offices to a library requiring a cash outflow of $100,000 a year in upkeep. A proposed capital budgeting project is expected to generate revenue equal to 5 percent of the firm's overall sales. An executive at the firm, H. Sears, argues that $5,000 (5% × 100,000) should be viewed as the proposed project's share of the library's costs. Is this appropriate for capital budgeting?

The answer is no. One must ask the question: What is the difference between the cash flows of the entire firm with the project and the cash flows of the entire firm without the project? The firm will spend $100,000 on library upkeep whether or not the proposed project is accepted. Since acceptance of the proposed project does not affect this cash flow, the cash flow should be ignored when calculating the NPV of the project.

? Concept Questions

- What are the four difficulties in determining incremental cash flows?
- Define sunk costs, opportunity costs, side effects, and allocated costs.

8.2 The Majestic Mulch and Compost Company: An Example

We next consider the example of a proposed investment in machinery and related items. Our example involves the Majestic Mulch and Compost Company (MMCC) and power mulching tools.

The MMCC, originally established in 1988 to make composting equipment, is now a leading producer of composters. In 1990 the company introduced "Friends of Grass," its first line of high-performance composters. The MMCC management has sought opportunities in whatever businesses seem to have some potential for cash flow. In 1993, World B. Clean, vice-president of MMCC, identified another segment of the compost market that looked promising and that he felt was not adequately served by larger manufacturers. That market was for power mulching tools, and he believed that a large number of composters valued a high-performance mulcher to aid in composting. He also believed that it would be difficult for competitors to take advantage of the opportunity because of MMCC's cost advantages and because of its highly developed marketing skills.

As a result, in late 2000 MMCC decided to evaluate the marketing potential of power mulching tools. MMCC sent a questionnaire to consumers in three markets: Vancouver, Toronto, and Montreal. The results of the three questionnaires were much better than expected and supported the conclusion that the power mulching tools could achieve a 10 to 15 percent share of the market. Of course, some people at MMCC complained about the cost of the test marketing, which was $250,000. However, Clean argued that it was a sunk cost and should not be included in project evaluation.

In any case, the MMCC is now considering investing in a machine to produce power mulching tools. The power mulchers would be produced in a building owned by the firm and located outside Prince George, B.C. It is currently vacant, and has no resale value due to its location. Working with his staff, Clean is preparing an analysis of the proposed new product. He summarizes his assumptions as follows: The cost of the tool-making machine is $800,000. The machine has an estimated market value at the end of eight years of $150,000. Production by year during the eight-year life of the machine is expected to be as follows: 6,000 units, 9,000 units, 12,000 units, 13,000 units, 12,000 units, 10,000 units, 8,000 units, and 6,000 units. The price of power mulchers in the first year will be $100. The power mulching tool market is highly competitive, so Clean believes that the price of power mulchers will increase only 2 percent per year, as compared to the anticipated general inflation rate of 5 percent. Conversely, the materials used to produce power mulchers are becoming more expensive. Because of this, variable production cash outflows are expected to grow 5 percent per year. First-year variable production costs will be $64 per unit, and fixed production costs will be $50,000 each year. The tax rate is 40 percent.

Net working capital is defined as the difference between current assets and current liabilities. Clean finds that the firm must maintain an investment in working capital. Like any manufacturing firm, it will purchase raw materials before production and sale, giving rise to an investment in inventory. It will maintain cash as a buffer against unforeseen expenditures. Its credit sales will generate accounts receivable. Management believes that the investment in the different items of working capital totals $40,000 in year 0, stays at 15 percent of sales at the end of each year, and falls to $0 by the project's end. In other words, the investment in working capital is completely recovered by the end of the project's life.

Projections based on these assumptions and Clean's analysis appear in Tables 8.1 through 8.4. In these tables all cash flows are assumed to occur at the *end* of the year. Because of the large amount of data in these tables, it is important to see how the tables are related. Table 8.1 shows the basic data for both investment and income. Supplementary schedules, as presented in Tables 8.2 and 8.3, help explain where the numbers in Table 8.1 come from. Our goal is to obtain projections of cash flow. The data in Table 8.1 are all that is needed to calculate the relevant cash flows, as shown in Table 8.4.

An Analysis of the Project

Investments   The investment outlays required for the project are summarized in the bottom segment of Table 8.1. They consist of two parts:[2]

1. *The power mulching tool machine.* The purchase requires a cash outflow of $800,000 at year 0. The firm realizes a cash inflow when the machine is sold in year 8. These cash flows are shown in lines 9 and 10 of Table 8.1.

2. *The investment in working capital.* Required working capital appears in line 7. Working capital rises over the early years of the project as expansion occurs. However, all working capital is assumed to be recovered at the end, a common assumption in capital budgeting. In other words, all inventory is sold by the end, the cash balance maintained as a buffer is liquidated, and all accounts receivable are collected. Increases in working capital in the early years must be funded by cash generated elsewhere in the firm. Hence, these increases are viewed as cash *outflows*. Conversely, decreases in working capital in the later years are viewed as cash inflows. All of these cash flows are presented in line 8. A more complete discussion of working capital is provided later in this section. The total cash flow from the above two investments is shown in line 11.

Income, Taxes, and Operating Cash Flow   Next, the determination of income and operating cash flow is presented in the top segment of Table 8.1. While we are ultimately interested in cash flow—not income—we need the income calculation in order to determine

---

TABLE 8.1	The Worksheet for Cash Flows of the MMCC*							
	Year 0	Year 1	Year 2	Year 3	Year 4	Year 5	Year 6	Year 7	Year 8
I. Income									
(1) Sales revenues		$600,000	$918,000	$1,248,480	$1,379,570	$1,298,919	$1,104,081	$900,930	$689,211
(2) Operating costs		434,000	654,800	896,720	1,013,144	983,509	866,820	736,129	590,327
(3) CCA		80,000	144,000	115,200	92,160	73,728	58,982	47,186	37,749
(4) EBIT		86,000	119,200	236,560	274,266	241,682	178,278	117,615	61,136
(5) Taxes		34,400	47,680	94,624	109,707	96,673	71,311	47,046	24,454
(6) Net income		51,600	71,520	141,936	164,560	145,009	106,967	70,569	36,682
II. Investments									
(7) NWC (end of year)	$40,000	$90,000	$137,700	$187,272	$206,936	$194,838	$165,612	$135,139	$0
(8) Change in NWC*	($40,000)	($50,000)	($47,700)	($49,572)	($19,664)	$12,098	$29,226	$30,473	$135,139
(9) Equipment†	($800,000)								
(10) Aftertax salvage									$150,000
(11) Investment cash flow	($840,000)	($50,000)	($47,700)	($49,572)	($19,664)	$12,098	$29,226	$30,473	$285,139

*All cash flows occur at the end of the year.
†A negative change in net working capital or equipment represents a cash outflow for the company.

---

[2] If the vacant building had a resale value, this would be included as a third part to this section. Recall from Section 8.1 the discussion of opportunity costs. A positive resale value would be a cash outflow in year 0.

TABLE 8.2   Operating Revenues and Costs of the MMCC

(1) Year	(2) Production	(3) Price*	(4) Sales Revenues	(5) Cost Per Unit†	(6) Variable Costs	(7) Fixed Costs	(8) Operating Costs
1	6,000	$100.00	$ 600,000	$64.00	$384,000	$50,000	$ 434,000
2	9,000	102.00	918,000	67.20	604,800	50,000	654,800
3	12,000	104.04	1,248,480	70.56	846,720	50,000	896,720
4	13,000	106.12	1,379,570	74.09	963,144	50,000	1,013,144
5	12,000	108.24	1,298,919	77.79	933,509	50,000	983,509
6	10,000	110.41	1,104,081	81.68	816,820	50,000	866,820
7	8,000	112.62	900,930	85.77	686,129	50,000	736,129
8	6,000	114.87	689,211	90.05	540,327	50,000	590,327

*Prices rise 2 percent a year.
†Unit costs rise 5 percent a year.

taxes. Lines 1 and 2 of Table 8.1 show sales revenues and operating costs, respectively. The projections in these lines are based on the sales revenues and operating costs computed in columns 4 and 8 of Table 8.2. The estimates of revenues and costs follow from assumptions made by the corporate planning staff at MMCC. In other words, the estimates critically depend on the fact that product prices are projected to increase at 2 percent per year and variable costs are projected to increase at 5 percent per year.

Capital cost allowance (depreciation for tax purposes and abbreviated as CCA) of the $800,000 capital investment is based on the amount allowed by the Canada Revenue Agency.[3] CCA calculations are shown in Table 8.3 and are based on a class 8, 20 percent rate. The column labelled CCA is reproduced in line 3 of Table 8.1. Earnings before interest and taxes (EBIT) are calculated in line 4 of Table 8.1. Taxes are provided in line 5 of this table, and net income is calculated in line 6.

Project Cash Flow   Project cash flow is finally determined in Table 8.4. It consists of operating cash flow and investment cash flow. Operating cash flow is determined by subtracting operating costs and taxes from sales revenues as shown in lines 1 through 4 in

TABLE 8.3   Annual Capital Cost Allowance, Power Mulcher Project (Class 8, 20 percent rate)

Year	Beginning UCC	CCA	Ending UCC
1	$400,000	$ 80,000	$320,000
2	720,000	144,000	576,000
3	576,000	115,200	460,800
4	460,800	92,160	368,640
5	368,640	73,728	294,912
6	294,912	58,982	235,930
7	235,930	47,186	188,744
8	188,744	37,749	150,995

[3]CCA rules are discussed in detail in Appendix 8A.

TABLE 8.4   Incremental Cash Flows for the MMCC

	Year 0	Year 1	Year 2	Year 3	Year 4	Year 5	Year 6	Year 7	Year 8
(1) Sales revenues [line 1, Table 8.1]		$600,000	$918,000	$1,248,480	$1,379,570	$1,298,919	$1,104,081	$900,930	$689,211
(2) Operating costs [line 2, Table 8.1]		434,000	654,800	896,720	1,013,144	983,509	866,820	736,129	590,327
(3) Taxes [line 5, Table 8.1]		34,400	47,680	94,624	109,707	96,673	71,311	47,046	24,454
(4) Operating cash flow [(1) − (2) − (3)]		131,600	215,520	257,136	256,720	218,737	165,949	117,755	74,430
(5) Investment cash flow	($840,000)	(50,000)	(47,700)	(49,572)	(19,664)	12,098	29,226	30,473	285,139
(6) Total project cash flow	($840,000)	$81,600	$167,820	$207,564	$237,056	$230,835	$195,175	$148,228	$359,570

NPV @ 4% $500,135
NPV @ 10% $188,042
NPV @ 15% $ 2,280
NPV @ 20%   ($137,896)

Table 8.4. Adding investment cash flow from line 11 in Table 8.1 gives total project cash flow on line 6 in Table 8.4.

Net Present Value   It is possible to calculate the NPV of the MMCC power mulcher tool project from these cash flows. As can be seen at the bottom of Table 8.4, the NPV is $188,042 if 10 percent is the appropriate discount rate and −$137,896 if 20 percent is the appropriate discount rate. If the discount rate is 15.07 percent, the project will have a zero NPV. In other words, the project's internal rate of return is 15.07 percent. If the discount rate of the MMCC power mulcher tool project is above 15.07 percent, it should not be accepted because its NPV would be negative.

Which Set of Books?

It should be noted that the firm's management generally keeps two sets of books, one for the Canada Revenue Agency (CRA) (called the *tax books*) and another for its annual report (called the *shareholders' books*). The tax books follow the rules of the *Income Tax Act*. The shareholders' books follow the rules of the Canadian Institute of Chartered Accountants (CICA), the governing body in accounting. The two sets of rules differ widely in certain areas. For example, deductible expenses as calculated according to CICA rules are often different from the calculations required by the Act.

Such differences result from the different purposes of the two sets of rules. CICA rules seek to represent the accounting income of the firm according to Generally Accepted Accounting Principles. Tax rules govern the calculation of corporate income tax. Appendix 8A gives a synopsis of the tax rules on CCA.

Which of the two sets of rules on depreciation do we want in order to create the previous tables for MMCC? Clearly, we're interested in the tax rules. Our purpose is to determine net cash flow, and tax payments are a cash outflow. The CICA regulations determine the calculation of accounting income, not cash flow.

A Note on Net Working Capital

The investment in net working capital is an important part of any capital budgeting analysis. While we explicitly considered net working capital in line 7 (Table 8.1) as 15 percent of sales, students may be wondering where such numbers come from. An investment in net working capital arises whenever (1) raw materials and other inventory are purchased prior to the sale of finished goods, (2) cash is kept in the project as a buffer against unexpected expenditures, and (3) credit sales are made, generating accounts receivable rather than cash. (The investment in net working capital is offset to the extent that purchases are made on credit, that is, when accounts payable are created.) This investment in net working capital represents a cash outflow, because cash generated elsewhere in the firm is tied up in the project.

To see how the investment in net working capital is built from its component parts, we focus on year 1. We see in Table 8.1 that MMCC's managers predict sales in year 1 to be $600,000 and operating costs to be $434,000. If both the sales and costs were cash transactions, the firm would receive $166,000 (or $600,000 − $434,000).

However, the managers:

1. Forecast that $100,000 of the sales will be on credit, implying that cash receipts in year 1 will be only $500,000 (or $600,000 − $100,000). The accounts receivable of $100,000 will be collected in year 2.

2. Believe that they can defer payment on $40,000 of the $434,000 of costs, implying that cash disbursements will be only $394,000 (or $434,000 − $40,000). Of course, MMCC will pay off the $40,000 of accounts payable in year 2.

3. Decide that inventory of $25,000 should be left on hand at year 1 to avoid *stockouts* (that is, running out of inventory) and other contingencies.

4. Decide that cash of $5,000 should be earmarked for the project at year 1 to avoid running out of cash.

Thus, net working capital in year 1 is

$$
\underset{\substack{\text{Accounts}\\\text{receivable}}}{\$100,000} - \underset{\substack{\text{Accounts}\\\text{payable}}}{\$40,000} + \underset{\text{Inventory}}{\$25,000} + \underset{\text{Cash}}{\$5,000} = \underset{\substack{\text{Net working}\\\text{capital}}}{\$90,000}
$$

Because $90,000 of cash generated elsewhere in the firm must be used to offset this requirement for net working capital, MMCC's managers correctly view the investment in net working capital as a cash outflow of the project. As the project grows over time, needs for net working capital increase. Changes in net working capital from year to year represent further cash flows, as indicated by the negative numbers for the first few years of line 8 of Table 8.1. However, in the declining years of the project, net working capital is reduced—ultimately to zero. That is, accounts receivable are finally collected, the project's cash buffer is returned to the rest of the corporation, and all remaining inventory is sold off. This frees up cash in the later years, as indicated by positive numbers in years 5, 6, 7, and 8 on line 8.

Typically, corporate worksheets (such as Table 8.1) treat net working capital as a whole. The individual components of net working capital (receivables, inventory, and so on) do not generally appear in the worksheets. However, the reader should remember that the net working capital numbers in the worksheets are not pulled out of thin air. Rather, they result from a meticulous forecast of the components, just as we illustrated for year 1.

Interest Expense

It may have bothered you that interest expense was ignored in the MMCC example. After all, many projects are at least partially financed with debt, particularly a power mulcher tool machine that is likely to increase the debt capacity of the firm. As it turns out, our approach of assuming no debt financing is rather standard in the real world. Firms typically calculate a project's cash flows under the assumption that the project is only financed with equity. Any adjustments for debt financing are reflected in the discount rate, not the cash flows. The treatment of debt in capital budgeting will be covered in depth later in the text. Suffice it to say at this time that the full ramifications of debt financing are well beyond our current discussion.

**Concept
Questions**

- **What are the items leading to cash flow in any year?**
- **Why did we determine taxable income when NPV analysis discounts cash flows, not income?**
- **Why is net working capital viewed as a cash outflow?**

8.3   The Boeing 777: A Real-World Example

Will the principles discussed in the previous sections of this chapter allow us to perform capital budgeting in the real world? Let's see by examining the Boeing 777 project, which we mentioned in the executive summary of this chapter. As stated there, the Boeing Company announced in late 1990 its intention to build the 777. The company anticipated selling several thousand of these planes over a 35-year period, beginning in 1995.

The relevant projected information is presented in Table 8.5, with the determination of annual net cash flow being the ultimate goal of the table. Net cash flow can be determined in three steps:[4]

1. *Taxes.* In order to determine taxes each year, we begin with taxable income, which can be expressed as:

Taxable income = Sales revenue − Operating costs − Depreciation

Choosing a representative year, say, 2005, we have:

Taxable income = $19,468.56 − $17,911.07 − $116.83 = $1440.66

Boeing forecasts a tax rate of 34 percent, implying taxes in 2005 of:

0.34 × $1440.66 = $489.82

2. *Investment.* Investment is the sum of the *change* in net working capital and the *amount* of capital expenditures, which is $450.88 ($431.41 + $19.47) for 2005.

3. *Final calculation.* We calculate net cash flow as:

Net cash flow = Sales revenue − Operating costs − Taxes − Investment

which for 2005 is:

$19,468.56 − $17,911.07 − $489.82 − $450.88 = $616.79

The last column in Table 8.5 provides net cash flow for each of the 35 years.

---

[4] Note that because Boeing is in the U.S., depreciation is based on different rules.

TABLE 8.5   Incremental Cash Flows: Boeing 777

Year	Number of Planes Delivered	Sales Revenue	Operating Costs	Tax Depreciation	Income Before Taxes	Taxes	Change in NWC	Capital Expenditure	Investment	Tax Depreciation Add-Back	Total Cash Flow
1991			$ 865.00	$ 40.00	$ (905.00)	$ (307.70)		$ 400.00	$ 400.00	$ 40.00	$ (957.30)
1992			1,340.00	96.00	(1,436.00)	(488.24)		600.00	600.00	96.00	(1,451.76)
1993			1,240.00	116.40	(1,356.40)	(461.18)		300.00	300.00	116.40	(1,078.82)
1994			840.00	124.76	(964.76)	(328.02)		200.00	200.00	124.76	(711.98)
1995	14	$ 1,847.55	1,976.69	112.28	(241.42)	(82.08)	181.06	1.85	182.91	112.28	(229.97)
1996	145	19,418.96	17,865.45	101.06	1,452.45	493.83	1,722.00	19.42	1,741.42	101.06	(681.74)
1997	140	19,244.23	16,550.04	90.56	2,603.24	885.10	(17.12)	19.42	2.30	90.56	1,806.79
1998	111	15,737.95	13,377.26	82.72	2,277.97	774.51	(343.62)	15.74	(327.88)	82.72	1,914.06
1999	107	16,257.35	13,656.17	77.75	2,523.43	857.97	50.90	16.26	67.16	77.75	1,676.05
2000	102	15,333.42	12,726.74	75.63	2,531.05	860.56	90.54	15.33	105.87	75.63	1,640.25
2001	92	14,289.29	11,860.11	75.00	2,354.18	800.42	(102.33)	14.29	(88.04)	75.00	1,716.80
2002	92	14,717.97	12,068.74	75.00	2,574.23	875.24	42.01	14.72	56.73	75.00	1,717.26
2003	105	17,233.97	14,131.85	99.46	3,002.66	1,020.90	246.57	244.64	491.21	99.46	1,590.01
2004	89	15,066.42	12,354.47	121.48	2,590.47	880.76	(212.42)	244.64	32.22	121.48	1,798.97
2005	111	19,468.56	17,911.07	116.83	1,440.66	489.82	431.41	19.47	450.88	116.83	616.79
2006	130	23,307.53	20,510.63	112.65	2,684.25	912.65	376.22	23.31	399.53	112.65	1,484.73
2007	118	21,911.40	18,843.81	100.20	2,967.39	1,008.91	(136.82)	21.91	(114.91)	100.20	2,173.59
2008	94	17,944.00	15,252.40	129.20	2,562.40	871.22	(388.81)	567.22	178.41	129.20	1,641.97
2009	123	24,103.23	22,174.99	96.99	1,831.25	622.63	603.60	24.10	627.70	96.99	677.92
2010	125	25,316.97	22,278.94	76.84	2,961.19	1,006.80	118.95	25.32	144.27	76.84	1,886.96
2011	125	26,076.48	22,425.77	65.81	3,584.90	1,218.87	74.43	26.08	100.51	65.81	2,331.33
2012	98	21,133.07	17,963.10	61.68	3,108.29	1,056.82	(484.45)	21.13	(463.32)	61.68	2,576.47
2013	84	18,550.25	15,582.21	57.96	2,910.08	989.43	(253.12)	18.55	(234.57)	57.96	2,213.18
2014	89	20,321.64	16,866.97	54.61	3,400.06	1,156.02	173.60	20.32	193.92	54.61	2,104.73
2015	89	20,931.29	17,372.97	52.83	3,505.49	1,191.87	59.75	20.93	80.68	52.83	2,285.77
2016	89	21,559.23	17,894.16	52.83	3,612.24	1,228.16	61.54	21.56	83.10	52.83	2,353.81
2017	89	22,206.00	18,430.98	52.83	3,722.19	1,265.54	63.38	22.21	85.59	52.83	2,423.89
2018	89	22,873.18	18,984.92	52.83	3,835.43	1,304.05	65.29	22.87	88.16	52.83	2,496.05
2019	89	23,558.35	19,553.43	47.52	3,957.40	1,345.52	67.24	23.56	90.80	47.52	2,568.60
2020	89	24,265.10	20,140.03	35.28	4,089.79	1,390.53	69.26	24.27	93.53	35.28	2,641.01
2021	89	24,993.05	20,744.23	28.36	4,220.46	1,434.96	71.34	24.99	96.33	28.36	2,717.53
2022	89	25,742.85	21,366.56	28.36	4,347.93	1,478.30	73.48	25.74	99.22	28.36	2,798.77
2023	89	26,515.13	22,007.56	28.36	4,479.21	1,522.93	75.68	26.52	102.20	28.36	2,882.44
2024	89	27,310.58	22,667.78	16.05	4,626.75	1,573.10	77.95	27.31	105.26	16.05	2,964.45

Notes:

Tax rate is 34 percent of taxable income.

Total cash flow can be determined by adding across the rows. Recall that total cash flow is equal to Sales revenue − Operating costs − Taxes − Investment.

Source: Robert Bruner, Case Studies in Finance, 4th edition (Burr Ridge, Ill.: Times Mirror/Irwin, 2003).

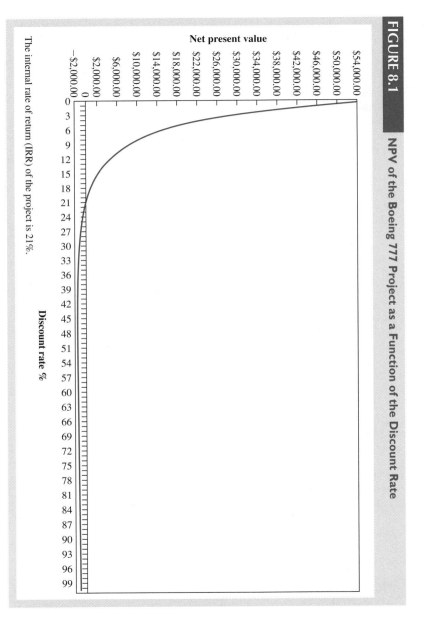

The internal rate of return (IRR) of the project is 21%.

In addition to the items in the table, Boeing invested several hundred million dollars in research and development prior to late 1990. Since these outflows were incurred prior to the decision to build the plane, they are sunk costs and should properly be excluded from the table.

The net present value (NPV) of the Boeing 777 project is calculated by discounting the net cash flows in the last column of the table. Of course, the NPV of any project is dependent on the discount rate. Figure 8.1 graphs NPV as a function of the discount rate. NPV must be negatively related to this rate, since there is only one change in the signs of the cash flows. The net present value of the project is 0 for a discount rate of 21 percent. Hence, the internal rate of return (IRR) of the project is 21 percent. Boeing should accept the project if its discount rate is less than 21 percent but should reject the project if its discount rate is above 21 percent.

It should be mentioned that the analysis in Table 8.5, as well as the analysis for any project, is entirely based on forecasts. The subsequent reality may be much different, as was the case with the 777. Though the table shows delivery of 711 planes by the end of 1999, only 282 planes had actually been delivered through May 2000.

8.4 Inflation and Capital Budgeting

Inflation is an important fact of economic life, and it must be considered in capital budgeting. We begin by considering the relationship between interest rates and inflation.

Interest Rates and Inflation

Suppose that the one-year interest rate that a financial institution pays is 10 percent. This means that an individual who deposits $1,000 at date 0 will get $1,100 (or $1,000 × 1.10) in one year. While 10 percent may seem like a handsome return, one can only put it in perspective after examining the rate of inflation.

Suppose that the rate of inflation is 6 percent over the year and it affects all goods equally. For example, a restaurant that charges $1.00 for a hamburger at date 0 charges $1.06 for the same hamburger at the end of the year. You can use your $1,000 to buy 1,000 hamburgers at date 0. Alternatively, if you put all of your money in the bank, you can buy 1,038 (or $1,100 / $1.06) hamburgers at date 1. Thus, you are only able to increase your hamburger consumption by 3.8 percent by lending to the bank. Since the prices of all goods rise at this 6 percent rate, lending lets you increase your consumption of any single good or any combination of goods by only 3.8 percent. Thus, 3.8 percent is what you are *really* earning through your savings account, after adjusting for inflation. Economists refer to the 3.8 percent number as the **real interest rate.** Economists refer to the 10 percent rate as the **nominal interest rate** or simply the *interest rate.* The above discussion is illustrated in Figure 8.2.

We have used an example with a specific nominal interest rate and a specific inflation rate. In general, the equation relating real and nominal cash flows can be written as

$$1 + \text{Nominal interest rate} = (1 + \text{Real interest rate}) \times (1 + \text{Inflation rate})$$

Rearranging terms, we have

$$\text{Real interest rate} = \frac{1 + \text{Nominal interest rate}}{1 + \text{Inflation rate}} - 1 \qquad (8.1)$$

The equation indicates that the real interest rate in our example is 3.8 percent (1.10/1.06 − 1).

This equation determines the real interest rate precisely. The following equation is an approximation:

$$\text{Real interest rate} \approx \text{Nominal interest rate} - \text{Inflation rate} \qquad (8.2)$$

The symbol ≈ indicates that the equation is approximately true. This latter equation calculates the real rate in our example as

$$4\% = 10\% - 6\%$$

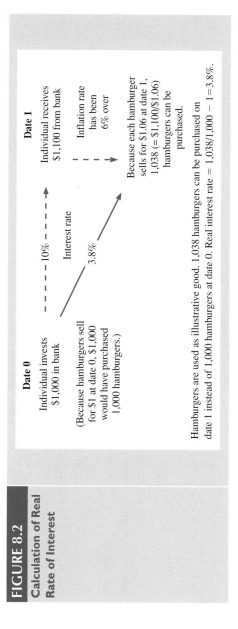

FIGURE 8.2

Calculation of Real Rate of Interest

Date 0

Individual invests $1,000 in bank

(Because hamburgers sell for $1 at date 0, $1,000 would have purchased 1,000 hamburgers.)

Interest rate ---- 10% ----

3.8%

Date 1

Individual receives $1,100 from bank

Inflation rate has been 6% over

Because each hamburger sells for $1.06 at date 1, 1,038 (= $1,100/$1.06) hamburgers can be purchased.

Hamburgers are used as illustrative good. 1,038 hamburgers can be purchased on date 1 instead of 1,000 hamburgers at date 0. Real interest rate = 1.038/1.000 − 1=3.8%.

The student should be aware that, while Equation (8.2) may seem more intuitive than Equation (8.1), (8.2) is only an approximation.

This approximation is reasonably accurate for low rates of interest and inflation. In our example, the difference between the approximate calculation and the exact one is only 0.2 percent (4 percent − 3.8 percent). Unfortunately, the approximation becomes poor when rates are higher.

The little-known monarchy of Gerberovia recently had a nominal interest rate of 300 percent and an inflation rate of 280 percent. According to Equation (8.2), the real interest rate is:

$$300\% - 280\% = 20\% \qquad \text{(Approximate formula)}$$

However, according to Equation (8.1), this rate is:

$$\frac{1 + 300\%}{1 + 280\%} - 1 = 5.26\% \qquad \text{(Exact formula)}$$

How do we know that the second formula is indeed the exact one? Let's think in terms of hamburgers again. Had you deposited $1,000 in a Gerberovian bank a year ago, the account would be worth $4,000 [$1,000 × (1 + 300%)] today. However, while a hamburger cost $1 a year ago, it costs $3.80 (1 + 280%) today. Therefore, you would now be able to buy 1052.6 (4,000/3.80) hamburgers, implying a real interest rate of 5.26 percent.

Cash Flow and Inflation

The above analysis defines two types of interest rates (nominal rates and real rates) and relates them through Equation (8.1). Capital budgeting requires data on cash flows as well as on interest rates. Like interest rates, cash flows can be expressed in either nominal or real terms.

A cash flow is expressed in nominal terms if the actual dollars to be received (or paid out) are given. A cash flow is expressed in real terms if the current or date 0 purchasing power of the cash flow is given.

Ottawa Publishing has just purchased the rights to the next book by famed romantic novelist Barbara Musk. Still unwritten, the book should be available to the public in four years. Currently, romantic novels sell for $10.00 in paperback. The publishers believe that inflation will be 6 percent a year over the next four years. Since romantic novels are so popular, the publishers anticipate that their prices will rise about 2 percent per year more than the inflation rate over the next four years. Not wanting to overprice, Ottawa Publishing anticipates pricing the novel at $13.60 [or (1.08)⁴ × $10.00] four years from now. In other words, the nominal value after four years is the future value calculated using the inflation rate of 8 percent. The firm anticipates selling 100,000 copies.

The expected cash flow in the fourth year of $1.36 million (or $13.60 × 100,000) is a **nominal cash flow** because the firm expects to receive $1.36 million at that time. In other words, a nominal cash flow reflects the actual dollars to be received in the future.

We determine the purchasing power of $1.36 million in four years as

$$\$1.08 \text{ million} = \frac{\$1.36 \text{ million}}{(1.06)^4}$$

The figure $1.08 million is a **real cash flow** since it is expressed in terms of date 0 purchasing power. Extending our hamburger example, the $1.36 million to be received in four years will only buy 1.08 million hamburgers because the price of a hamburger will rise from $1 to $1.26 [or $1 × (1.06)⁴] over the period.

EXAMPLE

Gatineau Booksellers, a customer of Ottawa Publishing, recently made leasehold improvements to its store for $2,000,000 to be depreciated by the straight-line method over five years. This implies yearly depreciation of $400,000 (or $2,000,000/5). Is this $400,000 figure a real or nominal quantity?

Depreciation is a *nominal quantity* because $400,000 is the actual tax deduction over each of the next four years. Depreciation becomes a real quantity if it is adjusted for purchasing power.[5] Hence, $316,837 [or $400,000/(1.06)⁵] is depreciation in the fourth year, expressed as a real quantity.

Discounting: Nominal or Real?

Our previous discussion showed that interest rates can be expressed in either nominal or real terms. Similarly, cash flows can be expressed in either nominal or real terms. Given these choices, how should one express interest rates and cash flows when performing capital budgeting?

Financial practitioners correctly stress the need to maintain *consistency* between cash flows and discount rates. That is,

Nominal cash flows must be discounted at the *nominal* rate.
Real cash flows must be discounted at the *real* rate.

As long as one is consistent, either approach is correct. In order to minimize computational error, it is generally advisable in practice to choose the approach that is easier. This idea is illustrated in the following two examples.

EXAMPLE

Shields Electric forecasts the following nominal cash flows on a particular project:

Date:	0	1	2
Cash flow	−$1,000	$600	$650

The nominal interest rate is 14 percent, and the inflation rate is forecast to be 5 percent. What is the value of the project?

Using Nominal Quantities   The NPV can be calculated as

$$\$26.47 = -\$1,000 + \frac{\$600}{1.14} + \frac{\$650}{(1.14)^2}$$

The project should be accepted.

---

[5]We use the word *quantity* not *cash flow*, because it is the CCA tax shield, not the depreciation itself, that is a cash flow. Tax shields are defined later in this chapter.

EXAMPLE

Using Real Quantities   The real cash flows are

Date:	0	1	2
Cash flow	–$1,000	$571.43 $\left(\dfrac{\$600}{1.05}\right)$	$589.57 $\left(\dfrac{\$650}{1.05^2}\right)$

The real interest rate is 8.57143 percent (1.14/1.05 – 1).
The NPV can be calculated as

$$\$26.47 = -\$1,000 + \frac{\$571.43}{1.0857143} + \frac{\$589.57}{(1.0857143)^2}$$

The NPV is the same when cash flows are expressed in real quantities. It must always be the case that the NPV is the same under the two different approaches.

Because both approaches always yield the same result, which one should be used? Students will be happy to learn the following rule: Use the approach that is simpler. In the Shields Electric case, nominal quantities produce a simpler calculation because the problem gave us nominal cash flows to begin with.

Altshuler, Inc., used the following data for a capital budgeting project:

	Year		
	0	1	2
Capital expenditure	$1,210		
Revenues (in real terms)		$1,900	$2,000
Cash expenses (in real terms)		950	1,000
Depreciation (straight line)		605	605

The president, David Altshuler, estimates inflation to be 10 percent per year over the next two years. In addition, he believes that the cash flows of the project should be discounted at the nominal rate of 15.5 percent. His firm's tax rate is 40 percent.

Mr. Altshuler forecasts all cash flows in *nominal* terms. Thus, he generates the following spreadsheet:

Year	0	1	2
Capital expenditure	–$1,210		
Revenues		$2,090 (= 1,900 × 1.10)	$2,420 (= 2,000 × (1.10)²)
–Expenses		–1,045 (= 950 × 1.10)	–1,210 (= 1,000 × (1.10)²)
–Depreciation		–605 (= 1,210/2)	–605
Taxable income		440	605
–Taxes (40%)		–176	–242
Income after taxes		264	363
+Depreciation		+605	+605
Cash flow		$ 869	$ 968

$$\text{NPV} = -\$1,210 + \frac{\$869}{1.155} + \frac{\$968}{(1.155)^2} = \$268$$

Mr. Altshuler's sidekick, Stuart Weiss, prefers working in real terms. He first calculates the real rate to be 5 percent ($= 1.155/1.10 − 1$). Next, he generates the following spreadsheet in *real* quantities:

Year	0	1	2
Capital expenditure	−$1,210		
Revenues		$1,900	$2,000
−Expenses		−950	−1,000
−Depreciation		−550 ($= 605/1.1$)	−500 ($= 605/1.1^2$)
Taxable income		400	500
−Taxes (40%)		−160	−200
Income after taxes		240	300
+Depreciation		+550	+500
Cash flow		$ 790	$ 800

$$NPV = -\$1,210 + \frac{\$790}{1.05} + \frac{\$800}{(1.05)^2} = \$268$$

In explaining his calculations to Mr. Altshuler, Mr. Weiss points out:

1. Since the capital expenditure occurs at date 0 (today), its nominal value and its real value are equal.

2. Since yearly depreciation of $605 is a nominal quantity, one converts it to a real quantity by discounting at the inflation rate of 10 percent.

3. It is no coincidence that both Mr. Altshuler and Mr. Weiss arrive at the same NPV number. Both methods must always give the same NPV.

? Concept Questions

- What is the difference between the nominal and the real interest rate?
- What is the difference between nominal and real cash flows?

8.5 A Capital Budgeting Simplification

Restating Operating Cash Flows

The MMCC example considered both investment outlays and operating cash flows. It is worthwhile to focus more closely on operating cash flows. In the MMCC example, we calculated operating cash flows after taxes as

$$\text{Operating cash flow after taxes} = \text{Revenues} - \text{Expenses} - \text{Taxes} \qquad (8.3)$$

Taxes can be rewritten as

$$\text{Taxes} = T_c \text{ [Revenues} - \text{Expenses} - \text{CCA]} \qquad (8.4)$$

where T_c is the corporate tax rate. The terms in the brackets in (8.4) represent taxable income.

Substituting (8.4) for Taxes in (8.3), we can rewrite cash flow as

$$\text{Operating cash flow} = \text{Revenues} - \text{Expenses} - T_c \text{ [Revenues} - \text{Expenses} - \text{CCA]}$$
after taxes

The above equation easily simplifies into

$$
\begin{matrix}
\text{Operating} \\
\text{cash flow} \\
\text{after taxes}
\end{matrix}
=
\begin{matrix}
\text{Revenues } (1 - T_c) \\
\text{After-tax} \\
\text{revenues}
\end{matrix}
-
\begin{matrix}
\text{Expenses } (1 - T_c) \\
\text{After-tax} \\
\text{expenses}
\end{matrix}
+
\begin{matrix}
T_c \text{ CCA} \\
\text{Tax shield} \\
\text{on CCA}
\end{matrix}
\qquad (8.5)
$$

Equation (8.5) states that operating cash flow after taxes is equal to after-tax revenues minus after-tax expenses plus the **tax shield on CCA**. Note that the coefficient on both revenues and expenses is $(1 - T_c)$ while the coefficient on CCA is T_c. As we will see, Equation (8.5) is very important for at least two reasons.

First, Equation (8.5) can answer the following questions on marginal contributions to cash flow:

1. How much will after-tax cash flow increase if revenues rise by $1? The formula tells us the answer must be $1 $\times (1 - T_c)$. If T_c equals 40 percent, we have $0.60 (or $1 - $0.40).

2. How much will after-tax cash flow decrease if costs rise by $1? The formula tells us the answer must be $-$1 $\times (1 - T_c)$. If T_c equals 40 percent, we have $-$0.60.

3. How much will after-tax cash flow increase for each dollar of CCA? The rise is $1 $\times T_c$. Thus, a dollar of CCA produces a CCA tax shield of $1 $\times T_c$. If T_c equals 40 percent, a dollar of CCA increases after-tax cash flow by $0.40.

Note that the coefficient of $(1 - T_c)$ applies to Questions (1) and (2), but the coefficient of T_c applies to Question (3).

Second, Equation (8.5) can help us perform capital budgeting more efficiently. This benefit is best seen through an example.

Applying the Tax Shield Approach to the Majestic Mulch and Compost Company Project

If you look back over our analysis of MMCC you will see that most of the number crunching involved finding CCA, EBIT, and net income figures. The tax shield approach has the potential to save us considerable time. To realize that potential, we do the calculations in a different order from Table 8.4. Instead of adding the cash flow components down the columns for each year and finding the present value of the total cash flows, we find the present values of each source of cash flows and add the present values. To find the present values we use a discount rate of 15 percent.

To begin, it will be helpful to define the following:

$$
\begin{aligned}
OCF &= \text{Operating cash flow} \\
R &= \text{Revenues} \\
E &= \text{Expenses (operating costs)} \\
D &= \text{Depreciation for tax purposes, i.e., } CCA^6 \\
T_c &= \text{Corporate tax rate}
\end{aligned}
$$

The first source of cash flow is $(R - E)(1 - T_c)$, as shown for each year on the first line of Table 8.6. The figure for the first year is $99,600. (The numbers come from Table 8.1.)

$$
\begin{aligned}
(R - E)(1 - T_c) &= (600,000 - 434,000)(1 - 0.40) \\
&= 99,600
\end{aligned}
$$

---

^{6}In this discussion we use the terms *depreciation* and *CCA* interchangeably.

TABLE 8.6   Tax Shield Solution, Power Mulcher Project

	Year 0	Year 1	Year 2	Year 3	Year 4	Year 5	Year 6	Year 7	Year 8
(1) $(R - E)(1 - T_c)$		$99,600	$157,920	$211,056	$219,856	$189,246	$142,356	$98,881	$59,331
(2) Changes in NWC	($40,000)	(50,000)	(47,700)	(49,572)	(19,664)	12,098	29,226	30,473	135,139
(3) Equipment expenditure:	(800,000)								150,000
Totals									
PV of $(R - E)(1 - T_c)$	$682,696								
PV of changes in NWC	(89,100)								
PV of equipment expenditure	(750,965)								
PV of CCA tax shield	159,649								
NPV	$2,280								

Calculating the present value of the $99,600 for the first year, and adding the present values of the other $(R - E)(1 - T_c)$ figures in Table 8.6 gives a total present value for this source of $682,696, as seen in the lower part of Table 8.6.

The second term is the tax shield on CCA for the first year. Table 8.7 reproduces the first year's tax shield of $32,000 along with the corresponding tax shields for each year. The total present value of the CCA tax shield is shown as $159,649.

The changes in net working capital and equipment expenditure are the same as in Table 8.4. Their present values are shown in the lower part of Table 8.6. The NPV is the sum of the present values of the four sources of cash flow. The answer, $2,280, is identical to what we found in Table 8.4 for a discount rate of 15 percent.

Present Value of the Tax Shield on CCA

Further time savings are made possible by using a formula that replaces the detailed calculation of yearly CCA. The formula is based on the idea that tax shields from CCA continue in perpetuity as long as there are assets remaining in the CCA class.[7] To calculate the present value of the tax shield on CCA, we first find the present value of an infinite stream

TABLE 8.7   Present Value of Tax Shield on CCA

Year	CCA	$0.40 \times CCA$	PV @ 15 percent
1	$ 80,000	$ 32,000	$ 27,826
2	144,000	57,600	43,554
3	115,200	46,080	30,298
4	92,160	36,864	21,077
5	73,728	29,491	14,662
6	58,982	23,593	10,200
7	47,186	18,874	7,096
8	37,749	15,099	4,936
		PV of tax shield on CCA	$159,649

[7] Strictly speaking, the UCC for a class remains positive as long as there are physical assets in the class and the proceeds from disposal of assets are less than total UCC for the class.

of tax shields abstracting from two practical implications: the 50 percent rule for CCA and disposal of the asset. We then adjust the formula.

C = Total capital cost of the asset that is added to the pool

d = CCA rate for the asset class

T_c = Company's marginal tax rate

k = Discount rate

S = Salvage or disposal value of the asset

n = Asset life in years

We can use the growing perpetuity formula from Chapter 5 (Equation 5.10) to derive the present value of the CCA tax shield. Recall that when cash flows grow at a constant rate g, the present value of the perpetuity at discount rate k is

$$PV = \frac{\text{1st payment}}{k - g}$$

Since we are temporarily ignoring the half-year rule, the growth rate in CCA payments is equal to $(-d)$, the CCA rate. Since CCA declines over time as the depreciable base (CC) reduces, the growth rate is negative. For example, in Table 8.7

$$
\begin{aligned}
CCA_3 &= CCA_2 \,[1 + (-d)] \\
&= 144{,}000\,[1 + (-0.20)] \\
&= 144{,}000\,(0.8) = 115{,}200
\end{aligned}
$$

Given the growth rate as $(-d)$, we need the first payment to complete the formula. This is the first year's tax shield calculating the CCA at rate d on the total cost of the asset added to the depreciation pool, C, and then multiplying by the tax rate, T_c.

$$\text{1st payment} = CdT_c$$

We can now complete the formula.

$$
\begin{aligned}
PV\,(\text{CCA tax shield}) &= \frac{\text{1st payment}}{k - g} \\
&= \frac{CdT_c}{k - (-d)} \\
&= \frac{CdT_c}{k + d}
\end{aligned}
$$

The next step is to extend the formula to adjust for Canada Revenue Agency's 50 percent rule. This rule states that a firm must add one-half of the incremental capital cost of a new project in year 1 and the other half in year 2. The result is that we now calculate present value of the tax shield in two parts. The present value of the stream starting the first year is simply one-half of the original value:

$$PV \text{ of 1st half} = 0.5 \,\frac{CdT_c}{k + d}$$

The PV of the second half (deferred one year) is the same quantity (bracketed term below) discounted back to time zero. The total present value of the tax shield on CCA under the 50 percent rule is the sum of the two present values.

$$PV \text{ tax shield on CCA} = \frac{0.5\,CdT_c}{k + d} + \frac{[0.5\,CdT_c]}{[k + d]}\,\frac{1}{(1 + k)}$$

With a little algebra we can simplify the formula to

$$PV = \frac{0.5\,CdT_c}{k+d}\,[1 + 1/(1+k)] = \frac{0.5\,CdT_c}{k+d}\left[\frac{1+k+1}{1+k}\right]$$

$$= \frac{CdT_c}{k+d}\,\frac{[1+0.5k]}{[1+k]}$$

The final adjustment for salvage value begins with the present value in the salvage year, n, of future tax shields beginning in year $n + 1$.

$$\frac{SdT_c}{k+d}$$

We discount this figure back to today and subtract it to get the complete formula.[8]

$$PV \text{ tax shield on CCA} = \frac{[CdT_c]}{k+d}\times\frac{[1+0.5k]}{1+k} - \frac{SdT_c}{k+d}\times\frac{1}{(1+k)^n} \qquad (8.6)$$

Using the first part of (8.6), the present value of the tax shield on MMCC's project is $170,932 assuming that the tax shield goes on in perpetuity.

$$= \frac{800,000\,(0.40)\,(0.20)}{0.15 + 0.20}\times\frac{1 + 0.5\times(0.15)}{1 + 0.15}$$

$$= 182.857 \times 1.075 \times 1.15 = \$170,932$$

The adjustment for the salvage value (second part of 8.6) is

$$\frac{150,000\,(0.40)\,(0.20)}{0.15 + 0.20}\times\frac{1}{(1+0.15)^8}$$

$$= -34,286 \times 1/(1.15)^8 = -\$11,208$$

The present value of the tax shield on CCA is the sum of the two present values.[9]

$$\text{Present value of tax shield from CCA} = \$170,932 - \$11,208$$
$$= \$159,724.$$

Total Project Cash Flow Versus Tax Shield Approach

The tax shield approach has three advantages over the total project cash flow approach:

1. Simplifying formulas such as annuities and growing annuities can be applied, where appropriate, to a cash flow source. This is not feasible for the approach we used in the first example, because cash flows from all sources were combined to determine net cash

---

[8] By not adjusting the salvage value for the 50 percent rule, we assume there will be no new investment in year n.

[9] There is a slight difference between this calculation for the present value of the tax shield on CCA and what we got in Table 8.7 by adding the tax shields over the project life. The difference arises whenever the salvage value of the asset differs from its UCC. The formula solution is more accurate as it takes into account the future CCA on this difference. In this case, the asset was sold for $150,000 and had UCC of $150,995. The $995 left in the pool after eight years creates an infinite stream of CCA. At time 8, this stream has a present value of [$995(0.20)(0.40)]/[0.15 + 0.20] = $227.43. At time 0, the present value of this stream at 15 percent is about $75. To get the precise estimate of the present value of the CCA tax shield, we need to add this to the approximation in Table 8.7: $159,649 + $75 = $159,724. This adjustment could be made initially by adding another line to Table 8.1.

flow for a year. Because the net cash flow for each year (as in line 4 of Table 8.4) is derived from so many sources, no simplifying formula can normally be used to calculate the net present value of all the yearly cash flows.

2. The approach used in the tax shield example can discount cash flows at different rates. This is often necessary due to varying risks associated with different cash flows.

3. The approach used in the first example cannot separate real and nominal flows because cash flows from all sources are combined each year. Thus, one must either make all flows nominal or make all flows real at the start.

It is our opinion that the tax shield approach is an improvement over the total project cash flow approach. In many cases, the improvement can be substantial, because both time savings and increases in accuracy are involved. The current example appears to allow both benefits. In some situations, however, there is only a slight improvement. For example, suppose that the cash flows from each source are irregular. The tax shield method would not save time, because the cash flows from the individual sources would not fit any simplifying formula. Also, suppose one were very unsure of the appropriate discount rates. Selecting a different discount rate for each cash flow might be unnecessary.[10]

We find that real-world companies use both approaches. Thus, the student should be aware of both procedures, always looking for practical situations where the latter method allows substantial benefits.

Concept
Questions

- **What is the basic difference between the discounting approach and the discounting approach in the total project cash flow example and the discounting approach in the tax shield example?**
- **What are the benefits of using each approach?**

8.6 Investments of Unequal Lives: The Equivalent Annual Cost Method

Suppose a firm must choose between two machines of unequal lives. Both machines can do the same job, but they have different operating costs and will last for different time periods. A simple application of the NPV rule suggests taking the machine whose costs have the lower present value. This choice might be a mistake, however, because the lower-cost machine may need to be replaced before the other one.

EXAMPLE

The Downtown Athletic Club must choose between two mechanical tennis ball throwers. Machine A costs less than machine B but will not last as long. The cash outflows from the two machines are:

Date:	0	1	2	3	4
Machine A	$500	$120	$120	$120	
Machine B	600	100	100	100	$100

[10]One of our colleagues in accounting is particularly critical of those who employ precise methodologies in situations with vague data. He tells the story of an accountant flying over the Grand Canyon who tells his seatmate, "I'll bet you didn't know that the Grand Canyon is two billion and two years old." The seatmate says, "Well, I can understand that it's around two billion years old, but how did you come up with two billion and two?" The accountant replied, "The pilot announced that the Grand Canyon was two billion years old when I took this same flight two years ago."

Machine A costs **$500** and lasts three years. There will be maintenance expenses of **$120** to be paid at the end of each of the three years. Machine B costs **$600** and lasts four years. There will be maintenance expenses of **$100** to be paid at the end of each of the four years. We place all costs in *real* terms, an assumption greatly simplifying the analysis. Revenues per year are assumed to be the same, regardless of machine, so they are ignored in the analysis. Note that all numbers in the above chart are *outflows*.

To get a handle on the decision, let's take the present value of the costs of each of the two machines. Assuming a discount rate of 10 percent, we have:

$$\text{Machine } A: \$798.42 = \$500 + \frac{\$120}{1.1} + \frac{\$120}{(1.1)^2} + \frac{\$120}{(1.1)^3} \tag{8.7}$$

$$\text{Machine } B: \$916.99 = \$600 + \frac{\$100}{1.1} + \frac{\$100}{(1.1)^2} + \frac{\$100}{(1.1)^3} + \frac{\$100}{(1.1)^4}$$

Machine B has a higher present value of outflows. A naive approach would be to select machine A because of its lower present value. However, machine B has a longer life so perhaps its cost per year is actually lower.

How might one properly adjust for the difference in useful life when comparing the two machines? Perhaps the easiest approach involves calculating something called the *equivalent annual cost* of each machine. This approach puts costs on a per-year basis.

Equation (8.7) showed that payments of ($500, $120, $120, $120) are equivalent to a single payment of $798.42 at date 0. We now wish to equate the single payment of $798.42 at date 0 with a three-year annuity. Using techniques of previous chapters, we have

$$798.42 = C \times A_{0.10}^3$$

$A_{0.10}^3$ is an annuity of $1 a year for three years, discounted at 10 percent. C is the unknown—the annuity payment per year such that the present value of all payments equals $798.42. Because $A_{0.10}^3$ equals 2.4869, C equals $321.05 ($798.42/2.4869). Thus, a payment stream of ($500, $120, $120, $120) is equivalent to annuity payments of $321.05 made at the *end* of each year for three years. We refer to $321.05 as the *equivalent annual cost* of machine A.

This idea is summarized in the little chart below:

Date	0	1	2	3
Cash outflows of Machine A	$500	$120	$120	$120
Equivalent annual cost of Machine A		$321.05	$321.05	$321.05

The Downtown Athletic Club should be indifferent between cash outflows of ($500, $120, $120, $120) and cash outflows of ($0, $321.05, $321.05, $321.05). Alternatively, one can say that the purchase of the machine is financially equivalent to a rental agreement calling for annual lease payments of $321.05. Because the club plans to replace the machine, these payments will go on indefinitely.

Now let's turn to machine B. We calculate its equivalent annual cost from

$$\$916.99 = C \times A_{0.10}^4$$

Because $A_{0.10}^4$ equals 3.1699, C equals $916.99/3.1699, or $289.28.

As we did above for machine A, the following chart can be created for machine B:

Date	0	1	2	3	4
Cash outflows of Machine B	$600	$100	$100	$100	$100
Equivalent annual cost of Machine B		$289.28	$289.28	$289.28	$289.28

The decision is easy once the charts of the two machines are compared. Would you rather make annual lease payments of $321.05 or $289.28? Put this way, the problem becomes a no-brainer. Clearly, a rational person would rather pay the lower amount. Thus, machine B is the preferred choice.

Two final remarks are in order. First, it is no accident that we specified the costs of the tennis ball machines in real terms. While B would still have been the preferred machine had the costs been stated in nominal terms, the actual solution would have been much more difficult. As a general rule, always convert cash flows to real terms when working through problems of this type.

Second, the above analysis applies only if one anticipates that both machines can be replaced. The analysis would differ if no replacement were possible. For example, imagine that the only company that manufactured tennis ball throwers just went out of business and no new producers are expected to enter the field. In this case, machine B would generate revenues in the fourth year whereas machine A would not. Here, simple net present value analysis for mutually exclusive projects including both revenues and costs would be appropriate.

The General Decision to Replace (Advanced)

The previous analysis concerned the choice between machine A and machine B, both of which were new acquisitions. More typically, firms must decide when to replace an existing machine with a new one. This decision is actually quite straightforward. One should replace if the annual cost of the new machine is less than the annual cost of the old machine. As with much else in finance, an example clarifies this approach better than further explanation.

Consider the situation of BIKE, which must decide whether to replace an existing machine. BIKE currently pays no taxes. The replacement machine costs $9,000 now and requires maintenance of $1,000 at the end of every year for eight years. At the end of eight years the machine would be sold for $2,000. All numbers are in real terms.

The existing machine requires increasing amounts of maintenance each year, and its salvage value falls each year, as shown:

Year	Maintenance	Salvage
Present	$ 0	$4,000
1	1,000	2,500
2	2,000	1,500
3	3,000	1,000
4	4,000	0

This chart tells us that the existing machine can be sold for $4,000 now. If it is sold one year from now, the resale price will be $2,500, and $1,000 must be spent on maintenance during the year to keep it running. For ease of calculation, we assume that this maintenance fee is paid at the end of the year. The machine will last for four more years before it falls apart. In other words, salvage value will be zero at the end of year 4. If BIKE faces an opportunity cost of capital of 15 percent, when should it replace the machine?

As we said above, our approach is to compare the annual cost of the replacement machine with the annual cost of the old machine. The annual cost of the replacement machine is simply its *equivalent annual cost* (EAC). Let's calculate that first.

Equivalent Annual Cost of New Machine   The present value of the cost of the new replacement machine is as follows:

$$PV_{costs} = \$9,000 + \$1,000 \times A^8_{0.15} - \frac{\$2,000}{(1.15)^8}$$

$$= \$9,000 + \$1,000 \times (4.4837) - \$2,000 \times (0.3269)$$

$$= \$12,833$$

Notice that the $2,000 salvage value is an inflow. It is treated as a *negative* number in the above equation because it *offsets* the cost of the machine.

The EAC of a new replacement machine equals

$$PV/\text{8-year annuity factor at }15\% = \frac{PV}{A^8_{0.15}} = \frac{\$12,833}{4.4873} = \$2,860$$

This calculation implies that buying a replacement machine is financially equivalent to renting this machine for $2,860 per year.

Cost of Old Machine   This calculation is a little trickier. If BIKE keeps the old machine for one year, the firm must pay maintenance costs of $1,000 a year from now. But this is not BIKE's only cost from keeping the machine for one year. BIKE will receive $2,500 at date 1 if the old machine is kept for one year but would receive $4,000 today if the old machine were sold immediately. This reduction in sales proceeds is clearly a cost as well.

Thus, the PV of the costs of keeping the machine one more year before selling it equals

$$\$4,000 + \frac{\$1,000}{1.15} - \frac{\$2,500}{1.15} = \$2,696$$

That is, if BIKE holds the old machine for one year, BIKE does *not* receive the $4,000 today. This $4,000 can be thought of as an opportunity cost. In addition, the firm must pay $1,000 a year from now. Finally, BIKE does receive $2,500 a year from now. This last item is treated as a negative number because it offsets the other two costs.

While we normally express cash flows in terms of present value, the analysis to come is made easier if we express the cash flow in terms of its future value one year from now. This future value is

$$\$2,696 \times 1.15 = \$3,100$$

In other words, the cost of keeping the machine for one year is equivalent to paying $3,100 at the end of the year.

Making the Comparison   Now let's review the cash flows. If we replace the machine immediately, we can view our annual expense as $2,860, beginning at the end of the year. This annual expense occurs forever, if we replace the new machine every eight years. This cash flow stream can be written as

	Year 1	Year 2	Year 3	Year 4	
Expenses from replacing machine immediately	$2,860	$2,860	$2,860	$2,860	. . .

If we replace the old machine in one year, our expense from using the old machine for that final year can be viewed as $3,100, payable at the end of the year. After replacement, our annual expense is $2,860, beginning at the end of two years. This annual expense occurs forever, if we replace the new machine every eight years. This cash flow stream can be written as

	Year 1	Year 2	Year 3	Year 4	
Expenses from using old machine for one year and then replacing it	$3,100	$2,860	$2,860	$2,860	...

Put this way, the choice is a no-brainer. Anyone would rather pay $2,860 at the end of the year than $3,100 at the end of the year. Thus, BIKE should replace[11] the old machine immediately in order to minimize the expense at year 1.

Two final points should be made on the decision to replace. First, we have examined a situation where both the old machine and the replacement machine generate the same revenues. Because revenues are unaffected by the choice of machine, revenues do not enter our analysis. This situation is common in business. For example, the decision to replace either the heating system or the air conditioning system in one's home office will likely not affect firm revenues. However, sometimes revenues will be greater with a new machine. The above approach can easily be amended to handle differential revenues.

Second, we want to stress the importance of the above approach. Applications of the above approach are pervasive in business, since every machine must be replaced at some point.

Concept
Question

- **What is the equivalent annual cost method of capital budgeting?**

8.7 SUMMARY AND CONCLUSIONS

This chapter discusses a number of practical applications of capital budgeting.

1. Capital budgeting must be conducted on an incremental basis. This means that sunk costs must be ignored, while opportunity costs, side effects, and allocated costs need to be considered.

2. Inflation should be handled consistently. One approach is to express both cash flows and the discount rate in nominal terms. The other approach is to express both cash flows and the discount rate in real terms. Because either approach yields the same NPV calculation, the simpler method should be used. Which method is simpler will generally depend on the nature of the capital budgeting problem.

---

[11] One caveat is in order. Perhaps the old machine's maintenance is high in the first year but drops after that. A decision to replace immediately might be premature in that case. Therefore, we need to check the cost of the old machine in future years.

The cost of keeping the existing machine a second year is

$$PV \text{ of costs at time } 1 = $2,500 + \frac{$2,000}{1.15} - \frac{$1,500}{1.15} = $2,935$$

which has future value of $3,375 ($2,935 × 1.15).

The costs of keeping the existing machine for years 3 and 4 are also greater than the EAC of buying a new machine. Thus, BIKE's decision to replace the old machine immediately is still valid.

3. In the total project cash flow example, we computed NPV using the following two steps:

   a. Calculate the net cash flow from all sources for each period.

   b. Calculate the NPV using the cash flows calculated above.

   In the tax shield example, we used two different steps:

   a. Calculate the present value of each source (for example, revenues and CCA tax shield).

   b. Add the present values across the different sources (including initial investment) in order to get NPV.

   The second approach has three benefits. Simplifying formulas can often be used. Nominal cash flows and real cash flows can be handled in the same example. Cash flows of varying risk can be used in the same example.

4. A firm should use the equivalent annual cost approach when choosing between two machines of unequal lives.

KEY TERMS

Allocated cost 206	Real cash flow 217
Erosion 206	Real interest rate 215
Incremental cash flow 205	Sunk cost 205
Nominal cash flow 216	Synergy 206
Nominal interest rate 215	Tax shield on CCA 220
Opportunity cost 205	

SUGGESTED READING

An excellent in-depth examination of the capital budgeting decision is contained in:
T. Copeland, T. Koller, and J. Murrin. *Valuation: Measuring and Managing the Value of Companies,* 3rd ed. The McKinsey Company, 1996.

QUESTIONS & PROBLEMS

Incremental Cash Flows

8.1 Which of the following should be treated as incremental cash flows when computing the NPV of an investment?

   a. The reduction in the sales of the company's other products.

   b. The expenditure on plant and equipment.

   c. The cost of research and development undertaken in connection with the product during the past three years.

   d. The annual CCA expense.

   e. Dividend payments.

   f. The resale value of plant and equipment at the end of the project's life.

   g. Salary and medical costs for production employees on leave.

Practical Application of NPV to Capital Budgeting (no inflation)

EXCEL

8.2 According to the February 7, 2002, issue of *The Sports Universe,* the Seattle Mariners' designated runner, Andy Schneider, signed a three-year contract in January 2002 with the following provisions:

   a. $1,400,000 signing bonus

   b. $2,500,000 salary per year for three years

   c. 10 years of deferred payments of $1,250,000 per year (these payments begin in year 4)

   d. Several bonus provisions that total as much as $750,000 per year for the three years of the contract

   Assume that Schneider received the bonuses each year, and that he signed the contract on January 1, 2002. Assume that cash flows are discounted at 12.36 percent. Ignore taxes. Schneider's signing bonus was paid on January 1, 2002. Schneider's salary and bonuses other than the signing bonus are paid at the end of the year. What was the present value of this contract in January when Schneider signed it?

Comparing Mutually Exclusive Projects

8.3   Victoria Enterprises, Inc. is evaluating alternative uses for a three-storey manufacturing and warehousing building that it has purchased for $745,000. The company could continue to rent the building to the present occupants for $45,000 per year. These tenants have indicated an interest in staying in the building for at least another 15 years. Alternatively, the company could make improvements to modify the existing structure to use for its own manufacturing and warehousing needs. Victoria's production engineer feels the building could be adapted to handle one of two new product lines. The cost and revenue data for the two product alternatives follow.

	Product A	Product B
Initial cash outlay for building modifications	$ 96,000	$177,500
Initial cash outlay for equipment	376,000	422,000
Annual pretax cash revenues (generated for 15 years)	300,500	373,600
Annual pretax cash expenditures (generated for 15 years)	170,000	212,000

The building will be used for only 15 years for either product A or product B. After 15 years, the building will be too small for efficient production of either product line. At that time, Victoria plans to rent the building to firms similar to the current occupants. To rent the building again, Victoria will need to restore the building to its present layout. The estimated cash cost of restoring the building if product A has been undertaken is $14,750; if product B has been produced, the cash cost will be $112,550. These cash costs can be deducted for tax purposes in the year the expenditures occur.

Victoria will depreciate the original building shell (purchased for $745,000) at a CCA rate of 5 percent, regardless of which alternative it chooses. The building modifications fall into CCA class 13 and are depreciated using the straight-line method over a 15-year life. Equipment purchases for either product are in class 8 and have a CCA rate of 20 percent. The firm's tax rate is 40 percent, and its required rate of return on such investments is 16 percent.

For simplicity, assume all cash flows for a given year occur at the end of the year. The initial outlays for modifications and equipment will occur at *t* = 0, and the restoration outlays will occur at the end of year 15. Also, Victoria has other profitable ongoing operations that are sufficient to cover any losses.

Which use of the building would you recommend to management?

Valuation of the Firm

8.4   The Regina Wheat Company (RWC) has wheat fields that currently produce annual profits of $660,000. These fields are expected to produce average annual profits of $660,000 in real terms forever. RWC has no depreciable assets, so the annual cash flow is also $660,000. RWC is an all-equity firm with 275,000 shares outstanding. The appropriate discount rate for its stock is 15 percent. RWC has an investment opportunity with a gross present value of $1,650,000. The investment requires a $1,100,000 outlay now. RWC has no other investment opportunities. Assume all cash flows are received at the end of each year. What is the price per share of RWC?

Capital Budgeting with Inflation

8.5   Consider the following cash flows on two mutually exclusive projects.

Year	Project A	Project B
0	–$40,000	–$50,000
1	20,000	10,000
2	15,000	20,000
3	15,000	40,000

Cash flows of project A are expressed in real terms while those of project B are expressed in nominal terms. The appropriate nominal discount rate is 15 percent, and inflation is 5 percent. Which project should you choose?

8.6   Phillips Industries runs a small manufacturing operation. For this year, it expects to have real net cash flows of $120,000. Phillips is an ongoing operation, but it expects competitive pressures to erode its (inflation-adjusted) net cash flows at 6 percent per year. The appropriate real discount rate for Phillips is 11 percent. All net cash flows are received at year-end. What is the present value of the net cash flows from Phillips' operations?

8.7   Larry, a small restaurant owner/manager, is contemplating the purchase of a larger restaurant from its owner, who is retiring. Larry would finance the purchase by selling his existing small restaurant, taking a second mortgage on his house, selling the stocks and bonds that he owns, and, if necessary, taking out a bank loan. Because Larry would have almost all of his wealth in the restaurant, he wants a careful analysis of how much he should be willing to pay for the business. The present owner of the larger restaurant has supplied the following information from the past five years.

Year	Gross Revenue	Profit
−5	$875,000	$ 62,000
−4	883,000	28,000
−3	828,000	4,400
−2	931,000	96,000
Last	998,000	103,000

As with many small businesses, the larger restaurant is structured as a sole proprietorship so no corporate taxes are deducted. The preceding figures have not been adjusted for changes in the price level. There is general agreement that the average profits for the past five years are representative of what can be expected in the future, after adjusting for inflation.

Larry is of the opinion that he could earn at least $3,000 in current dollars per month as a hired manager. Larry feels he should subtract this amount from profits when analyzing the venture. Furthermore, he is aware of statistics showing that for restaurants of this size, approximately 6 percent go out of business each year.

Larry has done some preliminary work to value the business. His analysis is as follows:

Year	Profits	Price-Level Factor	Profits (current dollars)	Imputed Managerial Wage	Net Profits
−5	$ 62,000	1.28	$ 79,400	$36,000	$ 43,400
−4	28,000	1.18	33,000	36,000	−3,000
−3	4,400	1.09	4,800	36,000	−31,200
−2	96,000	1.04	99,800	36,000	63,800
Last	103,000	1.00	103,000	36,000	67,000

The average profits for the past five years, expressed in current dollars, are $28,000. Using this average profit figure, Larry produced the following figures in current dollars.

Year	Expected Profits	Real Discount Factor 2%	Present Value
Next	$28,000	0.980	$27,440
+2	26,320	0.961	25,294
+3	24,752	0.942	23,316
+4	23,268	0.924	21,500
.	.	.	.
.	.	.	.
.	.	.	.

Based on these calculations, Larry has calculated that the value of the restaurant is $400,000.

a. Do you agree with Larry's assessment of the restaurant? In your answer, consider his treatment of inflation and his deduction of the managerial wage of $3,000 per month.

b. What present value would you place on the revenue stream; in other words, how much would you advise Larry to be willing to pay for the restaurant?

8.8 The Biological Insect Control Corporation (BICC) has hired you as a consultant to evaluate the NPV of its proposed toad ranch. BICC plans to breed toads and sell them as ecologically desirable insect-control mechanisms. It anticipates that the business will continue in perpetuity. Following the negligible start-up costs, BICC expects the following nominal cash flows at the end of the year:

Revenues	$150,000
Labour costs	80,000
Other costs	40,000

The company will rent machinery for $20,000 per year. The rental payments start at the end of year 1 and are expressed in nominal terms. Revenues will increase by 5 percent per year in real terms. Labour costs will increase by 3 percent per year in real terms. Other costs will decrease by 1 percent per year in real terms. The rate of inflation is expected to be 6 percent per year. BICC's required rate of return is 10 percent in real terms. There are no taxes. All cash flows occur at year-end. What is the NPV of BICC's proposed toad ranch today?

8.9 You are asked to evaluate the following project for a corporation with profitable ongoing operations. The required investment on January 1 of this year is $40,000. The firm will depreciate the investment at a CCA rate of 20 percent. The firm is in the 40 percent tax bracket.

The price of the product on January 1 will be $300 per unit. That price will stay constant in real terms. Labour costs will be $12 per hour on January 1. They will increase at 1 percent per year in real terms. Energy costs will be $5.15 per physical unit on January 1; they will increase at 3 percent per year in real terms. The inflation rate is 5 percent. Revenue is received and costs are paid at year-end.

	Year 1	Year 2	Year 3	Year 4
Physical production, in units	100	200	200	150
Labour input, in hours	2,000	2,000	2,000	2,000
Energy input, physical units	200	200	200	200

The riskless nominal discount rate is 7 percent. The real discount rate for costs and revenues is 3 percent. Calculate the NPV of this project.

8.10 Sparkling Water, Inc., sells 2 million bottles of drinking water each year. Each bottle sells at $2.50 in real terms and costs per bottle are $0.70 in real terms. Sales income and costs occur at year-end. Sales income is expected to rise at a real rate of 7 percent annually, while real costs are expected to rise at 5 percent annually. The relevant, real discount rate is 10 percent. The corporate tax rate is 40 percent. What is Sparkling worth today?

8.11 International Buckeyes is building a factory that can make 1 million buckeyes a year for five years. The factory costs $6 million. In year 1, each buckeye will sell for $3.15 in nominal terms. The price will rise 5 percent each year in real terms. During the first year, variable costs will be $0.2625 per buckeye in nominal terms and will rise by 2 percent each year in real terms. International Buckeyes will depreciate the factory at a CCA rate of 20 percent.

International Buckeyes expects to be able to sell the factory for $638,140.78 at the end of year 5 (or $500,000 in real terms). The proceeds will be invested in a new factory.

The nominal discount rate for risky cash flows is 25 percent. The nominal discount rate for riskless cash flows is 20 percent. The rate of inflation is 5 percent. Cash flows, except the initial investment, occur at the end of the year. The corporate tax rate is 40 percent. What is the net present value of this project?

8.12   Majestic Mining Company is negotiating for the purchase of a new piece of equipment for its current operations. MMC wants to know the maximum price that it should be willing to pay for the equipment. That is, how high must the price be for the equipment to have an NPV of zero? You are given the following facts:

1.   The new equipment would replace existing equipment that has a current market value of $20,000.

2.   The new equipment would not affect revenues, but before-tax operating costs would be reduced by $10,000 per year for eight years. These savings in cost would occur at year-end.

3.   The old equipment is now five years old. It is expected to last for another eight years, and to have no resale value at the end of those eight years. It was purchased for $40,000 and is being depreciated at a CCA rate of 20 percent.

4.   The new equipment will also be depreciated at a CCA rate of 20 percent. MMC expects to be able to sell the equipment for $5,000 at the end of eight years. At that time, the firm plans to reinvest in new equipment in the same CCA pool.

5.   MMC has profitable ongoing operations.

6.   The appropriate discount rate is 10 percent.

7.   The tax rate is 45 percent.

8.13   After extensive medical and marketing research, Pill Ltd. believes it can penetrate the pain reliever market. It can follow one of two strategies. The first is to manufacture a medication aimed at relieving headache pain. The second strategy is to make a pill designed to relieve headache and arthritis pain. Both products would be introduced at a price of $4 per package in real terms. The broader remedy would probably sell 10 million packages a year. This is twice the sales rate for the headache-only medication. Cash costs of production in the first year are expected to be $1.50 per package in real terms for the headache-only brand. Production costs are expected to be $1.70 in real terms for the more general pill. All prices and costs are expected to rise at the general inflation rate of 5 percent.

Either strategy would require further investment in plant. The headache-only pill could be produced using equipment that would cost $10.2 million, last three years, and have no resale value. The machinery required to produce the broader remedy would cost $12 million and last three years. At this time the firm would be able to sell it for $1 million (in real terms). The production machinery would need to be replaced every three years at constant real costs.

Suppose that, for both projects, the firm will use a CCA rate of 20 percent. The firm faces a corporate tax rate of 40 percent. Management believes the appropriate real discount rate is 13 percent. Which pain reliever should Pill Ltd. produce?

8.14   A machine that lasts four years has the following net cash outflows: $12,000 to purchase the machine and $6,000 for the annual year-end operating cost. At the end of four years, the machine is sold for $2,000; thus, the cash flow at year 4, C_4 is only $4,000.

C_0	C_1	C_2	C_3	C_4
$12,000	$6,000	$6,000	$6,000	$4,000

The cost of capital is 6 percent. What is the present value of the costs of operating a series of such machines in perpetuity?

Replacement with Unequal Lives

8.15   Office Automation, Inc., is obliged to choose between two copiers, XX40 or RH45. XX40 costs less than RH45, but its economic life is shorter. The costs and maintenance expenses of these two copiers are given as follows. These cash flows are expressed in real terms.

Copier	Year 0	Year 1	Year 2	Year 3	Year 4	Year 5
XX40	$1400	$200	$200	$200		
RH45	900	110	110	110	$110	$110

The inflation rate is 5 percent and the nominal discount rate is 14 percent. Assume that revenues are the same regardless of the copier, and that whichever copier the company chooses, it will buy the model forever. Which copier should the company choose? Ignore taxes and depreciation.

8.16   Station CIXT is considering the replacement of its old, fully depreciated sound mixer. Two new models are available. Mixer X has a cost of $400,000, a five-year expected life, and after-tax cash flow savings of $120,000 per year. Mixer Y has a cost of $600,000, an eight-year life, and after-tax cash flow savings of $130,000 per year. No new technological developments are expected. The cost of capital is 11 percent. Should CIXT replace the old mixer with X or Y?

8.17   Which is better: (1) investing $10,000 in a guaranteed investment certificate (GIC) for one year at 9 percent when expected inflation is 4 percent or (2) investing $10,000 in a GIC at 5 percent when expected inflation is 1 percent? In assessing these alternatives, assume that interest received is taxed at a rate of 40 percent.

8.18   A new electronic process monitor costs $140,000. This cost will be depreciated at 25 percent per year (class 9). The monitor will actually be worthless in five years. The new monitor would save us $50,000 per year before taxes in operating costs. If we require a 13 percent return, what is the NPV of the purchase? Assume a tax rate of 40 percent.

8.19   We believe we can sell 10,000 home security devices per year at $35 apiece. They cost $20 each to manufacture (variable cost). Fixed production costs will run $30,000 per year. The necessary equipment costs $150,000 to buy and will be depreciated at a 20 percent CCA rate. The equipment will have zero salvage value after the five-year life of the project. When this project is over, there will still be other assets in the CCA class. We would save $500,000 before taxes per year in order processing costs, and we would reduce working capital by $220,000 (a one-time reduction). What is the DCF return on this investment? The relevant tax rate is 40 percent.

8.20   This problem is much easier if you are working with a spreadsheet. We are contemplating the purchase of a $900,000 computer-based customer order management system. CCA on the system will be calculated at a rate of 30 percent. In five years it will be worth $330,000. When this project is over, there will still be other assets in the CCA class. We would save $500,000 before taxes per year in order processing costs, and we would reduce working capital by $220,000 (a one-time reduction). What is the DCF return on this investment? The relevant tax rate is 40 percent.

8.21   A proposed cost-saving device has an installed cost of $59,400. It is in class 9 for CCA purposes. (CCA rates are given in Table 8A.1.) It will actually function for five years, at which time it will have no value. When this project is over, there will still be other assets in the CCA class. There are no working capital consequences from the investment; the tax rate is 40 percent.

   a.   What must the annual pretax cost savings be for us to favour the investment? We require a 12 percent return. Hint: This is a variation on the problem of setting a bid price.

   b.   Suppose the device will be worth $11,000 in salvage (before taxes). How does this change your answer?

8.22   Klaatu Co. has recently completed a $400,000, two-year marketing study. Based on the results, Klaatu has estimated that 10,000 of its new RUR-class robots could be sold annually over the next eight years at a price of $9,615 each. Variable costs per robot are $7,400; fixed costs total $12 million per year.

Start-up costs include $40 million to build production facilities, $2.4 million in land, and $8 million in net working capital. The $40 million facility is made up of a building valued at $5 million that will belong to CCA class 3 and $35 million of manufacturing equipment (belonging to CCA class 8). (CCA rates are in Appendix 8A.) At the end of the project's life, the facilities (including the land) will be sold for an estimated $8.4 million, assuming the building's value will be $4 million. When this project is over, there will still be other assets in the CCA class. The value of the land is not expected to change.

Finally, start-up would also entail fully deductible expenses of $1.4 million at year 0. An ongoing, profitable business, Klaatu pays taxes at a 40 percent rate. Klaatu uses a 16 percent discount rate on projects such as this one. Should Klaatu produce the RUR-class robots?

MINICASE: Goodweek Tire, Inc.

After extensive research and development, Goodweek Tire, Inc., has recently developed a new tire, the SuperTread, and must decide whether to make the investments necessary to produce and market the SuperTread. The SuperTread would be ideal for drivers doing a large amount of wet weather and off-road driving in addition to normal highway usage. The research and development costs so far total about $10,000,000. The SuperTread would be put on the market beginning this year and Goodweek Tire expects it to stay on the market for a total of four years. Test marketing, costing $5,000,000, shows that there is a significant market for a SuperTread type tire.

As a financial analyst at Goodweek Tire, you are asked by your CFO, Adam Smith, to evaluate the SuperTread project and provide a recommendation on whether or not to go ahead with the investment. You are informed that all previous investments in the SuperTread are sunk costs and only future cash flows should be considered. Except for the initial investments, which occur immediately, assume all cash flows occur at year-end.

Goodweek Tire must initially invest $120,000,000 in production equipment to make the SuperTread. The equipment is expected to have a seven-year useful life. This equipment can be sold for $51,428,571 at the end of four years. Goodweek intends to sell the SuperTread to two distinct markets:

1. *The original equipment manufacturer (OEM) market.* The OEM market consists primarily of the large automobile companies (e.g., General Motors, Canada) who buy tires for new cars. In the OEM market, the SuperTread is expected to sell for $36 per tire. The variable cost to produce each SuperTread is $18.

2. *The replacement market.* The replacement market consists of all tires purchased after the automobile

has left the factory. This market allows higher margins, and Goodweek Tire expects to sell the SuperTread for $59 per tire. Variable costs are the same as in the OEM market.

Goodweek Tire intends to raise prices at 1 percent *above* the inflation rate. Variable costs will also increase 1 percent *above* the inflation rate. In addition, the SuperTread project will incur $25,000,000 in marketing and general administration costs the first year (expected to increase at the inflation rate in subsequent years).

Goodweek Tire's corporate tax rate is 40 percent. Annual inflation is expected to remain constant at 3.25 percent. Goodweek Tire uses a 15.9 percent discount rate to evaluate new product decisions.

The Tire Market Automotive industry analysts expect automobile manufacturers to have a production of 2 million new cars this year and for production to grow at 2.5 percent per year afterwards. Each new car needs four tires (the spare tires are undersized and are in a different category). Goodweek Tire expects the SuperTread to capture 11 percent of the OEM market.

Industry analysts estimate that the replacement tire market size will be 14 million tires this year and that it will grow at 2 percent annually. Goodweek Tire expects the SuperTread to capture an 8 percent market share.

You know that the investment in equipment is in class 8 for CCA purposes. Given Goodweek's ongoing operations, there will always be assets in class 8. You also decide to consider net working capital (NWC) requirements in this scenario. The immediate initial working capital requirement is $11,000,000, and thereafter the net working capital requirements will be 15 percent of sales. What will the NPV, payback period, discounted payback period, AAR, IRR, and PI on this project be?

MINICASE: I.Q., Inc.

In order to maintain its leadership position in the computer peripherals industry, particularly inkjet printers and accessories, I.Q. has begun to develop a new ink for its 8xx line of inkjet printers. As a marketing manager of the 8xx line of inkjet printers and accessories, you are in the position to make a decision whether or not to continue the development. The project is codenamed IQ8Ink.

Research efforts for the IQ8Ink have cost I.Q. $1 million so far, in addition to a positive test marketing effort costing $0.5 million. However, these are sunk costs and will not impact your decision making. What should be considered are the new investment and future cash inflows. From your observation, you know that you can invest immediately and start production now. You also know that the economic life of this effort is only four years, meaning potentially four years of production.

I.Q.'s CEO, K. Fione, is very pleased with the progress of the 8xx line so far and wishes to congratulate you on a job well done. So, the decision on the development of IQ8Ink is critical. From engineering, you know that you will need to invest another $1 million in production equipment to make this new ink. The equipment will have a useful life of five years and qualifies for a CCA rate of 20 percent. At year 4, you expect to sell the equipment for $0.3 million. For planning purposes, you believe that assets will remain in the equipment's CCA class. Furthermore, the net working capital

requirement will increase by $1 million immediately and will be recaptured at year 4.

As for the potential customers, there are two distinct segments:

1. New 8xx printers—For every new 8xx printer, one unit of this new ink will be used. (Assume complete retirement of old ink models with no costs associated.) Internal transfer price is at $2 now. The variable cost to produce per unit is $0.50.

2. Existing 8xx printers—While competitors exist, offering generic ink, IQ8Ink is superior and will take a large percentage of market share. Wholesale price is at $10 now. The variable cost to produce per unit is the same as above.

Note that on average, ink price and cost rise at 2 percent above the inflation rate. In addition, marketing and administration efforts will increase at inflation each subsequent year.

From economic data, inflation is expected to remain constant at 3 percent. I.Q.'s corporate tax rate is 40 percent and the division has a discount rate of 15 percent.

Last, you know that production of new 8xx printers will be 300,000 units in the first year and will increase by 10 percent per year. Additionally, the demand for ink from existing 8xx printers is 1 million units in the first year and increases by 10 percent per year. Out of the demand for ink from existing 8xx printers, I.Q. expects to capture 80 percent.

MINICASE: Jimmy's Hot Dog Stands

Jimmy Levitin owns a popular hot dog stand on a trendy section of Melrose Boulevard. Following the success of his first hot dog stand, "Jimmy's," which has been in operation for five years, Jimmy is now considering opening a second hot dog stand in another trendy location, on Sunset Boulevard in the Silver Lake area. Jimmy's market research shows that the clientele in both areas is similar: young professionals, typically without children, who like the traditional aspect of eating hot dogs, but also relish his gourmet, specially manufactured low-fat dogs and the healthy side dishes his stand also sells. Jimmy's overall plan is to get the second stand up and running for five years, and then sell both stands off to a new owner and retire.

Jimmy estimates that the cost of starting up a second stand will be as follows:

Purchase of real estate (retail food outlet)	$400,000
Installation of specialized kitchen equipment	40,000
Furniture and fittings	25,000

The cost of the real estate was allocated $250,000 to the land and $150,000 to the building. The Building CCA rate is 4 %.

On the sale of the building, the proceeds were allocated in the same ratio to land and building as they were in the purchase.

Jimmy estimates that net working capital will increase by $20,000 for the first year for the new outlet. He also estimates that yearly operating costs of the new location would be almost identical to those of his current stand:

Labour costs, inclusive of all overhead costs:

Kitchen and service staff (4 persons)	$ 96,000

Raw materials:

Hot dogs: 200 per day × 7 days	
× 52 weeks	$ 54,600
Drinks	18,400
Other food supplies	72,800
Nonfood supplies	22,200
Total raw materials	$168,000

The revenues at his current location are as follows:

Sales of hot dogs and other food items	$418,000
Drinks	92,000
Total revenues	$510,000

In addition to contributing profits, Jimmy expects that opening a second stand will decrease the cost of purchasing gourmet hot dogs from 75 cents to 60 cents in both locations. This is due to economies of scale, since the new outlet would double output over the current level of demand. Jimmy also expects that he will be able to manage both locations himself, avoiding hiring a second manager for the new location.

Assume that:

- The marginal tax rate is 40 percent.
- The required rate of return is 10 percent.
- The CCA rate is 30 percent.
- At the time the business is sold, the real estate will have increased in value at an annual rate of 10 percent and the kitchen equipment and furniture will have no value.
- The sale price of the business is the market value of the real estate plus one year's revenue.

What is the NPV of this investment?

Appendix 8A   Capital Cost Allowance

Under the *Income Tax Act*, accounting amortization cannot be used in the calculation of income for income tax purposes. Instead, the Act mandates the use of the Capital Cost Allowance (CCA) system.[12] Capital cost allowance is deducted in determining taxable income. CCA is not the same as depreciation under GAAP so there is no reason why calculation of a firm's income under tax rules has to be the same as under GAAP. For example, taxable corporate income may often be lower than accounting income because the company uses accelerated capital cost allowance rules in computing depreciation for tax purposes while using straight-line depreciation for GAAP reporting.[13]

CCA calculation begins by assigning every asset to a particular class. An asset's class establishes its maximum CCA rate for tax purposes. Leasehold improvements follow straight-line depreciation for CCA. For all other assets, CCA follows the declining balance method. The CCA for each year is computed by multiplying the asset's book value for tax purposes, called *undepreciated capital cost (UCC)*, by the appropriate rate.

Intangible assets, such as goodwill and patents, are particularly important to knowledge-based firms like software developers and pharmaceutical companies. Such assets are not subject to CCA. Instead, intangible assets are amortized at an effective rate of 5.25 percent on the declining balance.

The CCA system is unique to Canada and differs in many respects from the depreciation method used in the United States. One key difference is that, in the Canadian system, the expected salvage value (what we think the asset will be worth when we dispose

[12]Recall from Chapter 2 that accountants use the term *amortization* to refer to depreciation and depletion.

[13]Where taxable income is less than accounting income, total taxes (calculated from accounting income) are greater than current taxes (calculated from taxable income). The difference, deferred taxes (or future tax liability) for the year, is added to the deferred tax liability account on the balance sheet.

Part II *Value and Capital Budgeting*

TABLE 8A.1 Common CCA Classes

Class	Rate	Asset
1	4%	Brick buildings (acquired after 1987)
3	5	Brick buildings (acquired prior to 1988)
6	10	Fences and frame buildings
7	15	Canoes and boats, ships
8	20	Manufacturing and processing equipment
9	25	Electrical equipment and aircraft
10	30	Vans, trucks, tractors, and computer equipment
13	straight-line	Leasehold improvements
16	40	Taxicabs and rental cars
22	50	Excavating equipment

Source: *Income Tax Act 2001* (72nd edition).

of it) and the actual expected economic life (how long we expect the asset to be in service) are not considered in the calculation of capital cost allowance. (Some typical CCA classes and their respective CCA rates are described in Table 8A.1.) Another unique feature of the CCA system is the concept of pooling of assets described in detail below. Calculating CCA on pools of assets rather than for each item simplifies the system.

To illustrate how capital cost allowance is calculated, suppose your firm is considering buying a van costing $24,000, including any set-up costs that must (by law) be capitalized. (No rational, profitable business would capitalize, for tax purposes, anything that could legally be expensed.) Table 8A.1 shows that vans fall in class 10 with a 30 percent CCA rate. To calculate the CCA we need to follow the 50 percent rule, which requires us to figure CCA on only one-half of the asset's installed cost in the first year it is put in use. Notice that we add the other half in the second year. The UCC at the beginning of year 2 is:

$$\text{Beginning UCC} - \text{CCA} + \text{Remaining half of purchase price}$$
$$\$12,000 - 0.30 \times \$12,000 + \$12,000 = \$20,400$$

Table 8A.2 shows the CCA for our van for the first five years.

As we pointed out, in calculating CCA under current tax law, the economic life and future market value of the asset are not issues. As a result, an asset's UCC can differ substantially from its actual market value. With our $24,000 van, UCC after the first year is $8,400 (or $12,000 less the first year's CCA of $3,600). The remaining UCC values are summarized in Table 8A.2. After five years, the van's undepreciated capital cost is $4,898.

TABLE 8A.2 CCA for a Van

Year	Beginning UCC	CCA	Ending UCC
1	$12,000*	$3,600	$ 8,400
2	20,400†	6,120	14,280
3	14,280	4,284	9,996
4	9,996	2,999	6,997
5	6,997	2,099	4,898

*One-half of $24,000.
†Year 1 ending balance plus the remaining half of $24,000.

Capital Cost Allowance in Practice

Since capital cost allowance is deducted in computing taxable income, larger CCA rates reduce taxes and increase cash flows. To illustrate, in a federal budget a few years ago, the minister announced an increase in CCA rates from 25 to 30 percent for computer equipment. The combined federal/provincial corporate tax rate for this sector is 34.5 percent.

Mississauga Manufacturing was planning to acquire new processing equipment to enhance efficiency and its ability to compete with U.S. firms. The equipment had an installed cost of $1 million. How much additional tax did the new measure save Mississauga in the first year the equipment was put into use?

Under the 50 percent rule, UCC for the first year is $1/2 \times \$1$ million = $500,000. The CCA deductions under the old and new rates are

$$\text{Old rate: CCA} = 0.25 \times \$500,000 = \$125,000$$
$$\text{New rate: CCA} = 0.30 \times \$500,000 = \$150,000$$

Because the firm deducts CCA in figuring taxable income, taxable income will be reduced by the incremental CCA of $25,000. With $25,000 less in taxable income, Mississauga Manufacturing's combined tax bill will drop by $25,000 \times 0.345 = \$8,625$.

Asset Purchases and Sales

When an asset is sold, the UCC in its asset class (or pool) is reduced by what is realized on the asset or by its original cost, whichever is less. This amount is called the *adjusted cost of disposal*. Suppose that we want to sell the van in our earlier example after five years and find that it is worth $6,000. Since the $6,000 price is less than the original cost, the adjusted cost of disposal is $6,000 and the UCC in class 10 is reduced by this amount.

In this case, the $6,000 removed from the pool is $1,102 (or $6,000 − 4,898) more than the undepreciated capital cost of the van we are selling, and future CCA deductions will be reduced as the pool continues. On the other hand, if we sold the van for, say, $4,000, the UCC in class 10 would be reduced by $4,000 and the $898 excess (4,898 − 4,000) of UCC over the sale price would remain in the pool. In this case, future CCA increases as the declining balance calculations depreciate the $898 excess UCC to infinity.

So far, we have focused on CCA calculations for one asset. In practice, firms often buy and sell assets from a given class in the course of a year. In this case, we apply the net acquisitions rule. From the total installed cost of all acquisitions we subtract the adjusted cost of disposal of all assets in the pool. The result is net acquisitions for the asset class. If net acquisitions is positive, we apply the 50 percent rule and calculate CCA as above. If net acquisitions is negative, the 50 percent rule does not apply.

When an Asset Pool Is Terminated

Suppose your firm decides to contract out all transport and to sell all company vehicles. If the company owns no other class 10 assets, the asset pool in this class is terminated. As before, the adjusted cost of disposal is the net sales proceeds or the total installed cost of all the pool assets, whichever is less. This adjusted cost of disposal is subtracted from the total UCC in the pool. So far, the steps are exactly the same as in our van example where the pool continued. What happens next is different. Unless the adjusted cost of disposal just happens to equal the UCC exactly, a positive or negative UCC balance remains and this has tax implications.

A positive UCC balance remains when the adjusted cost of disposal is less than UCC before the sale. In this case, the firm has a terminal loss equal to the remaining UCC.

Because this loss is deductible from income for the year, it results in a tax saving. For example, if we sell the van after two years for $10,000, then the UCC exceeds the market value by $4,280 (or $14,280 − $10,000). In this case, the terminal loss of $4,280—assuming the tax rate is 40 percent—gives rise to a tax saving of 0.40 × $4,280 = $1,712.

A negative UCC balance occurs when the adjusted cost of disposal exceeds UCC in the pool. To illustrate, return to our example and suppose that this van is the only class 10 asset our company owns when it sells off the pool. In this case, we see that there is a $1,102 excess of adjusted cost of disposal ($6,000 − $4,898) over UCC so the final UCC balance is −$1,102.

The company must pay tax at its ordinary tax rate on this negative balance. Taxes must be paid in this case since the difference in adjusted cost of disposal and UCC is "excess" CCA recaptured when the asset is sold. We overdepreciated the asset by $6,000 − $4,898 = $1,102. Since we deducted $1,102 too much in CCA, we paid $440.80 ($1,102 × 0.4) too little in taxes, and we simply have to make up the difference.

Notice that this is not a tax on a capital gain. As a general rule, a capital gain only occurs if the market price exceeds the original cost. To illustrate a capital gain, suppose that instead of buying the van, our firm purchased a classic car for $50,000. After five years, the classic car will be sold for $75,000. In this case, the sale price exceeds the purchase price so the adjusted cost of disposal is $50,000 and the UCC pool is reduced by this amount. The total negative balance left in the UCC pool is $6,123 − $50,000 = −$43,877 and this is recaptured CCA. In addition, the firm has a capital gain of $75,000 − $50,000 = $25,000, the difference between the sale price and the original cost.

The company must pay tax on this capital gain of $25,000. As explained in Appendix 1A, at the time of writing, a corporation is taxed on 50 percent of any capital gains. Using a marginal corporate tax rate of 40 percent, the tax payable is $5,000 (or $25,000 × 0.50 × 0.40).

Staple Supply, Ltd., has just purchased a new computerized information system with an installed cost of $160,000. The computer is in class 10 for CCA purposes. What are the yearly capital cost allowances? Based on historical experience, we think that the system will be worth only $10,000 when we get rid of it in four years. What are the tax consequences of the sale if the company has several other computers that will still be in use in four years? Now suppose that Staple Supply will sell all its assets and wind up the company in four years. What is the total after-tax cash flow from the sale?

In Table 8A.3, at the end of year 4 the remaining balance for the specific computer system will be $46,648.[14] The pool is reduced by $10,000, but it will continue to be "depreciated." There are no tax consequences in year 4. This is only the case when the pool is active. If this is the only computer system, we close the pool and claim a terminal loss of $46,648 − $10,000 = $36,648.

TABLE 8A.3	CCA for a Computer System		
Year	Beginning UCC	CCA	Ending UCC
1	$ 80,000*	$24,000	$56,000
2	136,000†	40,800	95,200
3	95,200	28,560	66,640
4	66,640	19,992	46,648

[14] In actuality, the capital cost allowance for the entire pool will be calculated at once, without specific identification of each computer system.

Appendix Questions

8.A1 What is the difference between capital cost allowance and GAAP depreciation?

8.A2 A company has just invested $100,000 in new manufacturing equipment (class 8). Develop a CCA and UCC schedule (like Table 8A.2) for the first 10 years.

8.A3 Suppose the company decides to sell the equipment after three years for $30,000 and terminates the asset pool. Calculate the tax results.

Chapter 9

Risk Analysis, Real Options, and Capital Budgeting

EXECUTIVE SUMMARY

Chapters 7 and 8 covered the basic principles of capital budgeting, with particular emphasis on the net present value (NPV) approach. However, this is not the end of the story. Real-world practitioners often wonder how much confidence they should place in NPV calculations. This chapter examines sensitivity analysis, scenario analysis, break-even analysis, and Monte Carlo simulations, all of which recognize that, because it is based on estimates, NPV is really a distribution, not a single number. These techniques help the practitioner determine the degree of confidence to be placed in a capital budgeting calculation.

Information is uncovered as a project unfolds, allowing a manager to make sequential decisions over the life of the project. This chapter covers decision trees and real options, capital budgeting techniques that specifically take the sequential nature of decision making into account.

9.1 Decision Trees

There is usually a sequence of decisions in NPV project analysis. This section introduces the device of **decision trees** for identifying these sequential decisions.

Imagine you are the treasurer of the Solar Electronics Corporation (SEC), and the engineering group has recently developed the technology for solar-powered jet engines. The jet engine is to be used with 150-passenger commercial airplanes. The marketing staff has proposed that SEC develop some prototypes and conduct test marketing of the engine. A corporate planning group, including representatives from production, marketing, and engineering, estimates that this preliminary phase will take a year and will cost $100 million. Furthermore, the group believes there is a 75 percent chance that the marketing tests will prove successful.

If the initial marketing tests are *successful*, SEC can go ahead with full-scale production. This investment phase will cost $1,500 million. Production and sales will occur over the next five years. The preliminary cash flow projection appears in Table 9.1. Should SEC go ahead with investment and production on the jet engine, the NPV at a discount rate of 15 percent (in millions) is

$$\text{NPV} = -\$1,500 + \sum_{t=1}^{5} \frac{\$900}{(1.15)^t}$$
$$= -\$1,500 + \$900 \times A_{0.15}^5$$
$$= \$1,517$$

Note that the NPV is calculated as of date 1, the date at which the investment of $1,500 million is made. Later we bring this number back to date 0.

TABLE 9.1	Cash Flow Forecasts for Solar Electronics Corporation's Jet Engine Base Case (millions)*	
Investment	**Year 1**	**Years 2–6**
Revenues		$ 6,000
Variable costs		(3,000)
Fixed costs		(1,791)
Depreciation		(300)
Pretax profit		909
Tax ($T_c = 0.34$)		(309)
Net profit		$ 600
Cash flow		$ 900
Initial investment costs	–$1,500	

*Assumptions: (1) Investment is depreciated in years 2 through 6 using the straight-line method for simplicity; (2) tax rate is 34 percent; (3) the company receives no tax benefits on initial development costs.

If the initial marketing tests are *unsuccessful*, SEC's $1,500 million investment has an NPV of –$3,611 million. This figure is also calculated as of date 1. (To save space, we will not provide the raw numbers leading to this calculation.)

Figure 9.1 displays the problem concerning the jet engine as a decision tree. If SEC decides to conduct test marketing, there is a 75 percent probability that the test marketing will be successful. If the tests are successful, the firm faces a second decision: whether to

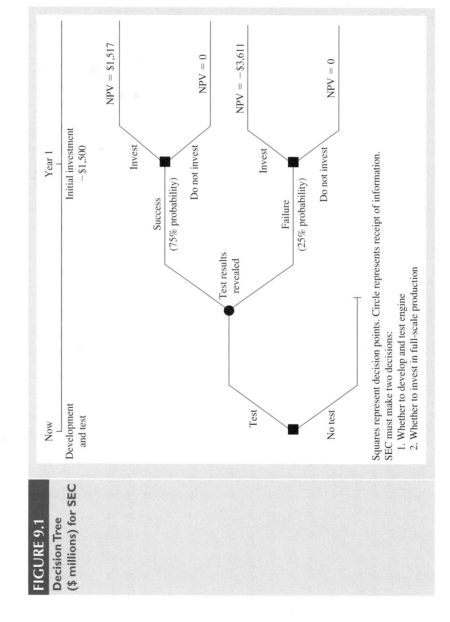

FIGURE 9.1
Decision Tree ($ millions) for SEC

Squares represent decision points. Circle represents receipt of information.
SEC must make two decisions:
1. Whether to develop and test engine
2. Whether to invest in full-scale production

invest $1,500 million in a project that yields $1,517 million NPV or to stop. If the tests are unsuccessful, the firm faces a different decision: whether to invest $1,500 million in a project that yields −$3,611 million NPV or to stop.

To review, SEC has the following two decisions to make:

1. Whether to develop and test the solar-powered jet engine.
2. Whether to invest in full-scale production following the results of the test.

One makes decisions in reverse order with decision trees. Thus we analyze the second-stage investment of $1,500 million first. If the tests are successful, should SEC make the second-stage investment? The answer is obviously yes, since $1,517 million is greater than zero. If the tests are unsuccessful, should the second-stage investment be made? Just as obviously, the answer is no, since −$3,611 million is below zero.

Now we move back to the first stage, where the decision boils down to the question: Should SEC invest $100 million now to obtain a 75 percent chance of $1,517 million one year later? The expected payoff evaluated at date 1 (in millions) is

$$
\begin{pmatrix} \text{Expected} \\ \text{payoff} \end{pmatrix} = \begin{pmatrix} \text{Probability} \\ \text{of} \\ \text{success} \end{pmatrix} \times \begin{pmatrix} \text{Payoff} \\ \text{if} \\ \text{successful} \end{pmatrix} + \begin{pmatrix} \text{Probability} \\ \text{of} \\ \text{failure} \end{pmatrix} \times \begin{pmatrix} \text{Payoff} \\ \text{if} \\ \text{failure} \end{pmatrix}
$$

$$
= (0.75 \times \$1,517) + (0.25 \times \$0)
$$

$$
= \$1,138
$$

The NPV of testing computed at date 0 (in millions) is

$$
\text{NPV} = -\$100 + \frac{\$1,138}{1.15}
$$

$$
= \$890
$$

Since the NPV is a positive number, the firm should test the market for solar-powered jet engines.

Warning   We have used a discount rate of 15 percent for both the testing and the investment decisions. Perhaps a higher discount rate should have been used for the initial test-marketing decision, which is likely to be riskier than the investment decision.

Concept
Questions

- What is a decision tree?
- How do decision trees handle sequential decisions?

9.2 Sensitivity Analysis, Scenario Analysis, and Break-Even Analysis

One thrust of this book is that NPV analysis is a superior capital budgeting technique. In fact, because the NPV approach uses cash flows rather than profits, uses all the cash flows, and discounts the cash flows properly, it is hard to find any theoretical fault with it. However, in our conversations with practical businesspeople, we hear the phrase "a false sense of security" frequently. These people point out that the documentation for capital budgeting proposals is often quite impressive. Cash flows are projected down to the last thousand dollars (or even the last dollar) for each year (or even each month). Opportunity costs and side effects are handled quite properly. Sunk costs are ignored—also quite properly. When a high net present value appears at the bottom, one's temptation is to say yes immediately. Nevertheless, the projected cash flow often goes unmet in practice, and the firm ends up with a money loser.

Sensitivity Analysis and Scenario Analysis

How can the firm get the net present value technique to live up to its potential? One approach is **sensitivity analysis** (a.k.a. *what-if analysis* and *bop analysis*[1]), which examines how sensitive a particular NPV calculation is to changes in underlying assumptions. We illustrate the technique with Solar Electronics' solar-powered jet engine from the previous section. As pointed out earlier, the cash flow forecasts for this project appear in Table 9.1. We begin by considering the assumptions underlying revenues, costs, and after-tax cash flows shown in the table.

Revenues   Sales projections for the proposed jet engine have been estimated by the marketing department as

$$
\begin{aligned}
\text{Number of jet} &= \text{Market share} \times \text{Size of jet} \\
\text{engines sold} && \text{engine market} \\
3,000 &= 0.30 \times 10,000
\end{aligned}
$$

$$
\begin{aligned}
\text{Sales revenues} &= \text{Number of jet} \times \text{Price per} \\
&\quad\ \text{engines sold} \qquad \text{engine} \\
\$6,000 \text{ million} &= 3,000 \times \$2 \text{ million}
\end{aligned}
$$

Thus, it turns out that the revenue estimates depend on three assumptions:

1. Market share
2. Size of jet engine market
3. Price per engine

Costs   Financial analysts frequently divide costs into two types: variable costs and fixed costs. **Variable costs** change as the output changes, and they are zero when production is zero. Costs of direct labour and raw materials are usually variable. It is common to assume that a variable cost is constant per unit of output, implying that total variable costs are proportional to the level of production. For example, if direct labour is variable and one unit of final output requires $10 of direct labour, then 100 units of final output should require $1,000 of direct labour.

Fixed costs are not dependent on the amount of goods or services produced during the period. Fixed costs are usually measured as costs per unit of time, such as rent per month or salaries per year. Naturally, fixed costs are not fixed forever. They are only fixed over a predetermined time period.

The engineering department has estimated variable costs to be $1 million per engine. Fixed costs are $1,791 million per year. The cost breakdowns are

$$
\begin{aligned}
\text{Variable} &= \text{Variable cost} \times \text{Number of jet} \\
\text{cost} &\quad\ \text{per unit} \qquad\ \text{engines sold} \\
\$3,000 \text{ million} &= \$1 \text{ million} \times 3,000
\end{aligned}
$$

$$
\begin{aligned}
\text{Total cost before taxes} &= \text{Variable cost} + \text{Fixed cost} \\
\$4,791 \text{ million} &= \$3,000 \text{ million} + \$1,791 \text{ million}
\end{aligned}
$$

---

[1]BOP stands for Best, Optimistic, Pessimistic.

TABLE 9.2   Different Estimates for Solar Electronics' Solar Jet Engine

Variable	Pessimistic	Expected or Best	Optimistic
Market size (per year)	5,000	10,000	20,000
Market share	20%	30%	50%
Price	$1.9 million	$2 million	$2.2 million
Variable cost (per plane)	$1.2 million	$1 million	$0.8 million
Fixed cost (per year)	$1,891 million	$1,791 million	$1,741 million
Investment	$1,900 million	$1,500 million	$1,000 million

The above estimates for market size, market share, price, variable cost, and fixed cost, as well as the estimate of initial investment, are presented in the middle column of Table 9.2. These figures represent the firm's expectations or best estimates of the different parameters. For purposes of comparison, the firm's analysts prepared both optimistic and pessimistic forecasts for the different variables. These are also provided in the table.

Standard sensitivity analysis calls for an NPV calculation for all three possibilities of a single variable, along with the expected forecast for all other variables. This procedure is illustrated in Table 9.3. For example, consider the NPV calculation of $8,154 million provided in the upper right-hand corner of this table. This occurs when the optimistic forecast of 20,000 units per year is used for market size. However, the expected forecasts from Table 9.2 are employed for all other variables when the $8,154 million figure is generated. Note that the same number of $1,517 million appears in each row of the middle column of Table 9.3. This occurs because the expected forecast is used for the variable that was singled out, as well as for all other variables.

Table 9.3 can be used for a number of purposes. First, taken as a whole, the table can indicate whether NPV analysis should be trusted. In other words, it reduces the false sense of security we spoke of earlier. Suppose that NPV is positive when the expected forecast for each variable is used. However, further suppose that every number in the pessimistic

TABLE 9.3   NPV Calculations as of Date 1 (in $ millions) for the Solar Jet Engine Using Sensitivity Analysis

	Pessimistic	Expected or Best	Optimistic
Market size	−$1,802*	$1,517	$8,154
Market share	−696*	1,517	5,942
Price	853	1,517	2,844
Variable cost	189	1,517	2,844
Fixed cost	1,295	1,517	1,628
Investment	1,208	1,517	1,903

Under sensitivity analysis, one input is varied while all other inputs are assumed to meet their expectation. For example, an NPV of −$1,802 occurs when the pessimistic forecast of 5,000 is used for market size. However, the expected forecasts from Table 9.2 are used for all other variables when −$1,802 is generated.

*We assume that the other divisions of the firm are profitable, implying that a loss on this project can offset income elsewhere in the firm, thereby reducing the overall taxes of the firm.

column is highly negative and every number in the optimistic column is highly positive. Even a single error in this forecast greatly alters the estimate, making one leery of the net present value approach. A conservative manager might well scrap the entire NPV analysis in this situation. Fortunately, this does not seem to be the case in Table 9.3, because all but two of the numbers are positive. Managers viewing the table will likely consider NPV analysis to be useful for the solar-powered jet engine.

Second, sensitivity analysis shows where more information is needed. For example, error in the estimate of investment appears to be relatively unimportant because, even under the pessimistic scenario, the NPV of $1,208 million is still highly positive. By contrast, the pessimistic forecast for market share leads to a negative NPV of −$696 million, and a pessimistic forecast for market size leads to a substantially negative NPV of −$1,802 million. Since the effect of incorrect estimates on revenues is so much greater than the effect of incorrect estimates on costs, more information on the factors determining revenues might be needed.

Because of these advantages, sensitivity analysis is widely used in practice. Graham and Harvey[2] report that slightly over 50 percent of the 392 firms in their sample subject their capital budgeting calculations to sensitivity analysis. This number is particularly large when one considers that only about 75 percent of the firms in their sample use NPV analysis.

Unfortunately, sensitivity analysis also suffers from some drawbacks. For example, sensitivity analysis may unwittingly *increase* the false sense of security among managers. Suppose all pessimistic forecasts yield positive NPVs. A manager might feel that there is no way the project can lose money. Of course, the forecasters may simply have an optimistic view of a pessimistic forecast. To combat this, some companies do not treat optimistic and pessimistic forecasts subjectively. Rather, their pessimistic forecasts are always, say, 20 percent less than expected. Unfortunately, the cure in this case may be worse than the disease, because a deviation of a fixed percentage ignores the fact that some variables are easier to forecast than others.

In addition, sensitivity analysis treats each variable in isolation when, in reality, the different variables are likely to be related. For example, if ineffective management allows costs to get out of control, it is likely that variable costs, fixed costs, and investment will all rise above expectation at the same time. If the market is not receptive to a solar-powered jet engine, both market share and price should decline together.

Managers frequently perform **scenario analysis,** a variant of sensitivity analysis, to minimize this problem. Simply put, this approach examines a number of different likely scenarios, where each scenario involves a confluence of factors. As a simple example, consider the effect of a few airline crashes. These crashes are likely to reduce flying in total, thereby limiting the demand for any new engines. Furthermore, even if the crashes did not involve solar-powered aircraft, the public could become more averse to any innovative and controversial technologies. Hence, SEC's market share might fall as well. Perhaps the cash flow calculations would look like those in Table 9.4 under the scenario of a plane crash. Given the calculations in the table, the NPV (in millions) would be

$$-\$2,023 = -\$1,500 - \$156 \times A_{0.15}^5$$

A series of scenarios like this might illuminate issues concerning the project better than the standard application of sensitivity analysis would.

---

[2] See Figure 2 of John Graham and Campbell Harvey, "The Theory and Practice of Corporate Finance: Evidence from the Field," *Journal of Financial Economics* (May/June 2001).

TABLE 9.4 Cash Flow Forecast (in $ millions) Under the Scenario of a Plane Crash*

	Year 1	Years 2–6
Revenues		$2,800
Variable costs		−1,400
Fixed costs		−1,791
Depreciation		−300
Pretax profit		−691
Tax ($T_c = 0.34$)†		235
Net profit		−456
Cash flow		−156
Initial investment cost	−$1,500	

*Assumptions are

Market size	7,000 (70 percent of expectation)
Market share	20% (2/3 of expectation)

Forecasts for all other variables are the expected forecasts as given in Table 9.2.

†Tax loss offsets income elsewhere in firm.

Break-Even Analysis

Our discussion of sensitivity analysis and scenario analysis suggests that there are many ways to examine variability in forecasts. We now present another approach, **break-even analysis**. As its name implies, this approach determines the sales needed to break even. The approach is a useful complement to sensitivity analysis, because it also sheds light on the severity of incorrect forecasts. We calculate the break-even point in terms of both accounting profit and present value.

Accounting Profit

Net profit under four different sales forecasts is

Unit Sales	Net Profit (in $ millions)
0	−$1,380
1,000	−720
3,000	600
10,000	5,220

A more complete presentation of costs and revenues appears in Table 9.5.

We plot the revenues, costs, and profits under the different assumptions about sales in Figure 9.2. The revenue and cost curves cross at 2,091 jet engines. This is the break-even point, i.e., the point where the project generates no profits or losses. As long as sales are above 2,091 jet engines, the project will make a profit.

This break-even point can be calculated very easily. Because the sale price is $2 million per engine and the variable cost is $1 million per engine, the after-tax difference per engine is

$$(\text{Sale price} - \text{Variable cost}) \times (1 - T_c) = (\$2 \text{ million} - \$1 \text{ million}) \times (1 - 0.34)$$

$$= \$0.66 \text{ million}$$

where T_c is the corporate tax rate of 34 percent. This after-tax difference is called the **contribution margin** because each additional engine contributes this amount to after-tax profit.[3]

---

[3]Though the previous section considered both optimistic and pessimistic forecasts for sale price and variable cost, break-even analysis uses just the expected or best estimates of these variables.

TABLE 9.5

Revenues and Costs of Project Under Different Sales Assumptions (in $ millions, except unit sales)

Year 1 Initial Investment	Annual Unit Sales	Years 2–6 Revenues	Variable Costs	Fixed Costs	Depreciation	Taxes* ($T_c = 0.34$)	Net Profit	Operating Cash Flows	NPV (evaluated date 1)
$1,500	0	$ 0	$ 0	-$1,791	-$300	$ 711	-$1,380	-$1,080	-$5,120
1,500	1,000	2,000	-1,000	-1,791	-300	371	-720	-420	-2,908
1,500	3,000	6,000	-3,000	-1,791	-300	-309	600	900	1,517
1,500	10,000	20,000	-10,000	-1,791	-300	-2,689	5,220	5,520	17,004

*Loss is incurred in the first two rows. For tax purposes, this loss offsets income elsewhere in the firm.

Fixed costs are $1,791 million and depreciation is $300 million, implying that the after-tax sum of these costs is

$$(\text{Fixed costs} + \text{Depreciation}) \times (1 - T_c) = (\$1,791 \text{ million} + \$300 \text{ million})$$
$$\times (1 - 0.34) = \$1,380 \text{ million}$$

That is, the firm incurs costs of $1,380 million, regardless of the number of sales. Because each engine contributes $0.66 million, sales must reach the following level to offset the above costs:

Accounting Profit Break-Even Point:

$$\frac{(\text{Fixed costs} + \text{Depreciation}) \times (1 - T_c)}{(\text{Sale price} - \text{Variable costs}) \times (1 - T_c)} = \frac{\$1,380 \text{ million}}{\$0.66 \text{ million}} = 2,091 \qquad (9.1)$$

Thus, 2,091 engines is the break-even point required for an accounting profit.

Present Value   As we stated many times in the text, we are more interested in present value than we are in net profits. Therefore, we must calculate the present value of the cash flows. Given a discount rate of 15 percent, we have

Unit Sales	NPV ($ millions)
0	-5,120
1,000	-2,908
3,000	1,517
10,000	17,004

FIGURE 9.2

Break-Even Point Using Accounting Numbers

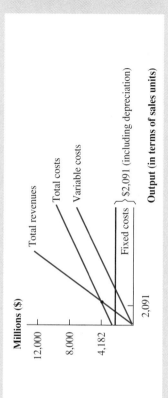

These NPV calculations are reproduced in the last column of Table 9.5. We can see that the NPV is negative if SEC produces 1,000 jet engines and positive if it produces 3,000 jet engines. Obviously, the zero NPV point occurs between 1,000 and 3,000 jet engines.

The present value break-even point can be calculated very easily. The firm originally invested $1,500 million. This initial investment can be expressed as a five-year equivalent annual cost (EAC), determined by dividing the initial investment by the appropriate five-year annuity factor:

$$\text{EAC} = \frac{\text{Initial investment}}{\text{5-year annuity factor at 15\%}} = \frac{\text{Initial investment}}{A_{0.15}^{5}}$$

$$= \frac{\$1,500 \text{ million}}{3.3522} = \$447.5 \text{ million}$$

Note that the EAC of $447.5 million is greater than the yearly depreciation of $300 million. This must occur since the calculation of EAC implicitly assumes that the $1,500 million investment could have been invested at 15 percent.

After-tax costs, regardless of output, can be viewed as

$$\$1,528 = \$447.5 + \$1,791 \times 0.66 - \$300 \times 0.34$$
$$\text{million} \quad \text{million} \quad \text{million} \qquad \text{million}$$

$$= \text{EAC} + \text{Fixed costs} \times (1 - T_c) - \text{Depreciation} \times T_c$$

That is, in addition to the initial investment's equivalent annual cost of $447.5 million, the firm pays fixed costs each year and receives a depreciation tax shield each year. The depreciation tax shield is written as a negative number since it offsets the costs in the equation. Because each engine contributes $0.66 million to after-tax profit, it will take the following sales to offset the above costs:

Present Value Break-Even Point:

$$\frac{\text{EAC} + \text{Fixed costs} \times (1 - T_c) - \text{Depreciation} \times T_c}{(\text{Sales price} - \text{Variable costs}) \times (1 - T_c)} = \frac{\$1,528 \text{ million}}{\$0.66 \text{ million}} = 2,315 \quad (9.2)$$

Thus, 2,315 engines is the break-even point from the perspective of present value.

Why is the accounting break-even point (Equation 9.1) different from the financial break-even point in Equation (9.2)? When we use accounting profit as the basis for the break-even calculation, we subtract depreciation. Depreciation for the solar jet engines project is $300 million. If 2,091 solar jet engines are sold, SEC will generate sufficient revenues to cover the $300 million depreciation expense plus other costs. Unfortunately, at this level of sales SEC will not cover the economic opportunity costs of the $1,500 million laid out for the investment. If we take into account that the $1,500 million could have been invested at 15 percent, the true annual cost of the investment is $447.5 million and not $300 million. Depreciation understates the true costs of recovering the initial investment. Thus, companies that break even on an accounting basis are really losing money. They are losing the opportunity cost of the initial investment.

Concept
Questions

- **What is a sensitivity analysis?**
- **Why is it important to perform a sensitivity analysis?**
- **What is a break-even analysis?**
- **Describe how sensitivity analysis interacts with break-even analysis.**

Break-Even Analysis, EAC, and Capital Cost Allowance

So far, in this chapter and the previous one, all our examples with EAC and break-even analysis have featured straight-line depreciation. While this had the advantage of simplifying the examples, it lacks realism for Canada. Here we show how to incorporate capital cost allowance into break-even analysis using the EAC approach.

Nack Trucks, Inc., is expanding into the business of buying stripped-down truck platforms, which it plans to customize to client specifications and resell. The company will rent its manufacturing facility for $6,000 per month. Truck platforms cost $20,000 each and the typical finished product sells for $42,000.

This new business line would require $60,000 in new equipment. This equipment falls into class 8 with a CCA rate of 20 percent and would be worth about $5,000 after four years. Nack's tax rate is 43.5 percent and the cost of capital is 20 percent.

There is only one major competitor and Nack's sales staff estimate that they could achieve annual sales of 12 units. In order to determine if this sales level will be profitable, we must find the NPV break-even point.

This problem is very similar to the one we solved for SEC in Equation (9.2) above. The key difference is that the depreciation here is based on CCA so we have to replace the term, Depreciation $\times T_c$, in (9.2) with the EAC of the present value of the CCA tax shield: $EAC_{PVCCATS}$. This requires first calculating PVCCATS and then converting to an EAC.

$$PVCCATS = \frac{60,000\,(0.20)\,(0.435)}{0.20 + 0.20} \times \frac{1 + 0.5\,(0.20)}{1 + 0.20} - \frac{5,000\,(0.20)\,(0.435)}{0.20 + 0.20}$$

$$\times \frac{1}{(1.20)^4} = \$11,438$$

$$EAC_{PVCCATS} = \$11,438/A^4_{0.20} = \$11,438/2.5887 = \$4,418.38$$

Next we find the EAC of the investment as:

$$[\$60,000 - \$5,000/(1.20)^4]/2.5887 = \$22,246.30$$

Fixed costs after tax are the rent of $6,000 \times 12 = \$72,000$ per year times $(1 - 0.435) = \$40,680$, and the after-tax contribution margin is $(\$42,000 - \$20,000)(1 - 0.435) = \$12,430$.

We can now rewrite Equation (9.2) and fill in the numbers:

Present Value Break-Even Point with CCA

$$\frac{EAC + \text{Fixed costs} \times (1 - T_c) - EAC_{PVCCATS}}{(\text{Sale price} - \text{Variable costs}) \times (1 - T_c)} = \frac{\$22,246.30 + \$40,680 - \$4,418.38}{\$12,430}$$

$$= 4.71 \text{ or } 5 \text{ trucks}$$

Our calculations show that the break-even point is 5 trucks. This is well below targeted sales of 12 trucks, so the expansion looks promising.

9.3 Monte Carlo Simulation

Both sensitivity analysis and scenario analysis attempt to answer the question, "What if?" However, while both analyses are frequently used in the real world, each has its own limitations. Sensitivity analysis allows only one variable to change at a time. By contrast, many variables are likely to move at the same time in the real world. Scenario analysis follows specific scenarios, such as changes in inflation, government regulation, or the number of competitors. While this methodology is often quite helpful, it cannot cover all sources of variability. In fact, projects are likely to exhibit a lot of variability under just one economic scenario.

Monte Carlo simulation is a further attempt to model real-world uncertainty. This approach takes its name from the famous European casino, because it analyzes projects the way one might analyze gambling strategies. Imagine a serious blackjack player who wonders if he should take a third card whenever his first two cards total 16. Most likely, a formal mathematical model would be too complex to be practical here. However, he could play thousands of hands in a casino, sometimes drawing a third card when his first two cards add to 16 and sometimes not drawing that third card. He could compare his winnings (or losses) under the two strategies in order to determine which was better. Of course, since he would probably lose a lot of money performing this test in a real casino, simulating the results from the two strategies on a computer might be cheaper. Monte Carlo simulation of capital budgeting projects is in this spirit.

Imagine that Backyard Barbecues, Inc. (BBI), a manufacturer of both charcoal and gas grills, has the blueprint for a new grill that cooks with compressed hydrogen. The CFO, Edward H. Comiskey, being dissatisfied with simpler capital budgeting techniques, wants a Monte Carlo simulation for this new grill. A consultant specializing in the Monte Carlo approach, Lester Mauney, takes him through the five basic steps of the method.

Step 1: Specify the Basic Model

Les Mauney breaks up cash flow into three components: annual revenue, annual costs, and initial investment. The revenue in any year is viewed as:

$$
\begin{array}{ccccc}
\text{Number of grills sold} & & \text{Market share of BBI's} & & \text{Price per} \\
\text{by entire industry} & \times & \text{hydrogen grill (in percent)} & \times & \text{hydrogen grill}
\end{array} \tag{9.3}
$$

The cost in any year is viewed as:

Fixed manufacturing costs + Variable manufacturing costs + Marketing costs
+ Selling costs

Initial investment is viewed as:

Cost of patent + Test-marketing costs + Cost of production facility

Step 2: Specify a Distribution for Each Variable in the Model

Here comes the hard part. Let's start with revenue, which has three components in (9.3). The consultant first models overall market size, that is, the number of grills sold by the entire industry. The trade publication, *Outdoor Food* (*OF*), reported that 10 million grills of all types were sold in North America last year and it forecasts sales of 10.5 million next year. Mr. Mauney, using *OF*'s forecast and his own intuition, creates the following distribution for next year's sales of grills by the entire industry:

Probability	20%	60%	20%
Next year's industrywide unit sales	10 million	10.5 million	11 million

The tight distribution here reflects the slow but steady historical growth in the grill market.

Lester Mauney realizes that estimating the market share of BBI's hydrogen grill is more difficult. Nevertheless, after a great deal of analysis, he determines the distribution of next year's market share to be:

Probability	10%	20%	30%	25%	10%	5%
Market share of BBI's hydrogen grill next year	1%	2%	3%	4%	5%	8%

While the consultant assumed a symmetrical distribution for industrywide unit sales, he believes a skewed distribution makes more sense for the project's market share. In his mind, there is always the small possibility that sales of the hydrogen grill will really take off.

The above forecasts assume that unit sales for the overall industry are unrelated to the project's market share. In other words, the two variables are *independent* of each other. Mr. Mauney reasons that, while an economic boom might increase industrywide grill sales and a recession might decrease them, the project's market share is unlikely to be related to economic conditions.

Now Mr. Mauney must determine the distribution of price per grill. Mr. Comiskey, the CFO, informs him that the price will be in the area of $200 per grill, given what other competitors are charging. However, the consultant believes that the price per hydrogen grill will almost certainly depend on the size of the overall market for grills. As in any business, you can usually charge more if demand is high.

After rejecting a number of complex models for price, Mr. Mauney settles on the following specification:

$$\text{Next year's price} = \$190 + \$1 \times \text{Industrywide unit sales (in millions)} +/- \$3 \quad\quad (9.4)$$
per hydrogen grill

The grill price in (9.4) is dependent on the unit sales of the industry. In addition, random variation is modelled via the term "+/−$3," where a drawing of +$3 and a drawing of −$3 each occur 50 percent of the time. For example, if industrywide unit sales are 11 million, the price per grill would be either:

$$\$190 + \$11 + \$3 = \$204 \quad (50\% \text{ probability})$$
$$\$190 + \$11 - \$3 = \$198 \quad (50\% \text{ probability})$$

The consultant now has distributions for each of the three components of next year's revenue. However, he needs distributions for future years as well. Using forecasts from *Outdoor Food* and other publications, Mr. Mauney forecasts the distribution of growth rates for the entire industry over the second year to be:

Probability	20%	60%	20%
Growth rate of industrywide unit sales in second year	1%	3%	5%

Given both the distribution of next year's industrywide unit sales and the distribution of growth rates for this variable over the second year, we can generate the distribution of industrywide unit sales for the second year. A similar extension should give Mr. Mauney a distribution for later years as well, though we won't go into the details here. And, just as the consultant extended the first component of revenue (industrywide unit sales) to later years, he would want to do the same thing for market share and unit price.

The above discussion shows how the three components of revenue can be modelled. Step 2 would be complete once the components of cost and of investment are modelled in a similar way. Special attention must be paid to the interactions between variables here, since ineffective management will likely allow the different cost components to rise together. However, since you are probably getting the idea now, we will skip the rest of this step.

Step 3: The Computer Draws One Outcome

As we said above, next year's revenue in our model is the product of three components. Imagine that the computer randomly picks industrywide unit sales of 10 million, a market share for BBI's hydrogen grill of 2 percent and a +$3 random price variation. Given these drawings, next year's price per hydrogen grill will be:

$$\$190 + \$10 + \$3 = \$203$$

and next year's revenue for BBI's hydrogen grill will be:

$$10 \text{ million} \times 0.02 \times \$203 = \$40.6 \text{ million}$$

Of course, we are not done with the entire outcome yet. We would have to perform drawings for revenue in each future year. In addition, we would perform drawings for costs in each future year. Finally, a drawing for initial investment would have to be made as well. In this way, a single outcome would generate a cash flow from the project in each future year.

How likely is it that the specific outcome above would be drawn? We can answer this because we know the probability of each component. Since industry sales of $10 million has a 20 percent probability, a market share of 2 percent also has a 20 percent probability, and a random price variation of +$3 has a 50 percent probability, the probability of these three drawings together in the same outcome is:

$$0.02 = 0.20 \times 0.20 \times 0.50 \qquad (9.5)$$

Of course, the probability would get even smaller once drawings for future revenues, future costs, and the initial investment are included in the outcome.

This step generates the cash flow for each year from a single outcome. What we are ultimately interested in is the *distribution* of cash flow each year across many outcomes. We ask the computer to randomly draw over and over again to give us this distribution, which is just what is done in the next step.

Step 4: Repeat the Procedure

While the above three steps generate one outcome, the essence of Monte Carlo simulation is repeated outcomes. Depending on the situation, the computer may be called on to generate thousands or even millions of outcomes. The result of all these drawings is a distribution of cash flow for each future year. This distribution is the basic output of Monte Carlo simulation.

Consider Figure 9.3. Here, repeated drawings have produced the simulated distribution of the third year's cash flow. There would be, of course, a distribution like the one in this figure for each future year. This leaves us with just one more step.

FIGURE 9.3

Simulated Distribution of the Third Year's Cash Flow for BBI's New Hydrogen Grill

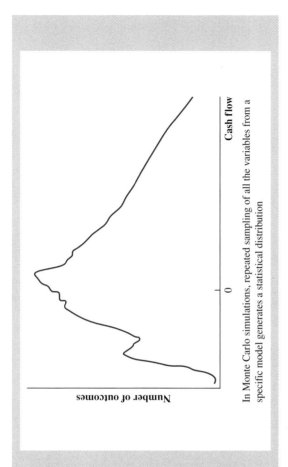

In Monte Carlo simulations, repeated sampling of all the variables from a specific model generates a statistical distribution

Step 5: Calculate NPV

Given the distribution of cash flow for the third year in Figure 9.3, one can determine the expected cash flow for this year. In a similar manner, one can also determine the expected cash flow for each future year and can then calculate the net present value of the project by discounting these expected cash flows at an appropriate rate.

Monte Carlo simulation is often viewed as a step beyond either sensitivity analysis or scenario analysis. Interactions between the variables are explicitly specified in Monte Carlo so, at least in theory, this methodology provides a more complete analysis. And, as a byproduct, having to build a precise model deepens the forecaster's understanding of the project.

Since Monte Carlo simulations have been around for at least 35 years, you might think that most firms would be performing them by now. Surprisingly, this does not seem to be the case. In our experience, executives are frequently skeptical of all the complexity. It is difficult to model either the distributions of all variables or the interactions between variables. In addition, the computer output is often devoid of economic intuition. Thus, while Monte Carlo simulations are used in certain real-world situations,[4] the approach is not likely to be "the wave of the future." In fact, Graham and Harvey[5] report that only about 15 percent of the firms in their sample use capital budgeting simulations.

9.4 Real Options

In Chapter 7, we stressed the superiority of net present value (NPV) analysis over other approaches when valuing capital budgeting projects. However, both scholars and practitioners have pointed out problems with NPV. The basic idea here is that NPV analysis, as

---

[4]More than perhaps any other, the pharmaceutical industry has pioneered applications of this methodology. For example, see, Nancy A. Nichols, "Scientific Management at Merck: An Interview with CFO Judy Lewent," *Harvard Business Review* (January/February 1994).

[5]See Figure 2 of Graham and Harvey, *op. cit.*

well as all the other approaches in Chapter 7, ignores the adjustments that a firm can make after a project is accepted. These adjustments are called **real options**. In this respect, NPV underestimates the true value of a project. NPV's conservatism here is best explained through a series of examples.

The Option to Expand

Conrad Willig, an entrepreneur, recently learned of a chemical treatment that causes water to freeze at 30°C, rather than 0°C. Of all the many practical applications for this treatment, Mr. Willig liked more than anything else the idea of hotels made of ice. Conrad estimated the annual cash flows from a single ice hotel to be $2 million, based on an initial investment of $12 million. He felt that 20 percent was an appropriate discount rate, given the risk of this new venture. Assuming that the cash flows were perpetual, Mr. Willig determined the NPV of the project to be:

$$-\$12,000,000 + \$2,000,000/0.20 = -\$2 \text{ million}$$

Most entrepreneurs would have rejected this venture, given its negative NPV. But Conrad was not your typical entrepreneur. He reasoned that NPV analysis missed a hidden source of value. While he was pretty sure that the initial investment would cost $12 million, there was some uncertainty concerning annual cash flows. His cash flow estimate of $2 million per year actually reflected his belief that there was a 50 percent probability that annual cash flows would be $3 million and a 50 percent probability that annual cash flows would be $1 million.

The NPV calculations for the two forecasts are:

Optimistic forecast: $-\$12$ million $+ \$3$ million$/0.20 = \$3$ million
Pessimistic forecast: $-\$12$ million $+ \$1$ million$/0.20 = -\$7$ million

On the surface, this new calculation doesn't seem to help Mr. Willig very much since an average of the two forecasts yields an NPV for the project of:

$$50\% \times \$3 \text{ million} + 50\% \times (-\$7 \text{ million}) = -\$2 \text{ million}$$

(which is just the value he calculated in the first place).

However, if the optimistic forecast turns out to be correct, Mr. Willig would want to *expand*. If he believes that there are, say, 10 locations in the country that can support an ice hotel, the true NPV of the venture would be:

$$50\% \times 10 \times \$3 \text{ million} + 50\% \times (-\$7 \text{ million}) = \$11.5 \text{ million}$$

The idea here, which is represented in Figure 9.4, is both basic and universal. The entrepreneur has the option to expand if the pilot location is successful. For example, think

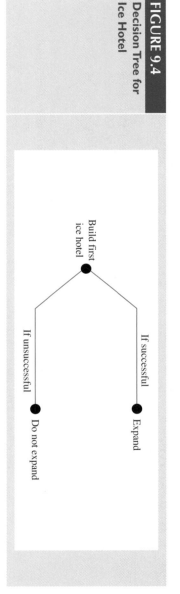

Build first ice hotel

If successful — Expand / Do not expand

If unsuccessful

of all the people that start restaurants, most of them ultimately failing. These individuals are not necessarily overly optimistic. They may realize the likelihood of failure but go ahead anyway because of the small chance of starting the next McDonald's or Burger King.

The Option to Abandon

Managers also have the option to abandon existing projects. While abandonment may seem cowardly, it can often save companies a great deal of money. Because of this, the option to abandon increases the value of any potential project.

The above example on ice hotels, which illustrated the option to expand, can also illustrate the option to abandon. To see this, imagine that Mr. Willig now believes that there is a 50 percent probability that annual cash flows will be $6 million and a 50 percent probability that annual cash flows will be −$2 million. The NPV calculations under the two forecasts become:

Optimistic forecast: −$12 million + $6 million/0.2 = $18 million
Pessimistic forecast: −$12 million − $2 million/0.2 = −$22 million

yielding an NPV for the project of:

$$50\% \times \$18 \text{ million} + 50\% \times (-\$22 \text{ million}) = -\$2 \text{ million} \qquad (9.6)$$

Furthermore, now imagine that Mr. Willig wants to own, at most, just one ice hotel, implying that there is no option to expand. Since the NPV in (9.6) is negative, it looks as if he will not build the hotel.

But things change when we consider the abandonment option. As of date 1, the entrepreneur will know which forecast has come true. If cash flows equal those under the optimistic forecast, Conrad will keep the project alive. If, however, cash flows equal those under the pessimistic forecast, he will abandon the hotel. Knowing these possibilities ahead of time, the NPV of the project becomes:

$$50\% \times \$18 \text{ million} + 50\% \times (-\$12 \text{ million} - \$2 \text{ million}/1.20) = \$2.17 \text{ million}$$

Since Mr. Willig abandons after experiencing the cash flow of −$2 million at date 1, he does not have to endure this outflow in any of the later years. Because the NPV is now positive, Conrad will accept the project.

The example here is clearly a stylized one. While many years may pass before a project is abandoned in the real world, our ice hotel was abandoned after just one year. And, while salvage values generally accompany abandonment, we assumed no salvage value for the ice hotel. Nevertheless, abandonment options are pervasive in the real world.

For example, consider the movie-making industry. As shown in Figure 9.5, movies begin with either the purchase or development of a script. A completed script might cost a movie studio a few million dollars and potentially lead to actual production. However, the great majority of scripts (perhaps well in excess of 80 percent) are abandoned. Why would studios abandon scripts that they had commissioned in the first place? While the studios know ahead of time that only a few scripts will be promising, they don't know which ones. Thus, they cast a wide net, commissioning many scripts to get a few good ones. And, the studios must be ruthless with the bad scripts, since the expenditure here pales in comparison to the huge losses from producing a bad movie.

The few lucky scripts will then move into production, where costs might be budgeted in the tens of millions of dollars, if not much more. At this stage, the dreaded phrase is that on-location production gets "bogged down," creating cost overruns. But the studios are equally ruthless here. Should these overruns become excessive, production is likely to be

FIGURE 9.5
The Abandonment
Option in the
Movie Industry

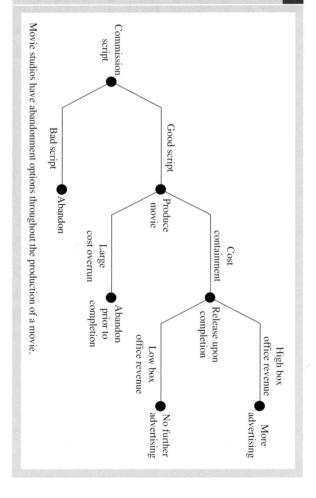

Movie studios have abandonment options throughout the production of a movie.

abandoned in midstream. Interestingly, abandonment almost always occurs due to high costs, not due to the fear that the movie won't be able to find an audience. Little information on that score will be obtained until the movie is actually released.

Release of the movie is accompanied by significant advertising expenditures, perhaps in the range of $10 to $20 million. Box office success in the first few weeks is likely to lead to further advertising expenditures. Again, the studio has the option, but not the obligation, to increase advertising here. It also has an option to produce a sequel.

Movie-making is one of the riskiest businesses around, with studios receiving hundreds of millions of dollars in a matter of weeks from a blockbuster while receiving practically nothing during this period from a flop. The above abandonment options contain costs that might otherwise bankrupt the industry.

Timing Options

One often finds urban land that has been vacant for many years. Yet this land is bought and sold from time to time. Why would anyone pay a positive price for land that has no source of revenue? Certainly one could not arrive at this positive value through NPV analysis. However, the paradox can easily be explained in terms of real options.

Suppose that the land's highest and best use is as an office building. Total construction costs for the building are estimated to be $1 million. Currently, net rents (after all costs) are estimated to be $90,000 per year in perpetuity and the discount rate is 10 percent. The NPV of this proposed building would be:

$$-\$1 \text{ million} + \$90,000/0.10 = -\$100,000$$

Since this NPV is negative, one would not currently want to build. In addition, it appears as if the land is worthless. However, suppose that the government is planning a bid for the 2012 Summer Olympics. Office rents will likely increase if the bid succeeds. In this case, the property's owner might want to erect the office building after all. Conversely, office rents will remain the same, or even fall, if the bid fails. The owner will not build in this case.

FIGURE 9.6
Decision Tree for Vacant Land

Rents rise substantially — Erect office building

Do not build yet, since rents are too low

Rents either stay the same or fall — Do not build yet

Vacant land may have value today, since the owner can erect a profitable office building if rents rise.

We say that the property owner has a *timing option*. While he does not currently want to build, he will want to build in the future should rents in the area rise substantially. This timing option explains why vacant land often has value. While there are costs, such as taxes, from holding raw land, the value of an office building after a substantial rise in rents may more than offset these holding costs. Of course, the exact value of the vacant land depends on both the probability of success in the Olympic bid and the extent of the rent increase. Figure 9.6 illustrates this timing option.

Mining operations almost always provide timing options as well. Suppose you own a copper mine where the cost of mining each tonne of copper exceeds the sales revenue. It's a no-brainer to say that you would not want to mine the copper currently. And since there are costs of ownership such as property taxes, insurance, and security, you might actually want to pay someone to take the mine off your hands. However, we would caution you not to do so hastily. Copper prices in the future might very well increase enough so that production is profitable. Given that possibility, you could likely find someone to pay a positive price for the property today.

Concept Questions

- What are the different types of real options?
- Why does traditional **NPV** analysis **tend** to **underestimate** the **true** value of a capital project?

9.5 SUMMARY AND CONCLUSIONS

This chapter discusses a number of practical applications of capital budgeting.

1. Though NPV is the best capital budgeting approach conceptually, it has been criticized in practice for providing managers with a false sense of security. Sensitivity analysis shows NPV under varying assumptions, giving managers a better feel for the project's risks. Unfortunately, sensitivity analysis modifies only one variable at a time, while many variables are likely to vary together in the real world. Scenario analysis examines a project's performance under different scenarios (e.g., war breaking out or oil prices skyrocketing). Finally, managers want to know how bad forecasts must be before a project loses money. Break-even analysis calculates the sales figure at which the project breaks even. Though break-even analysis is frequently performed on an accounting profit basis, we suggest that a net present value basis is more appropriate.

2. Monte Carlo simulation begins with a model of the firm's cash flows, based on both the interactions between different variables and the movement of each individual variable over time. Random sampling generates a distribution of these cash flows for each period, leading to a net present value calculation.

3. We analyze the hidden options in capital budgeting, such as the option to expand, the option to abandon, and timing options. We return to this topic in Chapter 25.

Part II   Value and Capital Budgeting

KEY TERMS

Break-even analysis 248	Real options 256
Contribution margin 248	Scenario analysis 247
Decision trees 242	Sensitivity analysis 245
Fixed costs 245	Variable costs 245
Monte Carlo simulation 252	

SUGGESTED READING

Two excellent sources on scenario analysis in corporate risk management are:

Rene Stulz, "Rethinking Risk Management," *Journal of Applied Corporate Finance*, 1996 (Fall), 8–24. Reprinted in *Corporate Hedging in Theory and Practice: Lessons from Metallgesellschaft*, Christopher L. Culp and Merton H. Miller, eds, Risk Publications, London, 1999.

Gregory W. Brown and Donald H. Chew, eds, *Corporate Risk: Strategies and Management*, Risk Publications, London, 1999.

An excellent book on real options is:

Martha Amran and Nalin Kulatilaka. *Real Options: Managing Strategic Investment in an Uncertain World.* Boston: Harvard Business School Press (1999).

A fascinating discussion of real options in the movie business can be found in:

Laura Martin, "Film Studio Reel Options." Unpublished manuscript, Credit Suisse First Boston (CSFB) (May 11, 2001). Obtainable at www.valuesweep.com.

QUESTIONS & PROBLEMS

Decision Trees

9.1   Sony Electronics, Inc., has developed a new DVD player. If the DVD player is successful, the present value of the payoff (at the time the product is brought to market) is $20 million. If the new player fails, the present value of the payoff is $5 million. If the product goes directly to market, there is a 50 percent chance of success. Alternatively, Sony can delay the launch by one year and spend $2 million to test market the DVD player. Test marketing allows the firm to improve the product and increase the probability of success to 75 percent. The appropriate discount rate is 15 percent. Should the firm conduct test marketing?

9.2   The manager for a growing firm is considering the launch of a new product. If the product goes directly to market, there is a 50 percent chance of success. For $120,000, the manager can conduct a focus group that will increase the product's chance of success to 70 percent. Alternatively, the manager has the option to pay a consulting firm $400,000 to research the market and refine the product. The consulting firm successfully launches new products 90 percent of the time. If the firm successfully launches the product, the payoff will be $1.2 million. If the product is a failure, the firm will receive $0. Which action will result in the highest expected payoff to the firm?

9.3   The sales of Tandem Bicycles, Inc., are decreasing because of foreign competition. The firm's chief financial officer (CFO) is considering the following mutually exclusive options to maintain market share this year:

• Price the products more aggressively. With this option, there is a 55 percent chance that Tandem will only lose $1.3 million in cash flow due to the decreased revenue. However, there is a 45 percent probability that Tandem's pricing strategy will fail, and the firm will lose a total of $1,850,000 in cash flow.

• Pay $800,000 for an Ottawa lobbyist to convince the regulators to impose tariffs on overseas bicycle manufacturers. With the lobbyist, there is a 75 percent chance that Tandem will lose no cash flow to the foreign competition. If the lobbyist does not succeed, Tandem Bicycles will lose $2 million in cash flow.

Assume all cash flows occur today, and that Tandem Bicycles will cease operations after this year. As the assistant to the CFO, which strategy would you recommend to maximize expected cash flow?

9.4 B&B has a new baby powder ready to market. If the firm goes directly to the market with the product, there is only a 55 percent chance of success. However, the firm can conduct customer segment research, which will take a year and cost $1 million. By going through research, B&B will be able to better target potential customers and will increase the probability of success to 70 percent. If successful, the baby powder will bring a present value profit (at time of initial selling) of $30 million. If unsuccessful, the present value payoff is only $3 million. Should the firm conduct customer segment research or go directly to market? The appropriate discount rate is 15 percent.

9.5 Young screenwriter Carl Draper has just finished his first script. It has action, drama, and humour, and he thinks it will be a blockbuster. He takes the script to every motion picture studio in town and tries to sell it but to no avail. Finally, ACME studios offers to buy the script, for either (a) $5,000, or (b) 1 percent of the movie's profits. There are two decisions that will take place for the studio: (1) Is the script good or bad? and (2) Is the movie good or bad? First, there is a 90 percent chance that the script is bad. If it is bad, the studio does nothing more and throws the script out. If the script is good, it will shoot the movie. After the movie is shot, the studio will review it and there is a 70 percent chance that the movie is bad. If the movie is bad, the movie will not be promoted and will not turn a profit. If the movie is good, the studio will promote it heavily and the average profit is $10 million. Carl rejects the $5,000 and says he wants the 1 percent of profits. Was this a good decision by Carl?

Accounting Break-Even Analysis

9.6 Samuelson, Inc., has just purchased a $600,000 machine to produce calculators. The machine qualifies for CCA at the rate of 30 percent and will be worth $50,000 after five years. It will produce 20,000 calculators each year. The variable production cost per calculator is $15 and total fixed costs are $900,000 per year. The corporate tax rate for the company is 40 percent. The cost of capital is 16%. (This is required for the PVCCATS calculation.) For the firm to break even (in terms of accounting profit), how much should the firm charge per calculator?

9.7 Consider the following information for a big-screen television distributor:

EXCEL

$$
\begin{aligned}
\text{Sales price per TV} &= \$1,500 \\
\text{Variable costs per TV} &= \$1,100 \\
\text{Fixed costs per year} &= \$120,000 \\
\text{EAC}_{\text{PVCCATS}} &= \$20,000 \\
\text{Tax rate} &= 35\%
\end{aligned}
$$

How many units must the distributor sell in a given year to break even (in terms of accounting profit)?

9.8 You are considering investing in a company that cultivates abalone for sale to local restaurants. Use the following information:

$$
\begin{aligned}
\text{Sales price per abalone} &= \$2.00 \\
\text{Variable costs per abalone} &= \$0.72 \\
\text{Fixed costs per year} &= \$340,000 \\
\text{EAC}_{\text{PVCCATS}} &= \$20,000 \\
\text{Tax rate} &= 35\%
\end{aligned}
$$

a. How many abalone must be harvested and sold per year for you to receive any profit (accounting break-even point)?

b. How much profit will you receive if 300,000 abalone are sold per year?

Part II *Value and Capital Budgeting*

9.9 What is the minimum number of times that a video arcade game must be played in a given period to break even?

Game price	= $0.50
Variable cost	= $0.02
Fixed costs	= $1,000
EAC$_{\text{PVCCATS}}$	= $50
Tax rate	= 34%

Present Value Break-Even Analysis

9.10 LJ's Toys Inc. just purchased a $200,000 machine to produce toy cars. The machine has a CCA rate of 20 percent and will be worth $20,000 after five years. Each toy sells for $25. The variable cost per toy is $5, and the firm incurs fixed costs of $350,000 each year. The corporate tax rate for the company is 25 percent. The appropriate discount rate is 12 percent. Assets will remain in the CCA class after the end of the project. What is the present value break-even point for the project?

9.11 The Cornchopper Company is considering the purchase of a new harvester. Cornchopper has hired you to determine the break-even purchase price (in terms of present value) of the harvester. This break-even purchase price is the price at which the project's NPV is zero. Base your analysis on the following facts:

- The new harvester is not expected to affect revenues, but pretax operating expenses will be reduced by $10,000 per year for 10 years.
- The old harvester is now five years old and has a UCC of $30,000.
- The old harvester can be sold for $20,000 today.
- The new harvester has a CCA rate of 20 percent and will be worthless after 10 years.
- The corporate tax rate is 40 percent.
- The firm's required rate of return is 15 percent.
- Assets will remain in the CCA class after the end of the project.

  The firm's required rate of return is 15 percent.

  Assume that the corporate tax rate is 40 percent and the appropriate discount rate is 8 percent. Assets will remain in the CCA class after the project ends. What is the present value break-even point?

9.12 Niko has purchased a brand new machine to produce its High Flight line of shoes. The machine has an economic life of five years and a CCA rate of 30 percent. The machine costs $300,000 and will be worth $10,000 in five years.

  The sale price per pair of shoes is $60, while the variable cost is $8. $100,000 of fixed cost per year is attributed to the machine.

  Assume that the corporate tax rate is 40 percent and the appropriate discount rate is 8 percent. Assets will remain in the CCA class after the project ends. What is the present value break-even point?

Scenario Analysis

9.13 The CFO of Mercer, Inc., is considering an investment of $420,000 in a machine with a CCA rate of 20 percent and a seven-year economic life. The appropriate discount rate is 13 percent, and the corporate tax rate for the company is 35 percent. Assume all revenues and expenses, which are presented below, are received and paid in cash. Assets will remain in the CCA class after the project ends.

	Pessimistic	Expected	Optimistic
Unit sales	23,000	25,000	27,000
Price	$38	$40	$42
Variable costs per unit	$21	$20	$19
Fixed costs per year	$320,000	$300,000	$280,000

a. Calculate the NPV of the project in each of the above scenarios.
b. If each scenario is equally likely, is the machine a worthwhile investment?

9.14 You are the financial analyst for a tennis racquet manufacturer. The company is considering a project using a graphite-like material in its racquets. Given the following information about the market for a racquet with the new material, will you recommend the project?

	Estimate		
	Pessimistic	Expected	Optimistic
Market size	110,000	120,000	130,000
Market share	22%	25%	27%
Selling price	$115	$120	$125
Variable costs per year	$72	$70	$68
Fixed costs per year	$850,000	$800,000	$750,000
Initial investment	$1,500,000	$1,500,000	$1,500,000

Assume the appropriate discount rate is 13 percent. The corporate tax rate is 40 percent. The CCA rate is 20 percent and salvage value after five years is $50,000. Assets will remain in the CCA class after the project ends. Each of the three scenarios is equally likely. Assume all revenues and expenses are received and paid in cash.

9.15 Xrco Petroleum has identified a new type of fuel additive and is considering launching this new product. As a marketing manager, you have come up with the following scenarios for the launch. From finance, you know that the tax rate for the company is 40 percent and the effective discount rate is 10 percent. You also know that the CCA rate is 20 percent and that production will occur over the next five years only. After five years, the salvage value will be $100,000. Assets will remain in the CCA class after the project ends. Will you undertake the project?

Probability of	Pessimistic	Expected	Optimistic	
scenario occuring	30%	40%	30%	
Market size	100,000	150,000	200,000	* Per year
Market share	20%	25%	30%	
Price	$100	$120	$140	
Variable cost	$80	$75	$70	
Fixed cost	$300,000	$250,000	$200,000	* Per year
Investment	$1,000,000	$1,000,000	$1,000,000	

9.16 The Big Burrito is planning to purchase a touch screen order system for its drive-thru window that would allow customers to select their order as soon as they arrive. This would reduce customer wait time and increase order accuracy. The touch screen and software would cost the Big Burrito $150,000 and would last five years. There would also be an annual maintenance cost of $5,000. In addition to improved customer service, the Big Burrito would gain two benefits. First, it could totally eliminate the full-time worker who used to accept and enter these orders. His annual salary plus benefits total $30,000 per year. Second, it expects drive-thru sales to increase but it doesn't know by how much. The estimates are:

	Pessimistic	Expected	Optimistic
Revenue increase (decrease)	$(5,000)	$15,000	$20,000
COGS, 25% of revenue increase	(1,250)	3,750	5,000

Net working capital (NWC) is expected to increase by $5,000 in the first year and be recovered at the end of year 5. If the appropriate discount rate is 15 percent and you ignore taxes, should the Big Burrito go ahead with this investment? (See p. 264 for a chart summarizing this information.)

Pessimistic

	Year 0	Year 1	Year 2	Year 3	Year 4	Year 5	NPV
Investments:							
Touch screen system	$(150,000)						
Annual maintenance		$(5,000)	$(5,000)	$(5,000)	$(5,000)	$(5,000)	
Change in NWC		(5,000)				5,000	
Wages saved		30,000	30,000	30,000	30,000	30,000	
Total cash flow from investments	$(150,000)	$20,000	$25,000	$25,000	$25,000	$30,000	
Income:							
Revenue		$(5,000)	$(5,000)	$(5,000)	$(5,000)	$(5,000)	
COGS		1,250	1,250	1,250	1,250	1,250	
Cash flow from operations		$(3,750)	$(3,750)	$(3,750)	$(3,750)	$(3,750)	
Total cash flow from project	$(150,000)	$16,250	$21,250	$21,250	$21,250	$26,250	
PV 15% (CF)	(150,000)	14,130	16,068	13,972	12,150	13,051	($80,629)

9.17 M.V.P. Games, Inc., has hired you to perform a feasibility study of a new video game that requires a $4 million initial investment. M.V.P. expects total annual operating cash flow of $750,000 for the next 10 years. The relevant discount rate is 10 percent. Ignore depreciation and taxes. Cash flows occur at year-end.

  a. What is the NPV of the new video game?

  b. After one year, the estimate of remaining annual cash flows will either be revised upward to $1.5 million or revised downward to $0. Each revision has an equal probability of occurring. At that time, the video game project can be sold for $200,000. What is the revised NPV, given that the firm can abandon the project after one year?

  c. What is the option value of abandonment?

9.18 Allied Products, Inc., is considering a new product launch. The firm expects to have annual operating cash flow of $200 million for the next ten years. Allied Products uses a discount rate of 20 percent for new product launches. The initial investment is $100 million. Ignore taxes and assume that the project has no salvage value at the end of its economic life.

  a. What is the NPV of the new product?

  b. After the first year, the project can be dismantled and sold for $50 million. If the estimate of remaining cash flows can be revised based on the first year's experience, at what level of expected cash flows does it make sense to abandon the project?

The Option To Abandon

9.19 Applied Nanotech is thinking about introducing a new surface cleaning machine. The marketing department has come up with the estimate that Applied Nanotech can sell 10 units per year at $0.3 million in net cash flow per unit for the next five years. The engineering department has come up with the estimate that developing the machine will take a $10 million initial investment. The finance department has estimated that a 25 percent discount rate should be used.

a. What is the base case NPV?

b. If unsuccessful, after the first year the project can be dismantled and sold for scrap for $5 million. Also, after the first year, expected cash flows will be revised up to 20 units per year or to 0 units, with equal probability. If so, what is the option value of abandonment? What is the revised NPV?

9.20 Snapplers are planning to enter the bottled water market. They expect to sell 5 million bottles per year at a net cash flow of $0.50 apiece for the next five years but they are unsure about the market. At the end of the first year, they will learn if the product is a success or failure. If it is a success, they can revise their forecast to 8 million bottles per year. If it is a failure, unit sales will be 1 million. Success and failure are equally likely. The relevant discount rate is 15 percent and the initial investment required is $3 million. If they abandon the project after year 1, they can recover $1.5 million of the initial investment.

a. What is the base case NPV?

b. What is the value of the option to abandon?

Part III

Risk

This part of the book examines the relationship between expected return and risk for portfolios and individual assets. When capital markets are in equilibrium, they determine a trade-off between expected return and risk. The return that shareholders can expect to obtain in the capital markets is the return firms require when evaluating risky investment projects. The shareholders' required return is the firm's cost of equity capital.

Chapter 10 examines the modern history of Canadian capital markets. A central fact emerges: The return on risky assets has been higher on average than the return on risk-free assets. This fact supports the perspective we use in examining risk and return. In Chapter 10, we introduce several key intuitions of modern finance.

Chapters 11 and 12 contain more advanced discussions of risk and expected return. The chapters are self-contained and elaborate on the material in Chapter 10.

Chapter 11 shows what determines the relationship between return and risk for portfolios. The model of risk and expected return used in the chapter is called the *capital asset pricing model* (CAPM).

Chapter 12 examines risk and return from another perspective: the arbitrage pricing theory (APT), which yields insights that one cannot get from the CAPM. The key concept is that the total risk of individual stocks can be divided into two parts: systematic and unsystematic. The fundamental principle of diversification is that, for highly diversified portfolios, unsystematic risk disappears; only systematic risk survives.

The section on risk concludes in Chapter 13 with a discussion of estimating a firm's cost of equity capital and some of the problems involved.

Chapter 10

Capital Market History: An Overview

EXECUTIVE SUMMARY

We learned in Chapter 5 that riskless cash flows should be discounted at the riskless rate of interest. Because most capital-budgeting projects involve risky flows, a different discount rate must be used. The next four chapters are devoted to determining the discount rate for risky projects.

Past experience indicates that students find the upcoming material among the most difficult in the entire textbook. Because of this, we always teach the material by presenting the results and conclusions first. By seeing where we are going ahead of time, it is easier to absorb the material when we get there. A synopsis of the four chapters follows:

1. Because our ultimate goal is to discount risky cash flows, we must first find a way to measure risk. In the current chapter we measure the variability of an asset by the variance or standard deviation of its returns. If an individual holds only one asset, its variance or standard deviation would be the appropriate measure of risk.

2. While Chapter 10 considers one type of asset in isolation, Chapter 11 examines a portfolio of many assets. In this case, we are interested in the *contribution* of the security to the risk of the entire portfolio. Because much of an individual security's variance is dispersed in a large, diversified portfolio, neither the security's variance nor its standard deviation can be viewed as the security's contribution to the risk of a large portfolio. Rather, this contribution is best measured by the security's beta (β). As an example, consider a stock whose returns are high when the returns on a large, diversified portfolio are low—and vice versa. This stock has a negative beta. In other words, it acts as a hedge, implying that the stock actually tends to reduce the risk of the portfolio. However, the stock could have a high variance, implying high risk for an investor holding only this security.

3. Investors will only hold a risky security if its expected return is high enough to compensate for its risk. Given the above, the expected return on a security should be positively related to the security's beta. In fact, the relationship between risk and expected return can be expressed more precisely by the following equation:

$$
\begin{pmatrix} \text{Expected return} \\ \text{on a security} \end{pmatrix} = \begin{pmatrix} \text{Risk-free} \\ \text{rate} \end{pmatrix} + \text{Beta} \times \begin{pmatrix} \text{Expected return on} \\ \text{market portfolio} \end{pmatrix} - \begin{pmatrix} \text{Risk-free} \\ \text{rate} \end{pmatrix}
$$

Because the term in parentheses on the right-hand side is positive, this equation says that the expected return on a security is a positive function of its beta. This equation is frequently referred to as the *capital asset pricing model* (CAPM).

4. We derive the relationship between risk and return in a different manner in Chapter 12. However, many of the conclusions are quite similar. This chapter is based on the *arbitrage pricing theory* (APT).

5. The theoretical ideas in Chapters 10, 11, and 12 are intellectually challenging. Fortunately, Chapter 13, which applies the above theory to the selection of discount rates, is much

simpler. In a world where (*a*) a project has the same risk as the firm, and (*b*) the firm has no debt, the expected return on the stock should serve as the project's discount rate. This expected return is taken from the capital asset pricing model, as presented above.

Because we have a long road ahead of us, the maxim that any journey begins with a single step applies here. We start with the perhaps mundane calculation of a security's return.

10.1 Returns

Dollar Returns

Suppose Canadian Atlantic Enterprises has several thousand shares of stock outstanding. You purchased some of these shares at the beginning of the year. It's now year-end, and you want to determine how well you've done on your investment.

Over the year, a company may pay cash *dividends* to its shareholders. As a shareholder in Canadian Atlantic Enterprises, you are a part owner of the company. If the company is profitable, it may choose to distribute some of its profits to shareholders. (Dividend policy is detailed in Chapter 19.)

In addition to the dividend, the other part of your return is the *capital gain* or *capital loss* on the stock arising from changes in the value of your investment. For example, consider the cash flows illustrated in Figure 10.1. The stock is selling for $37 per share. If you bought 100 shares, you had a total outlay of $3,700. Suppose that, over the year, the stock paid a dividend of $1.85 per share. By the end of the year, then, you would have received income of

$$\text{Dividend} = \$1.85 \times 100 = \$185$$

Also the value of the stock rose to $40.33 per share by the end of the year. Your 100 shares are now worth $4,033, so you have a capital gain of

$$\text{Capital gain} = (\$40.33 - \$37) \times 100 = \$333$$

On the other hand, if the price had dropped to, say, $34.78, you would have had a capital loss of

$$\text{Capital loss} = (\$34.78 - \$37) \times 100 = -\$222$$

Notice that a capital loss is the same thing as a negative capital gain.

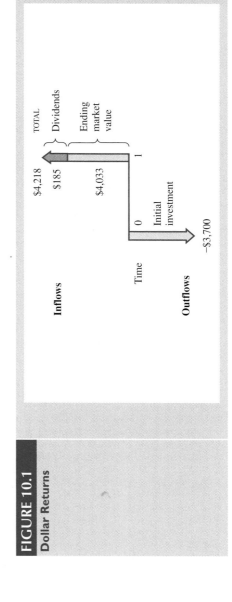

FIGURE 10.1
Dollar Returns

The total dollar return on your investment is the sum of the dividend and the capital gain:

$$\text{Total return} = \text{Dividend income} + \text{Capital gain (or loss)}$$

In our first example, the total dollar return is thus given by

$$\text{Total dollar return} = \$185 + 333 = \$518$$

Notice that, if you sold the stock at the end of the year, the total amount of cash you would have would be your initial investment plus the total return. In the preceding example, then, you would have:

$$
\begin{aligned}
\text{Total cash if stock is sold} &= \text{Initial investment} + \text{Total dollar return} \\
&= \$3,700 + \$518 \\
&= \$4,218
\end{aligned}
$$

As a check, notice that this is the same as the proceeds from the sale of the stock plus the dividends:

$$
\begin{aligned}
\text{Proceeds from stock sale} + \text{Dividends} &= \$40.33 \times 100 + \$185 \\
&= \$4,033 + \$185 \\
&= \$4,218
\end{aligned}
$$

Suppose you hold on to your Canadian Atlantic stock and don't sell it at the end of the year. Should you still consider the capital gain as part of your return? Isn't this only a paper gain and not really a cash flow if you don't sell it?

The answer to the first question is a strong yes; the answer to the second is an equally strong no. The capital gain is every bit as much a part of your return as the dividend, and you should certainly count it as part of your return. That you actually decided to keep the stock and not sell it or *realize* the gain in no way changes the fact that, if you want to, you could get the cash value of the stock.[1]

Percentage Returns

It is usually more convenient to summarize information about returns in percentage terms, rather than dollar terms, because that way your return does not depend on the amount invested. The question we want to answer is, How much do we get for each dollar we invest?

To answer this question, let P_t be the price of the stock at the beginning of the year and let D_{t+1} be the dividend paid on the stock during the year. Consider the cash flows in Figure 10.2. These are the same as those in Figure 10.1, except that we have now expressed everything on a per share basis.

In our example, the price at the beginning of the year was $37 per share and the dividend paid during the year on each share was $1.85. As we discussed in Chapter 5, expressing the dividend as a percentage of the beginning stock price results in the *dividend yield*:

$$\text{Dividend yield} = D_{t+1}/P_t = \$1.85/\$37 = 0.05 = 5\%$$

---

[1] After all, you could always sell the stock at year-end and immediately reinvest by buying the stock back. There is no difference between doing this and just not selling (assuming, of course, that there are no tax consequences from selling the stock). Again, the point is that whether you actually cash out or reinvest by not selling does not affect the return you earn.

FIGURE 10.2

Percentage Returns: Dollar Return and Per-Share Return

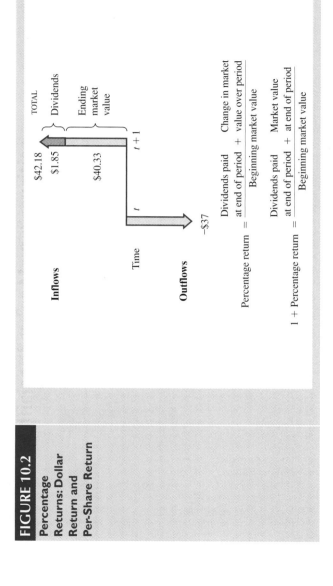

$$Percentage\ return = \frac{Dividends\ paid\ at\ end\ of\ period\ +\ Change\ in\ market\ value\ over\ period}{Beginning\ market\ value}$$

$$1\ +\ Percentage\ return = \frac{Dividends\ paid\ at\ end\ of\ period\ +\ Market\ value\ at\ end\ of\ period}{Beginning\ market\ value}$$

The second component of our percentage return is the capital gains yield. Recall (from Chapter 6) that this is calculated as the change in the price during the year (the capital gain) divided by the beginning price:

$$Capital\ gains\ yield = (P_{t+1} - P_t)/P_t$$
$$= (\$40.33 - \$37)/\$37 = \$3.33/\$37 = 0.09 = 9\%$$

Combining these two results, we find that the *total returns* on the investment in Canadian Atlantic stock during the year, which we will label R_{t+1}, was

$$R_{t+1} = \frac{Div_{t+1}}{P_t} + \frac{(P_{t+1} - P_t)}{P_t} = 5\% + 9\% = 14\%$$

From now on we will refer to returns in percentage terms.

EXAMPLE

Suppose a stock begins the year with a price of $25 per share and ends with a price of $35 per share. During the year it paid a $2 dividend per share. What are its dividend yield, its capital gain, and its total return for the year? We can imagine the cash flows in Figure 10.3.

$$R_1 = \frac{Div_1}{P_0} + \frac{P_1 - P_0}{P_0}$$
$$= \frac{\$2}{\$25} + \frac{\$35 - \$25}{\$25} = \frac{\$12}{\$25}$$
$$= 8\% + 40\% = 48\%$$

Thus, the stock's dividend yield, its capital gain, and its total return are 8 percent, 40 percent, and 48 percent, respectively.

FIGURE 10.3

Cash Flow—An
Investment
Example

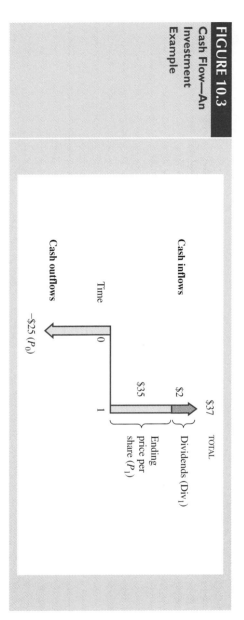

Cash inflows

$37   TOTAL

$2   Dividends (Div₁)

$35   Ending
price per
share (P₁)

Time   0 ⊢——————————⊣ 1

Cash outflows

−$25 (P₀)

Suppose you had invested $5,000. The total dollar proceeds you would have received on an investment in the stock are $5,000 × 1.48 = $7,400. If you know the total return on the stock, you do not need to know how many shares you would have had to purchase to figure out how much money you would have made on the $5,000 investment. You just use the total return.[2]

? **Concept**
Questions

- **What are the two parts of total return?**
- **Why are unrealized capital gains or losses included in the calculation of returns?**
- **What is the difference between a dollar return and a percentage return? Why are percentage returns more convenient?**

10.2 Holding-Period Returns

Investors look to capital market history as a guide to the risks and returns of alternative portfolio strategies. The data set in Table 10.1 could be used in advising large institutional investors. It draws on two major studies: Roger Ibbotson and Rex Sinquefield's examination of rates of return in U.S. financial markets and James Hatch and Robert White's

[2] Consider the stock in the previous example. We have ignored the question of when during the year you receive the dividend. Does it make a difference? To explore this question, suppose first that the dividend is paid at the very beginning of the year, and you receive it the moment after you have purchased the stock. Suppose, too, that interest rates are 10 percent, and that immediately after receiving the dividend you lend it out. What will be your total return, including the loan proceeds, at the end of the year?

Alternatively, instead of lending the dividend you could have reinvested it and purchased more of the stock. If that is what you do with the dividend, what will your total return be? (Warning: This does not go on forever, and when you buy more stock with the cash from the dividend on your first purchase, you are too late to get yet another dividend on the new stock.)

Finally, suppose the dividend is paid at year-end. What answer would you get for the total return? As you can see, by ignoring the question of when the dividend is paid when we calculate the return, we are implicitly assuming that it is received at the end of the year and cannot be reinvested during the year. The right way to figure out the return on a stock is to determine exactly when the dividend is received and to include the return that comes from reinvesting the dividend in the stock. This gives a pure stock return without confounding the issue by requiring knowledge of the interest rate during the year.

TABLE 10.1	Year-by-Year Total Percentage Returns, 1948–2003					
Year	Statistics Canada Inflation	Canadian Stocks S&P/TSX Composite	Scotia Capital Markets 91-Day T-Bill	Scotia Capital Markets Long Bonds	US Stocks S&P 500 (Cdn. $)	Nesbitt Burns Small Stocks
1948	8.88	12.25	0.4	-0.08	5.5	
1949	1.09	23.85	0.45	5.18	22.15	
1950	5.91	51.69	0.51	1.74	39.18	
1951	10.66	25.44	0.71	-7.89	15	
1952	-1.38	0.01	0.95	5.01	13.68	
1953	0	2.56	1.54	5	-0.99	
1954	0	39.37	1.62	12.23	52.62	
1955	0.47	27.68	1.22	0.13	35.51	
1956	3.24	12.68	2.63	-8.87	2.35	
1957	1.79	-20.58	3.76	7.94	-8.51	
1958	2.64	31.25	2.27	1.92	40.49	
1959	1.29	4.59	4.39	-5.07	10.54	
1960	1.27	1.78	3.66	12.19	5.15	
1961	0.42	32.75	2.86	9.16	32.85	
1962	1.67	-7.09	3.81	5.03	-5.77	
1963	1.64	15.6	3.58	4.58	23.19	
1964	2.02	25.43	3.73	6.16	15.75	
1965	3.16	6.67	3.79	0.05	12.58	
1966	3.45	-7.07	4.89	-1.05	-9.33	
1967	4.07	18.09	4.38	-0.48	23.61	
1968	3.91	22.45	6.22	2.14	10.26	
1969	4.79	-0.81	6.83	-2.86	-8.5	
1970	1.31	-3.57	6.89	16.39	-1.96	-11.69
1971	5.16	8.01	3.86	14.84	13.28	15.83
1972	4.91	27.37	3.43	8.11	18.12	44.72
1973	9.36	0.27	4.78	1.97	-14.58	-7.82
1974	12.3	-25.93	7.68	-4.53	-26.87	-26.89
1975	9.52	18.48	7.05	8.02	40.72	41
1976	5.87	11.02	9.1	23.64	22.97	22.77
1977	9.45	10.71	7.64	9.04	0.65	39.93
1978	8.44	29.72	7.9	4.1	15.5	44.41
1979	9.69	44.77	11.01	-2.83	16.52	46.04
1980	11.2	30.13	12.23	2.18	35.51	42.86
1981	12.2	-10.25	19.11	-2.09	-5.57	-15.1
1982	9.23	5.54	15.27	45.82	25.84	4.55
1983	4.51	35.49	9.39	9.61	24.07	44.3
1984	3.77	-2.39	11.21	16.9	12.87	-2.33
1985	4.38	25.07	9.7	26.68	39.82	38.98
1986	4.19	8.95	9.34	17.21	16.96	12.33
1987	4.12	5.88	8.2	1.77	-0.96	-5.47
1988	3.96	11.08	8.94	11.3	7.21	5.46
1989	5.17	21.37	11.95	15.17	27.74	10.66
1990	5	-14.8	13.28	4.32	-3.06	-27.32
1991	3.78	12.02	9.9	25.3	30.05	18.51
1992	2.14	-1.43	6.65	11.57	18.42	13.01
1993	1.7	32.55	5.63	22.09	14.4	52.26
1994	0.23	-0.18	4.76	-7.39	7.48	-9.21
1995	1.75	14.53	7.39	26.34	33.68	13.88
1996	2.17	28.35	5.02	14.18	23.62	28.66
1997	0.73	14.98	3.2	18.46	39.18	6.97
1998	1.02	-1.58	4.74	12.85	37.71	-17.9
1999	2.58	31.59	4.66	-5.98	14.14	20.29
2000	3.23	7.41	5.49	12.97	-5.67	-4.29
2001	0.6	-12.6	4.7	8.1	-7.5	0.7
2002	4.3	-12.4	2.5	8.7	-22.7	-0.9
2003	1.6	26.7	2.9	6.7	5.3	42.7

study of Canadian returns.[3] Our data present year-to-year historical rates of return on five important types of financial investments or asset classes:

1. *Canadian common stocks.* The common stock portfolio is based on a sample of the largest companies (in terms of total market value of outstanding stock) in Canada.[4]

2. *U.S. common stocks.* This portfolio consists of 500 of the largest U.S. companies. The full historical series is given in U.S. dollars and in Canadian dollars adjusting for shifts in exchange rates.

3. *Small stocks.* This portfolio, compiled by BMO Nesbitt Burns, includes the bottom fifth of stocks listed on the Toronto Stock Exchange (TSX). The ranking is by market value of equity capitalization—the price of the stock multiplied by the number of shares outstanding.

4. *Long bonds.* This portfolio includes high-quality, long-term corporate, provincial, and Government of Canada bonds.

5. *Canada Treasury bills.* This portfolio consists of Treasury bills (*T-bills* for short) with a three-month maturity.

These returns are not adjusted for transactions costs, inflation, or taxes; thus, they are nominal, pretax returns. In addition to the year-to-year returns on these financial instruments, the year-to-year percentage change in the Statistics Canada Consumer Price Index (CPI) is also computed. This is a commonly used measure of inflation, so we can calculate real returns using this as the inflation rate.

The five asset classes included cover a broad range of investments popular with Canadian individuals and financial institutions. We include U.S. stocks since Canadian investors often invest abroad—particularly in the United States.[5]

Before looking closely at the different portfolio returns, we take a look at the "big picture." Figure 10.4 shows what happened to $1 invested in three of these different portfolios at the beginning of 1957. We work with a sample period of 1957–2003 for two reasons: the years immediately after World War II do not reflect trends today and the TSE 300 (predecessor of the TSX) was introduced in 1956, making 1957 the first really comparable year. This decision is somewhat controversial and we return to it later as we draw lessons from our data. The growth in value for each of the different portfolios over the 47-year period ending in 2003 is given separately. Notice that, to get everything on a single graph, some modification in scaling is used. As is commonly done with financial series, the vertical axis is on a logarithmic scale such that equal distances measure equal percentage changes (as opposed to equal dollar changes) in values.

Looking at Figure 10.4, we see that the common stock investments did the best overall. Every dollar invested in Canadian stocks grew to $372.32 over the 47 years.

At the other end, the T-bill portfolio grew to only $23.72. Long bonds did better with an ending value of $51.51. These values are less impressive when we consider inflation

[3]The two classic studies are R. G. Ibbotson and R. A. Sinquefield, *Stocks, Bonds, Bills, and Inflation* (Charlottesville, Va.: Financial Analysts Research Foundation, 1982); and J. Hatch and R. White, *Canadian Stocks, Bonds, Bills, and Inflation: 1950–1983* (Charlottesville, Va.: Financial Analysts Research Foundation, 1985). Additional sources are BMO Nesbitt Burns for small stocks, Scotia Capital Markets for Canada Treasury bills and long bonds, and Statistics Canada CANSIM for rates of exchange and inflation.
[4]From 1956 on, the S&P/TSX 60 is used. For earlier years, the data used are a sample provided by the TSE.
[5]Chapter 32 discusses exchange-rate risk and other risks of foreign investments.

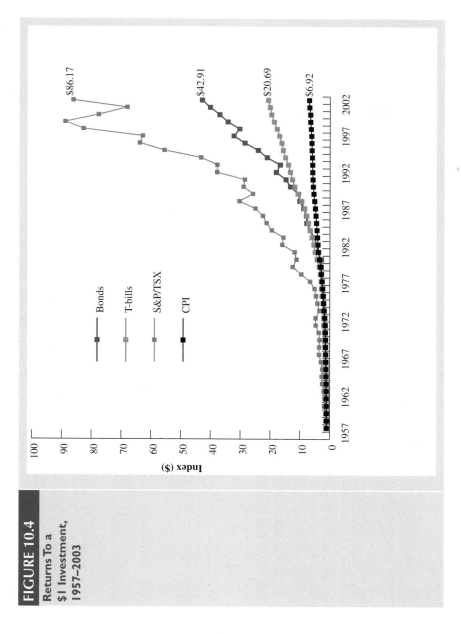

FIGURE 10.4

Returns To a
$1 Investment,
1957–2003

over this period. As illustrated, the price level climbed such that $9.30 is needed just to replace the original $1.

Figure 10.4 gives the total value of a $1 investment in the Canadian stock market from 1957 through 2003. In other words, it shows what the total return would have been if the dollar had been left in the stock market and if each year the dividends from the previous year had been reinvested in more stock. If R_t is the return in year t (expressed in decimals), the total you would have from year 1 to year T is the product of the returns in each of the years:

$$(1 + R_1) \times (1 + R_2) \ldots \times (1 + R_t) \times \ldots \times (1 + R_T)$$

For example, if the returns were 11 percent, −5 percent, and 9 percent in a three-year period, a $1 investment at the beginning of the period would, at the end of the three years, be worth

$$
\begin{aligned}
(1 + R_1) \times (1 + R_2) \times (1 + R_3) &= (\$1 + 0.11) \times (\$1 - 0.05) \times (\$1 + 0.09) \\
&= \$1.11 \times \$0.95 \times \$1.09 \\
&= \$1.15
\end{aligned}
$$

Notice that 0.15 (or 15 percent) is the total return and that it includes the return from reinvesting the first-year dividends in the stock market for two more years and reinvesting the second-year dividends for the final year. The 15 percent is called a three-year holding-period return. Table 10.1 gives annual holding-period returns from 1948 to 2003. From this table you can determine holding-period returns for any combination of years.

Concept Questions

- **What was the smallest return observed over the 56 years for each of these investments? When did it occur?**
- **How many times did large Canadian stocks (common stocks) return more than 30 percent? How many times did they return less than 20 percent?**
- **What was the longest winning streak (years without a negative return) for large Canadian stocks? For long-term bonds?**
- **How often did the T-bill portfolio have a negative return?**

10.3 Return Statistics

The history of capital market returns is too complicated to be useful in its undigested form. To use the history we must first find some manageable ways of describing it, dramatically condensing the detailed data into a few simple statements.

This is where two important numbers summarizing the history come in. The first and most natural number we want to find is some single measure that best describes the past annual returns on the stock market. In other words, what is our best estimate of the return that an investor could have realized in a particular year over the 1948–2003 period? This is the *average return*.

Figure 10.5 plots the histogram of the yearly stock market returns from 1957 to 2003. This plot is the **frequency distribution** of the numbers. The height of the graph gives the number of sample observations in the range on the horizontal axis.

Given a frequency distribution like that in Figure 10.5, we can calculate the **average** or **mean** of the distribution. To compute the arithmetic average of the distribution, we add up all of the values and divide the total number (47 in our case, because we have 47 years of data) by T. The bar over the R is used to represent the mean, and the formula is the ordinary formula for the average:

$$\text{Mean} = \bar{R} = \frac{(R_1 + \ldots + R_T)}{T}$$

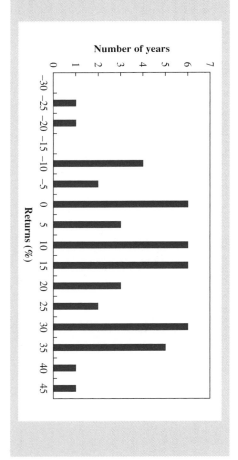

FIGURE 10.5
Frequency Distribution of Returns on Canadian Common Stocks, 1957–2003

The arithmetic mean of the 47 annual returns from 1957 to 2003 is 10.64 percent. The arithmetic mean return has the advantage of being easy to calculate and interpret so we use it here to measure expected return.[6]

The returns on Canadian common stocks from 1989 to 1992 were (in decimals) 0.2137, −0.1480, 0.1202, and −0.0143, respectively. The average or mean return over these four years is

$$\bar{R} = \frac{0.2137 - 0.1480 + 0.1202 - 0.0143}{4} = 0.0429$$

Concept
Question

• Why are return statistics useful?

10.4 Average Stock Returns and Risk-Free Returns

Now that we have computed the average return on the stock market, it seems sensible to compare it with the returns on other securities. The most obvious comparison is with the low variability returns in the government bond market. These are free of most of the volatility we see in the stock market.

The Government of Canada borrows money by issuing bonds, which the investing public holds. As we discussed in an earlier chapter, these bonds come in many forms. The ones we'll look at here are called *Treasury bills*, or *T-bills*. Once a week the government sells some bills at an auction. A typical bill is a pure discount bond that will mature in a year or less. Because the government can raise taxes to pay for the debt it incurs—a trick that many of us would like to be able to perform—this debt is virtually free of risk of default. Thus, we call the yield on T-bills the *risk-free return* over a short time (one year or less).[7]

An interesting comparison, then, is between the virtually risk-free return on T-bills and the very risky return on common stocks. This difference between risky returns and risk-free returns is often called the *excess return on the risky asset*. It is called *excess* because it is the additional return resulting from the riskiness of common stocks, and it is interpreted as a **risk premium.**

Table 10.2 shows the average stock return, bond return, T-bill return, and inflation rate from 1957 through 2003. From this we can derive risk premiums. We can see that the average risk premium for common stocks for the entire period was 3.84 percent (10.64 percent − 6.80 percent).

---

[6]We do have to admit that there is an alternative measure that is more accurate for present purposes: the geometric mean. To compute the geometric mean we link the returns in each of our 47 years geometrically: $[(1+R_1)(1+R_2)\ldots(1+R_{46})]^{1/46} - 1$. This is a superior formula because it reflects mathematically the fact that returns are compounded. The difference between the arithmetic and geometric averages is proportionate to variance. This means that high-variance investments like risky shares will result in the greatest error when using the simplified arithmetic method.

[7]A Treasury bill with a 90-day maturity is risk-free only during that particular time period.

TABLE 10.2   Average Annual Returns, 1957–2003

Investment	Arithmetic Average Return (%)	Risk Premium (%)	Standard Deviation (%)	Distribution
Canadian common stocks	10.64	3.84	16.41	
US common stocks (CDN $)	12.69	5.88	17.25	
Long bonds	8.96	2.16	10.36	
Small stocks	4.17	7.37	23.25	
Inflation	4.29		3.26	
Treasury bills	6.80	0.00	3.63	

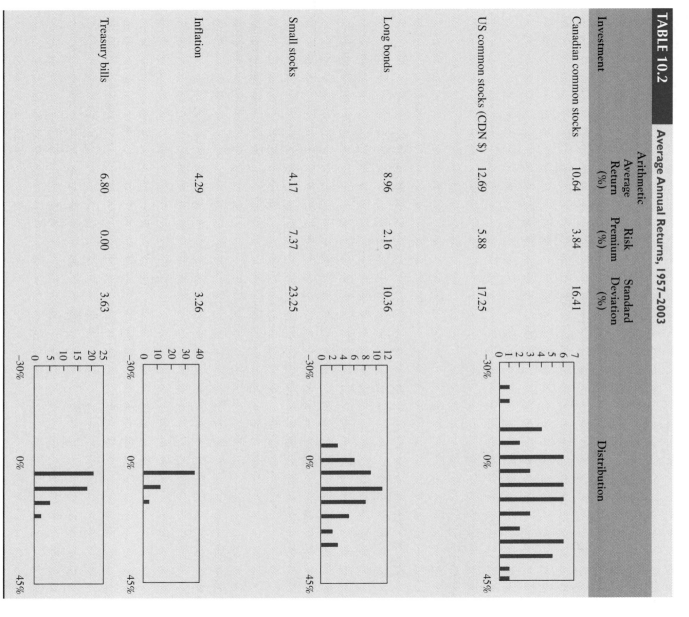

One of the most significant observations of stock market data is this long-run excess of the stock return over the risk-free return. An investor for this period was rewarded for investment in the stock market with an extra or excess return over what would have been achieved by simply investing in T-bills.

Why was there such a reward? Does it mean that it never pays to invest in T-bills and that someone who invested in them instead of in the stock market needs a course in finance? A complete answer to these questions lies at the heart of modern finance, and Chapter 11 is devoted entirely to them. However, part of the answer can be found in the variability of the various types of investments. We see in Table 10.1 many years when an investment in T-bills achieved higher returns than an investment in common stocks. Also, we note that the returns from an investment in common stocks are frequently negative, whereas an investment in T-bills never produces a negative return.[8] So, we now turn our attention to measuring the variability of returns and an introductory discussion of risk.

By looking more closely at Table 10.2, we see that the standard deviation of T-bills is substantially less than that of common stocks. This suggests that the risk of T-bills is below that of common stocks. Because the answer turns on the riskiness of investments in common stock, we now shift our attention to measuring this risk.

Concept Questions

- **What is the major observation about capital markets that we will seek to explain?**
- **What does the observation tell us about investors for the period from 1957 through 2003?**

10.5 Risk Statistics

The second number that we use to characterize the distribution of returns is a measure of risk. There is no universally agreed upon definition of risk. One way to think about the risk of returns on common stock is in terms of how spread out the frequency distribution in Figure 10.5 is.[9] The spread or dispersion of a distribution is a measure of how much a particular return can deviate from the mean return. If the distribution is very spread out, the returns that will occur are very uncertain. By contrast, a distribution whose returns are all within a few percentage points of each other is tight, and the returns are less uncertain. The measures of risk we will discuss are variance and standard deviation.

Variance and Standard Deviation

The **variance** and its square root, the **standard deviation,** are the most common measures of variability or dispersion. We will use Var to denote the variance and SD to represent the standard deviation.

The returns on Canadian common stocks from 1989 to 1992 were (in decimals) 0.2137, −0.1480, 0.1202, and −0.0143, respectively. The variance of this sample is computed as

$$\text{Var} = \frac{1}{T-1}[(R_1 - \bar{R})^2 + (R_2 - \bar{R})^2 + (R_3 - \bar{R})^2 + (R_4 - \bar{R})^2]$$

$$0.0250 = \frac{1}{3}[(0.2137 - 0.0429)^2 + (-0.1480 - 0.0429)^2 + (0.1202 - 0.0429)^2 + (-0.0143 - 0.0429)^2]$$

$$\text{SD} = \sqrt{0.0250} = 0.1508 = 15.80\%$$

This formula tells us just what to do: Take each of the T individual returns $(R_1, R_2, \ldots)$ and subtract the average return, $\bar{R}$; square the result, and add them all up. Finally, divide this

---

[8] All our returns are nominal and before-tax. The real, after-tax return on T-bills can be negative.

[9] Several condensed frequency distributions are also in the extreme right column of Table 10.2.

total by the number of returns less 1 ($T-1$). The standard deviation is always just the square root of the variance.[10]

Using the actual stock returns in Table 10.1 for the 47-year period 1957–2003 in the above formula, the resulting standard deviation of stock returns is 16.41 percent. The standard deviation is the standard statistical measure of the spread of a sample, and it will be the measure we use most of the time. Its interpretation is facilitated by a discussion of the normal distribution.

Normal Distribution and Its Implications for Standard Deviation

A large enough sample drawn from a **normal distribution** looks like the bell-shaped curve drawn in Figure 10.6. As you can see, this distribution is *symmetric* about its mean, not *skewed*, and it has a much cleaner shape than the actual distribution of yearly returns drawn in Figure 10.5.[11] Of course, if we had been able to observe stock market returns for 1,000 years, we might have filled in a lot of the jumps and jerks in Figure 10.5 and had a smoother curve.

In classical statistics, the normal distribution plays a central role, and the standard deviation is the usual way of representing the spread of a normal distribution. For the normal distribution, the probability of having a return that is above or below the mean by a certain amount depends only on the standard deviation. For example, the probability of having a return that is within one standard deviation of the mean of the distribution is approximately 0.68 or ⅔, and the probability of having a return that is within two standard deviations of the mean is approximately 0.95.

The 16.41 percent standard deviation we found for stock returns from 1957 through 2003 can now be interpreted in the following way: If stock returns are roughly normally distributed, the probability that a yearly return will fall in the range −5.77 percent to 27.05 percent (10.64 percent plus or minus one standard deviation, 16.41 percent) is about 67 percent. This range is illustrated in Figure 10.6. In other words, there is about one chance in three that the return will be *outside* this range. Based on historical experience and assuming that the past is a good guide to the future, investors who buy shares in large Canadian companies should expect to be outside this range in one year out of every three.

---

[10]For small samples, as in this example, you can use a financial calculator to compute the variance and standard deviation. For example, using the Sharp Business/Financial calculator, the steps are:

1. Clear the calculator.
2. Set the calculator to statistics mode by pressing *2nd F MODE* until STAT appears on the display.
3. Set the calculator for statistical calculations by pressing *2nd F TAB decimal point*. The calculator responds by displaying 0.
4. Enter the first observation, 0.2137, and press *M+*. The calculator displays 1, showing that it has recorded the first observation.
5. Enter the second observation, −0.1480, using the +/− key to enter the sign. The calculator displays 2, showing that it has recorded the second observation.
6. Enter the remaining observations.
7. Ask the calculator for the expected return (R in the formula) by pressing x.
8. Ask the calculator for the standard deviation by pressing σ.

For larger samples, you should use the STDEV command in Excel.

[11]Some people define risk as the possibility of obtaining a return below the average. Some measures of risk, such as semivariance, use only the negative deviations from the average return. However, for symmetric distributions, such as the normal distribution, this method of measuring downside risk is equivalent to measuring risk with deviations from the mean on both sides.

This reinforces our earlier observations about stock market volatility. However, there is only a 5 percent chance (approximately) that we would end up outside the range −22.18 percent to 43.46 percent (10.64 percent plus or minus 2 × 16.41%). These points are also illustrated in Figure 10.6.

The distribution in Figure 10.6 is a theoretical distribution, sometimes called the *population*. There is no assurance that the actual distribution of observations in a given sample will produce a histogram that looks exactly like the theoretical distribution. We can see how messy the actual frequency function of historical observations is by observing Figure 10.5. If we were to keep on generating observations for a long enough period of time, however, the aberrations in the sample would disappear, and the actual historical distribution would start to look like the underlying theoretical distribution.

Our comparison illustrates how sampling error exists in any individual sample. In other words, the distribution of the sample only approximates the true distribution; we always measure the truth with some error. For example, we do not know what the true expected return was for common stocks in the 47-year history. However, we are sure that 10.64 percent is a good estimate.

Value at Risk

Figure 10.6 provides the basis for calculating **value at risk (VaR)**, a popular risk measurement tool used by banks, insurance companies, and other financial institutions. VaR represents the maximum possible loss in dollars for a given confidence level. To explain where VaR comes from, we start with Figure 10.6, which shows that there is a 95.44 percent probability that the annual return on common stock will lie between a loss of −22.18 percent and a gain of 43.46 percent. This means that there is a 4.56 percent probability that the

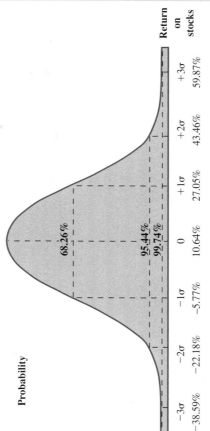

Probability

68.26%

95.44%
99.74%

| −3σ | −2σ | −1σ | 0 | +1σ | +2σ | +3σ | **Return on stocks** |
| −38.59% | −22.18% | −5.77% | 10.64% | 27.05% | 43.46% | 59.87% | |

In the case of a normal distribution, there is a 68.26 percent probability that a return will be within one standard deviation of the mean. In this example, there is a 68.26 percent probability that a yearly return will be between −5.77 percent and 27.05 percent.

There is a 95.44 percent probability that a return will be within two standard deviations of the mean. In this example, there is a 95.44 percent probability that a yearly return will be between −22.18 percent and 43.46 percent.

Finally, there is a 99.74 percent probability that a return will be within three standard deviations of the mean. In this example, there is a 99.74 percent probability that a yearly return will be between −38.59 percent and 59.87 percent.

FIGURE 10.6
The Normal Distribution

return will lie outside this range. Given that the normal distribution is symmetric, it follows that half that probability (or 2.28 percent) is attached to returns below −22.18 percent. (There is a similar probability of returns higher than 43.46 percent but because we are measuring risk, it is not of concern here.) In brief, if we pick 2.28 percent as our confidence level, Figure 10.6 tells us that returns lower than −22.18 percent will occur only 2.28 percent of the time.

VaR is expressed in dollars so the final piece of information needed is our total exposure to Canadian equities. Suppose that this is $200 million. Multiplying $200 million by a loss of 22.18 percent gives $44.36 million for VaR. In other words, $44.36 million is the most we can lose in one year on our Canadian equity exposure provided we are willing to accept a 2.28 percent chance that our loss could be higher. Canadian banks are required to report VaR in their annual reports.

Further Perspective on Returns and Risk

Table 10.2 presents returns and risks for major asset classes over a reasonably long period of Canadian history. Our discussion of these data suggested that the greater the potential reward, the greater is the risk. In particular, the equity risk premium was 3.84 percent over this period for Canadian stocks.

This may strike you as low as during the 1990s, as well as in the years immediately after World War II, double-digit returns on Canadian and U.S. stocks were common, as Table 10.1 shows. Currently most financial executives and professional investment managers expect lower returns and smaller risk premiums in the future.[12] We agree with their expectation and this relates to our earlier discussion of which data to use to calculate the market risk premium. In Table 10.1 we display returns data back to 1948 but only go back to 1957 when we calculate risk premiums in Table 10.2. This drops off the high returns experienced in many of the post-war years. If we recalculate the returns and risk premiums in Table 10.2 going all the way back to 1948, we arrive at a market risk premium of 6.53 percent. We discuss the relationship between risk and required return in more detail in the next chapter.

Using U.S. data including the years immediately following World War II and going back to 1926, Appendix 10A shows a similar result. The risk premium for this period is higher than for other historical periods.

All this suggests that our estimate of around 4 percent is quite a reasonable prediction for the equity risk premium in Canada looking to the future. However, we do have to acknowledge that this remains a controversial issue about which experts disagree.

- **Define sample estimates of variance and standard deviation.**
- **How does the normal distribution help us interpret standard deviation?**
- **Assuming that long-term bonds have an approximately normal distribution, what is the approximate probability of earning 17 percent or more in a given year? With T-bills, what is this probability?**
- **Real estate returns appear to be an anomaly, with higher returns and lower standard deviation than common stocks. What factors could explain this?**

12 A survey of academic views on the market risk premium is in I. Welch, "Views of Financial Economists on the Equity Risk Premium and Other Issues," *Journal of Business* 73 (October 2000), pp. 501–537. William Mercer surveys professional investment managers in Canada in its annual *Fearless Forecast* available in the Knowledge Center at *http://mercerric.com*.

10.6 SUMMARY AND CONCLUSIONS

1. This chapter explores capital market history. Such history is useful because it tells us what to expect in the way of returns from risky assets. We summed up our study of market history with two key lessons:

   a. Risky assets, on average, earn a risk premium. There is a reward for bearing risk.

   b. The greater the risk from a risky investment, the greater is the required reward.

   These lessons' implications for the financial manager are discussed in the chapters ahead.

2. The statistical measures in this chapter are necessary building blocks for the next three chapters. Standard deviation and variance measure the variability of the return on an individual security. We will argue that standard deviation and variance are appropriate measures of the risk of an individual security only if an investor's portfolio is composed exclusively of that security.

KEY TERMS

Average (mean) 276
Frequency distribution 276
Normal distribution 280
Risk premium 277

Standard deviation 279
Value at risk (VAR) 281
Variance 279

SUGGESTED READING

An important record of the performance of financial investments in Canadian capital markets can be found in:

J. E. Hatch and R. W. White. *Canadian Stocks, Bonds, Bills and Inflation: 1950–1983.* Charlottesville, Va.: Financial Analysts Research Foundation, 1985.

The corresponding study for the United States is:

R. G. Ibbotson and R. A. Sinquefield. *Stocks, Bonds, Bills and Inflation* (SBBI). Charlottesville, Va.: Financial Analysts Research Foundation, 1982. (Updated in *SBBI 2003 Yearbook*™. Chicago: Ibbotson Associates.)

What is the equity risk premium? This is the question addressed by:

Bradford Cornell. *The Equity Risk Premium: The Long Term Future of the Stock Market,* New York: John Wiley, 1999; and Robert S. Shiller, "*Irrational Exuberance.*" Princeton, N.J.: Princeton University Press, 2000.

QUESTIONS & PROBLEMS

Returns

10.1 One year ago, you bought 500 shares of Webster, Inc., stock at $37 per share. You just received a dividend of $1,000 and Webster stock now sells for $38.

    a. How much did you earn in capital gains?

    b. What was your total dollar return?

    c. What was your percentage return?

    d. Must you sell the stock to include the capital gain in your return?

10.2 One year ago, Mr. Seth Cohen invested $10,400 in 200 shares of First Industries, Inc., stock and just received a dividend of $600. Today, he sold the 200 shares at $54.25 per share.

    a. What was his capital gain?

    b. What was his total dollar return?

    c. What was his percentage return?

    d. What was the stock's dividend yield?

10.3 You purchased a stock one year ago at $42 per share. The stock just paid a dividend of $2.40 per share. Today, you sold the stock at $31 per share. What is the percentage return on this stock?

10.4 Lydian Stock currently trades at $52 per share. You intend to buy the stock today and hold it for two years. Two years from today, you expect to sell the stock at $54.75 per share. What is the expected holding period return on the stock?

10.5 Use the information provided in Table 10.1 to compute the nominal and real annual returns from 1979 to 2003 for

a. Canadian common stock.

b. Long-term bonds.

c. Canada Treasury bills.

10.6 Suppose the current interest rate on Canada Treasury bills is 4.2 percent. Table 10.2 shows the average return on Treasury bills from 1957 through 2003 to be 6.80 percent. The average return on common stock during the same period was 10.64 percent. Given this information, what is the current expected return on common stocks?

10.7 Two years ago, General Materials and Standard Fixtures' stock prices were the same. Over the first year, General Materials' stock price increased by 10 percent while Standard Fixtures' stock price decreased by 10 percent. Over the second year, General Materials' stock price decreased by 10 percent and Standard Fixtures' stock price increased by 10 percent. Do these two stocks have the same prices today? Explain.

Average Returns, Expected Returns, and Variance

10.8 During the past seven years, the returns on a portfolio of long-term bonds were the following:

Year	Long-Term Bonds
−7	−3.5%
−6	−1.3
−5	61.9
−4	6.1
−3	21.3
−2	40.0
Last	25.9

a. Calculate the average return for long-term bonds over this period.

b. Calculate the variance and the standard deviation of the returns for long-term bonds during this period.

10.9 The following are the returns during the past seven years on a market portfolio of common stocks and on Treasury bills.

Year	Common Stocks	Treasury Bills
−7	35.6%	12.3%
−6	−5.4	16.2
−5	23.5	11.6
−4	57.5	9.7
−3	6.9	10.9
−2	52.9	8.5
Last	−20.4	6.8

The realized risk premium is the return on the common stocks less the return on the Treasury bills.

a. Calculate the realized risk premium of common stocks over T-bills in each year.

b. Calculate the average risk premium of common stocks over T-bills during the period.

c. Is it possible that this observed risk premium can be negative? Explain.

Average Returns, Expected Returns, and Variance

10.10 The returns on both a portfolio of common stocks and a portfolio of Treasury bills are contingent on the state of the economy, as shown below.

Economic Condition	Probability	Market Return	Treasury Bills
Recession	0.25	−8.2%	3.5%
Normal	0.50	12.3	3.5
Boom	0.25	25.8	3.5

a. Calculate the expected returns on the Treasury bills and on the market.

b. Calculate the expected risk premium.

10.11 Tabulated below are the returns from 1935 through 1939 on small-company stocks and on large-company common stocks.

Year	Small-Company Stocks (%)	Large-Company Common Stocks (%)
1935	47.7	46.9
1936	33.9	32.4
1937	−35.0	−35.7
1938	31.0	32.3
1939	−0.5	−1.5

a. Calculate the average return for the small-company stocks and for the large-company common stocks.

b. Calculate the variance and standard deviation of the small-company returns and the large company returns.

10.12 The following data are the returns for 1998 through 2003 on four types of capital market instruments: Canadian common stocks, small-capitalization stocks, long-term bonds, and Canada Treasury bills.

Year	Canadian Common Stocks	Small-Cap Stocks	Long-Term Bonds	Canada T-Bills
1998	−1.58	−17.9	−12.9	4.8
1999	31.6	20.3	−6.0	4.7
2000	7.41	−4.3	13.0	5.5
2001	−12.6	0.7	8.1	4.7
2002	−12.4	−0.9	8.7	2.5
2003	26.7	42.7	6.7	2.9

Calculate the average return and variance for each type of security.

10.13 Suppose International Trading Company's stock returns follow a normal distribution with a mean of 17.5 percent and a standard deviation of 8.5 percent. What is the range in which roughly 95 percent of the returns fall?

10.14 Go to the "Excel Analytics" link for BCE Inc (BCE) and download the monthly adjusted stock prices. Assuming you invested $1,000 in BCE at the close 12 months ago, what is your ending investment value? What was the average monthly geometric return over this period? What was the average monthly arithmetic return?

10.15 Go to the "Excel Analytics" link for Encana (ECA) and download the monthly adjusted stock prices. What was the average monthly return for Encana over the past year? What was the monthly variance of returns? The monthly standard deviation?

EXCEL

**S & P
PROBLEMS**

STANDARD
&POOR'S

Appendix 10A   The Historical Market Risk Premium: The Very Long Run

The data in Chapter 10 indicate that the returns on common stock have historically been much higher than the returns on short-term government securities. This phenomenon has bothered economists, since it is difficult to justify why large numbers of rational investors purchase the lower yielding bills and bonds.

In 1985 Mehra and Prescott published a very influential paper that showed that, for the United States, the historical returns for common stocks are far too high when compared to the rates of return on short-term government securities.[13] They point out that the difference in returns (frequently called the *equity premium*) implies a very high degree of risk aversion on the part of investors. Since the publication of the Mehra and Prescott research, financial economists have tried to explain the so-called equity risk premium puzzle. The high historical equity risk premium is especially intriguing compared to the very low historical rate of return on Treasury securities. This seems to imply behaviour that has not actually happened. For example, if people have been very risk-averse and historical borrowing rates have been low, it suggests that persons should have been willing to borrow in periods of economic uncertainty and downturn to avoid the possibility of a reduced standard of living. However, we do not observe increased borrowing during recessions.

The equity risk premium puzzle of Mehra and Prescott has been generally viewed as an unexplained paradox. However, recently, Jeremy Seigel has shown that the historical risk premium may be substantially lower than previously realized (see Table 10A.1). He shows that, while the risk premium averaged 8.4 percent from 1926 to 2002, it averaged only 2.9 percent from 1802 to 1870, and 4.6 percent from 1871 to 1925.[14] It is puzzling that the trend has been rising over the last 200 years. It has been especially high since 1926. However, the key point is that historically the risk premium has been lower than in more recent times and we should be somewhat cautious about assumptions we make concerning the current risk premium.

Appendix Question

What lesson can be drawn from studying historical risk premiums dating back 200 years?

TABLE 10A.1	Historical U.S. Risk Premiums				
	1802–1870	1871–1925	1926–2002	1802–2002	Overall
Common stock	8.1	8.4	12.2	9.7	
Treasury bills	5.2	3.8	3.8	4.3	
Risk premium	2.9	4.6	8.4	5.4	

[13]Rajnish Mehra and Edward C. Prescott, "The Equity Premium: A Puzzle," *Journal of Monetary Economics* 15 (1985), pp. 145–61.

[14]Jeremy J. Seigel, *Stocks for the Long Run*, 3rd ed. (New York: McGraw-Hill, 2002).

Chapter 11

Return and Risk: The Capital Asset Pricing Model (CAPM)

EXECUTIVE SUMMARY

The previous chapter achieved two purposes. First, we acquainted you with the history of Canadian capital markets. Second, we presented statistics such as expected return, variance, and standard deviation. Our ultimate goal in the next three chapters is to determine the appropriate discount rate for capital budgeting projects. Because the discount rate on a project is a function of its risk, the discussion in the previous chapter on standard deviation is a necessary first step. However, we shall see that standard deviation is not the final word on risk.

Our next step is to investigate the relationship between the risk and the return of individual securities when these securities are part of a large portfolio. This task is taken up in Chapter 11. The actual treatment of the appropriate discount rate for capital budgeting is reserved for Chapter 13.

The crux of the current chapter can be summarized as follows: An individual who holds one security should use expected return as the measure of the security's return. Standard deviation or variance is the proper measure of the security's risk. An individual who holds a diversified portfolio cares about the *contribution* of each security to the expected return and the risk of the portfolio. It turns out that a security's expected return is the appropriate measure of the security's contribution to the expected return on the portfolio. However, neither the security's variance nor the security's standard deviation is an appropriate measure of a security's contribution to the risk of a portfolio. The contribution of a security to the risk of a portfolio is best measured by beta.

11.1 Individual Securities

In the first part of Chapter 11 we will examine the characteristics of individual securities. In particular, we will discuss:

1. *Expected return.* This is the return that an individual expects a stock to earn over the next period. Of course, because this is only an expectation, the actual return may be either higher or lower. An individual's expectation may simply be the average return per period a security has earned in the past. Alternatively, it may be based on a detailed analysis of a firm's prospects, on some computer-based model, or on special (or inside) information.

2. *Variance and standard deviation.* There are many ways to assess the volatility of a security's return. One of the most common is variance, which is a measure of the squared deviations of a security's return from its expected return. Standard deviation, which is the square root of the variance, may be thought of as a standardized version of the variance.

11.2 Expected Return, Variance, and Covariance

Expected Return and Variance

Suppose financial analysts believe that there are four equally likely states of the economy: depression, recession, normal, and boom times. The returns on the Supertech Company are expected to follow the economy closely, while the returns on the Slowpoke Company are not. The return predictions are given below:

	Supertech Returns R_{At}	Slowpoke Returns R_{Bt}
Depression	−20%	5%
Recession	10	20
Normal	30	−12
Boom	50	9

Variance can be calculated in four steps. Calculating expected return is the first step.[1] An additional step is needed to calculate standard deviation. (The calculations are presented in Table 11.1.)

1. Calculate the expected return:

Supertech:

$$\frac{-0.20 + 0.10 + 0.30 + 0.50}{4} = 0.175 = 17.5\%$$

Slowpoke:

$$\frac{0.05 + 0.20 - 0.12 + 0.09}{4} = 0.055 = 5.5\%$$

2. For each company, calculate the deviation of each possible return from the company's expected return given above. This is presented in the third column of Table 11.1.

3. The deviations we have calculated are indications of the dispersion of returns. However, because some are positive and some are negative, it is difficult to work with them in this form. For example, if we were to add up all the deviations for a single company, we would get zero as the sum.

To make the deviations more meaningful, we multiply each one by itself. Now all the numbers are positive, implying that their sum must be positive as well. The squared deviations are presented in the last column of Table 11.1.

---

[1] If the probabilities of all the states are not the same, find the expected return (standard deviation) by multiplying each return (deviation) by its probability.

---

3. *Covariance and correlation*. Returns on individual securities are related to one another. Covariance is a statistic measuring the interrelationship between two securities. Alternatively, this relationship can be restated in terms of the correlation between the two securities. Covariance and correlation are building blocks to an understanding of the beta coefficient.

TABLE 11.1	Calculating Variance and Standard Deviation		
(1) State of Economy	(2) Rate of Return	(3) Deviation from Expected Return	(4) Squared Value of Deviation
Supertech*	R_{At} (Expected return = 0.175)	$(R_{At} - \bar{R}_A)$	$(R_{At} - \bar{R}_A)^2$
Depression	-0.20	-0.375 $(= -0.20 - 0.175)$	0.140625 $[= (-0.375)^2]$
Recession	0.10	-0.075	0.005625
Normal	0.30	0.125	0.015625
Boom	0.50	0.325	0.105625
			0.267500
Slowpoke†	R_{Bt} (Expected return = 0.055)	$(R_{Bt} - \bar{R}_B)$	$(R_{Bt} - \bar{R}_B)^2$
Depression	0.05	-0.005 $(= 0.05 - 0.055)$	0.000025 $[= (-0.005)^2]$
Recession	0.20	0.145	0.021025
Normal	-0.12	-0.175	0.030625
Boom	0.09	0.035	0.001225
			0.052900

$$* \ \bar{R}_A = \frac{-0.20 + 0.10 + 0.30 + 0.50}{4} = 0.175 = 17.5\%$$

$$\text{Var}(R_A) = \sigma_A^2 = \frac{0.2675}{4} = 0.066875$$

$$\text{SD}(R_A) = \sigma_A = \sqrt{0.066875} = 0.2586 = 25.86\%$$

$$† \ \bar{R}_B = \frac{0.05 + 0.20 - 0.12 + 0.09}{4} = 0.055 = 5.5\%$$

$$\text{Var}(R_B) = \sigma_B^2 = \frac{0.0529}{4} = 0.013225$$

$$\text{SD}(R_B) = \sigma_B = \sqrt{0.013225} = 0.1150 = 11.50\%$$

4. For each company, calculate the average squared deviation, which is the variance:[2]

Supertech:

$$\frac{0.140625 + 0.005625 + 0.015625 + 0.105625}{4} = 0.066875$$

Slowpoke:

$$\frac{0.000025 + 0.021025 + 0.030625 + 0.001225}{4} = 0.013225$$

Thus, the variance of Supertech is 0.066875, and the variance of Slowpoke is 0.013225.

---

[2]In this example, the four states give rise to four possible outcomes for each stock. Had we used past data, the outcomes would have actually occurred. In that case, statisticians argue that the correct divisor is $N - 1$, where N is the number of observations. Thus, the denominator would be 3 (or $4 - 1$) in the case of past data, not 4. Note that the example in Section 10.5 involved past data and we used a divisor of $N - 1$. While this difference causes grief to both students and textbook writers, it is a minor point in practice. In the real world, samples are generally so large that using N or $N - 1$ in the denominator has virtually no effect on the calculation of variance.

5. Calculate standard deviation by taking the square root of the variance:

Supertech:

$$\sqrt{0.066875} = 0.2586 = 25.86\%$$

Slowpoke:

$$\sqrt{0.013225} = 0.1150 = 11.50\%$$

Algebraically, the formula for variance can be expressed as

$$\text{Var}(R) = \text{Expected value of } (R - \overline{R})^2$$

where $\overline{R}$ is the security's expected return and R is the actual return.

A look at the four-step calculation for variance makes it clear why it is a measure of the spread of the sample of returns. For each observation, we square the difference between the actual return and the expected return. We then take an average of these squared differences.

However, because the variance is still expressed in squared terms, it is difficult to interpret. Standard deviation has a much simpler interpretation, which we will provide shortly. Standard deviation is simply the square root of the variance. The general formula for the standard deviation is

$$SD(R) = \sqrt{\text{Var}(R)}$$

Covariance and Correlation

The statistical estimates variance and standard deviation measure the variability of individual stocks. We now wish to measure the relationship between the return on one stock and the return on another. To make our discussion more precise, we need a statistical measure of the relationship between two variables. Enter **covariance** and **correlation.**

Covariance and correlation are ways of measuring whether or not two random variables are related and how. We explain these terms by extending an example presented earlier in this chapter.

We have already determined the expected returns and standard deviations for both Supertech and Slowpoke. (The expected returns are 0.175 and 0.055 for Supertech and Slowpoke, respectively. The standard deviations are 0.2586 and 0.1150, respectively.) In addition, we calculated for each firm the deviation of each possible return from the expected return. Using these data, covariance can be calculated in two steps. An extra step is needed to calculate correlation.

1. For each state of the economy, multiply Supertech's deviation from its expected return and Slowpoke's deviation from its expected return together. For example, Supertech's rate of return in a depression is −0.20, which is −0.375 (or −0.20 − 0.175) from its expected return. Slowpoke's rate of return in a depression is 0.05, which is −0.005 (or 0.05 − 0.055) from its expected return. Multiplying the two deviations together yields 0.001875 [or (−0.375) × (−0.005)]. The actual calculations are given in the last column of Table 11.2. This procedure can be written algebraically as

$$(R_{At} - \overline{R}_A) \times (R_{Bt} - \overline{R}_B) \tag{11.1}$$

where R_{At} and R_{Bt} are the returns on Supertech and Slowpoke in state t. $\overline{R}_A$ and $\overline{R}_B$ are the expected returns on the two securities.

2. Calculate the average value of the four states in the last column. This average is the covariance. That is,[3]

$$\sigma_{AB} = \text{Cov}(R_A, R_B) = \frac{-0.195}{4} = -0.004875$$

Note that we represent the covariance between Supertech and Slowpoke as either $\text{Cov}(R_A, R_B)$ or σ_{AB}. Equation (11.1) illustrates the intuition of covariance. Suppose Supertech's return is generally above its average when Slowpoke's return is above its average, and Supertech's return is generally below its average when Slowpoke's return is below its average. This is indicative of a positive dependency or a positive relationship between the two returns. Note that the term in Equation (11.1) will be *positive* in any state where both returns are *above* their averages. In addition, (11.1) will still be *positive* in any state where both terms are *below* their averages. Thus, a positive relationship between the two returns will give rise to a positive calculation for covariance.

Conversely, suppose Supertech's return is generally above its average when Slowpoke's return is below its average, and Supertech's return is generally below its average when Slowpoke's return is above its average. This is indicative of a negative dependency or a negative relationship between the two returns. Note that the term in Equation (11.1) will be *negative* in any state where one return is above its average and the other return is below its average. Thus, a negative relationship between the two returns will give rise to a negative calculation for covariance.

Finally, suppose there is no relation between the two returns. In this case, knowing whether the return on Supertech is above or below its expected return tells us nothing about the return

TABLE 11.2	**Calculating Covariance and Correlation**			
State of Economy	Rate of Return of Supertech R_{At}	Deviation from Expected Return $(R_{At} - \overline{R_A})$	Rate of Return of Slowpoke R_{Bt}	Deviation from Expected Return $(R_{Bt} - \overline{R_B})$	Product of Deviations $(R_{At} - \overline{R_A}) \times (R_{Bt} - \overline{R_B})$
---	---	---	---	---	---
		(Expected return = 0.175)		(Expected return = 0.055)	
Depression	−0.20	−0.375 (= −0.20 − 0.175)	0.05	−0.005 (= 0.05 − 0.055)	0.001875 (= −0.375 × −0.005)
Recession	0.10	−0.075	0.20	0.145	−0.010875 (= −0.075 × 0.145)
Normal	0.30	0.125	−0.12	−0.175	−0.021875 (= 0.125 × −0.175)
Boom	0.50	0.325	0.09	0.035	0.011375 (= 0.325 × 0.035)
	$\overline{0.70}$		$\overline{0.22}$		$\overline{-0.0195}$

$$\sigma_{AB} = \text{Cov}(R_A, R_B) = \frac{-0.0195}{4} = -0.004875$$

$$\rho_{AB} = \text{Corr}(R_A, R_B) = \frac{\text{Cov}(R_A, R_B)}{\text{SD}(R_A) \times \text{SD}(R_B)} = \frac{-0.004875}{0.2586 \times 0.1150} = -0.1639$$

---

[3]As with variance, we divide by N (4 in this example) because the four states give rise to four possible outcomes. However, had we used past data, the correct divisor would be $N - 1$ (3 in this example).

on Slowpoke. In the covariance formula, then, there will be no tendency for the terms to be positive or negative, and on average they will tend to offset each other and cancel out. This will make the covariance zero.

Of course, even if the two returns are unrelated to each other, the covariance formula will not equal zero exactly in any actual history. This is due to sampling error; randomness alone will make the calculation positive or negative. But for a historical sample that is long enough, if the two returns are not related to each other, we should expect the formula to come close to zero.

The covariance formula seems to capture what we are looking for. If the two returns are positively related to each other, they will have a positive covariance, and if they are negatively related to each other, the covariance will be negative. Last, and very important, if they are unrelated, the covariance should be zero.

The formula for covariance can be written algebraically as

$$\sigma_{AB} = \text{Cov}(R_A, R_B) = \text{Expected value of } [(R_A - \overline{R_A}) \times (R_B - \overline{R_B})]$$

where $\overline{R_A}$ and $\overline{R_B}$ are the expected returns for the two securities, and R_A and R_B are the actual returns. The ordering of the two variables is unimportant. That is, the covariance of A with B is equal to the covariance of B with A. This can be stated more formally as $\text{Cov}(R_A, R_B)$ = $\text{Cov}(R_B, R_A)$ or $\sigma_{AB} = \sigma_{BA}$.

The covariance we calculated is -0.004875. A negative number like this implies that the return on one stock is likely to be above its average when the return on the other stock is below its average, and vice versa. However, the size of the number is difficult to interpret. Like the variance figure, the covariance is in squared deviation units. Until we can put it in perspective, we don't know what to make of it.

We solve the problem by computing the correlation.

3. To calculate the correlation, divide the covariance by the standard deviations of both of the two securities. For our example, we have

$$\rho_{AB} = \text{Corr}(R_A, R_B) = \frac{\text{Cov}(R_A, R_B)}{\sigma_A \times \sigma_B} = \frac{-0.004875}{0.2586 \times 0.1150} = -0.1639 \quad \textbf{(11.2)}$$

where σ_A and σ_B are the standard deviations of Supertech and Slowpoke, respectively. Note that we represent the correlation between Supertech and Slowpoke either as $\text{Corr}(R_A, R_B)$ or ρ_{AB}. As with covariance, the ordering of the two variables is unimportant. That is, the correlation of A with B is equal to the correlation of B with A. More formally, $\text{Corr}(R_A, R_B) = \text{Corr}(R_B, R_A)$ or $\rho_{AB} = \rho_{BA}$.

Because the standard deviation is always positive, the sign of the correlation between two variables must be the same as that of the covariance between the two variables. If the correlation is positive, we say that the variables are *positively correlated*; if it is negative, we say that they are *negatively correlated*; and if it is zero, we say that they are *uncorrelated*. Furthermore, it can be proven that the correlation is always between +1 and −1. This is due to the standardizing procedure of dividing by the two standard deviations.

We can compare the correlation between different pairs of securities. For example, it turns out that the correlation between Bank of Montreal and Royal Bank of Canada is much higher than the correlation between Bank of Montreal and Nortel. Hence, we can state that the first pair of securities is more interrelated than the second pair.

Figure 11.1 shows the three benchmark cases for two assets, A and B. The figure shows two assets with return correlations of +1, −1, and 0. This implies perfect positive

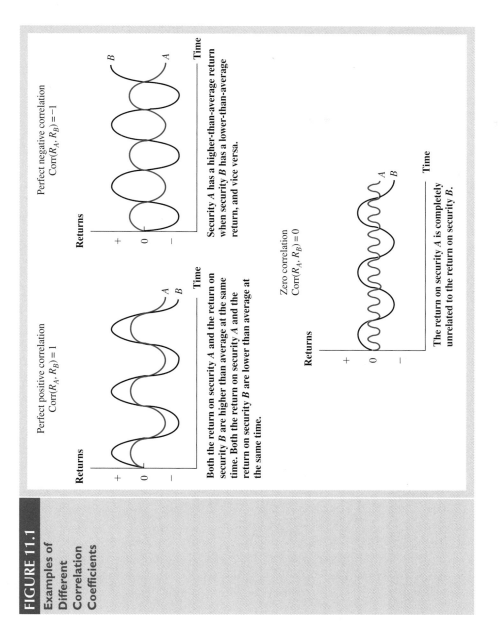

FIGURE 11.1

Examples of Different Correlation Coefficients

Perfect positive correlation
$\mathrm{Corr}(R_A, R_B) = 1$

Both the return on security *A* and the return on security *B* are higher than average at the same time. Both the return on security *A* and the return on security *B* are lower than average at the same time.

Perfect negative correlation
$\mathrm{Corr}(R_A, R_B) = -1$

Security *A* has a higher-than-average return when security *B* has a lower-than-average return, and vice versa.

Zero correlation
$\mathrm{Corr}(R_A, R_B) = 0$

The return on security *A* is completely unrelated to the return on security *B*.

correlation, perfect negative correlation, and no correlation, respectively. The graphs in the figure plot the separate returns on the two securities through time.

11.3 The Return and Risk for Portfolios

Suppose that an investor has estimates of the expected returns and standard deviations on individual securities and the correlations between securities. How then does the investor choose the best combination or **portfolio** of securities to hold? Obviously, the investor would like a portfolio with a high expected return and a low standard deviation of return. It is therefore worthwhile to consider

1. The relationship between the expected return on individual securities and the expected return on a portfolio made up of these securities.

2. The relationship between the standard deviations of individual securities, the correlations between these securities, and the standard deviation of a portfolio made up of these securities.

The Example of Supertech and Slowpoke

In order to analyze the above two relationships, we will use the Supertech and Slowpoke example presented previously. The relevant data are in the box below.[4]

The Expected Return on a Portfolio

The formula for expected return on a portfolio is very simple:

The expected return on a portfolio is simply a weighted average of the expected returns on the individual securities.

Relevant Data from Example of Supertech and Slowpoke

Item	Symbol	Value
Expected return on Supertech	$\overline{R}_{Super}$	$0.175 = 17.5\%$
Expected return on Slowpoke	$\overline{R}_{Slow}$	$0.055 = 5.5\%$
Variance of Supertech	σ^2_{Super}	0.066875
Variance of Slowpoke	σ^2_{Slow}	0.013225
Standard deviation of Supertech	σ_{Super}	$0.2586 = 25.86\%$
Standard deviation of Slowpoke	σ_{Slow}	$0.1150 = 11.50\%$
Covariance between Supertech and Slowpoke	$\sigma_{Super, Slow}$	-0.004875
Correlation between Supertech and Slowpoke	$\rho_{Super, Slow}$	-0.1639

Consider Supertech and Slowpoke. From the box above, we find that the expected returns on these two securities are 17.5 percent and 5.5 percent, respectively.

The expected return on a portfolio of these two securities alone can be written as

$$\text{Expected return on portfolio} = X_{Super}\,(17.5\%) + X_{Slow}\,(5.5\%)$$

where X_{Super} is the percentage of the portfolio in Supertech and X_{Slow} is the percentage of the portfolio in Slowpoke. If the investor can only invest with $100 invests $60 in Supertech and $40 in Slowpoke, the expected return on the portfolio can be written as

$$\text{Expected return on portfolio} = 0.6 \times 17.5\% + 0.4 \times 5.5\% = 12.7\%$$

Algebraically, we can write

$$\text{Expected return on portfolio} = X_A\overline{R}_A + X_B\overline{R}_B \tag{11.3}$$

where X_A and X_B are the proportions of the total portfolio in the assets A and B, respectively. (Because our investor can only invest in two securities, $X_A + X_B$ must equal 1 or 100 percent.) $\overline{R}_A$ and $\overline{R}_B$ are the expected returns on the two securities.

Now consider two stocks, each with an expected return of 10 percent. The expected return on a portfolio composed of these two stocks must be 10 percent, regardless of the

[4]See Tables 11.1 and 11.2 for actual calculations.

proportions of the two stocks held. This result may seem obvious at this point, but it will become important later. The result implies that you do not reduce or *dissipate* your expected return by investing in a number of securities. Rather, the expected return on your portfolio is simply a weighted average of the expected returns on the individual assets in the portfolio.

Variance and Standard Deviation of a Portfolio

The Variance   The formula for the variance of a portfolio composed of two securities, A and B, is

The Variance of the Portfolio:

$$\text{Var(portfolio)} = X_A^2 \sigma_A^2 + 2X_A X_B \sigma_{A,B} + X_B^2 \sigma_B^2$$

Note that there are three terms on the right-hand side of the equation. The first term involves the variance of $A(\sigma_A^2)$, the second term involves the covariance between the two securities ($\sigma_{A,B}$), and the third term involves the variance of $B(\sigma_B^2)$. (It should be noted that $\sigma_{A,B} = \sigma_{B,A}$. That is, the ordering of the variables is not relevant when expressing the covariance between two securities.)

The formula indicates an important point. The variance of a portfolio depends on both the variances of the individual securities and the covariance between the two securities. The variance of a security measures the variability of an individual security's return. Covariance measures the relationship between the two securities. For given variances of the individual securities, a positive relationship or covariance between the two securities increases the variance of the entire portfolio. A negative relationship or covariance between the two securities decreases the variance of the entire portfolio. This important result seems to square with common sense. If one of your securities tends to go up when the other goes down, or vice versa, your two securities are offsetting each other. You are achieving what we call a *hedge* in finance, and the risk of your entire portfolio will be low. However, if both your securities rise and fall together, you are not hedging at all. Hence, the risk of your entire portfolio will be higher.

The variance formula for our two securities, Super and Slow, is

$$\text{Var(portfolio)} = X_{\text{Super}}^2 \sigma_{\text{Super}}^2 + 2X_{\text{Super}} X_{\text{Slow}} \sigma_{\text{Super,Slow}} + X_{\text{Slow}}^2 \sigma_{\text{Slow}}^2 \quad \textbf{(11.4)}$$

Given our earlier assumption that an individual with \$100 invests \$60 in Supertech and \$40 in Slowpoke, $X_{\text{Super}} = 0.6$ and $X_{\text{Slow}} = 0.4$. Using this assumption and the relevant data from the box on page 294, the variance of the portfolio is

$$0.023851 = 0.36 \times 0.066875 + 2 \times [0.6 \times 0.4 \times (-0.004875)] + \quad \textbf{(11.4')}$$
$$0.16 \times 0.013225$$

The Matrix Approach   Alternatively, Equation (11.4) can be expressed in the following matrix format:

	Supertech	Slowpoke
Supertech	$X_{\text{Super}}^2\ \sigma_{\text{Super}}^2$ $0.024075 = 0.36 \times 0.066875$	$X_{\text{Super}}X_{\text{Slow}}\sigma_{\text{Super, Slow}}$ $-0.00117 = 0.6 \times 0.4 \times (-0.004875)$
Slowpoke	$X_{\text{Super}}X_{\text{Slow}}\sigma_{\text{Super, Slow}}$ $-0.00117 = 0.6 \times 0.4 \times (-0.004875)$	$X_{\text{Slow}}^2\ \sigma_{\text{Slow}}^2$ $0.002116 = 0.16 \times 0.013225$

There are four boxes in the matrix. We can add the terms in the boxes to obtain Equation (11.4), the variance of a portfolio composed of the two securities. The term in the upper left-hand corner contains the variance of Supertech. The term in the lower right-hand corner contains the variance of Slowpoke. The other two boxes contain the covariance terms. These two boxes are identical, indicating why the covariance term is multiplied by 2 in Equation (11.4).

At this point, students often find the box approach to be more confusing than Equation (11.4). However, the box approach is easily generalized to more than two securities, a task we perform later in this chapter.

Standard Deviation of a Portfolio   Given (11.4'), we can now determine the standard deviation of the portfolio's return. This is

$$\sigma_P = \text{SD(portfolio)} = \sqrt{\text{Var(portfolio)}} = \sqrt{0.023851} = 0.1544 = 15.44\% \quad (11.5)$$

The interpretation of the standard deviation of the portfolio is the same as the interpretation of the standard deviation of an individual security. The expected return on our portfolio is 12.7 percent. A return of -2.74 percent ($12.7\% - 15.44\%$) is one standard deviation below the mean and a return of 28.14 percent ($12.7\% + 15.44\%$) is one standard deviation above the mean. If the return on the portfolio is normally distributed, a return between -2.74 percent and $+28.14$ percent occurs about 68 percent of the time. [5]

The Diversification Effect   It is instructive to compare the standard deviation of the portfolio with the standard deviation of the individual securities. The weighted average of the standard deviations of the individual securities is

$$\text{Weighted average of standard deviations} = X_{\text{Super}}\sigma_{\text{Super}} + X_{\text{Slow}}\sigma_{\text{Slow}} \quad (11.6)$$
$$0.2012 = 0.6 \times 0.2586 + 0.4 \times 0.115$$

One of the most important results in this chapter relates to the difference between Equations (11.5) and (11.6). In our example, the standard deviation of the portfolio is *less* than a weighted average of the standard deviations of the individual securities.

We pointed out earlier that the expected return on the portfolio is a weighted average of the expected returns on the individual securities. Thus, we get a different type of result for the standard deviation of a portfolio than we do for the expected return on a portfolio.

It is generally argued that our result for the standard deviation of a portfolio is due to diversification. For example, Supertech and Slowpoke are slightly negatively correlated ($\rho = -0.1639$). Supertech's return is likely to be a little below average if Slowpoke's return is above average. Similarly, Supertech's return is likely to be a little above average if Slowpoke's return is below average. Thus, the standard deviation of a portfolio composed of the two securities is less than a weighted average of the standard deviations of the two securities.

The above example has negative correlation. Clearly, there will be less benefit from diversification if the two securities exhibit positive correlation. How high must the positive correlation be before all diversification benefits vanish?

To answer this question, let us rewrite (11.4) in terms of correlation rather than covariance. The covariance can be rewritten as [6]

$$\sigma_{\text{Super, Slow}} = \rho_{\text{Super, Slow}}\sigma_{\text{Super}}\sigma_{\text{Slow}} \quad (11.7)$$

___
[5] There are only four equally probable returns for Supertech and Slowpoke, so neither security possesses a normal distribution. Thus, probabilities would be slightly different in our example.

[6] As with covariance, the ordering of the two securities is not relevant when expressing the correlation between the two securities. That is, $\rho_{\text{Super, Slow}} = \rho_{\text{Slow, Super}}$.

The formula states that the covariance between any two securities is simply the correlation between the two securities multiplied by the standard deviations of each. In other words, covariance incorporates both (1) the correlation between the two assets and (2) the variability of each of the two securities as measured by standard deviation.

From our calculations earlier in this chapter we know that the correlation between the two securities is −0.1639. Given the variances used in Equation (11.4′), the standard deviations are 0.2586 and 0.115 for Supertech and Slowpoke, respectively. Thus, the variance of a portfolio can be expressed as

Variance of the portfolio's return:

$$= X^2_{Super}\sigma^2_{Super} + 2X_{Super}X_{Slow}\rho_{Super,\,Slow}\sigma_{Super}\sigma_{Slow} + X^2_{Slow}\sigma^2_{Slow} \quad (11.8)$$

$$0.023851 = 0.36 \times 0.066875 + 2 \times 0.6 \times 0.4 \times (-0.1639) \times$$
$$0.2586 \times 0.115 + 0.16 \times 0.013225$$

The middle term on the right-hand side is now written in terms of correlation, ρ, not covariance.

Suppose $\rho_{Super,\,Slow} = 1$, the highest possible value for correlation. Assume all the other parameters in the example are the same. The variance of the portfolio is

$$\text{Variance of the portfolio's return} = 0.040466 = 0.36 \times 0.066875 + 2 \times$$
$$(0.6 \times 0.4 \times 1 \times 0.2586 \times 0.115) +$$
$$0.16 \times 0.013225$$

The standard deviation is

Standard deviation of portfolio's return $= \sqrt{0.040466} = 0.2012 = 20.12\%$ **(11.9)**

Note that (11.9) and (11.6) are equal. That is, the standard deviation of a portfolio's return is equal to the weighted average of the standard deviations of the individual returns when $\rho = 1$. Inspection of (11.8) indicates that the variance and hence the standard deviation of the portfolio must drop as the correlation drops below 1. This leads to:

As long as $\rho < 1$, the standard deviation of a portfolio of two securities is less than the weighted average of the standard deviations of the individual securities.

In other words, the diversification effect applies as long as there is less than perfect correlation (as long as $\rho < 1$). Thus, our Supertech–Slowpoke example is a case of overkill. We illustrated diversification with an example with negative correlation. We could have illustrated diversification with an example with positive correlation—as long as it was not perfect positive correlation.

An Extension to Many Assets   The preceding insight can be extended to the case of many assets. That is, as long as correlations between pairs of securities are less than 1, the standard deviation of a portfolio of many assets is less than the weighted average of the standard deviations of the individual securities.

Now consider Table 11.3, which shows the standard deviation of some of the individual securities listed in the index over a recent 25-year period. Note that all of the individual securities in the table have higher standard deviations than that of the index. In general, the standard deviations of most of the individual securities in an index will be above the standard deviation of the index itself, though a few of the securities could have lower standard deviations than that of the index.

TABLE 11.3   Standard Deviations for Annual Returns of Selected TSX Companies over a 25-Year Period

Abitibi Price Inc.	30.88%
Bank of Montreal	24.23
Bell Canada Enterprises Inc.	21.47
Canadian Pacific Ltd.	26.16
Imperial Oil Ltd.	24.84
Molson Companies Ltd.	24.79
MacMillan Bloedel Ltd.	27.04
Placer Dome Inc.	42.33
S&P/TSX 60	17.04

Source: Calculated from the Canadian Financial Markets Research Centre tape.

Concept Questions

- What are the formulas for the expected return, variance, and standard deviation of a portfolio of two assets?
- What is the diversification effect?
- What are the highest and lowest possible values for the correlation coefficient?

11.4 The Efficient Set for Two Assets

Our results on expected returns and standard deviations are graphed in Figure 11.2. In the figure, there is a dot labelled Slowpoke and a dot labelled Supertech. Each dot represents both the expected return and the standard deviation for an individual security. As can be seen, Supertech has both a higher expected return and a higher standard deviation.

The box or "□" in Figure 11.2 represents a portfolio with 60 percent invested in Supertech and 40 percent invested in Slowpoke. You will recall that we have previously calculated both the expected return and the standard deviation for this portfolio.

FIGURE 11.2

Expected Return and Standard Deviation for (1) Supertech, (2) Slowpoke, and (3) A Portfolio Composed of 60 Percent in Supertech and 40 Percent in Slowpoke

Expected return

17.5 —

12.7 —

5.5 —

● 2 Slowpoke

□ 3

● 1 Supertech

| 11.50 | 15.44 | 25.86 |

Standard deviation (%)

FIGURE 11.3

Set of Portfolios Composed of Holdings in Supertech and Slowpoke (correlation between the two securities is −0.16)

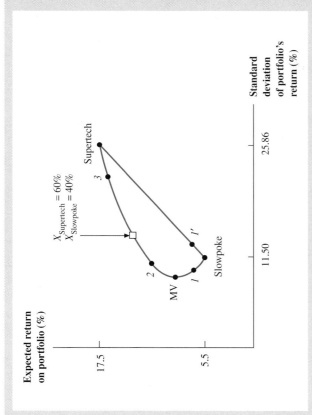

Portfolio *1* is composed of 90 percent Slowpoke and 10 percent Supertech ($\rho = -0.16$).
Portfolio 2 is composed of 50 percent Slowpoke and 50 percent Supertech ($\rho = -0.16$).
Portfolio 3 is composed of 10 percent Slowpoke and 90 percent Supertech ($\rho = -0.16$).
Portfolio *1'* is composed of 90 percent Slowpoke and 10 percent Supertech ($\rho = 1$).
Point MV denotes the minimum variance portfolio. This is the portfolio with the lowest possible variance. By definition, the same portfolio must also have the lowest possible standard deviation.

The choice of 60 percent in Supertech and 40 percent in Slowpoke is just one of an infinite number of portfolios that can be created. The set of portfolios is sketched by the curved line in Figure 11.3.

Consider portfolio 1. This is a portfolio composed of 90 percent Slowpoke and 10 percent Supertech. Because it is weighted so heavily toward Slowpoke, it appears close to the Slowpoke point on the graph. Portfolio 2 is higher on the curve because it is composed of 50 percent Slowpoke and 50 percent Supertech. Portfolio 3 is close to the Supertech point on the graph because it is composed of 90 percent Supertech and 10 percent Slowpoke.

There are a few important points concerning this graph.

1. We argued that the diversification effect occurs whenever the correlation between the two securities is below 1. The correlation between Supertech and Slowpoke is −0.1639. The diversification effect can be illustrated by comparison with the straight line between the Supertech point and the Slowpoke point. The straight line represents points that would have been generated had the correlation coefficient between the two securities been 1. The diversification effect is illustrated in the figure since the curved line is always to the left of the straight line. Consider point 1'. This represents a portfolio composed of 90 percent in Slowpoke and 10 percent in Supertech if the correlation between the two were exactly 1. We argue that there is no diversification effect if $\rho = 1$. However, the diversification effect applies to the curved line, because point 1 has the same expected return as point 1' but has a lower standard deviation. (Points 2' and 3' are omitted to reduce the clutter in Figure 11.3.)

Though the straight line and the curved line are both represented in Figure 11.3, they do not exist simultaneously. Either ρ = −0.1639 and the curve exists or ρ = 1 and the straight line exists. In other words, though an investor can choose between different points on the curve if ρ = −0.1639, he or she cannot choose between points on the curve and points on the straight line.

2. The point MV represents the minimum variance portfolio. This is the portfolio with the lowest possible variance. By definition, this portfolio must also have the lowest possible standard deviation. (The term *minimum variance portfolio* is standard in the literature, and we will use that term. Perhaps *minimum standard deviation* would actually be better, because standard deviation, not variance, is measured on the horizontal axis of Figure 11.3.)

3. An investor considering a portfolio of Slowpoke and Supertech faces an **opportunity set** or **feasible set** represented by the curved line in Figure 11.3. That is, the investor can achieve any point on the curve by selecting the appropriate mix between the two securities. He or she cannot achieve any points above the curve because the investor cannot increase the return on the individual securities, decrease the standard deviations of the securities, or decrease the correlation between the two securities. Neither can the investor achieve points below the curve because he or she cannot lower the returns on the individual securities, increase the standard deviations of the securities, or increase the correlation. (Of course, the investor would not want to achieve points below the curve, even if it were possible to do so.)

Were the investor relatively tolerant of risk, he or she might choose portfolio 3. (In fact, the investor could even choose the end point by investing all his or her money in Supertech.) An investor with less tolerance for risk might choose point 2. An investor wanting as little risk as possible would choose MV, the portfolio with minimum variance or minimum standard deviation.

4. Note that the curve is backward bending between the Slowpoke point and MV. This indicates that, for a portion of the feasible set, standard deviation actually decreases as one increases expected return. Students frequently ask, "How can an increase in the proportion of the risky security, Supertech, lead to a reduction in the risk of the portfolio?"

This surprising finding is due to the diversification effect. The returns on the two securities are negatively correlated. One security tends to go up when the other goes down. Thus, an addition of a small amount of Supertech acts as a hedge to a portfolio composed only of Slowpoke. The risk of the portfolio is reduced, implying a backward bending curve. Actually, backward bending always occurs if ρ ≤ 0. It may or may not occur when ρ > 0. Of course, the curve bends backward only for a portion of its length. As one continues to increase the percentage of Supertech in the portfolio, the high standard deviation of this security eventually causes the standard deviation of the entire portfolio to rise.

5. No investor would want to hold a portfolio with an expected return below that of the minimum variance portfolio. For example, no investor would choose portfolio 1. This portfolio has less expected return but more standard deviation than the minimum variance portfolio has. We say that portfolios such as portfolio 1 are *dominated* by the minimum variance portfolio.

Though the entire curve from Slowpoke to Supertech is called the *feasible set*, investors only consider the curve from MV to Supertech. Hence, the curve from MV to Supertech is called the **efficient set.**

Figure 11.3 represents the opportunity set when ρ = −0.1639. It is worthwhile to examine Figure 11.4, which shows different curves for different correlations. As can be seen, the lower the correlation, the more bend there is in the curve. This indicates that the

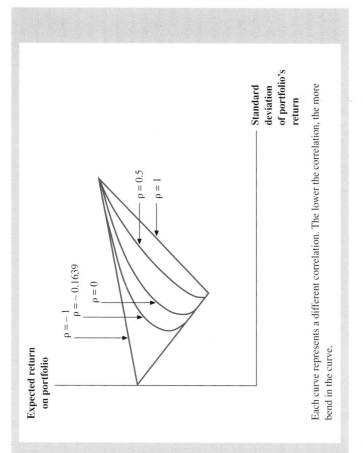

Each curve represents a different correlation. The lower the correlation, the more bend in the curve.

diversification effect rises as ρ declines. The greatest bend occurs in the limiting case where ρ = −1. This is perfect negative correlation. While this extreme case where ρ = −1 seems to fascinate students, it has little practical importance. Most pairs of securities exhibit positive correlation. Strong negative correlation, let alone perfect negative correlation, is an unlikely occurrence indeed.[7]

Note that there is only one correlation between a pair of securities. We stated earlier that the correlation between Slowpoke and Supertech is −0.1639. Thus, the curve in Figure 11.4 representing this correlation is the correct one and the other curves should be viewed as merely hypothetical.

The graphs we examined are not mere intellectual curiosities. Rather, efficient sets can easily be calculated in the real world. As mentioned earlier, data on returns, standard deviations, and correlations are generally taken from past data, though subjective notions can be used to calculate the values of these statistics as well. Once the statistics have been determined, any one of a whole host of software packages can be purchased to generate an efficient set. However, the choice of the preferred portfolio within the efficient set is up to you. As with other important decisions like what job to choose, what house or car to buy, and how much time to allocate to this course, there is no computer program to choose the preferred portfolio.

Application to International Diversification

Research on diversification extends our discussion of historical average returns and risks in Chapter 11 to include foreign investment portfolios. It turns out that the feasible set looks like Figure 11.5, where points like *U* and *L* represent portfolios instead of

---

[7]A major exception occurs with derivative securities. For example, the correlation between a stock and a put option on the stock is generally strongly negative. Puts will be treated later in the text.

FIGURE 11.5

Efficient Frontier

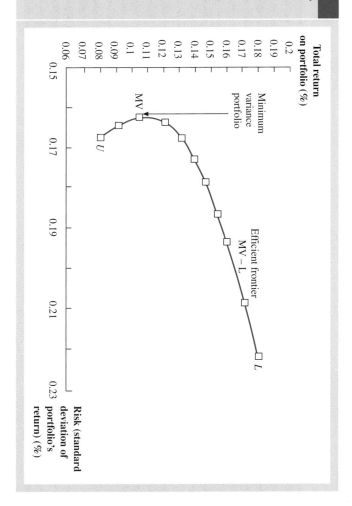

individual stocks. Portfolio U represents 100 percent investment in Canadian equities and portfolio L represents 100 percent in foreign equities. The domestic stock portfolio is less risky than the foreign portfolio. Does this mean that Canadian portfolio managers should invest entirely in Canada?

The answer is no because the minimum variance portfolio with approximately 20 percent foreign content dominates portfolio U, the 100 percent domestic portfolio. Going from 0 percent to around 20 percent foreign content actually reduces portfolio standard deviation due to the diversification effect. However, portfolio MV is not necessarily optimal. Recognizing these points led pension managers to lobby successfully in 2000 for an increase in allowable foreign content to 30 percent.[8]

Another point worth pondering concerns the potential pitfalls of using only past data to estimate future returns and correlations. The stock markets of many foreign countries—such as Korea, Thailand, and Indonesia—had phenomenal growth in the early 1990s. Thus, a graph like Figure 11.5 makes a large investment in these foreign markets seem attractive. However, abnormally high returns and low correlations cannot be sustained forever, and the Asian stock markets suffered major declines in the late 1990s. To avoid the forecaster's trap inherent in blind reliance on historical returns, some subjectivity must be used when forecasting future expected returns and correlations. Scenario analysis is a useful tool here.

Concept Question

- What is the relationship between the shape of the efficient set for two assets and the correlation between the two assets?

[8]These data come from H. S. Marmer, "International Investing: A New Canadian Perspective," *Canadian Investment Review* (Spring 1991), pp. 47–53; and *Canadian Investment Review* (Winter 1998), pp. 49–51. B. Bruce, "Why Diversify?" *Canadian Investment Review* (Summer 2000), pp. 40–44, takes this case further, arguing for foreign content of 70 percent.

11.5 The Efficient Set for Many Securities

The previous discussion concerned two securities. We found that a simple curve sketched out all the possible portfolios. Because investors generally hold more than two securities, we should examine the same feasible set when more than two securities are held. The shaded area in Figure 11.6 represents the opportunity set or feasible set when many securities are considered. The shaded area represents all the possible combinations of expected return and standard deviation for a portfolio. For example, in a universe of 100 securities, point 1 might represent a portfolio of, say, 40 securities. Point 2 might represent a portfolio of 80 securities. Point 3 might represent a different set of 80 securities or the same 80 securities held in different proportions. Obviously, the combinations are virtually endless. However, note that all possible combinations fit into a confined region. No security or combination of securities can fall outside of the shaded region. That is, no one can choose a portfolio with an expected return above that given by the shaded region because the expected returns on individual securities cannot be altered. Furthermore, no one can choose a portfolio with a standard deviation below that given in the shaded area. Perhaps more surprisingly, no one can choose an expected return below that given in the curve. In other words, the capital markets actually prevent a self-destructive person from taking on a guaranteed loss.[9]

So far, Figure 11.6 is different from the earlier graphs. When only two securities are involved, all the combinations lie on a single curve. Conversely, with many securities the combinations cover an entire area. However, notice that an individual will want to be somewhere on the upper edge between MV and X. The upper edge, which we indicate in Figure 11.6 by a thick line, is called the *efficient set*. Any point below the efficient set would receive less expected return and the same standard deviation as a point on the efficient set. For example, consider R on the efficient set and W directly below it. If W contains the risk you desire, you should choose R instead in order to receive a higher expected return.

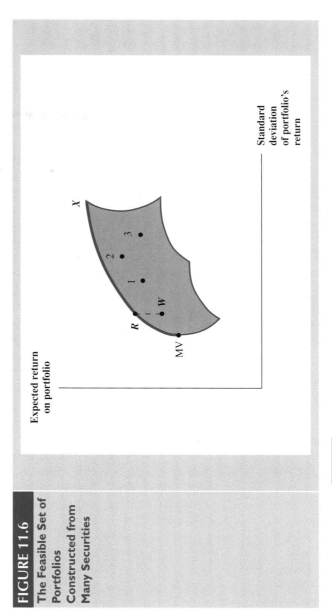

FIGURE 11.6

The Feasible Set of Portfolios Constructed from Many Securities

Expected return on portfolio

Standard deviation of portfolio's return

---

[9]Of course, someone dead set on parting with his money can do so. For example, he can trade frequently without purpose, so that commissions more than offset the positive expected returns on the portfolio.

In the final analysis, Figure 11.6 is quite similar to Figure 11.3. The efficient set in Figure 11.3 runs from MV to Supertech. It contains various combinations of the securities Supertech and Slowpoke. The efficient set in Figure 11.6 runs from MV to X. It contains various combinations of many securities. The fact that a whole shaded area appears in Figure 11.6 but not in Figure 11.3 is not an important difference; no investor would choose any point below the efficient set in Figure 11.6 anyway.

We mentioned earlier that an efficient set for two securities can be traced out easily in the real world. The task becomes more difficult when additional securities are included because the number of observations grows. For example, using subjective analysis to estimate expected returns and standard deviations for, say, 100 or 500 securities may very well become overwhelming, and the difficulties with correlations may be greater still. There are almost 5,000 correlations between pairs of securities from a universe of 100 securities.

Though much of the mathematics of efficient set computation had been derived in the 1950s,[10] the high cost of computer time restricted application of the principles. In recent years, the cost has been drastically reduced and a number of software packages allow the calculation of an efficient set for portfolios of moderate size. By all accounts, these packages sell quite briskly, so that our discussion above would appear to be important in practice.

Variance and Standard Deviation in a Portfolio of Many Assets

Earlier, we calculated the formulas for variance and standard deviation in the two-asset case. Because we considered a portfolio of many assets in Figure 11.6, it is worthwhile to calculate the formulas for variance and standard deviation in the many-asset case. The formula for the variance of a portfolio of many assets can be viewed as an extension of the formula for the variance of two assets.

To develop the formula, we employ the same type of matrix that we used in the two-asset case. This matrix is displayed in Table 11.4. Assuming that there are N assets, we write the numbers 1 through N on the horizontal axis and 1 through N on the vertical axis. This creates a matrix of $N \times N = N^2$ boxes.

TABLE 11.4		Matrix Used to Calculate the Variance of a Portfolio			
Stock	**1**	**2**	**3**	**...**	**N**
1	$X_1^2\sigma_1^2$	$X_1X_2\mathrm{Cov}(R_1,R_2)$	$X_1X_3\mathrm{Cov}(R_1,R_3)$		$X_1X_N\mathrm{Cov}(R_1,R_N)$
2	$X_2X_1\mathrm{Cov}(R_2,R_1)$	$X_2^2\sigma_2^2$	$X_2X_3\mathrm{Cov}(R_2,R_3)$		$X_2X_N\mathrm{Cov}(R_2,R_N)$
3	$X_3X_1\mathrm{Cov}(R_3,R_1)$	$X_3X_2\mathrm{Cov}(R_3,R_2)$	$X_3^2\sigma_3^2$		$X_3X_N\mathrm{Cov}(R_3,R_N)$
.					
.					
.					
N	$X_NX_1\mathrm{Cov}(R_N,R_1)$	$X_NX_2\mathrm{Cov}(R_N,R_2)$	$X_NX_3\mathrm{Cov}(R_N,R_3)$		$X_N^2\sigma_N^2$

- The variance of the portfolio is the sum of the terms in all the boxes.
- σ_i is the standard deviation of stock i.
- $\mathrm{Cov}(R_i, R_j)$ is the covariance between stock i and stock j.
- Terms involving the standard deviation of a single security appear on the diagonal. Terms involving covariance between two securities appear off the diagonal.

---

[10]The classic is Harry Markowitz, *Portfolio Selection* (New York: John Wiley & Sons, 1959). Markowitz shared the Nobel Prize in Economics in 1990 (with William Sharpe) for his work on modern portfolio theory.

Consider, for example, the box with a horizontal dimension of 2 and a vertical dimension of 3. The term in the box is $X_3 X_2 \text{Cov}(R_3, R_2)$. X_3 and X_2 are the percentages of the entire portfolio that are invested in the third asset and the second asset, respectively. For example, if an individual with a portfolio of $1,000 invests $100 in the second asset, $X_2 = 10\%$ (or $100/$1,000). $\text{Cov}(R_3, R_2)$ is the covariance between the returns on the third asset and the returns on the second asset. Next, note the box with a horizontal dimension of 3 and a vertical dimension of 2. The term in the box is $X_2 X_3 \text{Cov}(R_2, R_3)$. Because $\text{Cov}(R_3, R_2) = \text{Cov}(R_2, R_3)$, the two boxes have the same value. The second security and the third security make up one pair of stocks. In fact, every pair of stocks appears twice in the table: once in the lower left-hand side and once in the upper right-hand side.

Suppose that the vertical dimension equals the horizontal dimension. For example, the term in the box is $X_1^2 \sigma_1^2$ when both dimensions are 1. Here, σ_1^2 is the variance of the return on the first security.

Thus, the diagonal terms in the matrix contain the variances of the different stocks. The off-diagonal terms contain the covariances. Table 11.5 relates the numbers of diagonal and off-diagonal elements to the size of the matrix. The number of diagonal terms (number of variance terms) is always the same as the number of stocks in the portfolio. The number of off-diagonal terms (number of covariance terms) rises much faster than the number of diagonal terms. For example, a portfolio of 100 stocks has 9,900 covariance terms. Since the variance of a portfolio's returns is the sum of all the boxes, it follows that:

> The variance of the return on a portfolio with many securities is more dependent on the covariances between the individual securities than on the variances of the individual securities.

In a large portfolio, the number of terms involving covariance between two securities is much greater than the number of terms involving variance of a single security.

- **What is the formula for the variance of a portfolio for many assets?**
- **How can the formula be expressed in terms of a box or matrix?**

TABLE 11.5	Number of Variance and Covariance Terms as a Function of the Number of Stocks in the Portfolio		
Number of Stocks in Portfolio	Total Number of Terms	Number of Variance Terms (number of terms on diagonal)	Number of Covariance Terms (number of terms off diagonal)
1	1	1	0
2	4	2	2
3	9	3	6
10	100	10	90
100	10,000	100	9,900
.	.	.	.
.	.	.	.
N	N^2	N	$N^2 - N$

In a large portfolio, the number of terms involving covariance between two securities is much greater than the number of terms involving variance of a single security.

11.6 Diversification: An Example

The above point can be illustrated by altering the matrix in Table 11.4 slightly. Suppose that we make the following three assumptions:

1. All securities possess the same variance, which we write as $\overline{\text{var}}$. In other words, $\sigma_i^2 = \overline{\text{var}}$ for every security.

2. All covariances in Table 11.4 are the same. We represent this uniform covariance as $\overline{\text{cov}}$. In other words, $\text{Cov}(R_i, R_j) = \overline{\text{cov}}$ for every pair of securities. It can easily be shown that $\overline{\text{var}} > \overline{\text{cov}}$.

3. All securities are equally weighted in the portfolio. Because there are N assets, the weight of each asset in the portfolio is $1/N$. In other words, $X_i = 1/N$ for each security i.

Table 11.6 is the matrix of variances and covariances under these three simplifying assumptions. Note that all of the diagonal terms are identical. Similarly, all of the off-diagonal terms are identical. As with Table 11.4, the variance of the portfolio is the sum of the terms of the boxes in Table 11.6. We know that there are N diagonal terms involving variance. Similarly, there are $N \times (N - 1)$ off-diagonal terms involving covariance. Summing across all the boxes in Table 11.6, we can express the variances of the portfolio as

$$
\begin{aligned}
\text{Variance of portfolio} \;=\; & N \quad\; \times \left(\frac{1}{N^2}\right)\overline{\text{var}} + N(N-1) \;\times\; \left(\frac{1}{N^2}\right)\overline{\text{cov}} \qquad (11.10) \\[4pt]
& \underset{\substack{\text{Number of} \\ \text{diagonal} \\ \text{terms}}}{} \;\; \underset{\substack{\text{Each} \\ \text{diagonal} \\ \text{term}}}{} \qquad \underset{\substack{\text{Number of} \\ \text{off-diagonal} \\ \text{terms}}}{} \qquad \underset{\substack{\text{Each} \\ \text{off-diagonal} \\ \text{term}}}{} \\[6pt]
=\; & \left(\frac{1}{N}\right)\overline{\text{var}} + \left(\frac{N^2 - N}{N^2}\right)\overline{\text{cov}} \\[6pt]
=\; & \left(\frac{1}{N}\right)\overline{\text{var}} + \left(1 - \frac{1}{N}\right)\overline{\text{cov}}
\end{aligned}
$$

Equation (11.10) expresses the variance of our special portfolio as a weighted sum of the average security variance and the average covariance.[11] The intuition is confirmed when

TABLE 11.6	Matrix Used to Calculate the Variance of a Portfolio*				
Stock	1	2	3	...	N
1	$(1/N^2)\overline{\text{var}}$	$(1/N^2)\overline{\text{cov}}$	$(1/N^2)\overline{\text{cov}}$		$(1/N^2)\overline{\text{cov}}$
2	$(1/N^2)\overline{\text{cov}}$	$(1/N^2)\overline{\text{var}}$	$(1/N^2)\overline{\text{cov}}$		$(1/N^2)\overline{\text{cov}}$
3	$(1/N^2)\overline{\text{cov}}$	$(1/N^2)\overline{\text{cov}}$	$(1/N^2)\overline{\text{var}}$		$(1/N^2)\overline{\text{cov}}$
.					
.					
.					
N	$(1/N^2)\overline{\text{cov}}$	$(1/N^2)\overline{\text{cov}}$	$(1/N^2)\overline{\text{cov}}$		$(1/N^2)\overline{\text{var}}$

*When
a. All securities possess the same variance, which we represent as $\overline{\text{var}}$.
b. All pairs of securities possess the same covariance, which we represent as $\overline{\text{cov}}$.
c. All securities are held in the same proportion, which is 1/N.

we increase the number of securities in the portfolio without limit. The variance of the portfolio becomes

$$\text{Variance of portfolio (when } N \rightarrow \infty) = \overline{\text{cov}} \qquad (11.11)$$

This occurs because (1) the weight on the variance term, $1/N$, goes to 0 as N goes to infinity and (2) the weight on the covariance term, $1 - 1/N$, goes to 1 as N goes to infinity.

Equation (11.11) provides an interesting and important result. In our special portfolio, the variances of the individual securities completely vanish as the number of securities becomes large. However, the covariance terms remain. In fact, the variance of the portfolio becomes the average covariance, $\overline{\text{cov}}$. One often hears that one should diversify. You should not put all your eggs in one basket. The effect of diversification on the risk of a portfolio can be illustrated in this example. The variances of the individual securities are diversified away, but the covariance terms cannot be diversified away.

The fact that part, but not all, of one's risk can be diversified away should be explored. Consider Mr. Smith, who brings $1,000 to the roulette table at a casino. It would be very risky if he put all his money on one spin of the wheel. For example, imagine that he put the full $1,000 on red at the table. If the wheel showed red, he would get $2,000, but if the wheel showed black, he would lose everything. Suppose, instead, that he divided his money over 1,000 different spins by betting $1 at a time on red. Probability theory tells us that he could count on winning about 50 percent of the time. In other words, he could count on pretty nearly getting all his original $1,000 back.[12]

Now, let's contrast this with our stock market example, which we illustrate in Figure 11.7. The variance of the portfolio with only one security is, of course, var, because the variance of a portfolio with one security is the variance of the security. The variance of the portfolio drops as more securities are added, which is evidence of the diversification effect. However, unlike Mr. Smith's roulette example, the portfolio's variance can never drop to zero. Rather it reaches a floor of $\overline{\text{cov}}$, which is the covariance of each pair of securities.[13]

Because the variance of the portfolio asymptotically approaches $\overline{\text{cov}}$, each additional security continues to reduce risk. Thus, if there were neither commissions nor other transactions costs, it could be argued that one can never achieve too much diversification. However, there is a cost to diversification in the real world. Commissions per dollar invested fall as one makes larger purchases in a single stock. Unfortunately, one must buy fewer shares of each security when buying more and more different securities. Comparing the costs and benefits of diversification, Meir Statman argues that a portfolio of about 30 stocks is needed to achieve optimal diversification. Sean Cleary and David Copp find that, for Canadian investors, the number of stocks needed is 30 to 50. This higher number is likely because Canadian stocks are more concentrated in a few industries.[14]

We mentioned earlier that $\overline{\text{var}}$ must be greater than $\overline{\text{cov}}$. Thus, the variance of a security's return can be broken down in the following way:

Total risk of individual security	=	Portfolio risk	+	Unsystematic or diversible risk
($\overline{\text{var}}$)		($\overline{\text{cov}}$)		($\overline{\text{var}} - \overline{\text{cov}}$)

---

[11] Equation (11.10) is actually a weighted average of the variance and covariance terms because the weights, $1/N$ and $1 - 1/N$, sum to 1.

[12] This example ignores the casino's cut.

[13] Though it is harder to show, this risk reduction effect also applies to the general case where variances and covariances are *not* equal.

[14] Meir Statman, "How Many Stocks Make a Diversified Portfolio?" *Journal of Financial and Quantitative Analysis* (September 1987); Sean Cleary and David Copp, "Diversification with Canadian Stocks: How Much Is Enough?" *Canadian Investment Review* (Fall 1999).

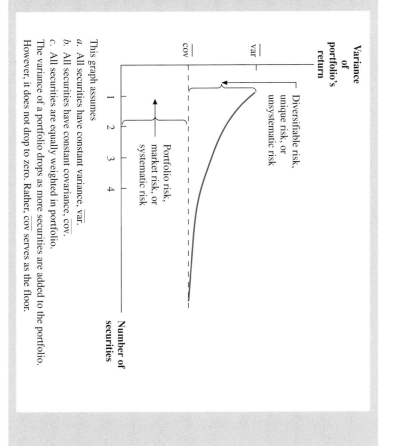

This graph assumes

a. All securities have constant variance, $\overline{\text{var}}$.
b. All securities have constant covariance, $\overline{\text{cov}}$.
c. All securities are equally weighted in portfolio.

The variance of a portfolio drops as more securities are added to the portfolio. However, it does not drop to zero. Rather, $\overline{\text{cov}}$ serves as the floor.

Total risk, which is $\overline{\text{var}}$ in our example, is the risk that one bears by holding one security only. *Portfolio risk* is the risk that one still bears after achieving full diversification, which is $\overline{\text{cov}}$ in our example. Portfolio risk is often called **systematic** or **market risk** as well. **Diversifiable, unique,** or **unsystematic risk** is that risk that can be diversified away in a large portfolio, which must be $(\overline{\text{var}} - \overline{\text{cov}})$ by definition.

To an individual who selects a diversified portfolio, the total risk of an individual security is not important. When considering adding a security to a diversified portfolio, the individual cares about that portion of the risk of a security that cannot be diversified away. This risk can alternatively be viewed as the *contribution* of a security to the risk of an entire portfolio. We will talk later about the case where securities make different contributions to the risk of the entire portfolio.

Risk and the Sensible Investor

Having gone to all this trouble to show that unsystematic risk disappears in a well-diversified portfolio, how do we know that investors even want such portfolios? Suppose they like risk and don't want it to disappear?

We must admit that, theoretically at least, this is possible, but we will argue that it does not describe what we think of as the typical investor. Our typical investor is **risk averse.** Risk-averse behaviour can be defined in many ways, but we prefer the following example: A fair gamble is one with zero expected return; a risk-averse investor would prefer to avoid fair gambles.

Why do investors choose well-diversified portfolios? Our answer is that they are risk averse, and risk-averse people avoid unnecessary risk, such as the unsystematic risk on a stock. If you do not think this is much of an answer to why investors choose well-diversified portfolios and avoid unsystematic risk, consider whether you would take on such a risk. For example, suppose you had worked all summer and had saved $5,000, which you intended to use for university expenses. Now, suppose someone came up to you and offered to flip a coin for the money: heads, you would double your money, and tails, you would lose it all.

Would you take such a bet? Perhaps you would, but the average investor would not. To induce the typical risk-averse investor to take a fair gamble, you must sweeten the pot. For example, you might need to raise the odds of winning from 50–50 to 70–30 or higher. The risk-averse investor can be induced to take fair gambles only if they are sweetened so that they become unfair to the investor's advantage.

Beyond risk aversion, the tremendous growth of mutual funds and exchange-traded funds in recent years strongly suggests that investors want diversified portfolios. *Mutual funds* pool funds from individual investors, allowing them to own units in large, diversified portfolios. Exchange-traded funds (ETFs) are trusts that track a market index such as the Standard & Poor's 500, the S&P/TSX 60, or the Nikkei. They trade on the New York Stock Exchange and the TSX. By holding such funds, individuals can achieve wide diversification across securities and markets around the world.

- **What are the two components of the total risk of a security?**
- **Why doesn't diversification eliminate all risk?**
- **How is risk aversion defined?**

11.7 Riskless Borrowing and Lending

In constructing Figure 11.6, we assume that all the securities on the efficient set are risky. Alternatively, an investor could easily combine a risky investment with an investment in a riskless or risk-free security, such as an investment in Canada Treasury bills. This is illustrated in the following example.

EXAMPLE

Zorana Sadiq is considering investing in the common stock of Princess Enterprises. In addition, Ms. Sadiq will either borrow or lend at the risk-free rate. The relevant parameters are

	Expected Return on Common Stock of Princess	Guaranteed Return on Risk-Free Asset
Return	14%	3%
Standard deviation	0.20	0

Suppose Ms. Sadiq chooses to invest a total of $1,000: $350 is invested in Princess Enterprises and $650 in the risk-free asset. The expected return on her total investment is simply a weighted average of the two returns:

Expected return on portfolio
composed of one riskless $= 0.069 = (0.35 \times 0.14) + (0.65 \times 0.03)$ **(11.12)**
and one risky asset

Because the expected return on the portfolio is a weighted average of the expected return on the risky asset (Princess Enterprises) and the risk-free return, the calculation is analogous to the way we treated two risky assets. In other words, Equation (11.3) applies here.

Using Equation (11.4), the formula for the variance of the portfolio can be written as

$$X^2_{\text{Princess}}\sigma^2_{\text{Princess}} + 2X_{\text{Princess}}X_{\text{Risk-free}}\sigma_{\text{Princess,Risk-free}} + X^2_{\text{Risk-free}}\sigma^2_{\text{Risk-free}}$$

However, by definition, the risk-free asset has no variability. Thus, both $\sigma_{\text{Princess,Risk-free}}$ and $\sigma^2_{\text{Risk-free}}$ are equal to zero, reducing the above expression to

Variance of portfolio
composed of one $= X^2_{\text{Princess}}\sigma^2_{\text{Princess}} = (0.35)^2 \times (0.20)^2 = 0.0049$ (11.13)
riskless and one
risky asset

The standard deviation of the portfolio is

Standard deviation of
portfolio composed $= X_{\text{Princess}}\sigma_{\text{Princess}} = 0.35 \times 0.20 = 0.07$ (11.14)
of one riskless and
one risky asset

The relationship between risk and return for one risky and one riskless asset can be seen in Figure 11.8. Ms. Sadiq's split of 35–65 percent between the two assets is represented on a *straight* line between the risk-free rate and a pure investment in Princess Enterprises. Note that, unlike the case of two risky assets, the opportunity set is straight, not curved.

Suppose that, alternatively, Ms. Sadiq borrows $200 at the risk-free rate. Combining this with her original sum of $1,000, she invests a total of $1,200 in Princess Enterprises. Her expected return would be

The standard deviation is

Expected return on portfolio
formed by borrowing $= 14.8\% = 1.20 \times 0.14 + (-0.2) \times 0.10$
to invest in risky asset

Here, she invests 120 percent of her original investment of $1,000 by borrowing 20 percent of her original investment. Note that the return of 14.8 percent is greater than the 14 percent expected return on Princess Enterprises. This occurs because she is borrowing at 3 percent to invest in a security with an expected return greater than 3 percent.

The standard deviation is

Standard deviation of portfolio formed
by borrowing to invest in risky asset $= 1.20 \times 0.2 = 0.24$

The standard deviation of 0.24 is greater than 0.20, the standard deviation of Princess Enterprises, because borrowing increases the variability of the investment. This investment also appears in Figure 11.8.

So far, we have assumed that Ms. Sadiq is able to borrow at the same rate at which she can lend.[15] Now let us consider the case where the borrowing rate is above the lending rate. The dotted line in Figure 11.8 illustrates the opportunity set for borrowing opportunities in this case. The dotted line is below the solid line because a higher borrowing rate lowers the expected return on the investment.

---

[15]Surprisingly, this appears to be a decent approximation because a large number of investors are able to borrow on margin when purchasing stocks. The borrowing rate on the margin is very near the riskless rate of interest, particularly for large investors. More will be said about this in a later chapter. Also note that portfolio weights can be negative when investors sell a stock short. Short selling involves borrowing the stock and selling it today with the plan to cover the short in the future by buying back the stock at a lower price. With short selling, the line in Figure 11.8 extends to the left of the vertical axis.

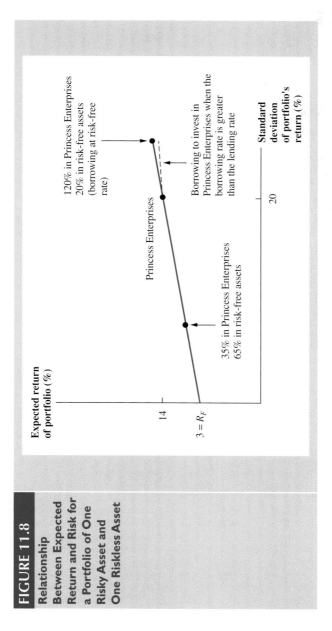

FIGURE 11.8

Relationship Between Expected Return and Risk for a Portfolio of One Risky Asset and One Riskless Asset

Expected return of portfolio (%)

120% in Princess Enterprises
20% in risk-free assets
(borrowing at risk-free rate)

Princess Enterprises

Borrowing to invest in Princess Enterprises when the borrowing rate is greater than the lending rate

35% in Princess Enterprises
65% in risk-free assets

14

$3 = R_F$

20

Standard deviation of portfolio's return (%)

The Optimal Portfolio

The previous section analyzed a portfolio of one riskless asset and one risky asset. In reality, an investor is likely to combine an investment in the riskless asset with a portfolio of risky assets. This is illustrated in Figure 11.9.

Consider point Q, representing a portfolio of securities. Point Q is in the interior of the feasible set of risky securities. Let us assume the point represents a portfolio of 30 percent in BCE Inc. (BCE), 45 percent in Canadian Imperial Bank of Commerce (CIBC), and 25 percent in Inco. Individuals combining investments in Q with investments in the riskless asset would achieve points along the straight line from R_F to Q. We refer to this as line I. For example, point 1 represents a portfolio of 70 percent in the riskless asset and 30 percent in stocks represented by Q. An investor with $100 choosing point 1 as his portfolio would put $70 in the risk-free asset and $30 in Q. This can be restated as $70 in the riskless asset, $9 (or $0.3 × $30) in BCE, $13.50 (or $0.45 × $30) in CIBC, and $7.50 (or $0.25 × $30) in Inco. Point 2 also represents a portfolio of the risk-free asset and Q, with more (65 percent) being invested in Q.

Point 3 is obtained by borrowing to invest in Q. For example, an investor with $100 of his or her own would borrow $40 from the bank or broker in order to invest $140 in Q. This can be stated as borrowing $40 and contributing $100 of one's own money in order to invest $42 (or $0.3 × $140) in BCE, $63 (or $0.45 × $140) in CIBC, and $35 (or $0.25 × $140) in Inco.

Though any investor can obtain any point on line I, no point on the line is optimal. To see this, consider line II, a line running from R_F through A. Point A represents another portfolio of risky securities. Line II represents portfolios formed by combinations of the risk-free asset and the securities in A. Points between R_F and A are portfolios in which some money is invested in the riskless asset and the rest is placed in A. Points past A are achieved by borrowing at the riskless rate to buy more of A than one could with one's original funds alone.

As drawn, line II is tangent to the efficient set of risky securities. Whatever point an individual can obtain on line I, he or she can obtain a point with the same standard deviation and a higher expected return on line II. In fact, because line II is tangent to the efficient

FIGURE 11.9
Relationship Between Expected Return and Standard Deviation for an Investment in a Combination of Risky Securities and the Riskless Asset

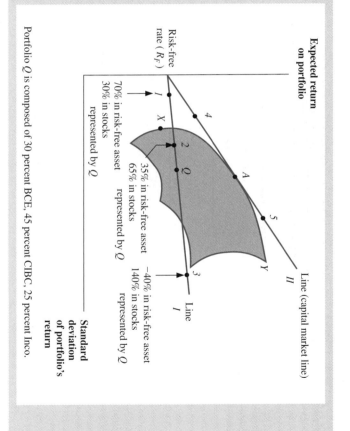

Expected return on portfolio

Line (capital market line)

Risk-free rate (R_F)

Line *II*

1

X

4

2

Q

35% in risk-free asset
65% in stocks
represented by *Q*

70% in risk-free asset
30% in stocks
represented by *Q*

A

5

Y

3

Line *I*

−40% in risk-free asset
140% in stocks
represented by *Q*

Standard deviation of portfolio's return

Portfolio *Q* is composed of 30 percent BCE, 45 percent CIBC, 25 percent Inco.

---

set, it provides the investor with the best possible opportunities. In other words, line *II*, which is frequently called the **capital market line**, can be viewed as the efficient set of all assets, both risky and riskless. An investor with a fair degree of risk aversion might choose a point between R_F and *A*, perhaps point 4. An individual with a lower degree of risk aversion might choose a point closer to *A* or even beyond *A*. For example, point 5 is achieved when an individual borrows money to increase an investment in *A*.

The graph illustrates an important point. With riskless borrowing and lending, the portfolio of risky assets held by any investor would always be point *A*. Regardless of the investor's tolerance for risk, he or she would never choose any other point on the efficient set of risky assets (represented by curve *XAY*) or any point in the interior of the feasible region. Rather, the investor would combine the securities of *A* with the riskless assets if he or she had high aversion to risk and would borrow the riskless asset to invest more funds in *A* if he or she had low aversion to risk.

This result establishes what financial economists call the **separation principle**. That is, the investor makes two separate decisions:

1. After estimating (a) the expected return and variances of individual securities and (b) the covariances between pairs of securities, the investor calculates the efficient set of risky assets, represented by curve *XAY* in Figure 11.9, and determines point *A*, the tangency between the risk-free rate and the efficient set of risky assets (curve *XAY*). Point *A* represents the portfolio of risky assets that the investor will hold. This point is determined solely from estimates of returns, variances, and covariances. No personal characteristics, such as degree of risk aversion, are needed in this step.

2. The investor must now determine how to combine point *A*, the portfolio of risky assets, with the riskless asset. He or she could invest some of the funds in the riskless asset and some in portfolio *A*. The investor would end up at a point on the line between R_F and *A* in this case. Alternatively, the investor could borrow at the risk-free rate and contribute some personal funds as well, investing the sum in portfolio *A*. He or she would end up at a point on line *II* beyond *A*. The investor's position in the riskless asset (that is, the choice

of where on the line he or she wants to be) is determined by internal characteristics, such as the investor's ability to tolerate risk.

Concept Questions

- **What is the formula for the standard deviation of a portfolio composed of one riskless and one risky asset?**
- **How does one determine the optimal portfolio among the efficient set of risky assets?**

11.8 Market Equilibrium

Definition of the Market Equilibrium Portfolio

The above analysis concerns one investor. Estimates of the expected returns and variances for individual securities and the covariances between pairs of securities are unique to this individual. Other investors would obviously have different estimates of these variables. However, the estimates might not vary much because all investors would be forming expectations from the same data on past price movement and other publicly available information.

Financial economists often imagine a world where all investors possess the same estimates of expected returns, variances, and covariances. Though this can never be literally true, it can be thought of as a useful simplifying assumption in a world where investors have access to similar sources of information. This assumption is called **homogeneous expectations**.[16]

If investors have homogeneous expectations, Figure 11.9 would be the same for all individuals. That is, all investors would sketch out the same efficient set of risky assets because they would be working with the same inputs. This efficient set of risky assets is represented by the curve *XAY*. Because the same risk-free rate would apply to everyone, all investors would view point *A* as the portfolio of risky assets to be held.

This point *A* takes on great importance because all investors would purchase the risky securities that it represents. Those investors with a high degree of risk aversion might combine *A* with an investment in the riskless asset, achieving point 4, for example. Others with low aversion to risk might borrow to achieve, say, point 5. Because this is a very important conclusion, we restate it:

In a world with homogeneous expectations, all investors would hold the portfolio of risky assets represented by point *A*.

If all investors choose the same portfolio of risky assets, it is possible to determine what that portfolio is. Common sense tells us that it is a market-value weighted portfolio of all existing securities. It is the **market portfolio**.[17]

In practice, financial economists use a broad-based index such as the S&P/TSX 60 as a proxy for the market portfolio. Of course, all investors do not hold the same portfolio in practice. However, we know that a large number of investors hold diversified portfolios, particularly when mutual funds or pension funds are included. A broad-based index is a good proxy for the highly diversified portfolios of many investors.

---

[16]The assumption of homogeneous expectations states that all investors have the same beliefs concerning returns, variances, and covariances. It does not say that all investors have the same aversion to risk.

[17]By "market-value weighted," we mean that the percentage weight of each stock is the market value of the company's equity divided by the total market capitalization.

Definition of Risk When Investors Hold the Market Portfolio

The previous section states that many investors hold diversified portfolios similar to broad-based indexes. This result allows us to measure the risk of a security in the context of a diversified portfolio as the *beta* of the security. We illustrate beta by an example.

Consider the following possible returns on both the stock of Jelco, Inc., and on the market:

State	Type of Economy	Return on Market (percent)	Return on Jelco, Inc. (percent)
I	Bull	15	25
II	Bull	15	15
III	Bear	−5	−5
IV	Bear	−5	−15

Though the return on the market has only two possible outcomes (15 percent and −5 percent), the return on Jelco has four possible outcomes. It is helpful to consider the expected return on a security for a given return on the market. Assuming each state is equally likely, we have

Type of Economy	Return on Market (percent)	Expected Return on Jelco, Inc. (percent)
Bull	15%	20% = 25% × ½ + 15% × ½
Bear	−5%	−10% = −5% × ½ + (−15%) × ½

Jelco, Inc., responds to market movements because its expected return is greater in bullish states than in bearish states. We now calculate exactly how responsive the security is to market movements. The market's return in a bullish economy is 20 percent [15% − (−5%)] greater than the market's return in a bearish economy. However, the expected return on Jelco in a bullish economy is 30 percent [20% − (−10%)] greater than its expected return in a bearish state. Thus, Jelco, Inc., has a responsiveness coefficient of 1.5 (30%/20%).

This relationship appears in Figure 11.10. The returns for both Jelco and the market in each state are plotted as four points. In addition, we plot the expected return on the security for each of the two possible returns on the market. These two points, each of which we designate by an X, are joined by a line called the **characteristic line** of the security. The slope of the line is 1.5, the number calculated in the previous paragraph. This responsiveness coefficient of 1.5 is the **beta** of Jelco.

The interpretation of beta from Figure 11.10 is intuitive. The graph tells us that the returns of Jelco are magnified 1.5 times over those of the market. When the market does well, Jelco's stock is expected to do even better. When the market does poorly, Jelco's stock is expected to do even worse. Now imagine an individual with a portfolio near that of the market who is considering the addition of Jelco to his portfolio. Because of Jelco's *magnification factor* of 1.5, he will view this stock as contributing much to the risk of the portfolio. (We will show shortly that the beta of the average security in the market is 1.) Jelco contributes more to the risk of a large, diversified portfolio than does an average security because Jelco is more responsive to movements in the market.

FIGURE 11.10

Performance of Jelco, Inc., and the Market Portfolio

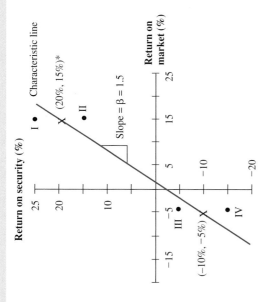

The two points marked X represent the expected return on Jelco for each possible outcome of the market portfolio. The expected return on Jelco is positively related to the return on the market. Because the slope is 1.5, we say that Jelco's beta is 1.5. Beta measures the responsiveness of the security's return to movement in the market.
*(20%, 15%) refers to the point where the return on the security is 20 percent and the return on the market is 15 percent.

Further insight can be gleaned by examining securities with negative betas. One should view these securities as either hedges or insurance policies. The security is expected to do well when the market does poorly and vice versa. Because of this, adding a negative-beta security to a large, diversified portfolio actually reduces the risk of the portfolio.[18]

Table 11.7 presents empirical estimates of betas for individual securities. As can be seen, some securities are more responsive to the market than others. For example, Research

TABLE 11.7   **Estimates of Beta for Selected Individual Stocks**

Stock	Beta
High-beta stocks	
Research in Motion	3.04
Nortel Networks	3.61
Average-beta stocks	
Bank of Nova Scotia	0.28
Bombardier	1.48
Investors Group	0.36
Maple Leaf Foods	0.25
Rogers Communication	1.17
Low-beta stocks	
Canadian Utilities	0.08
TransCanada Power	0.08

Source: *Financial Post Investor Suite*

---

[18]Unfortunately, empirical evidence shows that virtually no stocks have negative betas.

in Motion (RIM) has a beta of 3.04. This means that, for every 1 percent movement in the market,[19] RIM is expected to move 3.04 percent in the same direction. Conversely, Canadian Utilities has a beta of only 0.08. This means that, for every 1 percent movement in the market, Canadian Utilities is expected to move 0.08 percent in the same direction.

We can summarize our discussion of beta by saying:

> Beta measures the responsiveness of a security to movements in the market portfolio.

The Formula for Beta

Our discussion so far has stressed the intuition behind beta. The actual definition of beta is

$$\beta_i = \frac{\text{Cov}(R_i, R_M)}{\sigma^2(R_M)} \quad (11.15)$$

where $\text{Cov}(R_i, R_M)$ is the covariance between the return on asset i and the return on the market portfolio and $\sigma^2(R_M)$ is the variance of the market.

One useful property is that the average beta across all securities, when weighted by the proportion of each security's market value to that of the market portfolio, is 1. That is,

$$\sum_{i=1}^{N} X_i \beta_i = 1 \quad (11.16)$$

where X_i is the proportion of security i's market value to that of the entire market and N is the number of securities in the market.

Equation (11.16) is intuitive, once you think about it. If you weight all securities by their market values, the resulting portfolio is the market. By definition, the beta of the market portfolio is 1. That is, for every 1 percent movement in the market, the market must move 1 percent—*by definition*.

A Test

We have put these questions on past corporate finance examinations:

1. What sort of investor rationally views the variance (or standard deviation) of an individual security's return as the security's proper measure of risk?

2. What sort of investor rationally views the beta of a security as the security's proper measure of risk?

A good answer might be something like the following:

> A rational, risk-averse investor views the variance (or standard deviation) of her portfolio's return as the proper measure of the risk of her portfolio. If for some reason or another the investor can hold only one security, the variance of that security's return becomes the variance of the portfolio's return. Hence, the variance of the security's return is the security's proper measure of risk.
>
> If an individual holds a diversified portfolio, she still views the variance (or standard deviation) of her portfolio's return as the proper measure of the risk of her portfolio. However, she is no longer interested in the variance of each individual security's return. Rather, she is interested in the contribution of an individual security to the variance of the portfolio.

---

[19] Table 11.7 uses the S&P/TSX 60 as the proxy for the market portfolio and obtains betas from the *Financial Post Investor Suite*. Other sources include Bloomberg and Yahoo Finance.

Under the assumption of homogeneous expectations, all individuals hold the market portfolio. Thus, we measure risk as the contribution of an individual security to the variance of the market portfolio. This contribution, when standardized properly, is the beta of the security. While very few investors hold the market portfolio exactly, many hold reasonably diversified portfolios. These portfolios are close enough to the market portfolio so that the beta of a security is likely to be a reasonable measure of its risk.

? Concept Questions

- If all investors have homogeneous expectations, what portfolio of risky assets do they hold?
- What is the formula for beta?
- Why is beta the appropriate measure of risk for a single security in a large portfolio?

11.9 Relationship Between Risk and Expected Return (CAPM)

It is commonplace to argue that the expected return on an asset should be positively related to its risk. That is, individuals will hold a risky asset only if its expected return compensates for its risk. In this section, we first estimate the expected return on the stock market as a whole. Next, we estimate expected returns on individual securities.

Expected Return on Market

Financial economists frequently argue that the expected return on the market can be represented as:

$$\overline{R}_M = R_F + \text{Risk premium}$$

In words, the expected return on the market is the sum of the risk-free rate plus some compensation for the risk inherent in the market portfolio. Note that the equation refers to the *expected* return on the market, not the actual return in a particular month or year. Because stocks have risk, the actual return on the market over a particular period can, of course, be below R_F, or can even be negative.

Since investors want compensation for risk, the risk premium is presumably positive. But exactly how positive is it? It is generally argued that the best estimate for the risk premium in the future is the average risk premium in the past. As reported in Chapter 10, the expected return on common stocks was 10.64 percent over 1957–2003. The average risk-free rate over the same time interval was 6.80 percent. Thus, the average difference between the two was 3.84 percent (10.64% − 6.80%). Financial economists find this to be a useful estimate of the difference to occur in the future. We will use it frequently in this text.[20]

For example, if the risk-free rate, generally estimated by the yield on a one-year Treasury bill, is 5 percent, the expected return on the market is

$$5\% + 3.84\% = 8.84\%$$

---

[20]This is not the only way to estimate the market-risk premium. In fact, there are several useful ways to estimate the market-risk premium. One could argue that the long-term government bond return is the best measure of the long-term historical risk-free rate. With this empirical version of the CAPM, one would use the current long-term government bond return to estimate the current risk-free rate.

Expected Return on an Individual Security

Now that we have estimated the expected return on the market as a whole, what is the expected return on an individual security? We have argued that the beta of a security is the appropriate measure of risk in a large, diversified portfolio. Since most investors are diversified, the expected return on a security should be positively related to its beta. This is illustrated in Figure 11.11.

Actually, financial economists can be more precise about the relationship between expected return and beta. They posit that, under plausible conditions, the relationship between expected return and beta can be represented by the following equation.[21]

Capital Asset Pricing Model:

$\overline{R}$	=	R_F	+	β	$\times$	$(\overline{R}_M - R_F)$	(11.17)
Expected return on a security	=	Risk-free rate	+	Beta of the security	$\times$	Difference between expected return on market and risk-free rate	

This formula, which is called the **capital asset pricing model** (or CAPM for short), implies that the expected return on a security is linearly related to its beta. Since the average return on the market has been higher than the average risk-free rate over long periods of time, $\overline{R}_M - R_F$ is presumably positive. Thus, the formula implies that the expected return on a security is *positively* related to its beta. The formula can be illustrated by assuming a few special cases:

- *Assume that* $\beta = 0$. Here $\overline{R} = R_F$, that is, the expected return on the security is equal to the risk-free rate. Because a security with zero beta has no relevant risk, its expected return should equal the risk-free rate.

- *Assume that* $\beta = 1$. Equation (11.17) reduces to $\overline{R} = \overline{R}_M$. That is, the expected return on the security is equal to the expected return on the market. This makes sense since the beta of the market portfolio is also 1.

---
[21] This relationship was first proposed independently by John Lintner and William F. Sharpe.

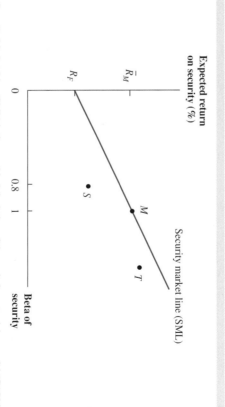

The Security Market Line (SML) is the graphical depiction of the capital asset pricing model (CAPM). The expected return on a stock with a beta of 0 is equal to the risk-free rate. The expected return on a stock with a beta of 1 is equal to the expected return on the market.

Formula (11.17) can be represented graphically by the upward sloping line in Figure 10.11. Note that the line begins at R_F and rises to $\overline{R}_M$ when beta is 1. This line is frequently called the **security market line** (SML).

As with any line, the SML has both a slope and an intercept. R_F, the risk-free rate, is the intercept. Because the beta of a security is the horizontal axis, $\overline{R}_M - R_F$ is the slope. The line will be upward sloping as long as the expected return on the market is greater than the risk-free rate. Because the market portfolio is a risky asset, theory suggests that its expected return is above the risk-free rate. In addition, the empirical evidence of the previous chapter showed that the average return per year on the market portfolio over the past 50 years was 3.84 percent above the risk-free rate.

EXAMPLE

The stock of Aardvark Enterprises has a beta of 1.5 and that of Zebra Enterprises has a beta of 0.7. The risk-free rate is 5 percent, and the difference between the expected return on the market and the risk-free rate is 3.84 percent. The expected returns on the two securities are:

Expected Return for Aardvark:

$$10.76\% = 5\% + 1.5 \times 3.84\% \tag{11.18}$$

Expected Return for Zebra:

$$7.69\% = 5\% + 0.7 \times 3.84\%$$

Three additional points concerning the CAPM should be mentioned:

1. *Linearity.* The intuition behind an upwardly sloping curve is clear. Because beta is the appropriate measure of risk, high-beta securities should have an expected return above that of low-beta securities. However, both Figure 11.11 and Equation (11.17) show something more than an upwardly sloping curve; the relationship between expected return and beta corresponds to a *straight* line.

It is easy to show that the line of Figure 11.11 is straight. To see this, consider security S with, say, a beta of 0.8. This security is represented by a point below the security market line in the figure. Any investor could duplicate the beta of security S by buying a portfolio with 20 percent in the risk-free asset and 80 percent in a security with a beta of 1. However, the homemade portfolio would itself lie on the SML. In other words, the portfolio dominates security S because the portfolio has a higher expected return and the same beta.

Now consider security T with, say, a beta greater than 1. This security is also below the SML in Figure 11.11. Any investor could duplicate the beta of security T by borrowing to invest in a security with a beta of 1. This portfolio must also lie on the SML, thereby dominating security T.

Because no one would hold either S or T, their stock prices would drop. This price adjustment would raise the expected returns on the two securities. The price adjustment would continue until the two securities lay on the security market line. The preceding example considered two overpriced stocks and a straight SML. Securities lying above the SML are *underpriced*. Their prices must rise until their expected returns lie on the line. If the SML is itself curved, many stocks would be mispriced. In equilibrium, all securities would be held only when prices changed so that the SML became straight. In other words, linearity would be achieved.

2. *Portfolios as well as securities.* Our discussion of the CAPM considered individual securities. Does the relationship in Figure 11.11 and Equation (11.17) hold for portfolios as well?

Yes. To see this, consider a portfolio formed by investing equally in our two securities, Aardvark and Zebra. The expected return on the portfolio is

Expected Return on Portfolio:

$$9.23\% = 0.5 \times 10.76\% + 0.5 \times 7.69\%$$ (11.19)

The beta of the portfolio is simply a weighted average of the betas of the two securities. Thus we have

Beta of Portfolio:

$$1.1 = 0.5 \times 1.5 + 0.5 \times 0.7$$

Under the CAPM, the expected return on the portfolio is

$$9.23\% = 5\% + 1.1 \times 3.84\%$$ (11.20)

Because the expected return in (11.19) is the same as the expected return in (11.20), the example shows that the CAPM holds for portfolios as well as for individual securities.

3. A potential confusion. Students often confuse the SML in Figure 11.11 with line *II* in Figure 11.9. Actually, the lines are quite different. Line *II* traces the efficient set of portfolios formed from both risky assets and the riskless asset. Each point on the line represents an entire portfolio. Point A is a portfolio composed entirely of risky assets. Every other point on the line represents a portfolio of the securities in A combined with the riskless asset. The axes on Figure 11.9 are the expected return on a *portfolio* and the standard deviation of a *portfolio*. Individual securities do not lie along line *II*.

The SML in Figure 11.11 relates expected return to beta. Figure 11.11 differs from Figure 11.9 in at least two ways. First, beta appears in the horizontal axis of Figure 11.11, but standard deviation appears in the horizontal axis of Figure 11.9. Second, the SML in Figure 11.11 holds both for all individual securities and for all possible portfolios, whereas line *II* in Figure 11.9 holds only for efficient portfolios.

We stated earlier that, under homogeneous expectations, point A in Figure 11.9 becomes the market portfolio. In this situation, line *II* is referred to as the capital market line (CML).

11.10   SUMMARY AND CONCLUSIONS

This chapter sets forth the fundamentals of modern portfolio theory and the pricing of capital assets. Our basic points are these:

1. This chapter shows us how to calculate the expected return and variance for individual securities, and the covariance and correlation for pairs of securities. Given these statistics, the expected return and variance for a portfolio of two securities A and B can be written as

$$\text{Expected return on portfolio} = X_A \bar{R}_A + X_B \bar{R}_B$$

$$\text{Var(portfolio)} = X_A^2 \sigma_A^2 + 2X_A X_B \sigma_{AB} + X_B^2 \sigma_B^2$$

Concept Questions

- Why is the SML a straight line?
- What is the capital asset pricing model?
- What are the differences between the capital market line and the security market line?

2. In our notation, X stands for the proportion of a security in one's portfolio. By varying X, one can trace out the efficient set of portfolios. We graphed the efficient set for the two-asset case as a curve, pointing out that the degree of curvature or bend in the graph reflects the diversification effect: The lower the correlation between the two securities, the greater the bend. The same general shape of the efficient set holds in a world of many assets.

3. Just as the formula for variance in the two-asset case is computed from a 2×2 matrix, the variance formula is computed from an $N \times N$ matrix in the N-asset case. We show that, with a large number of assets, there are many more covariance terms than variance terms in the matrix. In fact, the variance terms are effectively diversified away in a large portfolio but the covariance terms are not. Thus, a diversified portfolio can only eliminate some, but not all, of the risk of the individual securities.

4. The efficient set of risky assets can be combined with riskless borrowing and lending. In this case, a rational investor will always choose to hold the portfolio of risky securities represented by point A in Figure 11.9. Then he or she can either borrow or lend at the riskless rate to achieve any desired point on line II in the figure.

5. The contribution of a security to the risk of a large, well-diversified portfolio is proportional to the covariance of the security's return with the market's return. This contribution, when standardized, is called the beta. The beta of a security can also be interpreted as the responsiveness of a security's return to that of the market.

6. The CAPM states that

$$\overline{R} = R_F + \beta(\overline{R}_M - R_F)$$

In other words, the expected return on a security is positively (and linearly) related to the security's beta.

KEY TERMS

Beta 314	Homogeneous expectations 313
Capital asset pricing model (CAPM) 318	Market portfolio 313
Capital market line 312	Opportunity (feasible) set 300
Characteristic line 314	Portfolio 293
Correlation 290	Risk averse 308
Covariance 290	Security market line (SML) 319
Diversifiable (unique) (unsystematic)	Separation principle 312
risk 308	Systematic (market) risk 308
Efficient set 300	

SUGGESTED READING

The capital asset pricing model was originally published in two classic articles:

W. F. Sharpe. "Capital Asset Prices: A Theory of Market Equilibrium Under Conditions of Risk." *Journal of Finance* (September 1964). (William F. Sharpe shared the Nobel Prize in economics in 1990 with Harry Markowitz for his development of CAPM.)

J. Lintner. "Security Prices, Risk and Maximal Gains from Diversification." *Journal of Finance* (December 1965).

The seminal influence of Harry Markowitz is described in:

"Travels along the Efficient Frontier," *Dow Jones Asset Management* (May/June 1997).

Canadian tests of the capital asset pricing model are reviewed in current investment texts:

Z. Bodie, A. Kane, A. Marcus, S. Perrakis, and P. Ryan. *Investments*, 4th Canadian ed. Whitby, Ontario: McGraw-Hill Ryerson, 2002.

W. F. Sharpe, G. F. Alexander, J. V. Bailey, and D. J. Fowler. *Investments*, 3rd Canadian ed. Scarborough, Ontario: Prentice Hall Canada, 1999.

The Canadian Investment Review is a source for less technical articles on asset pricing.

QUESTIONS & PROBLEMS

Expected Return, Variance, and Covariance

11.1 Ms. Sharp thinks that the distribution of rates of return on Q-mart stock is as follows:

State of Economy	Probability of State Occurring	Q-Mart Stock Return (%)
Depression	0.1	−4.5
Recession	0.2	4.6
Normal	0.5	12.5
Boom	0.2	20.7

a. What is the expected return on the stock?

b. What is the standard deviation of returns on the stock?

11.2 The probability that the economy will contract is 0.2. The probability of moderate growth is 0.6, and the probability of a rapid expansion is 0.2. If the economy contracts, you can expect a return on your portfolio of 5 percent. With moderate growth, your return will be 8 percent. If there is a rapid expansion, your portfolio will return 15 percent.

a. What is your expected return?

b. What is the standard deviation of the return?

11.3 Below are the probabilities for the economy's five possible states next year, with the corresponding returns on the market and on Trebli, Inc., stock.

Economic Condition	Probability	Market Return	Trebli Return
Rapid expansion	0.12	0.23	0.12
Moderate expansion	0.40	0.18	0.09
No growth	0.25	0.15	0.05
Moderate contraction	0.15	0.09	0.01
Serious contraction	0.08	0.03	−0.02

a. What is the expected return on the market?

b. What is the expected return on Trebli stock?

11.4 Four equally likely states of the economy may occur next year. Below are the returns on the stocks of Belinkie Enterprises and Overlake Company under each of the possible states.

State	Belinkie Enterprises	Overlake Company
1	0.04	0.05
2	0.06	0.07
3	0.09	0.10
4	0.04	0.14

a. What is the expected return on each stock?

b. What is the variance of the returns on each stock?

11.5 The returns on the market of common stocks and on the Treasury bills are contingent on the economy as follows.

Economic Condition	Probability	Market Return	Treasury Bills
Recession	0.20	−8.2%	3.5%
Normal	0.60	12.3	3.5
Boom	0.20	25.8	3.5

a. Calculate the expected returns on the market and Treasury bills.

b. Calculate the expected risk premium.

EXCEL

Chapter 11 Return and Risk: The Capital Asset Pricing Model (CAPM)   **323**

11.6 Suppose you have invested only in two stocks, *A* and *B*. The returns on the two stocks depend on the following three states of the economy, which are equally likely to happen:

State of Economy	Return on Stock A (%)	Return on Stock B (%)
Bear	6.30	−3.70
Normal	10.50	6.40
Bull	15.60	25.30

  a. Calculate the expected return on each stock.
  b. Calculate the standard deviation of returns on each stock.
  c. Calculate the covariance and correlation between the returns on the two stocks.

11.7 Mr. Henry can invest in Highbull stock and Slowbear stock. His projection of the returns on these two stocks is as follows:

State of Economy	Probability of State Occurring	Return on Highbull Stock (%)	Return on Slowbear Stock (%)
Recession	0.25	−2.00	4.50
Normal	0.60	9.20	5.70
Boom	0.15	15.40	6.90

  a. Calculate the expected return on each stock.
  b. Calculate the standard deviation of returns on each stock.
  c. Calculate the covariance and correlation between the returns on the two stocks.

Portfolios

11.8 A portfolio consists of 120 shares of Atlas stock, which sells for $50 per share, and 150 shares of Babcock stock, which sells for $20 per share. What are the weights of the two stocks in this portfolio?

11.9 Security *F* has an expected return of 12 percent and a standard deviation of 9 percent per year. Security *G* has an expected return of 18 percent and a standard deviation of 25 percent per year.
  a. What is the expected return on a portfolio composed of 30 percent of security *F* and 70 percent of security *G*?
  b. If the correlation between the returns of security *F* and security *G* is 0.3, what is the standard deviation of the portfolio described in part (*a*)?

11.10 Suppose the expected returns and standard deviations of stocks *A* and *B* are $E(R_A) = 0.15$, $E(R_B) = 0.25$, $\sigma_A = 0.1$, and $\sigma_B = 0.2$, respectively.
  a. Calculate the expected return and standard deviation of a portfolio that is composed of 40 percent *A* and 60 percent *B* when the correlation between the returns on *A* and *B* is 0.5.
  b. Calculate the standard deviation of a portfolio that is composed of 40 percent *A* and 60 percent *B* when the correlation coefficient between the returns on *A* and *B* is −0.5.
  c. How does the correlation between the returns on *A* and *B* affect the standard deviation of the portfolio?

11.11 Suppose Janet Smith holds 100 shares of Macrosoft stock and 300 shares of Intelligence stock. Macrosoft's stock currently sells at $80 per share, while Intelligence's stock sells at $40 per share. The expected return on Macrosoft's stock is 15 percent, while the expected return on Intelligence's stock is 20 percent. The standard deviation of Macrosoft is 8 percent, while that of Intelligence is 20 percent. The correlation between the returns on the two stocks is 0.38. $\sigma_A = 0.08$, and $\sigma_B = 0.20$.
  a. Calculate the expected return and standard deviation of her portfolio.
  b. Today she sold 200 shares of Intelligence stock in order to pay her tuition. Calculate the expected return and standard deviation of her new portfolio.

EXCEL

11.12 Consider the possible rates of return on stocks *A* and *B* over the next year:

State of Economy	Probability of State Occurring	Stock *A* Return If State Occurs (%)	Stock *B* Return If State Occurs (%)
Recession	0.2	7	−5
Normal	0.5	7	10
Boom	0.3	7	25

a. Determine the expected returns, variances, and standard deviations for stock *A* and stock *B*.

b. Determine the covariance and correlation between the returns of stock *A* and stock *B*.

c. Determine the expected return and standard deviation of an equally weighted portfolio of stock *A* and stock *B*.

11.13 Suppose there are only two stocks in the world: stock *A* and stock *B*. The expected returns on these two stocks are 10 percent and 20 percent, while the standard deviations of the stocks are 5 percent and 15 percent, respectively. The correlation between the returns on the two stocks is 0.

a. Calculate the expected return and standard deviation of a portfolio that is composed of 30 percent *A* and 70 percent *B*.

b. Calculate the expected return and standard deviation of a portfolio that is composed of 90 percent *A* and 10 percent *B*.

c. Suppose you are risk averse. Would you hold 100 percent in stock *A*? How about 100 percent stock *B*? Explain.

11.14 If a portfolio has a positive weight for each asset, can the expected return on the portfolio be greater than the expected return on the asset in the portfolio with the highest expected return? Can the expected return on the portfolio be less than the expected return on the asset in the portfolio with the lowest expected return? Explain.

11.15 Miss Maple is considering two securities, *A* and *B*, with the relevant information given below:

State of Economy	Probability	Return on Security *A* (%)	Return on Security *B* (%)
Bear	0.3	3.0	6.5
Bull	0.7	15.0	6.5

a. Calculate the expected return and standard deviation of each of the two securities.

b. Suppose Miss Maple invested $2,500 in security *A* and $3,500 in security *B*. Calculate the expected return and standard deviation of her portfolio.

11.16 A broker has advised you not to invest in oil industry stocks because they have high standard deviations. Is the broker's advice sound for a risk-averse investor like yourself? Why or why not?

11.17 There are three securities in the market. The following chart shows their possible payoffs.

State	Probability of Outcome	Return on Security 1 (%)	Return on Security 2 (%)	Return on Security 3 (%)
1	0.1	0.25	0.25	0.10
2	0.4	0.20	0.15	0.15
3	0.4	0.15	0.20	0.20
4	0.1	0.10	0.10	0.25

EXCEL

a. What is the expected return and standard deviation of each security?

b. What are the covariances and correlations between the pairs of securities?

c. What is the expected return and standard deviation of a portfolio with half of its funds invested in security 1 and half in security 2?

d. What is the expected return and standard deviation of a portfolio with half of its funds invested in security 1 and half in security 3?

e. What is the expected return and standard deviation of a portfolio with half of its funds invested in security 2 and half in security 3?

f. What do your answers in parts (a), (c), (d), and (e) imply about diversification?

11.18 The return on stock A is uncorrelated with the return on stock B. Stock A has a 40 percent chance of having a return of 15 percent and a 60 percent chance of a return of 10 percent. Stock B has a one-half chance of a 35 percent return and a one-half chance of a −5 percent return.

a. Write a list of all of the possible outcomes and their probabilities.

b. What is the expected return on a portfolio with 50 percent invested in stock A and 50 percent invested in stock B?

11.19 Assume there are N securities in the market. The expected return on every security is 10 percent. All securities also have the same variance of 0.0144. The covariance between any pair of securities is 0.0064.

a. What is the expected return and variance of an equally weighted portfolio containing all N securities? Note: the weight of each security in the portfolio is 1/N.

b. What will happen to the variance of the portfolio as N approaches infinity?

c. What characteristics of a security are most important in the determination of the variance of a well-diversified portfolio?

11.20 Is the following statement true or false? Explain.

The most important characteristic in determining the variance of a well-diversified portfolio is the variance of each of the individual stocks.

11.21 Briefly explain why the covariance of a security with the rest of a well-diversified portfolio is a more appropriate measure of the risk of the security than the security's variance.

11.22 Consider the following quotation from a leading investment manager:

The shares of Southern Co. have traded close to $12 for most of the past three years. Since Southern's stock has demonstrated very little price movement, the stock has a low beta. Texas Instruments, on the other hand, has traded as high as $150 and as low as its current $75. Since TI's stock has demonstrated a large amount of price movement, the stock has a very high beta.

Do you agree with this analysis? Explain.

11.23 The market portfolio has an expected return of 12 percent and a standard deviation of 10 percent. The risk-free rate is 5 percent.

a. What is the expected return on a well-diversified portfolio with a standard deviation of 7 percent?

b. What is the standard deviation of a well-diversified portfolio with an expected return of 20 percent?

11.24 Consider the following information on the returns on the market and Fuji stock.

Type of Economy	Return on Market (%)	Expected Return on Fuji (%)
Bear	2.5	3.4
Bull	16.3	12.8

Calculate the beta of Fuji.

EXCEL

CAPM

11.25 William Shakespeare's character Polonius in *Hamlet* says: "Neither a borrower nor a lender be." Under the assumptions of the capital asset pricing model, what would be the composition of Polonius' portfolio?

11.26 Securities *A*, *B*, and *C* have the following characteristics:

Security	Expected Return (%)	Beta
A	10	0.7
B	14	1.2
C	20	1.8

a. What is the expected return on a portfolio with equal weights?

b. What is the beta of a portfolio with equal weights?

c. Are the three securities priced correctly according to the capital asset pricing model?

11.27 Holup, Inc., makes pneumatic equipment. The beta of Holup's stock is 1.2. The expected market risk premium is 8.5 percent, and the current risk-free rate is 6 percent. Assume the capital asset pricing model holds. What is the expected return on Holup's stock?

11.28 The beta of stock *A* is 0.80. The risk-free rate is 6 percent, and the market risk premium is 8.5 percent. Assume the capital asset pricing model holds. What is the expected return on stock *A*?

11.29 The risk-free rate is 8 percent. The beta of stock *B* is 1.5, and the expected return on the market portfolio is 15 percent. Assume the capital asset pricing model holds. What is the expected return on stock *B*?

11.30 Suppose the expected market risk premium is 7.5 percent and the risk-free rate is 3.7 percent. The expected return on TriStar's stock is 14.2 percent. Assume the capital asset pricing model holds. What is the beta of TriStar's stock?

11.31 Consider the following two stocks:

	Beta	Expected Return
Murck Pharmaceutical	1.4	30%
Pizer Drug Corp	0.7	19%

Assume the capital asset pricing model holds. Based on the CAPM, what is the risk-free rate? What is the expected return on the market portfolio?

11.32 Suppose you observe the following situation:

State of Economy	Probability of State	Return If State Occurs	
		Stock A	Stock B
Bust	0.15	−0.1	−0.3
Normal	0.70	0.1	0.05
Boom	0.15	0.2	0.4

a. Calculate the expected return on each stock.

b. Assuming the capital asset pricing model holds and stock *A*'s beta is greater than stock *B*'s beta by 0.25, what is the expected market risk premium?

11.33 Assume the capital asset pricing model holds.

a. Draw the security market line for the case where the expected market risk premium is 5 percent and the risk-free rate is 7 percent.

b. Suppose that an asset has a beta of 0.8 and an expected return of 9 percent. Does the expected return of this asset lie above or below the security market line that you drew in part (*a*)? Is the security properly priced? If not, explain what will happen in this market.

c. Suppose that an asset has a beta of 3 and an expected return of 25 percent. Does the expected return of this asset lie above or below the security market line that you drew in part (*a*)? Is the security properly priced? If not, explain what will happen in this market.

Chapter 11   Return and Risk: The Capital Asset Pricing Model (CAPM)   **327**

11.34 A stock has a beta of 1.8. A security analyst who specializes in studying this stock expects its return to be 18 percent. Suppose the risk-free rate is 5 percent and the expected market risk premium is 8 percent. Is the analyst pessimistic or optimistic about this stock relative to the market's expectations?

11.35 Suppose the expected return on the market portfolio is 13.8 percent and the risk-free rate is 6.4 percent. Solomon Inc. stock has a beta of 1.2. Assume the capital asset pricing model holds.

 a. What is the expected return on Solomon's stock?

 b. If the risk-free rate decreases to 3.5 percent, what is the expected return on Solomon's stock?

11.36 A portfolio that combines the risk-free asset and the market portfolio has an expected return of 25 percent and a standard deviation of 4 percent. The risk-free rate is 5 percent, and the expected return on the market portfolio is 20 percent. Assume the capital asset pricing model holds. What expected rate of return would a security earn if it had a 0.5 correlation with the market portfolio and a standard deviation of 2 percent?

11.37 The risk-free rate is 7.6 percent. Potpourri Inc. stock has a beta of 1.7 and an expected return of 16.7 percent. Assume the capital asset pricing model holds.

 a. What is the expected market risk premium?

 b. Magnolia Industries stock has a beta of 0.8. What is the expected return on the Magnolia stock?

 c. Suppose you have invested $10,000 in a combination of Potpourri and Magnolia stock. The beta of the portfolio is 1.07. How much did you invest in each stock? What is the expected return of the portfolio?

11.38 Suppose the risk-free rate is 6.3 percent and the market portfolio has an expected return of 14.8 percent. The market portfolio has a variance of 0.0121. Portfolio Z has a correlation coefficient with the market of 0.45 and a variance of 0.0169. According to the capital asset pricing model, what is the expected return on portfolio Z?

11.39 You have access to the following data concerning the Durham Company and the market portfolio:

Variance of returns on the market portfolio = 0.04326
Covariance between the returns on Durham and the market portfolio = 0.0635

The expected market risk premium is 9.4 percent and the expected return on Treasury bills is 4.9 percent.

 a. Write the equation of the security market line.

 b. What is the required return on Durham Company's stock?

11.40 Johnson Paint stock has an expected return of 19 percent and a beta of 1.7, while Williamson Tire stock has an expected return of 14 percent and a beta of 1.2. Assume the capital asset pricing model holds. What is the expected return on the market? What is the risk-free rate?

11.41 Is the following statement true or false? Explain.

 A risky security cannot have an expected return that is less than the risk-free rate because no risk-averse investor would be willing to hold this asset in equilibrium.

11.42 Suppose you have invested $30,000 in the following four stocks:

Security	Amount Invested	Beta
Stock A	$ 5,000	0.75
Stock B	10,000	1.1
Stock C	8,000	1.36
Stock D	7,000	1.88

The risk-free rate is 4 percent and the expected return on the market portfolio is 15 percent. Based on the capital asset pricing model, what is the expected return on the above portfolio?

EXCEL

Part III   Risk

11.43 You have been provided the following data on the securities of three firms, the market portfolio, and the risk-free asset:

Security	Expected Return	Standard Deviation	Correlation*	Beta
Firm A	0.13	0.12	(i)	0.9
Firm B	0.16	(ii)	0.4	1.1
Firm C	0.25	0.24	0.75	(iii)
The market portfolio	0.15	0.1	(iv)	(v)
The risk-free asset	0.05	(vi)	(vii)	(viii)

*With the market portfolio.

a. Fill in the missing values in the table.
b. Is the stock of firm A correctly priced according to the capital asset pricing model (CAPM)? What about the stock of firm B? firm C? If these securities are not correctly priced, what is your investment recommendation for someone with a well-diversified portfolio?

EXCEL

11.44 There are two stocks in the market: stock A and stock B. The price of stock A today is $50. The price of stock A next year will be $40 if the economy is in a recession, $55 if the economy is normal, and $60 if the economy is expanding. The probabilities of recession, normal times, and expansion are 0.1, 0.8, and 0.1, respectively. Stock A pays no dividends and has a correlation of 0.8 with the market portfolio. Stock B has an expected return of 9 percent, a standard deviation of 12 percent, a correlation with the market portfolio of 0.2, and a correlation with stock A of 0.6. The market portfolio has a standard deviation of 10 percent. Assume the CAPM holds.

a. If you are a typical, risk-averse investor with a well-diversified portfolio, which stock would you prefer? Why?
b. What are the expected return and standard deviation of a portfolio consisting of 70 percent of stock A and 30 percent of stock B?
c. What is the beta of the portfolio in part (b)?

Advanced (requires calculus)

11.45 Assume stocks A and B have the following characteristics:

Stock	Expected Return (%)	Standard Deviation %
A	5	10
B	10	20

The covariance between the returns on the two stocks is 0.001.

a. Suppose an investor holds a portfolio consisting of only stock A and stock B. Find the portfolio weights, X_A and X_B, such that the variance of his portfolio is minimized. (Hint: Remember that the sum of the two weights must equal 1.)
b. What is the expected return on the minimum variance portfolio?
c. If the covariance between the returns on the two stocks is −0.02, what are the minimum variance weights?
d. What is the variance of the portfolio in part (c)?

NOTE: While these problems can be calculated manually, it is recommended that a spreadsheet program such as Excel® be used for calculations.

S & P
PROBLEMS
STANDARD & POOR'S

11.46 Go to the "Excel Analytics" link for Nexen Inc. (NXY) and Thomson Corp. (TOC) and download the monthly adjusted stock prices. Copy the monthly returns for each stock into a new spreadsheet. Calculate the covariance and correlation between the two stock returns. Would you expect a higher or lower correlation if you had chosen Petro-Canada (PCA) instead of Thomson Corp.? What is the standard deviation of a portfolio 75 percent invested in NXY and 25 percent in TOC? What about a portfolio equally invested in the two stocks? What about a portfolio 25 percent in NXY and 75 percent in TOC?

11.47 Go to the "Excel Analytics" link for Encana Corp (ECA) and download the monthly adjusted stock prices. Copy the monthly returns for ECA and the monthly S&P 500 returns in a new spreadsheet. Calculate the beta of ECA for the entire period of data available. Now download the monthly stock prices for Research In Motion Limited (RIM) and calculate the beta for this company. Are the betas similar? Would you have expected the beta for ECA to be higher or lower than the beta for RIM? Why?

Appendix 11A

Is Beta Dead?

The capital asset pricing model represents one of the most important advances in financial economics. It is clearly useful for investment purposes, since it shows how the expected return on an asset is related to its beta. In addition, we will show in Chapter 12 that it is useful in corporate finance, since the discount rate on a project is a function of the project's beta. However, one must never forget that, as with any other model, the CAPM is not revealed truth but, rather, a construct to be empirically tested.

The first empirical tests of the CAPM occurred over 20 years ago and were quite supportive. Using data from the 1930s to the 1960s, researchers showed that the average return on a portfolio of stocks was positively related to the beta of the portfolio,[22] a finding consistent with the CAPM. Though some evidence in these studies was less consistent with the CAPM,[23] financial economists were quick to embrace the CAPM following these empirical papers.

While a large body of empirical work developed in the following decades, often with varying results, the CAPM was not seriously called into question until recently. Two papers by Fama and French[24] (yes, the same Fama whose joint paper in 1973 with James MacBeth supported the CAPM) present evidence inconsistent with the model. Their work has received a great deal of attention, both in academic circles and in the popular press, with

[22]Perhaps the two most well-known papers were Fischer Black, Michael C. Jensen, and Myron S. Scholes, "The Capital Asset Pricing Model: Some Empirical Tests," in M. Jensen, ed. *Studies in the Theory of Capital Markets* (New York: Praeger, 1972); and Eugene F. Fama and James MacBeth, "Risk, Return and Equilibrium: Some Empirical Tests," *Journal of Political Economy* 8 (1973), pp. 607–36.

[23]For example, the studies suggest that the average return on a zero-beta portfolio is above the risk-free rate, a finding inconsistent with the CAPM. Two Canadian studies raising questions about the CAPM's accuracy are: J. D. Jobson and R. M. Korkie, "Some Tests of Linear Asset Pricing with Multivariate Normality," *Canadian Journal of Administrative Sciences* 2 (June 1985), and A. L. Calvet and J. Lefoll, "Risk and Return on Canadian Capital Markets," *Canadian Journal of Administrative Science* 5 (March 1988).

[24]Eugene F. Fama and Kenneth R. French, "The Cross-Section of Expected Stock Returns," *Journal of Finance* 47 (1992), pp. 427–66; and E. F. Fama and K. R. French, "Common Risk Factors in the Returns on Stocks and Bonds," *Journal of Financial Economics* 17 (1993), pp. 3–56.

Part III   *Risk*

newspaper articles displaying headlines such as "Beta Is Dead!" These papers make two related points. First they conclude that the relationship between average return and beta is weak over the period from 1941 to 1990 and virtually nonexistent from 1963 to 1990. Second, they argue that the average return on a security is negatively related to both the firm's price-to-earnings (P/E) ratio and the firm's market value-to-book value (M/B) ratio. These contentions, if confirmed by other research, would be quite damaging to the CAPM. After all, the CAPM states that the expected returns on stocks should be related *only* to beta, and not to other factors such as P/E and M/B.

However, a number of researchers have criticized the Fama–French papers. While we avoid an in-depth discussion of the fine points of the debate, we mention a few issues. First, although Fama and French cannot reject the hypothesis that average returns are unrelated to beta, one can also not reject the hypothesis that average returns are related to beta exactly as specified by the CAPM. In other words, while 50 years of data seem like a lot, they may simply not be enough to test the CAPM properly. Second, the result with P/E and M/B may be due to a statistical fallacy called a hindsight bias.[25] Third, P/E and M/B are merely two of an infinite number of possible factors. Thus, the relationship between average return and both P/E and M/B may be spurious, being nothing more than the result of data dredging. Fourth, average returns are positively related to beta over the period from 1927 to 1990. There appears to be no compelling reason for emphasizing a shorter period than this one. Fifth, average returns are actually positively related to beta over shorter periods when annual data, rather than monthly data, are used to estimate beta.[26] There appears to be no compelling reason for preferring either monthly data over annual data or vice versa. Thus, we believe that, while the results of Fama and French are quite intriguing, they cannot be viewed as the final word.

[25] For example, see William J. Breen and Robert A. Koraczyk, "On Selection Biases in Book-to-Market Based Tests of Asset Pricing Models," unpublished paper. Northwestern University, November 1993; and S. P. Kothari, Jay Shanken, and Richard G. Sloan. "Another Look at the Cross-Section of Expected Stock Returns," *Journal of Finance* 50 (March 1995), pp. 185–224.

[26] Points 4 and 5 are addressed in the Kothari, Shanken, and Sloan paper.

Chapter 12

An Alternative View of Risk and Return: The Arbitrage Pricing Theory

EXECUTIVE SUMMARY

The previous two chapters showed how variable returns on securities are. This variability is measured by variance and by standard deviation. Next, we discussed how the returns on securities are interdependent. We measured the degree of interdependence between a pair of securities by covariance and by correlation. This interdependence led to a number of interesting results. First, we showed that diversification in stocks can eliminate some, but not all, risk. By contrast, we showed that diversification in a casino can eliminate all risk. Second, the interdependence of returns led to the capital asset pricing model (CAPM). This model posits a positive (and linear) relationship between the beta of a security and its expected return.

The CAPM was developed in the early 1960s.[1] An alternative to the CAPM, called the *arbitrage pricing theory* (APT), has been developed more recently.[2] For our purposes, the differences between the two models stem from the APT's treatment of the interrelationship among the returns on securities.[3] The APT assumes that returns on securities are generated by a number of industrywide and marketwide factors. Correlation between a pair of securities occurs when these two securities are affected by the same factor or factors. By contrast, though the CAPM allows correlation among securities, it does not specify the underlying factors causing the correlation.

Both the APT and the CAPM imply a positive relationship between expected return and risk. In our (perhaps biased) opinion, the APT allows this relationship to be developed in a particularly intuitive manner. In addition, the APT views risk more generally than just as the standardized covariance or beta of a security with the market portfolio. Therefore, we offer this approach as an alternative to the CAPM.

[1] In particular, see Jack Treynor, "Toward a Theory of the Market Value of Risky Assets," unpublished manuscript (1961); William F. Sharpe, "Capital Asset Prices: A Theory of Market Equilibrium Under Conditions of Risk," *Journal of Finance* (September 1964); and John Lintner, "The Valuation of Risky Assets and the Selection of Risky Investments in Stock Portfolios and Capital Budgets," *Review of Economics and Statistics* (February 1965).

[2] See Stephen A. Ross, "The Arbitrage Theory of Capital Asset Pricing," *Journal of Economic Theory* (December 1976).

[3] This is by no means the only difference in the assumptions of the two models. For example, the CAPM usually assumes either that the returns on assets are normally distributed or that investors have quadratic utility functions. The APT does not require either assumption. Instead it is based on the more general principle that when assets are priced correctly, it is not possible to make arbitrage profits without taking on risk. While this and other differences are quite important in research, they are not relevant to the material presented in our text.

12.1 Factor Models: Announcements, Surprises, and Expected Returns

We learned in the previous chapter how to construct portfolios and how to evaluate their returns. We now step back and examine the returns on individual securities more closely. By doing this we will find that the portfolios inherit and alter the properties of the securities they comprise.

To be concrete, let us consider the return on the stock of a company called Quebec Supply. What will determine this stock's return in, say, the coming month?

The return on any stock traded in a financial market consists of two parts. First, the *normal* or *expected return* from the stock is the part of the return that shareholders in the market predict or expect. It depends on all of the information shareholders have that bears on the stock, and it uses all of our understanding of what will influence the stock in the next month.

The second part is the *uncertain* and *risky return* on the stock. This is the portion that comes from information that will be revealed within the month. The list of such information is endless, but here are some examples:

- News about Quebec Supply's research.
- Statistics Canada figures released on the gross national product (GNP).
- Announcement of the latest federal deficit-reduction plans.
- Discovery that a rival's product has been tampered with.
- News that Quebec Supply's sales figures are higher than expected.
- A sudden drop in interest rates.
- The unexpected retirement of Quebec Supply's founder and president.

A way to write the return on Quebec Supply's stock in the coming month, then, is

$$R = \bar{R} + U$$

where R is the actual total return in the month, $\bar{R}$ is the expected part of the return, and U stands for the unexpected part of the return.

Some care must be exercised in studying the effects of these and other news items on the return. For example, Statistics Canada might give us GNP or unemployment figures for this month, but how much of that is new information for shareholders? Surely, at the beginning of the month, shareholders will have some idea or forecast of what the monthly GNP will be. To the extent to which the shareholders had forecast the government's announcement, that forecast should be factored into the expected part of the return as of the beginning of the month, $\bar{R}$. On the other hand, insofar as the announcement by the government is a surprise and to the extent to which it influences the return on the stock, it will be part of U, the unanticipated part of the return.

As an example, suppose shareholders in the market had forecast that the GNP increase this month would be 0.5 percent. If GNP influences our company's stock, this forecast will be part of the information shareholders use to form the expectation, $\bar{R}$, of monthly return. If the actual announcement this month is exactly 0.5 percent, the same as the forecast, then the shareholders learned nothing new, and the announcement is not news. It is like hearing a rumour about a friend when you knew it all along. Another way of saying this is that shareholders had already discounted the announcement. This use of the word *discount* is different from that in computing present value, but the spirit is similar. When we discount a dollar in the future, we say that it is worth less to us because of the time value of money.

When we discount an announcement or a news item in the future, we mean that it has less impact on the market because the market already knew much of it.

On the other hand, suppose Statistics Canada announced that the actual GNP increase during the month was 1.5 percent. Now shareholders have learned something—that the increase is one percentage point higher than they had forecast. This difference between the actual result and the forecast, one percentage point in this example, is sometimes called the *innovation* or *surprise*.

Any announcement can be broken into two parts: the anticipated or expected part, and the surprise or innovation:

$$\text{Announcement} = \text{Expected part} + \text{Surprise}$$

The expected part of any announcement is part of the information the market uses to form the expectation, $\bar{R}$, of the return on the stock. The surprise is the news that influences the unanticipated return on the stock, U.

To take another example, if shareholders know in January that the president of a firm is going to resign, the official announcement in February will be fully expected and will be discounted by the market. Because the announcement was expected before February, its influence on the stock will have taken place before February. The announcement itself in February will contain no surprise, and the stock's price should not change at all at the announcement in February.

When we speak of news, then, we refer to the surprise part of any announcement and not to the portion that the market has expected and therefore has already discounted.

? Concept Questions

- What are the two basic parts of a return?
- Under what conditions will some news have no effect on common stock prices?

12.2 Risk: Systematic and Unsystematic

The unanticipated part of the return, that portion resulting from surprises, is the true risk of any investment. After all, if we had already got what we had expected, there would be no risk and no uncertainty.

There are important differences, though, among various sources of risk. Look at our previous list of news stories. Some of these stories are directed specifically at Quebec Supply, and some are more general. Which of the news items are of specific importance to Quebec Supply?

Announcements about interest rates or GNP are clearly important for nearly all companies, whereas the news about Quebec Supply's president, its research, its sales, or the affairs of a rival company are of specific interest to Quebec Supply. We will divide these two types of announcements and the resulting risk, then, into two components: a systematic portion, called *systematic risk*, and the remainder, which we call *specific* or *unsystematic risk*. The following definitions describe the difference:

- A *systematic risk* is any risk that affects a large number of assets, each to a greater or lesser degree.
- An *unsystematic risk* is a risk that specifically affects a single asset or a small group of assets.[4]

---

[4]In the previous chapter, we briefly mentioned that unsystematic risk is risk that can be diversified away in a large portfolio. This result will also follow from the present analysis.

Uncertainty about general economic conditions, such as GNP, interest rates, or inflation, is an example of systematic risk. These conditions affect nearly all stocks to some degree. An unanticipated or surprise increase in inflation affects wages and the costs of the supplies that companies buy, the value of the assets that companies own, and the prices at which companies sell their products. These forces to which all companies are susceptible are the essence of systematic risk.

In contrast, the announcement of a small oil strike by a company may very well affect that company alone or a few other companies. Certainly, it is unlikely to have an effect on the world oil market. To stress that such information is unsystematic and affects only some specific companies, we sometimes call it an *idiosyncratic risk*.

The distinction between a systematic risk and an unsystematic risk is never as exact as we make it out to be. Even the most narrow and peculiar bit of news about a company ripples through the economy. It reminds us of the tale of the war that was lost because one horse lost a shoe; even a minor event may have an impact on the world. But this degree of hair-splitting should not trouble us much. To paraphrase a judge's comment on pornography, we are not able to define systematic and unsystematic risk exactly, but we know them when we see them.

This permits us to break down the risk of Quebec Supply's stock into its two components: the systematic and the unsystematic. As is traditional, we will use the Greek epsilon, ε, to represent the unsystematic risk and write

$$R = \bar{R} + U$$
$$= \bar{R} + m + \varepsilon$$

where we have used the letter m to stand for the systematic risk. Sometimes systematic risk is referred to as *market risk*. This emphasizes the fact that m influences all assets in the market to some extent.

The important point about the way we have broken the total risk, U, into its two components, m and ε, is that ε, because it is specific to the company, is unrelated to the specific risk of most other companies. For example, the unsystematic risk on Quebec Supply's stock, ε_Q, is unrelated to the unsystematic risk of Bank of Montreal's stock, ε_{BMO}. The risk that Quebec Supply's stock will go up or down because of a discovery by its research team—or its failure to discover something—probably is unrelated to any of the specific uncertainties that affect Bank of Montreal's stock.

Using the terms of the previous chapter, this means that the unsystematic risks of Quebec Supply's stock and Bank of Montreal's stock are unrelated to each other, or uncorrelated. In the symbols of statistics,

$$\mathrm{Corr}(\varepsilon_Q, \varepsilon_{BMO}) = 0$$

**? Concept
Questions**

• Describe the difference between systematic risk and unsystematic risk.
• Why is unsystematic risk sometimes referred to as *idiosyncratic risk?*

12.3 Systematic Risk and Betas

The fact that the unsystematic parts of the returns on two companies are unrelated to each other does not mean that the systematic portions are unrelated. On the contrary, because both companies are influenced by the same systematic risks, individual companies' systematic risks and, therefore, their total returns will be related.

For example, a surprise about inflation will influence almost all companies to some extent. How sensitive is Quebec Supply's stock return to unanticipated changes in inflation? If Quebec Supply's stock tends to go up on news that inflation is exceeding expectations, we would say that it is positively related to inflation. If the stock goes down when inflation exceeds expectations and up when inflation falls short of expectations, it is negatively related. In the unusual case where a stock's return is uncorrelated with inflation surprises, inflation has no effect on it.

We capture the influence of a systematic risk like inflation on a stock by using the **beta coefficient.** The beta coefficient, β, tells us the response of the stock's return to a systematic risk. In the previous chapter, beta measured the responsiveness of a security's return to a specific risk factor, the return on the market portfolio. We used this type of responsiveness to develop the capital asset pricing model. Because we now consider many types of systematic risks, our current work can be viewed as a generalization of what we did in the previous chapter.

If a company's stock is positively related to the risk of inflation, that stock has a positive inflation beta. If it is negatively related to inflation, its inflation beta is negative, and if it is uncorrelated with inflation, its inflation beta is zero.

It is not hard to imagine stocks with positive and negative inflation betas. The stock of a company owning gold mines will probably have a positive inflation beta because an unanticipated rise in inflation is usually associated with an increase in gold prices. On the other hand, an automobile company facing stiff foreign competition might find that an increase in inflation means that the wages it pays are higher, but that it cannot raise its prices to cover the increase. This profit squeeze, as the company's expenses rise faster than its revenues, would give its stock a negative inflation beta.

Some companies that have few assets and that act as brokers—buying items in competitive markets and reselling them in other markets—might be relatively unaffected by inflation, because their costs and their revenues would rise and fall together. Their stocks would have an inflation beta of zero.

Some structure is useful at this point. Suppose we have identified three systematic risks on which we want to focus. We may believe that these three are sufficient to describe the systematic risks that influence stock returns. Three likely candidates are inflation, GNP, and interest rates. Thus, every stock will have a beta associated with each of these systematic risks: an inflation beta, a GNP beta, and an interest-rate beta. We can write the return on the stock, then, in the following form:

$$R = \bar{R} + U$$
$$= \bar{R} + m + \varepsilon$$
$$= \bar{R} + \beta_I F_I + \beta_{GNP} F_{GNP} + \beta_r F_r + \varepsilon$$

where we have used β_I to denote the stock's inflation beta, β_{GNP} for its GNP beta, and β_r to stand for its interest-rate beta. In the equation, F stands for a surprise, whether it be in inflation, GNP, or interest rates.

Let us go through an example to see how the surprises and the expected return add up to produce the total return, R, on a given stock. To make it more familiar, suppose that the return is over a horizon of a year and not just a month. Suppose that at the beginning of the year, inflation is forecast to be 5 percent for the year. GNP is forecast to increase by 2 percent, and interest rates are expected not to change. Suppose the stock we are looking at has the following betas:

$$\beta_I = 2.0$$
$$\beta_{GNP} = 1.0$$
$$\beta_r = -1.8$$

The magnitude of the beta describes how great an impact a systematic risk has on a stock's returns. A beta of $+1$ indicates that the stock's return rises and falls one for one with the systematic factor. This means, in our example, that because the stock has a GNP beta of 1, it experiences a 1 percent increase in return for every 1 percent surprise increase in GNP. If its GNP beta were -2, it would fall by 2 percent when there was an unanticipated increase of 1 percent in GNP, and it would rise by 2 percent if GNP experienced a surprise 1 percent decline.

Next let's suppose that during the year the following occurs: Inflation rises by 7 percent, GNP rises by only 1 percent, and interest rates fall by 2 percent. Lastly, suppose that we learn some good news about the company (perhaps that it's succeeding rapidly with some new business strategy) and that this unanticipated development contributes 5 percent to its return. In other words,

$$\varepsilon = 5\%$$

Let us assemble all of this information to find what return the stock had during the year.

First, we must determine what news or surprises took place in the systematic factors. From our information we know that

$$\text{Expected inflation} = 5\%$$
$$\text{Expected GNP change} = 2\%$$
$$\text{Expected change in interest rates} = 0\%$$

This means that the market had discounted these changes, and the surprises will be the difference between what actually takes place and these expectations:

$$
\begin{aligned}
F_I &= \text{Surprise in inflation} \\
&= \text{Actual inflation} - \text{Expected inflation} \\
&= 7\% - 5\% \\
&= 2\%
\end{aligned}
$$

Similarly,

$$
\begin{aligned}
F_{\text{GNP}} &= \text{Surprise in GNP} \\
&= \text{Actual GNP} - \text{Expected GNP} \\
&= 1\% - 2\% \\
&= -1\%
\end{aligned}
$$

and

$$
\begin{aligned}
F_r &= \text{Surprise in change in interest rates} \\
&= \text{Actual change} - \text{Expected change} \\
&= -2\% - 0\% \\
&= -2\%
\end{aligned}
$$

The total effect of the systematic risks on the stock return, then, is

$$
\begin{aligned}
m &= \text{Systematic risk portion of return} \\
&= \beta_I F_I + \beta_{\text{GNP}} F_{\text{GNP}} + \beta_r F_r \\
&= [2 \times 2\%] + [1 \times (-1\%)] + [(-1.8) \times (-2\%)] \\
&= 6.6\%
\end{aligned}
$$

Combining this with the unsystematic risk portion, the total risky portion of the return on the stock is

$$m + \varepsilon = 6.6\% + 5\% = 11.6\%$$

Last, if the expected return on the stock for the year is, say, 4 percent, the total return from all three components is

$$R = \overline{R} + m + \varepsilon$$
$$= 4\% + 6.6\% + 5\%$$
$$= 15.6\%$$

The model we have been looking at is called a **factor model**, and the systematic sources of risk, designated F, are called the *factors*. To be perfectly formal, a *k-factor model* is a model where each stock's return is generated by

$$R = \overline{R} + \beta_1 F_1 + \beta_2 F_2 + \ldots + \beta_k F_k + \varepsilon$$

where ε is specific to a particular stock and uncorrelated with the ε-term for other stocks. In our preceding example, we had a three-factor model. We used inflation, GNP, and the change in interest rates as examples of systematic sources of risk (or factors). Researchers have not settled on what is the correct set of factors. Like so many other questions, this might be one of those matters that never are laid to rest.

In practice, researchers frequently use a one-factor model for returns. They do not use all of the sorts of economic factors we used previously as examples; instead, they use an index of stock market returns—like the S&P/TSX 60 or even a more broadly based index with more stocks in it—as the single factor. Using the single-factor model we can write returns as

$$R = \overline{R} + \beta(R_{S\&P/TSX\ 60} - \overline{R}_{S\&P/TSX\ 60}) + \varepsilon$$

Where there is only one factor (the returns on the S&P/TSX 60 Index), we do not need to put a subscript on the beta. In this form (with minor modifications) the factor model is called a **market model**. This term is employed because the index that is used for the factor is an index of returns on the whole (stock) market. The market model is written as

$$R = \overline{R} + \beta(R_M - \overline{R}_M) + \varepsilon$$

where R_M is the return on the market portfolio.[5] The single β is called the *beta coefficient*.

Concept Questions

- **What is an inflation beta? A GNP beta? An interest-rate beta?**
- **What is the difference between a *k*-factor model and the market model?**
- **Define the beta coefficient.**

12.4 Portfolios and Factor Models

Now let us see what happens to portfolios of stocks when each of the stocks follows a one-factor model. For purposes of discussion, we will take the coming one-month period and examine returns. We could have used a day, a year, or any other time period. If the period represents the time between decisions, however, we would rather it be short than long—a month is a reasonable time frame to use.

---

[5] Alternatively, the market model could be written as

$$R = \alpha + \beta R_M + \varepsilon$$

Here alpha (α) is an intercept term equal to $\overline{R} - \beta \overline{R}_M$.

Part III *Risk*

We will create portfolios from a list of N stocks, and we will use a one-factor model to capture the systematic risk. The ith stock in the list will therefore have returns

$$R_i = \bar{R}_i + \beta_i F + \varepsilon_i \qquad (12.1)$$

where we have subscripted the variables to indicate that they relate to the ith stock. Notice that the factor F is not subscripted. The factor that represents systematic risk could be a surprise in GNP, or we could use the market model and let the factor be the difference between the S&P/TSX 60 return and what we expect that return to be, $R_{S\&P/TSX\ 60} - \bar{R}_{S\&P/TSX\ 60}$. In either case, the factor applies to all stocks.

The β_i is subscripted because it represents the unique way the factor influences the ith stock. To recapitulate our discussion of factor models, if β_i is zero, the returns on the ith stock are

$$R_i = \bar{R} + \varepsilon_i$$

In words, the ith stock's returns are unaffected by the factor, F, if β_i is zero. If β_i is positive, positive changes in the factor raise the ith stock's returns, and declines lower them. Conversely, if β_i is negative, its returns and the factor move in opposite directions.

Figure 12.1 illustrates the relationship between a stock's excess returns, $R_i - \bar{R}_i$, and the factor F for different betas, where $\beta_i > 0$. The lines in Figure 12.1 plot Equation (12.1) on the assumption that there has been no unsystematic risk. That is, $\varepsilon_i = 0$. Because we are assuming positive betas, the lines slope upward, indicating that the return on the stock rises with F. Notice that, if the factor is zero ($F = 0$), the line passes through zero on the y-axis.

Now let us see what happens when we create stock portfolios where each stock follows a one-factor model. Let x_i be the proportion of security i in the portfolio. That is, if

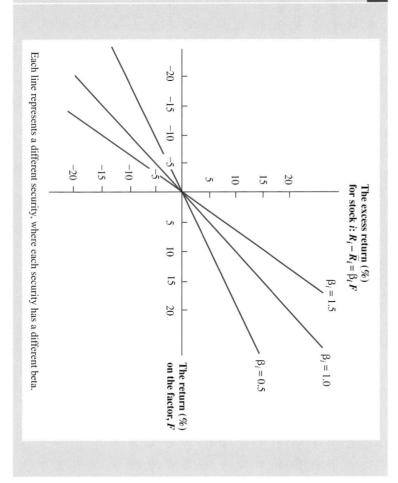

FIGURE 12.1

The One-Factor Model for Stock i

**The excess return (%)
for stock i: $R_i - \bar{R}_i = \beta_i F$**

$\beta_i = 1.5$

$\beta_i = 1.0$

$\beta_i = 0.5$

**The return (%)
on the factor, F**

Each line represents a different security, where each security has a different beta.

an individual with a portfolio of $100 wants $20 in TransCanada Pipelines Ltd., we say $X_{\text{TCPL}} = 20\%$. Because the Xs represent the proportions of wealth we are investing in each of the stocks, we know that they must add up to 100 percent or 1. That is,

$$X_1 + X_2 + X_3 + \ldots + X_N = 1$$

We know that the portfolio return is the weighted average of the returns on the individual assets in the portfolio:

$$R_P = X_1 R_1 + X_2 R_2 + X_3 R_3 + \ldots + X_N R_N \tag{12.2}$$

Equation (12.2) expresses the return on the portfolio as a weighted average of the returns on the individual assets. We saw from Equation (12.1) that each asset's return is determined by both the factor F and the unsystematic risk of ε_i. Thus, by substituting Equation (12.1) for each R_i in Equation (12.2), we have

$$R_P = X_1(\overline{R}_1 + \beta_1 F + \varepsilon_1) + X_2(\overline{R}_2 + \beta_2 F + \varepsilon_2) + \tag{12.3}$$
$$\text{(Return on stock 1)} \qquad \text{(Return on stock 2)}$$
$$X_3(\overline{R}_3 + \beta_3 F + \varepsilon_3) + \ldots + X_N(\overline{R}_N + \beta_N F + \varepsilon_N)$$
$$\text{(Return on stock 3)} \qquad \qquad \text{(Return on stock } N)$$

Equation (12.3) shows us that the return on a portfolio is determined by three sets of parameters:

1. The expected return on each individual security, $\overline{R}_i$.
2. The beta of each security multiplied by the factor F.
3. The unsystematic risk of each individual security, ε_i.

We express Equation (12.3) in terms of these three sets of parameters as

Weighted Average of Expected Returns:

$$R_P = X_1 \overline{R}_1 + X_2 \overline{R}_2 + X_3 \overline{R}_3 + \ldots + X_N \overline{R}_N \tag{12.4}$$

(Weighted Average of Betas)F:
$$+ (X_1\beta_1 + X_2\beta_2 + X_3\beta_3 + \ldots + X_N\beta_N)F$$

Weighted Average of Unsystematic Risks:
$$+ X_1\varepsilon_1 + X_2\varepsilon_2 + X_3\varepsilon_3 + \ldots + X_N\varepsilon_N$$

This rather imposing equation is actually straightforward. The first row is the weighted average of each security's expected return. The items in the parentheses in the second row represent the weighted average of each security's beta. This weighted average is, in turn, multiplied by the factor F. The third row represents a weighted average of the unsystematic risks of the individual securities.

Where does uncertainty appear in Equation (12.4)? There is no uncertainty in the first row because only the expected value of each security's return appears there. Uncertainty in the second row is reflected by only one item, F. That is, while we know that the expected value of F is zero, we do not know what its value will be over a particular time period. Uncertainty in the third row is reflected by each unsystematic risk, ε_i.

Portfolios and Diversification

In the previous sections of this chapter, we expressed the return on a single security in terms of our factor model. Portfolios were treated next. Because investors generally hold

Part III   Risk

diversified portfolios, we now want to know what Equation (12.4) looks like in a large or diversified portfolio. [6]

As it turns out, something unusual happens to Equation (12.4)—the third row actually *disappears* in a large portfolio. To see this, consider the gambler of the previous chapter who divides $1,000 by betting on red over many spins of the roulette wheel. For example, he may participate in 1,000 spins, betting $1 at a time. Though we do not know ahead of time whether a particular spin will yield red or black, we can be confident that red will win about 50 percent of the time. Ignoring the house take, the investor can be expected to end up with just about his original $1,000.

Though we are concerned with stocks, not roulette wheels, the same principle applies. Each security has its own unsystematic risk, where the surprise for one stock is unrelated to the surprise of another stock. By investing a small amount in each security, the weighted average of the unsystematic risks will be very close to zero in a large portfolio. [7]

Although the third row completely vanishes in a large portfolio, nothing unusual occurs in either row 1 or row 2. Row 1 remains a weighted average of the expected returns on the individual securities as securities are added to the portfolio. Because there is no uncertainty at all in the first row, there is no way for diversification to cause this row to vanish. The terms inside the parentheses of the second row remain a weighted average of the betas. They do not vanish, either, when securities are added. Because the factor *F* is unaffected when securities are added to the portfolios, the second row does not vanish.

Why does the third row vanish while the second row does not, though both rows reflect uncertainty? The key is that there are many unsystematic risks in row 3. Because these risks are independent of each other, the effect of diversification becomes stronger as we add more assets to the portfolio. The resulting portfolio becomes less and less risky, and the return becomes more certain. However, the systematic risk, *F*, affects all securities because it is outside the parentheses in row 2. Because one cannot avoid this factor by investing in many securities, diversification does not occur in this row.

The above material can be further explained by an example similar in spirit to the diversification example of the previous chapter. We keep our one-factor model but make three specific assumptions:

1. All securities have the same expected return of 10 percent. This assumption implies that the first row of Equation (12.4) must also equal 10 percent because this row is a weighted average of the expected returns of the individual securities.

2. All securities have a beta of 1. The sum of the terms inside the parentheses in the second row of (12.4) must equal 1 because these terms are a weighted average of the individual betas. Since the terms inside the parentheses are multiplied by *F*, the value of the second row is
   $1 \times F = F.$

3. In this example, we focus on the behaviour of one individual, Walter Bagehot. Being a new observer of the economic scene, Mr. Bagehot decides to hold an equally weighted portfolio. That is, the proportion of each security in his portfolio is 1/*N*.

---

[6] Technically, we can think of a large portfolio as one where an investor keeps increasing the number of securities without limit. In practice, effective diversification would occur if at least a few dozen securities were held.

[7] More precisely, we say that the weighted average of the unsystematic risk approaches zero as the number of equally weighted securities in a portfolio approaches infinity.

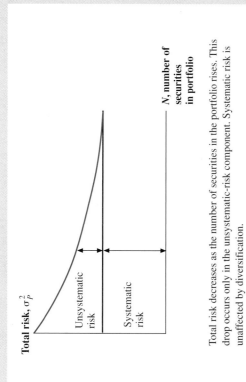

Total risk decreases as the number of securities in the portfolio rises. This
drop occurs only in the unsystematic-risk component. Systematic risk is
unaffected by diversification.

We can express the return on Mr. Bagehot's portfolio as

Return on Walter Bagehot's Portfolio:

$$R_P = 10\% + F + \left(\frac{1}{N}\varepsilon_1 + \frac{1}{N}\varepsilon_2 + \frac{1}{N}\varepsilon_3 + \ldots + \frac{1}{N}\varepsilon_N \right) \qquad (12.4')$$

From   From   From row 3 of (12.4)
row 1   row 2
of (12.4)   of (12.4)

We mentioned above that, as N increases without limit, row 3 of (12.4) becomes equal to
zero. Thus, the return to Walter Bagehot's portfolio when the number of securities is very
large is

$$R_P = 10\% + F \qquad (12.4'')$$

The key to diversification is exhibited in (12.4''). The unsystematic risk of row 3 vanishes,[8]
while the systematic risk of row 2 remains.

This is illustrated in Figure 12.2. Systematic risk, captured by variation in the factor,
F, is not reduced through diversification. Conversely, unsystematic risk diminishes as securities are added, vanishing as the number of securities becomes infinite. Our result is analogous to the diversification example of the previous chapter. In that chapter, we said that
undiversifiable or systematic risk arises from positive covariances between securities. In
this chapter, we say that systematic risk arises from a common factor F. Because a common
factor causes positive covariances, the arguments of the two chapters are parallel.

• **How can the return on a portfolio be expressed in terms of a factor model?**
• **What risk is diversified away in a large portfolio?**

---

[8]The variance of row 3 is

$$\frac{1}{N^2}\sigma_\varepsilon^2 + \frac{1}{N^2}\sigma_\varepsilon^2 + \frac{1}{N^2}\sigma_\varepsilon^2 + \ldots + \frac{1}{N^2}\sigma_\varepsilon^2 = \frac{1}{N^2}N\sigma_\varepsilon^2$$

where σ_ε^2 is the variance of each ε. This can be rewritten as σ_ε^2/N, which tends to 0 as N goes to infinity.

12.5 Betas and Expected Returns

The Linear Relationship

We have argued many times that the expected return on a security compensates for its risk. In the previous chapter we showed that market beta (the standardized covariance of the security's returns with those of the market) was the appropriate measure of risk under the assumptions of homogeneous expectations and riskless borrowing and lending. The capital asset pricing model, which posited these assumptions, implied that the expected return on a security was positively (and linearly) related to its beta. We will find a similar relationship between risk and return in the one-factor model of this chapter.

We begin by noting that the relevant risk in large and well-diversified portfolios is all systematic because unsystematic risk is diversified away. An implication is that, when a well-diversified shareholder considers changing holdings of a particular stock, the security's unsystematic risk can be ignored.

Notice that we are not claiming that stocks, like portfolios, have no unsystematic risk. Neither are we saying that the unsystematic risk of a stock will not affect its returns. Stocks do have unsystematic risk, and their actual returns do depend on the unsystematic risk. Because this risk washes out in a well-diversified portfolio, however, shareholders can ignore this unsystematic risk when they consider whether or not to add a stock to their portfolio. Therefore, if shareholders are ignoring the unsystematic risk, only the systematic risk of a stock can be related to its *expected* return.

This relationship is illustrated in the security market line of Figure 12.3. Points *P*, *C*, *A*, and *L* all lie on the line emanating from the risk-free rate of 10 percent. The points representing each of these four assets can be created by combinations of the risk-free rate and any of the other three assets. For example, since *A* has a beta of 2.0 and *P* has a beta of 1.0, a portfolio of 50 percent in asset *A* and 50 percent in the riskless rate has the same beta as asset *P*. The risk-free rate is 10 percent and the expected return on security *A* is 35 percent, implying that the combination's return of 22.5 percent [or $(10\% + 35\%)/2$] is identical to security *P*'s expected return. Because security *P* has both the same beta and the same expected return as a combination of the riskless asset and security *A*, an individual is equally inclined to add a small amount of security *P* and to add a small amount of this

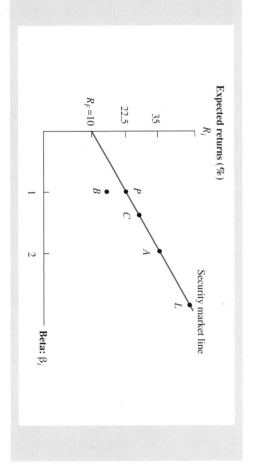